CORPORATE FINANCE

PRINCIPLES & PRACTICE

Denzil Watson and Antony Head
Sheffield Hallam University

FINANCIAL TIMES
PITMAN PUBLISHING

To Lesley, Aidan and Rosemary
for their love and patience,
and to Dora, Hugh and Doreen
for their unrelenting support and care.

Pearson Education Limited
Edinburgh Gate
Harlow
Essex CM20 2JE
England

and Associated Companies throughout the world

Visit us on the World Wide Web at:
http://www.pearsoneduc.com

First published in Great Britain in 1998

ISBN 0 273 63008 3

British Library Cataloguing in Publication Data
A CIP catalogue record for this book can be obtained from the British Library.

10 9 8 7 6 5 4 3
04 03 02 01 00 99

Typeset by M Rules
Printed and bound in Great Britain by Redwood Books, Trowbridge, Wiltshire

The Publishers' policy is to use paper manufactured from sustainable forests.

CONTENTS

PREFACE

Introduction

Corporate finance is concerned with the financing and investment decisions made by the management of companies in pursuit of corporate goals. As a subject, corporate finance has a theoretical base which has evolved over many years and which continues to evolve as we write. It has a practical side too, concerned with the study of how companies actually make financing and investment decisions, and it is often the case that theory and practice disagree!

The fundamental problem that faces financial managers is how to secure the greatest possible return in exchange for accepting the smallest amount of risk. This necessarily requires that financial managers have available to them (and are able to use!) a range of appropriate tools and techniques. These will help them to value the different decision options that are open to them and assess the risk of those options. The value of an option depends upon the extent to which it contributes towards the achievement of corporate goals. In corporate finance, the fundamental goal is usually taken to be to increase the wealth of shareholders.

Aim of the book

The aim of this text is to provide an introduction to the core concepts and key topic areas of corporate finance in an approachable, 'user-friendly' style. Many texts on corporate finance adopt a theory-based or mathematical approach which is not appropriate for those approaching the subject for the first time. This book covers the core concepts and key topic areas without burdening the reader with what we regard as unnecessary detail or too heavy a dose of theory.

Flexible course design

Many undergraduate courses are now delivered on a modular or unit basis over one teaching semester of 12 twelve weeks' duration. In order to meet the constraints imposed by such courses, this book has been designed as far as possible to support self-study and directed learning. There is a choice of integrated topics for the end of the course.

Each chapter offers:

- questions, with answers at the back of the text, to check comprehension of concepts and computational techniques;

- questions for review, with answers at the end of the text, to aid in deepening understanding of particular topic areas;
- questions for discussion, answers for which are available in the Lecturer's Guide;
- a comprehensive list of key points to check understanding and aid revision;
- suggestions for further reading to guide readers who wish to study further;
- comprehensive references to guide the reader to key texts and articles.

A comprehensive glossary is included at the end of the text to assist the reader in grasping any unfamiliar terms that may be encountered in the study of corporate finance.

Target readership

This book has been written primarily for students taking a course in corporate finance in their second or final year of undergraduate study on business studies, accounting and finance-related degree programmes. It may also be suitable for students on professional and postgraduate business and finance courses where corporate finance or financial management are taught at introductory level.

Acknowledgements

We are grateful to our reviewer for helpful comments and suggestions. We are also grateful to the undergraduate students of Sheffield Hallam University who have taken our courses and, thereby, helped in developing our approach to the teaching and learning of the subject. We are particularly grateful to Pat Bond of Financial Times Pitman Publishing for his patience and encouragement and to Julianne Mulholland and Nikki Bowen who were responsible for the editing of the text. We also extend our gratitude to colleagues at Sheffield Hallam University, with special thanks going to Willie Seal, David Holmes and Peter McGregor. Denzil would also like to extend his thanks to Geoff Thomas, the treasurer at Rugby Group plc, for a most fascinating and enjoyable insight into the practical world of finance over the summer of 1994.

CHAPTER 1

THE FINANCE FUNCTION

INTRODUCTION

Corporate finance is concerned with the efficient and effective management of the finances of an organisation in order to achieve the objectives of that organisation. This involves planning and controlling the provision of resources (where funds are raised from), the allocation of resources (where funds are deployed to) and finally the control of resources (whether funds are being used effectively or not). The fundamental objective that faces financial managers is to achieve an optimal allocation of the scarce resources that are available to them – the scarce resource being money. Therefore, corporate finance theory draws heavily upon the subject of economics.

The discipline of corporate finance is frequently associated with that of accountancy. However, while financial managers do need to have a firm understanding of management accounting (in order to make decisions) and a good understanding of financial accounting (in order to have an awareness of how financial decisions and their results are presented to the outside world), corporate finance and accounting are fundamentally different in nature. Corporate finance is inherently forward looking and based on cash flows, and this differentiates it from financial accounting, which is historic in nature and focuses on profit rather than cash. Corporate finance is concerned with raising funds and providing a return to investors, and this differentiates it from management accounting, which is primarily concerned with the provision of information for management to assist it in making decisions within the company. However, having highlighted differences between these disciplines, there is no doubt that corporate finance borrows extensively from both.

In the following chapters we give detailed consideration to the many and varied problems and tasks faced by financial managers. A common strand that runs through all the chapters is an awareness of the dual concepts of valuation and decision making, i.e. corporate finance is concerned with placing values on the alternative courses of action that a company can take, deciding which is the best of the alternatives and considering the effects the decision will have on the value of the company itself.

LEARNING OBJECTIVES

After studying this chapter, you should have achieved the following learning objectives:

- an appreciation of the three decision areas concerning the financial manager;
- an understanding of the reasons why shareholder wealth maximisation is the primary financial objective of a company, rather than other objectives of which a company needs to take account;
- an understanding of why the surrogate objective of maximisation of a company's share price is preferred to the objective of maximisation of shareholder wealth;
- an understanding of how the concept of agency theory can be used to analyse the relationship between shareholders and managers and an understanding of the ways in which it has been suggested that agency problems may be overcome;
- an appreciation of the developing role of institutional investors in overcoming agency problems;
- an appreciation of the contribution made to the corporate governance debate by the proposals of the Cadbury Report and the Greenbury Report.

1.1 THE ROLE OF THE FINANCIAL MANAGER

Financial managers are central to the management of a company's funds. They are responsible for a company's investment decisions, advising on the allocation of funds in terms of the total amount of assets, the composition of fixed and current assets, and the consequent risk profile of the choices. They are also responsible for raising funds, choosing from a wide variety of institutions and markets, with each source of finance having different criteria as regards cost, availability, maturity and risk. The place where supply meets demand for finance is called the financial market, which is made up of the short-term money markets and the longer-term capital markets. A major source of finance available to a company is internal rather than external, i.e. to retain part of the earnings generated by its business activities. The managers of the company, however, will have to strike a balance between the amount of earnings they retain and the amount paid out to shareholders as a dividend.

We can see, therefore, that a financial manager's decisions can be divided into three general areas: *investment* decisions; *financing* decisions; and *dividend* decisions. The position of the financial manager as a person central to these decisions and their associated cash flows is illustrated in Exhibit 1.1.

EXHIBIT 1.1

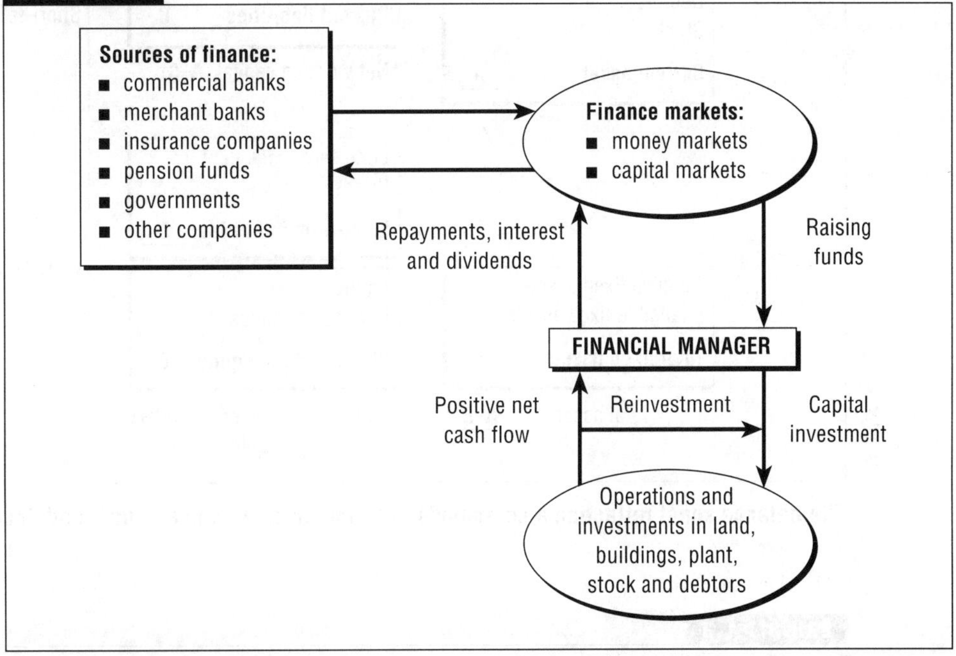

The role of the financial manager as a person central to a company's financing, investment and reinvestment decisions

These decision areas will be reflected in the company's financial statements. Investment decisions will be reflected on the asset side of the balance sheet while the financing decisions of the company and its dividend policy are reflected by the liabilities side of the balance sheet. This is illustrated in Exhibit 1.2.

While it is convenient to split a financial manager's decisions into three compartments for discussion purposes, it is very important to stress the high level of interdependence that exists between these decision areas. A financial manager making a decision in one of these three key areas, therefore, should always take into account the effect of that decision on the other two areas. Examples of possible knock-on effects of taking a decision in one of the three areas on the other two are indicated in Exhibit 1.3.

So who makes corporate finance decisions in practice? In most companies there will be no one individual who is solely responsible for corporate financial management. The more strategic dimensions of the three decision areas tend to be considered at board level, with an important contribution coming from the *finance director*, who oversees the finance function. Any financial decisions taken will be arrived at after considerable consultation with accountants, tax experts and legal counsel. The daily cash and treasury management duties of the company and its

EXHIBIT 1.2

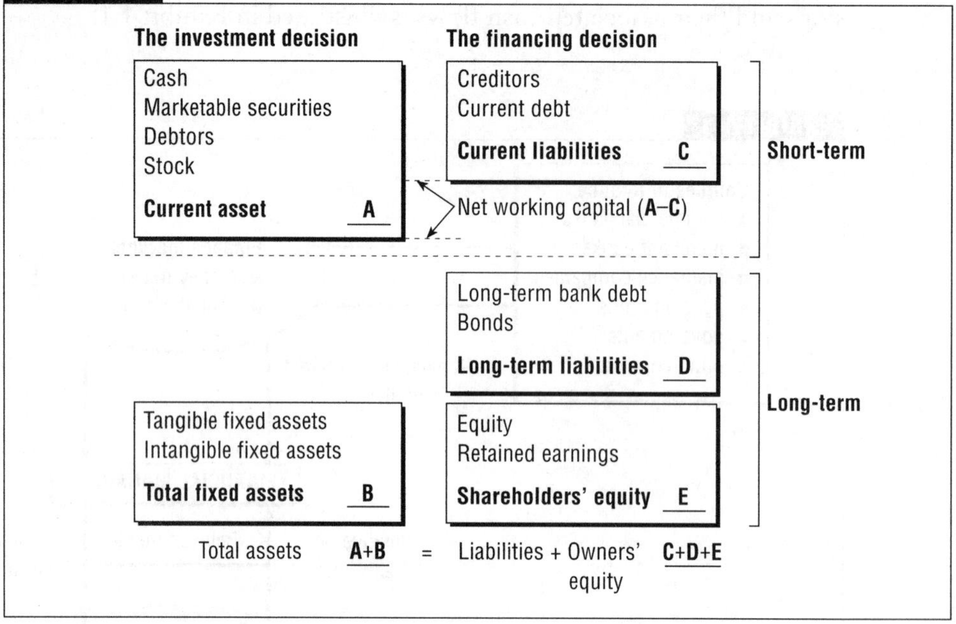

The balance sheet reflecting a company's investment, financing and dividend decisions

EXHIBIT 1.3

Investment: company decides to take on a large number of attractive new investment projects	**Finance:** company will need to raise finance in order to take up projects	**Dividends:** if finance is not available from external sources, dividends may need to be cut in order to increase internal financing
Dividends: company decides to pay higher levels of dividends to its shareholders	**Finance:** lower level of retained earnings available for investment means company may have to find finance from external sources	**Investment:** if finance is not available from external sources the company may have to postpone future investment projects
Finance: company finances itself using more expensive sources, resulting in a higher cost of capital	**Investment:** due to a higher cost of capital the number of projects attractive to the company decreases	**Dividends:** the company's ability to pay dividends in the future will be adversely affected

Table showing the inter-relationship between financing, dividend and investment decisions

liaison with financial institutions such as banks will be undertaken by the *corporate treasurer*. It is common for both finance director and corporate treasurer to have an accounting background. An increasingly important role of the corporate treasurer in the modern corporate finance climate is to hedge interest and exchange rate risk. An illustration of the various functions within the finance department of a large company is given in Exhibit 1.4.

EXHIBIT 1.4

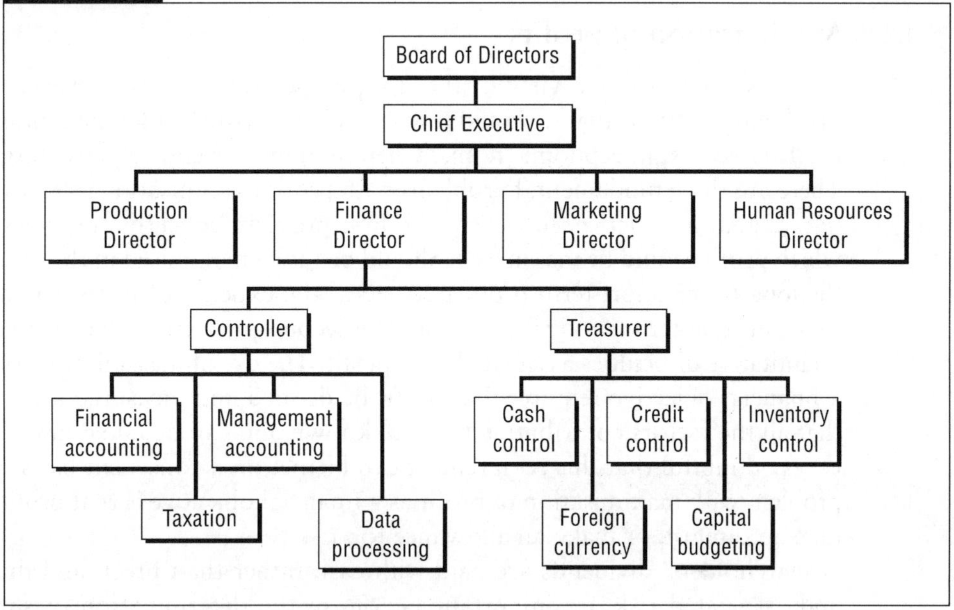

Tree diagram showing how the finance function fits within a company's management structure

1.2 CORPORATE OBJECTIVES

So what should be the primary financial objective of corporate finance and, therefore, the main objective of the financial manager? The answer to this question is that their objective should be to make decisions that maximise the value of the company for its owners. As the owners of the company are its shareholders, the primary financial objective of corporate finance is usually stated to be the maximisation of shareholder wealth. Since shareholders receive their wealth through dividends and capital gains, shareholders' wealth will be maximised by maximising the value of dividends and capital gains that shareholders receive over time. How financial managers go about achieving this objective of maximising shareholder wealth will be considered in the next section.

Due to the rather vague and complicated nature of the concept of shareholder wealth maximisation, other objectives are commonly suggested as possible substitutes or surrogates. Alternative objectives for a company to shareholder wealth maximisation also exist, due to the existence of a number of other interest groups with stakes in the company, such as employees, the local community, and creditors, who all have differing views on what the company should achieve. It is important to stress, however, that while companies do have to consider other stakeholders and may adopt one or several surrogate objectives over shorter time periods, from a corporate finance perspective such objectives should only be pursued in support of the overriding long-term objective of maximising their shareholders' wealth. We shall now consider some of these other possible objectives for a company.

1.2.1 Maximisation of profits

The classical economic view of the firm, as put forward by Hayek (1960) and Friedman (1970), is that it should be operated in a manner that maximises its profits. This occurs, in economic terms, when marginal revenue equals marginal cost. There are three fundamental problems with profit maximisation as an overall corporate goal in practice, however. The first problem concerns the timescale over which profit should be maximised. Should profit be maximised in the short term or the long term? Short-term profit pursued at the expense of necessary investment may put long-term survival in doubt. The second problem is that there are many quantitative difficulties associated with profit. The use of maximisation of profit as a financial objective requires that profit be defined and measured accurately and that all the factors contributing to it are known and can be taken into account. It is very doubtful that this requirement can be met on a consistent basis. The third problem with maximisation of profit as a financial objective is that profit does not take account of, or make an allowance for, risk.

Shareholders' dividends are paid with cash rather than profit and their timing and associated risk are important factors in the determination of shareholder wealth. When we consider this, together with the problems discussed in the previous paragraph, we can conclude that the maximisation of profit is not a suitable surrogate objective for the maximisation of shareholder wealth. That is not to say that a company does not need to pay any attention to its profit figures, however, as falling profits are taken by the financial markets to be a sign of financial weakness. In addition, profitability targets serve a useful purpose in helping to achieve short-term or operational objectives within the overall strategic plan of a company.

1.2.2 Maximisation of sales

If a company were solely to pursue sales maximisation as its overriding long-term objective, it would probably result in the company overtrading (*see* Chapter 10) and it might lead eventually to liquidation. Sales may not necessarily be at a profit, and sales targets could be disastrous if products are not correctly priced. Maximisation of sales can be useful as a short-term objective, though. As an example, a company entering a new market and trying to establish a market share could follow a policy of sales maximisation.

1.2.3 Survival

Survival cannot be accepted as a satisfactory long-term objective. Will investors want to invest in a company whose main objective is merely to survive? The answer to this question has to be an emphatic no. In the long term, a company must attract capital investment by holding out the prospect of gains which are at least as great as those offered by comparable alternative investment opportunities. Survival may be a key short-term objective though, especially in times of economic recession. If a company were to go into liquidation, by the time assets have been distributed to stakeholders higher up in the creditor hierarchy there may be little if any money to distribute to ordinary shareholders. If liquidation were a possibility, short-term survival as an objective would be consistent with shareholder wealth maximisation.

1.2.4 Social responsibility

Some organisations adopt an altruistic social purpose as a corporate objective. They may be concerned with improving working conditions for their employees, providing a wholesome product for their customers, or avoiding anti-social actions such as environmental pollution or undesirable promotional practices. While it is important not to upset other interest groups such as employees and the local community, social responsibility should not be a company's overriding goal but rather play a supporting role within its overall objectives. On the other hand, while a company is not merely in existence to please its employees, the consequences of having a workforce that is both demotivated and unhappy will be detrimental to the long-term prosperity of the company.

1.3 HOW IS SHAREHOLDERS' WEALTH MAXIMISED?

We have already mentioned that shareholder wealth maximisation is a rather vague and complicated concept. We have also stated that shareholders' wealth is derived through the cash they receive via dividend payments and the capital gains associated with the ownership of their shares. It follows logically that the maximisation of shareholders' wealth can be achieved by maximising the purchasing power they derive through dividend payments and capital gains over time. From this view of shareholder wealth maximisation we can identify three variables that directly affect shareholders' wealth:

- the magnitude of cash flows accumulating to the company;
- the timing of such cash flows;
- the risk associated with them.

Having established the factors that affect shareholders' wealth we now have to decide what to take as an indicator of shareholder wealth. The surrogate that is usually taken is a company's ordinary share price, which should reflect expectations about future dividend payments as well as investor views about the long-term prospects of the company and its expected cash flows. The surrogate objective, therefore, becomes to maximise the current market price of the company's ordinary shares and hence to maximise the total market value of the company. The link between the cash flows coming in from a company's projects all the way through to the wealth of its shareholders is indicated in Exhibit 1.5.

EXHIBIT 1.5

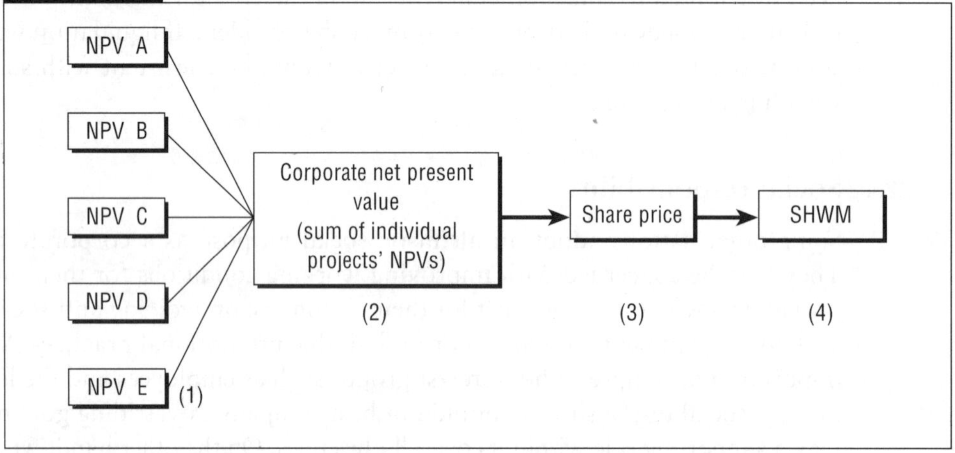

Diagram showing the links between the investment projects of a company and shareholder wealth

At stage (1) a company takes on all projects with a positive net present value. By using net present value to appraise the desirability of potential projects the company is taking into account the three variables that affect shareholder wealth, i.e. the size of expected cash flows, their timing through discounting at the company's cost of capital, and finally their associated risk through the selected discount rate. At stage (2) the net present value of the company as a whole should be equal to the sum of the net present values of the projects it has undertaken. Stage (3) is for the net present value of the company as a whole to be accurately reflected by the market value of the company through its share price. The link between stages (2) and (3) (i.e. the market value of the company reflecting the true value of the company) will heavily depend upon the efficiency of the stock market and hence on the speed and accuracy with which share prices change to reflect new information about companies. The importance of stock market efficiency to corporate finance will be considered in Chapter 2. Finally, at stage (4), share price is taken to be a surrogate for shareholder wealth, and so shareholder wealth will be maximised when the market capitalisation of the company is maximised.

Now that we have established the factors that affect shareholder wealth and have decided that maximisation of a company's share price is an acceptable surrogate objective for maximisation of shareholder wealth, we need to consider how a financial manager can go about achieving such an objective. The factors that affect shareholder wealth are largely under the financial manager's control, even though the outcome of any decisions made will also be affected by the conditions prevailing in the financial markets. In the terms of our earlier discussion, a company's value will be maximised if the financial manager makes 'good' investment, financing and dividend decisions. Examples of 'good' financial decisions, in the sense of financial decisions that promote maximisation of a company's share price, include the following:

- using net present value to assess all potential projects and then accepting all projects with positive net present values;
- raising finance using the most appropriate mixture of debt and equity in order to minimise a company's cost of capital;
- adopting the most appropriate dividend policy, which reflects the amount of dividends a company can afford to pay, given its level of profits, and the amount of retained earnings it requires for reinvestment;
- managing a company's working capital efficiently by striking a balance between the need to maintain liquidity within the company and the opportunity cost of holding liquid assets;
- taking account of the risk associated with financial decisions and where possible guarding against it, e.g. hedging interest and exchange rate risk.

1.4 AGENCY THEORY

1.4.1 Why does agency exist?

While managers should make decisions that are consistent with the objective of maximising shareholder wealth, whether this actually happens in practice is another matter. The problem of 'agency' is said to occur when managers are clearly not acting in the best interest of their shareholders. Three important features that contribute to the existence of the agency problem within public limited companies are as follows:

- there exists a divergence of ownership and control whereby those who own the company (shareholders) do not manage it, but appoint agents (management) to run the company on their behalf;
- the goals of the management differ from those of the owners (shareholders). Human nature being what it is, managers are likely to look to maximising their own wealth rather than the wealth of shareholders;
- asymmetry of information exists between the two parties. Management, as a consequence of running the company on a day-to-day basis, has access to both management accounting data and financial reports, while shareholders only receive annual reports, which may, themselves, be subject to manipulation by the management.

When these three factors are considered together, it should become apparent that company management is both in the position to, and has the incentive to, pursue the maximisation of its own wealth without detection from the owners of the company. It is this asymmetry of information which makes it difficult for shareholders to monitor managerial decisions, allowing managers to follow their own welfare-maximising decisions. Examples of possible management goals include the following:

- growth or size maximisation of the company;
- managerial power;
- creation of job security;
- increasing managerial reward and emoluments;
- pursuing their own social objectives or pet projects.

The potential problems between a company's management and its shareholders is not the only agency problem that exists. It was argued by Jensen and Meckling (1976) that the company can be viewed as a whole series of agency relationships between the different interest groups involved. These agency relationships are shown in Exhibit 1.6. The arrows point away from the principal towards the agent. For example, as customers pay for goods and services from the company, they are the principal, and the supplying company their agent. While company management is the agent of the shareholders, the relationship is reversed between creditors and shareholders, with shareholders becoming, through the actions of the management they appoint and direct, the agents of the creditors.

EXHIBIT 1.6

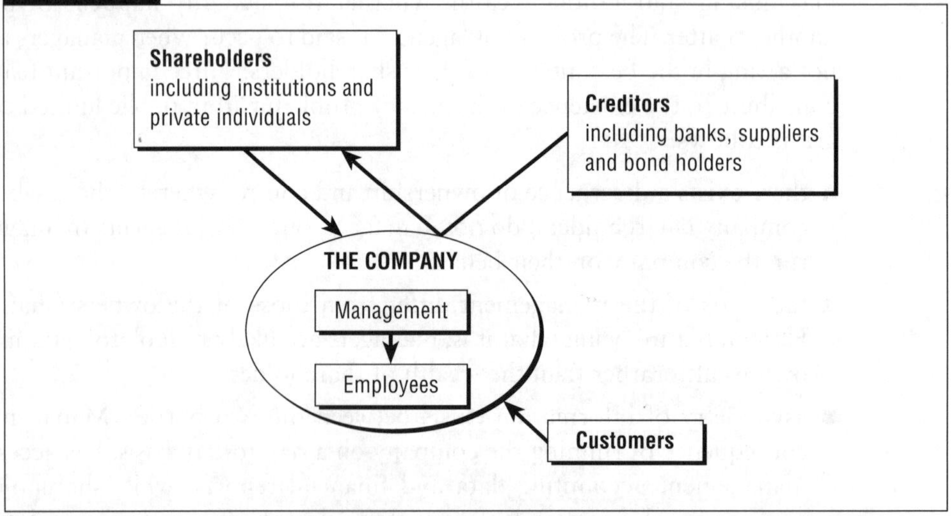

Diagram showing the agency relationships that exist between the various stakeholders of a company

From a corporate finance perspective, an important agency relationship is that which exists between shareholders, now as the agents, and the providers of debt finance as principals. The agency problem here is that shareholders will have a preference for using debt holders' money for progressively riskier projects, as it is shareholders who will gain from the success of such projects but debt holders who bear the risk.

1.4.2 How does agency manifest itself with a company?

Areas of conflict between managers and shareholders include investment decisions and risk. Managerial reward schemes are often based on short-term performance measures and managers therefore tend to use the payback method when appraising possible projects, since this technique emphasises short-term returns. With respect to risk, managers may make investments to decrease unsystematic risk through diversification, in order to reduce the risk of the company. Unsystematic risk, which is discussed in Chapter 9, is the risk associated with undertaking particular business activities. By reducing the risk of the company through diversification, managers hope to safeguard their job prospects. However, investors have probably diversified away unsystematic risk themselves by investing in portfolios containing the shares of many different companies. The wealth of shareholders is not increased, therefore, by the diversifying activities of managers. Another agency problem in the area of risk can arise if managers undertake low-risk projects, when the preference of shareholders is for higher-risk projects.

Conflict arises between shareholders and debt holders because, as we mentioned earlier, shareholders have a preference for higher-risk projects when compared to debt holders. Here, the return of shareholders is unlimited, whereas their loss is limited to the value of their shares. The risk of bankruptcy is also borne by debt holders but their return is not unlimited, since they are only entitled to a fixed return.

1.4.3 Dealing with the agency problem between shareholders and managers

Jensen and Meckling (1976) suggested that there are two ways of seeking to optimise managerial behaviour in order to encourage 'goal congruence' between shareholders and managers. The first way is for shareholders to monitor the actions of management. There are a number of possible monitoring devices that can be used, although they all incur costs in terms of both time and money. These monitoring devices include the use of independently audited financial statements and additional reporting requirements, the shadowing of senior managers, and the use of external analysts. The costs of monitoring management must be weighed against the benefits accruing from a decrease in sub-optimal managerial behaviour (i.e. managerial behaviour which does not aim to maximise shareholder wealth). A major difficulty associated with monitoring as a method of solving the agency problem is the existence of what are known as 'free riders'. Smaller investors may allow larger shareholders, who are keener to monitor managerial behaviour due to their larger stake in the company, to incur the bulk of monitoring costs, while reaping the benefits of the corrected management behaviour. The smaller investors, then, obtain a 'free ride'.

An alternative to the monitoring approach is for shareholders to incorporate clauses into managerial contracts which encourage goal congruence. Such clauses may formalise constraints, incentives and punishments. When shareholders are formulating managerial contracts, the 'optimal' contract will be one which minimises all of the costs associated with agency. These costs include:

- financial contracting costs, such as transaction and legal costs;
- the opportunity cost of any contractual constraints;
- the cost of managers' incentive and bonus fees;
- monitoring costs, such as the cost of reports and audits;
- the loss of wealth due to sub-optimal behaviour by the agent.

It is important that managerial contracts reflect the needs of individual companies. For certain companies, for example, monitoring may be both difficult and costly. Managerial contracts for such companies may choose to include bonuses for improved performance. Due to the difficulties associated with monitoring managerial behaviour, such incentives could represent a far more practical way of encouraging goal congruence. The two most common incentives offered to managers are performance-related pay and executive share options. These methods are not without their drawbacks.

Performance-related pay

Managerial remuneration can be linked to performance indicators such as profit, earnings per share and return on capital employed. The major problem here is the difficulty in finding an accurate measure of managerial performance. There are a number of difficulties associated with using the performance measures mentioned since, being accounting measures, they may be subject to manipulation by management and may not be good indicators of shareholder wealth in the first place.

Executive share option schemes

Due to the problems associated with performance-related pay, share option schemes now represent the most frequently used incentive to encourage goal congruence among senior management. Share options allow managers to purchase a specified number of their company's shares at a fixed price over a specified time period. The options only have value when the market price of the company's shares exceeds the price at which they can be bought by using the option. The aim of share option schemes is that, by giving managers share options and making them potential shareholders themselves, they will be encouraged to maximise the company's share price and hence to maximise shareholder wealth.

Share option schemes are not without their problems. First, while good financial management does increase share prices, there are a number of external factors that affect share prices too. If the country is experiencing an economic boom, share prices will increase across the board. Managers will then benefit through increases in the value of their share options, but this is not necessarily down to their good managerial performance. Second, problems with share option schemes arise because of their allocation and terms: share options are not seen as an immediate cost to the company, and so the terms of the options (i.e. the number of shares that can be purchased and the price at which they can be bought) may sometimes be set at too generous a level.

Shareholders, in addition to using monitoring and managerial incentives, have other ways of keeping managers 'on their toes'. They can exercise their right to remove directors by voting them out of office at the company's annual general meeting. Whether this represents a viable 'threat' to management or not depends heavily upon the ownership structure of the company's share capital, i.e. whether there are a few large influential shareholders holding over half of the company's shares. Alternatively, shareholders can 'vote with their feet' and sell their shares on the capital markets. This has the effect of depressing the company's share price, making it a possible target for take-over. The fact that target company management usually lose their jobs after a take-over may provide an incentive for managers to run their company more in the interests of shareholders.

1.4.4 The agency problem between debt holders and shareholders

The simplest way for debt holders to protect their interests in a company is to secure their debt against the company's assets. Should the company go into liquidation, debt holders will have a prior claim over assets which they can then sell in order to recover their initial investment.

An alternative way for debt holders to protect their interests and limit the amount of risk they face is for them to use restrictive covenants. These take the form of clauses written into bond agreements which restrict a company's decision-making process. They may prevent a company from investing in high-risk projects or from paying out excessive levels of dividends and may limit its future gearing levels. Restrictive covenants are discussed in more detail in Section 6.1.1.

1.4.5 The influence of institutional investors

In Section 1.4.4 we implied that an increase in the concentration of share ownership may potentially lead to a reduction in the problems associated with agency. In recent years in the UK, especially over the late 1970s and to a lesser extent subsequently, there has been an increase in shareholdings by large institutional investors. This trend is clearly apparent in Exhibit 1.7, where it can be seen that institutional shareholders now account for the ownership of approximately 62 per cent of all ordinary share capital.

In the past, while institutional investors have not been overtly interested in becoming involved with companies' operational decisions, they have been placing

EXHIBIT 1.7

	1963	1969	1975	1981	1990	1993	1996
Public sector	1.5	2.6	3.6	3.0	2.0	1.2	0.1
Banks	1.3	1.7	0.7	0.3	0.7	0.3	0.5
Institutional investors	29.0	34.2	47.3	57.6	60.6	61.1	61.8
Industrial and commercial companies	5.1	5.4	3.0	5.1	2.8	1.0	1.6
Personal sector	56.1	49.5	39.8	30.4	22.1	20.4	19.4
Overseas sector	7.0	0.6	5.6	3.6	11.8	16.0	16.6
Total	100.0	100.0	100.0	100.0	100.0	100.0	100.0

The beneficial ownership of UK quoted ordinary shares in percentage terms according to classification of owner over the period 1963–96

Source: Office for National Statistics

pressure on companies to maintain their dividend payments in an adverse macroeconomic environment. The irony here is that, rather than reducing the agency problem, institutional investors are exacerbating it by pressing companies to pay dividends which they can ill afford. However, recent years have seen a number of incidents where institutional investors have 'got tough' with companies in which they invest which do not comply with corporate governance standards. The example of one such institutional investor acting in this way, insurance company Standard Life, is the subject of Vignette 1.1.

A recent development in the US has been the increase in pressure on companies, from both a performance and an accountability perspective, which has been generated by shareholder coalitions such as the Council of Institutional Investors (CII) and the California Public Employees' Retirement System (CalPERS), which is the largest US pension fund. These organisations publish, on a regular basis, lists of companies which they consider to have been under-performing, due to bad management, over the last five years. The publication of these lists is a tactic to force such companies to take steps to improve their future performance.

1.5 CORPORATE GOVERNANCE

Corporate governance is concerned with the relationship between company management and its owners and the structure and nature of the mechanisms by which owners 'govern' management. The importance of corporate governance has been highlighted in the UK by recent concerns about the way in which remuneration packages for senior executives have been determined, and by the spectacular collapse of a number of large companies (such as Polly Peck in 1990, Maxwell Communications Corporation in 1991 and the Bank of Credit and Commerce International (BCCI), also in 1991). Doubts have been raised about whether the interests of shareholders are being met by executive remuneration packages which

VIGNETTE 1.1

Standard Life issues governance guidelines

FT

Standard Life, one of the UK's largest life assurers, has notified chairmen of the UK's biggest companies that it is prepared to vote against directors' contracts which fall short of its corporate governance standards. The group, a leading institutional shareholder which owns roughly two per cent of the UK stock market, is the first life assurer to set out a formal corporate governance policy. Several large pension schemes have previously taken a strong public line on corporate governance matters, but life assurance and fund managers – who typically are run by corporate boards – have generally eschewed public comment.

In a letter to chairmen of FT-SE 100 companies, dated 17 January, Mr Dick Barfield, Chief Investment Manager of the £42bn fund, outlined the corporate government issues which it mostly endorses.

Mr Barfield said that Standard Life had published details of the letter because it believes that 'as a leading institutional investor, we have the responsibility to our customers to encourage improved performance of the companies in which we invest'.

It says that if companies fail to disclose directors' remuneration in line with the Greenbury Committee two years running, Standard Life will vote against the adoption of the annual report and accounts and the appointment of any director standing for re-election.

Also, Standard Life will oppose any contracts for directors that are longer than one year unless there are 'exceptional and justifiable circumstances'. The life assurer said that it was only minded to approve long-term incentive schemes for directors which offer rewards for high performance only, 'but not for mediocrity'.

Specifically, Standard Life opposes the increasingly common measure of total shareholder return – which takes into account both share price increases and dividends – because both may rise for reasons which have little to do with the success of the management.

The letter also makes clear that the independence of non-executive directors is critical and that remuneration and audit committees should consist only of genuinely independent non-executives.

Source: Norma Cohen, *Financial Times*, 19 January 1996

are not only complex, but have been formulated by the very executives expected to enjoy their benefits.

The corporate governance system in the UK has traditionally stressed the importance of internal controls and the importance of the role of financial reporting and accountability, as opposed to a large amount of external legislation. The agency problem in the UK was addressed in 1992 by a committee chaired by Sir Adrian Cadbury. The resulting Cadbury Report (1992) recommended a Code of Best Practice. The main proposals of this voluntary code were:

- the posts of chief executive officer and chairman, the two most powerful positions within a company, should not be held by the same person;
- company boards should include non-executive directors of 'sufficient calibre' who are independent of management, appointed for specified terms after being selected through a formal process;
- executive directors' contracts should be no longer than three years without shareholder approval;

- there should be full disclosure of directors' remunerations, including any pensions contributions and share options;
- executive directors' pay should be subject to the recommendations of a remuneration committee made up wholly, or mainly, of non-executive directors;
- the relationship between a company and its auditor should be professional and objective;
- companies should establish an audit committee including at least three non-executive directors.

The committee recommended a greater role for non-executive directors on remuneration committees in order to avoid potential conflicts of interest. The Stock Exchange requires its member companies to state in their accounts whether or not they comply with the Cadbury Code of Best Practice and, if not, to explain the reasons behind their non-compliance. The code also encouraged the 'constructive involvement' of institutional investors, suggesting they use their influence to ensure that companies comply with the code.

Many commentators have been critical of the effectiveness of the Cadbury Report, focusing on the market-based nature of the proposed process of self-regulation. The efficacy of these proposals will depend, to a great extent, on the manner in which non-executive directors are selected for appointment. In particular, the use of the 'old boy network' to select potential candidates would run contrary to the spirit of the Cadbury proposals. The effectiveness of these proposals was questioned in a paper on the issues of corporate governance by Forbes and Watson (1993). They argued that any scheme attempting to increase the accountability of senior management to shareholders would require the active involvement of institutional shareholders if it were to be effective.

The approach of the Cadbury Committee was reinforced by the Code of Best Practice produced as part of the Greenbury Report (1995). This report specifically criticised what it considered to be the over-generous remuneration packages awarded to directors of the privatised utilities. Its recommendations were:

- directors' contracts should be reduced to one-year rolling contracts;
- remuneration committees, when setting pay levels, should be more sensitive to company-wide pay settlements and avoid 'excessive payments'. These committees should be made up exclusively of non-executive directors;
- companies should abandon directors' performance-related bonus schemes and phase out executive share option schemes. These should be replaced with long-term incentive plans which reward directors through the payment of shares if they reach 'stretching' financial or share-price targets.

Evidence since the Greenbury Report suggests that some elements of the committee's code on executive pay are largely being ignored by UK companies. According to research carried out by the corporate governance consultancy Pension & Investment Research Consultants (1996), 60 per cent of the directors in the UK's 350 biggest companies had contracts in excess of one year, while approximately 50 per cent of companies surveyed had *added* long-term incentive plans to existing share option schemes, rather than replacing them with the new incentive plans. One can only conclude that the problems of corporate governance in the UK still have a long way to go before they are totally solved.

1.6 CONCLUSION

In this chapter we have identified the role of the financial manager within a public company. We have established that a financial manager's overriding aim should be to maximise the wealth of the company's shareholders; other objectives which are often cited, such as profit maximisation, survival and social responsibility, are of secondary importance. Shareholders' wealth is maximised through company management making sound investment, financing and dividend decisions. These decisions should take account of expected company cash flows and their timing and associated risk, as these are the key variables driving shareholders' wealth.

Unfortunately, managers are in a position to maximise their own wealth rather than that of shareholders. This problem of 'agency' can be tackled in a number of ways; the two most common being performance-related pay schemes and managerial share options, although these are far from perfect solutions. The terms and conditions of managers' pay and the topical issue of corporate governance have been the subject of recent reports by the Cadbury and Greenbury committees. The recommendations of these committees have gone some way towards eradicating the problem of agency.

KEY POINTS

1. While accountancy plays an important role within corporate finance, the fundamental problem addressed by corporate finance is economic, i.e. how best to allocate the scarce resource of money.

2. Financial managers are responsible for making decisions about raising funds (the financing decision), allocating funds (the investment decision) and how much to distribute to shareholders (the dividend decision).

3. While objectives such as profit maximisation, social responsibility and survival represent important supporting objectives, the overriding objective of a company must be that of shareholder wealth maximisation.

4. Maximisation of a company's ordinary share price is used as a surrogate objective to that of maximisation of shareholder wealth.

5. A financial manager can maximise a company's market value by making good investment, financing and dividend decisions.

6 Managers do not always act in the best interest of their shareholders, giving rise to what is called 'the agency problem'.

7 Agency is most likely to be a problem when there is a divergence of ownership and control, when the goals of management differ from those of shareholders and when asymmetry of information exists.

8 An example of how the agency problem can manifest itself within a company is where managers diversify away unsystematic risk to reduce the risk of the company, thereby safeguarding their job prospects.

9 Monitoring and performance-related benefits are two potential ways to optimise managerial behaviour and encourage 'goal congruence'.

10 Due to difficulties associated with monitoring, incentives such as performance-related pay and executive share options can be a more practical way of encouraging goal congruence.

11 Institutional shareholders now own approximately 60 per cent of all UK ordinary share capital. Recently, they have brought pressure to bear on companies who do not comply with corporate governance standards.

12 The problem of corporate governance has received a lot of attention following a number of high-profile corporate collapses and a plethora of self-serving executive remuneration packages.

13 The UK corporate governance system has traditionally stressed internal controls and financial reporting rather than external legislation.

14 Corporate governance in the UK was addressed by the 1992 Cadbury Report and its Code of Best Practice, and the 1995 Greenbury Report.

QUESTIONS

Answers to these questions can be found on pages 391–2.

1 What are the functions and areas of responsibility that fall under the control of the financial manager?

2 Give examples to illustrate the high level of interdependence existing between the different decision areas of corporate finance.

3 Given the following possible corporate objectives, provide a rational argument explaining which of them should be the main goal of the financial manager:

(a) profit maximisation;

(b) sales maximisation;

(c) maximisation of benefit to employees and the local community;

(d) maximisation of shareholder wealth.

4 Explain how a financial manager can, in practice, maximise the wealth of shareholders.

5 Give some examples of good financial management.

6 Which of the following will not lead to a reduction of agency problems experienced by shareholders?
   (a) increased monitoring by shareholders;
   (b) salary bonuses for management based on financial performance;
   (c) the granting of share options to management;
   (d) the use of restrictive covenants in bond deeds;
   (e) the use of shorter contracts for management.

7 What is meant by the 'agency problem' in the context of a public limited company?

8 How is it possible for the agency problem to be reduced in a company?

9 What goals might be pursued by managers instead of maximisation of shareholder wealth?

10 Do you consider the agency problem to be of particular relevance to UK public limited companies?

QUESTIONS FOR REVIEW

Answers to these questions can be found on page 393.

1 The primary financial objective of a company is stated by corporate finance theory to be the maximisation of the wealth of its shareholders, but this objective is usually replaced by the surrogate objective of maximisation of the company's share price. Discuss the ways in which this substitution can be justified.

2 Explain why maximisation of a company's share price is preferred as a financial objective to the maximisation of its sales.

3 Discuss the ways in which the concepts of agency theory can be used to explain the relationships that exist between the managers of a listed company and the providers of its equity finance. Your answer should include an explanation of the following terms:
   (a) asymmetry of information;
   (b) agency costs;
   (c) the free-rider problem.

QUESTIONS FOR DISCUSSION

1 Discuss ways in which the shareholders of a company can encourage its managers to act in a way which is consistent with the objective of maximisation of shareholder wealth.

2 The primary financial objective of financial management is usually taken to be the maximisation of shareholder wealth. Discuss what other objectives may be important to a public limited company and whether such objectives are consistent with the primary objective of shareholder wealth maximisation.

3 Discuss the significance of the Cadbury Report in the context of corporate governance in the UK. Have its recommendations led to improvements?

REFERENCES

Cadbury Committee (1992) *Committee on the Financial Aspects of Corporate Governance: Final Report*, Dec.

Hayek, F. (1960) 'The corporation in a democratic society – in whose interest ought it and should it be run?' in Asher, M. and Bach, C. (eds) *Management and Corporations*, New York, McGraw-Hill.

Forbes, W. and Watson, R. (1993) 'Managerial remuneration and corporate governance: a review of the issues, evidence and Cadbury Committee proposals', *Journal of Accounting and Business Research: Corporate Governance Special Issue*.

Friedman, M. (1970) 'The social responsibility of business is to increase its profits', *New York Magazine*, 30 Sept.

Greenbury, R. (1995) *Directors' Remuneration: Report of a Study Group chaired by Sir Richard Greenbury*, London, Gee and Co.

Jensen, M. and Meckling, W. (1976) 'Theory of the firm: managerial behaviour, agency costs and ownership structure', *Journal of Financial Economics*, Vol. 3, pp. 305–60.

Pension & Investment Research Consultants (1996) *After Greenbury: Contracts and Compensation*, Aug.

RECOMMENDED READING

For informative chapters which give an American perspective on the problem of agency and how it can be solved by financial contracting *see*:

Diacogniannis, G. (1994) *Financial Management*, London, McGraw-Hill, Chapter 2.

Emery, D. and Finnerty, J. (1991) *Principles of Finance*, Minnesota, West Publishing Company, Chapter 9.

Important and informative papers and articles recommended for further reading include:

Andrews, G. (1982) 'What should a company's objectives be?' *Managerial Finance*, Vol. 8, pp. 1–4.

Barfield, R. (1995) 'Shareholder value in practice', *The Treasurer*, Jan, pp. 31–4.

Charkham, J. (1993) 'The Bank and corporate governance: past, present and future', *Bank of England Quarterly Bulletin*, Aug, pp. 388–92.

Fama, E. (1980) 'Agency problems and the theory of the firm', *Journal of the Political Economy*, Vol. 88, April, pp. 288–307.

Grinyer, J. (1986) 'Alternatives to maximisation of shareholder wealth', *Accounting and Business Research*, Autumn.

Marsh, P. (1997) 'Myths surrounding short-termism', in *Mastering Finance*, Issue 6, *Financial Times*.

Zingales, L. (1997) 'Why it's worth being in control', in *Mastering Finance*, Issue 5, *Financial Times*.

CHAPTER 2

CAPITAL MARKETS, MARKET EFFICIENCY AND RATIO ANALYSIS

INTRODUCTION

At one level, capital markets are places where companies who need long-term finance can meet investors who have finance to offer. This finance may be equity finance, involving the issue of new ordinary shares, or it may be debt finance, in which case companies can choose from a wide range of loans and debt securities. At another level, capital markets are places where investors buy and sell company and government securities, with their trading decisions reflecting information on company performance, insight provided by financial analysts, dividend announcements by companies, expectations on the future levels of interest rates and inflation, the investment decisions of financial managers, and so on.

At both levels, companies and investors will want the capital markets to assign fair prices to the financial securities being traded. In the language of corporate finance, companies and investors want the capital markets to be *efficient*. It is possible to describe the characteristics of an efficient capital market by considering the relationship between market prices and the information available to the market. Whether capital markets are in fact efficient has been studied extensively for many years and, in the first part of this chapter, we shall focus on the key topic of the efficient market hypothesis.

Investors, financial managers and the capital markets obtain a great deal of information about companies from their financial statements, from financial databases, from the financial press, and so on. Through the application of ratio analysis, financial statements can be made to yield useful information concerning the profitability, solvency, performance, efficiency of operations and risk of individual companies. This information will be used, for example, by investors when reaching decisions about whether, and at what price, to offer finance to companies; by financial managers in making decisions in the key areas of investment, financing and dividends; and by shareholders making decisions on which securities to add or remove from their portfolios.

LEARNING OBJECTIVES

After studying this chapter, you should have achieved the following learning objectives:

- an appreciation of the range of internal and external sources of finance available to a company, and of the factors influencing the relative proportions of internal and external finance used to fund investment;
- an understanding of the significance of the capital markets to a company;
- a firm understanding of the importance of the efficient market hypothesis to corporate finance and an ability to explain the difference between the various forms of market efficiency;
- an appreciation of the empirical research that has been undertaken to establish the extent to which capital markets may be considered to be efficient in practice;
- the ability to calculate key ratios from the financial statements of companies and an understanding of their significance in corporate finance;
- an appreciation of the difficulties that may be encountered when calculating and interpreting financial ratios.

2.1 SOURCES OF BUSINESS FINANCE

One of the key decision areas for corporate finance is the question of how a company finances its operations. If finance is not raised efficiently, the ability of a company to accept desirable projects will be affected and the profitability of its existing operations may suffer. The aims of an efficient financing policy will be to raise the appropriate level of funds, at the time they are required, at the lowest possible cost. It is not difficult, then, to see a link between the financing decisions made by a company's managers and the wealth of the company's shareholders. For a financing policy to be efficient, however, companies need to be aware of the sources of finance available to them.

2.1.1 Retained earnings

Sources of finance can be split into two broad classifications, namely *external* finance and *internal* finance. By internal finance we mean cash generated by a company which is not needed to meet operating costs, interest payments, tax liabilities, cash dividends or fixed asset refurbishment. In corporate finance, this surplus cash is usually called retained earnings. It is important not to confuse the idea of retained earnings with the accounting term 'retained profit', which is found in both profit and loss accounts and balance sheets. Retained profit in the profit and loss account is not necessarily cash, and retained profit in the balance sheet does not represent funds that can be invested. Only cash can be invested: a company with substantial retained profits, no cash in hand and a substantial overdraft will clearly be unable to finance investment from retained earnings.

Another internal source of finance that is often overlooked is the savings generated by more efficient management of working capital. This is the capital associated with short-term assets and liabilities (*see* Chapter 10). More efficient management of trade debtors, stocks, cash and trade creditors can reduce bank overdrafts and interest charges and increase cash reserves.

EXHIBIT 2.1

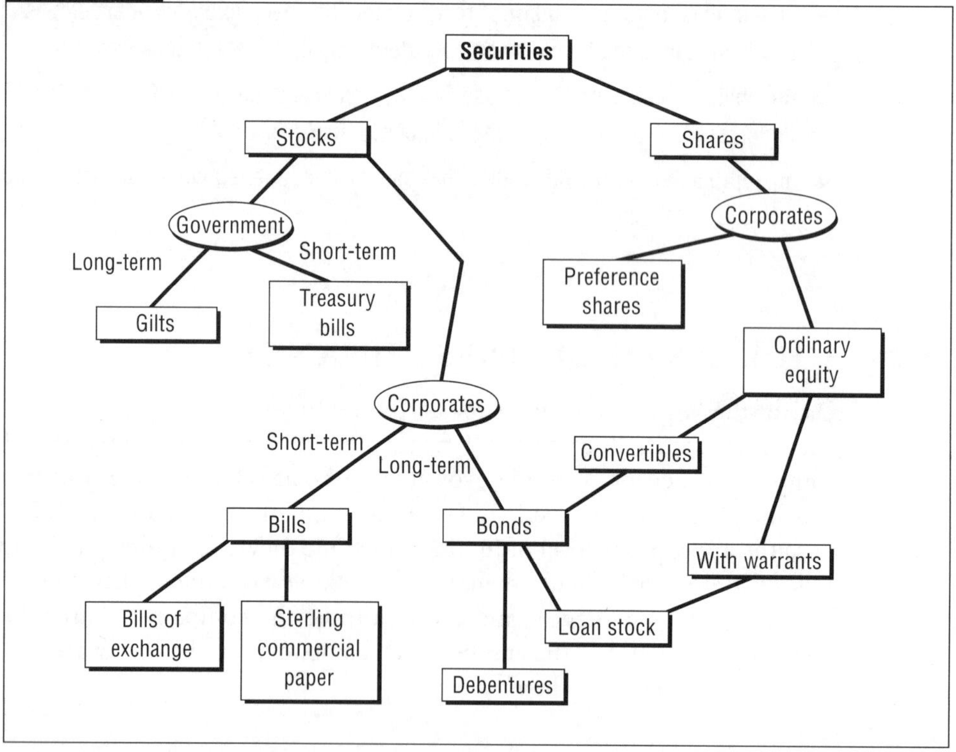

An illustration of the variety of financial instruments that can be used by a company to raise finance

There are a multitude of different types of external finance available, which can be broadly split into debt and equity finance. External finance can also be classified according to whether the finance is short term or long term, and according to whether it has been raised via financial markets or via financial institutions. The range of financial instruments associated with external finance and their interrelationships are illustrated in Exhibit 2.1; you may find it useful to refer back to this exhibit as you study this and subsequent chapters. As far as long-term sources of finance are concerned, ordinary shares and preference shares are discussed in Chapter 5, while corporate bonds are discussed in Chapter 6. Short-term finance is discussed in Chapter 10.

2.1.2 The relative proportions of internal and external finance

Exhibit 2.2 illustrates that retained earnings and other internal sources of finance account for the bulk of capital funds used by UK companies. Over the five-year period 1992 to 1995, the proportion of total capital funds derived from internal sources was less than 50 per cent in only one year and in 1994 exceeded 70 per cent. On average over the period, internal funds accounted for 60 per cent of total capital funds or £50bn per year. Between 1992 and 1994, there was a net repayment of long-term bank and other borrowings by UK companies of some £12.3bn. Even though these borrowings increased quite significantly in 1995 (£17bn) and 1996 (£23bn) as the UK economy recovered from recession, they remained less important than internal finance as a source of capital funds. More significant than borrowings over the period were capital market issues, which accounted for an average of 28 per cent of capital funds raised over the period, or approximately £24bn per year. On this evidence, the central role currently played by retained earnings in the financing of investment by UK companies is clear. This was also the case in the period 1980 to 1989, as described by Foley (1991).

EXHIBIT 2.2

	1992	*1993*	*1994*	*1995*	*1996*
Total (£m)	55 021	78 920	83 746	104 848	110 565
Internal sources of funds(per cent)	65.5	62.4	70.7	51.6	48.5
External sources of funds(per cent)	34.5	37.6	29.2	48.4	51.5
consisting of:					
Capital market issues (per cent)	29.1	33.8	27.2	29.8	21.1
Bank and other borrowing (per cent)	(5.3)	(9.9)	(1.9)	16.0	20.8
Others (per cent)*	10.7	13.7	3.9	2.6	9.6

*'Others' consists of overseas investment, capital transfers, and import and other credit received

Sources of capital funds for UK industrial and commercial companies, 1992–6
Source: Office for National Statistics – adapted

Companies prefer to use retained earnings as a source of finance for investment projects because they are in some ways cheaper, but the amount of retained earnings available will not be unlimited. Most companies, as a consequence, will need at some stage to consider external sources of finance if they are looking to raise funds for investment projects or for an expansion of operating activities. The decision as to the relative proportions of internal and external finance to be used for a capital investment project will depend upon a number of factors, as follows.

The level of finance required

It may be possible for a company to meet small investment finance needs from retained earnings, for example funds needed for the refurbishment of existing fixed assets or for undertaking minor new investment projects. Larger projects will require funds from outside the company.

The level of profitability of existing operations

If profitability is high, with a high level of retained earnings to match, a higher proportion of the finance needed for investment projects can be met from internal sources. If profitability is low, a company will be more dependent upon external financing.

The opportunity cost of retained earnings

Retained earnings, a company liability, belong to shareholders. This means that they are not costless, but have a cost which is equal to the best return that shareholders could obtain on their funds elsewhere in the financial markets. The best alternative return obtainable by shareholders is called the 'opportunity cost' of retained earnings and, as discussed in Chapters 5 and 8, the required return on equity is greater than the required return on debt. The relative proportions of internal and external finance used for investment projects must be chosen so as to minimise the overall cost of finance.

The costs associated with external finance

By using retained earnings, companies can avoid incurring the issue costs associated with raising external finance and will not make commitments to servicing fixed interest debt.

The availability of external sources to the company

The range of sources of finance available to a company will depend upon its individual circumstances. A company which is not listed on a recognised stock exchange, for example, will find it difficult to raise large amounts of equity finance, while a company which has a large proportion of debt finance and is therefore seen as somewhat risky will find it difficult to raise further bank loans.

The dividend policy of the company

As discussed in detail in Chapter 7, the dividend policy of a company will have a direct impact on the amount of retained earnings available for investment. Companies which consistently pay out a high proportion of distributable profits as dividends will need to utilise a higher proportion of external finance when funding investment projects.

2.2 THE CAPITAL MARKETS

The capital markets are markets for trading in long-term financial instruments or securities. These capital market securities were illustrated in Exhibit 2.1, but the most important ones for companies are ordinary shares or ordinary equity, preference shares and debt securities such as debentures, unsecured loan stock and convertible loan stock. Capital markets also exist for public sector securities and for Eurobonds.

For companies, the capital markets have two main functions. First, they act as a means whereby long-term funds can be raised by companies from those with funds to invest, such as financial institutions and private investors. In fulfilling this function, they act as a *primary market* for new issues of equity or debt. New issue methods for equity, whether to new or existing shareholders, are discussed in Chapter 5. Second, capital markets provide a ready means for investors to sell their existing holdings of shares and bonds or to increase their portfolios by buying additional ones. Here, they act as a *secondary market* for dealing in existing securities. The secondary market plays an important role in corporate financial management, because by facilitating the ready buying and selling of securities, it increases their liquidity and hence their value. Investors would pay less for a security that was difficult to dispose of. The secondary market is also a source of pricing information for the primary market, increasing the efficiency with which new funds are allocated.

The International Stock Exchange is the main market for equity, and methods of obtaining a listing or 'quotation' on this market are considered in Chapter 5.

Smaller companies who are unable to seek a listing on the Stock Exchange can apply for a listing on the Alternative Investment Market (AIM), which is a new market that has been operated by the Stock Exchange since June 1995. The AIM has replaced the Unlisted Securities Market (USM), which had been declining in importance for some time due to a lack of new entrants and investors. The AIM functions as both a primary and a secondary market in the shares of small and growing companies and has been quite successful to date. Unlike the Stock Exchange, the AIM does not have any qualifying restrictions on capitalisation, length of trading record, or percentage of shares to be held in public hands.

2.2.1 Market efficiency

What are the desirable characteristics of capital markets? Dixon and Holmes (1992) suggest that transaction costs should be as low as possible, so that barriers to trading in capital markets are reduced and *operational efficiency* is promoted. Primary markets should direct funds to their most productive uses, so that capital markets have *allocational efficiency*. This calls for fair prices to be provided by the secondary market, so activity on the primary market should have only a minimal effect on secondary market prices. This points to the need for *pricing efficiency*, which means that the prices of securities should reflect all relevant available information. The common thread that runs through this discussion is that capital markets should be *efficient* in the transfer and use of funds.

2.2.2 Perfect markets and efficient markets

The are many references in corporate finance theory to perfect markets and efficient markets. A perfect market has the following characteristics:

- trading is costless. This means that there are no taxes or transaction costs, and entry and exit from the market is free;
- information is costless and freely available to all market participants; and
- there are many buyers and sellers, and no one investor is dominant.

Clearly, no stock market anywhere in the world is a perfect market. However, companies and investors do not need capital markets to be perfect; rather, they need capital markets to offer fair prices so that they can make reasoned investment and financing decisions. From our earlier discussion, an efficient capital market will need to have the following features.

- *Operational efficiency*. This means that transaction costs in the market should be as low as possible and that required trading should be quickly effected.
- *Pricing efficiency*. This means that the prices of capital market securities fully and fairly reflect all information concerning past events and all events that the market expects to occur in the future. The prices of securities are therefore fair prices.
- *Allocational efficiency*. This means that the capital market, through the medium of pricing efficiency, allocates funds to where they can best be used.

The efficient market hypothesis (EMH) is concerned with establishing the prices of capital market securities and states that 'the prices of securities fully and fairly reflect all relevant available information'. In that case, as Keane (1983) points out, market efficiency refers to the speed and quality of the price adjustment to new information. The testing of markets for efficiency has led to the recognition of three different levels or forms of market efficiency.

2.2.3 Different forms of market efficiency

Empirical tests of the efficiency of capital markets have examined the extent to which the prices of securities reflect relevant information, i.e. pricing efficiency, because of a lack of data for testing allocational efficiency and operational efficiency. Many studies have examined the extent to which it is possible to make abnormal returns, that is, to make returns in excess of expected returns.

Weak form efficiency

Markets are said to be 'weak form efficient' if current share prices reflect all past movements of share prices. This means that it is not possible to make abnormal returns by studying past share price movements using Technical Analysis (*see* Section 2.2.6) in such a market. The empirical evidence strongly suggests that capital markets are weak form efficient.

Semi-strong form efficiency

Markets are said to be 'semi-strong form efficient' if share prices reflect all historic information and all publicly available information, and react quickly and accurately to reflect any new information as it becomes available. This means that, in a market which is semi-strong form efficient, abnormal returns cannot be made by studying available company information and so cannot be made using Fundamental Analysis (*see* Section 2.2.6). Empirical studies support the proposition that capital markets are semi-strong form efficient.

Strong form efficiency

Markets are said to be 'strong form efficient' if share prices reflect *all* information, whether it is publicly available or not. If markets are strong form efficient, then *no one* can make abnormal returns from share dealing, not even people who are able to act upon 'insider information'. Capital markets do not satisfy all the conditions for strong form efficiency, as some people do manage to make abnormal returns through insider dealing, as witnessed by some highly publicised prosecutions in recent years. However, it has to be said that these cases are relatively small in number when one considers the volume of transactions in the market as a whole.

2.2.4 Testing for market efficiency

Weak form tests

If a capital market is weak form efficient, so that security prices fully reflect past information, it will not be possible to predict future security prices by studying past movements. Many empirical studies have supported the proposition that the movement of capital market security prices over time is very like a 'random walk'. The random walk hypothesis suggests that, if we know the price of a security at the end of one time period, it is not possible for us to predict accurately its price at the end of the next time period. The empirical evidence indicates that the relationship between today's and tomorrow's security prices is indeed random, in which case capital markets are weak form efficient.

Empirical studies of weak form market efficiency have employed serial correlation tests, run tests and filter tests. Studies testing for *serial correlation*, one of the earliest of which was carried out by Kendall (1953), look for any correlation between the price changes of securities at different points in time. The evidence from such studies tends to support the random walk hypothesis. Studies using *run tests*, such as the one reported by Fama (1965), examine whether any significance can be attached to the direction of price changes by examining the length of the runs of successive price changes of the same sign. The empirical evidence indicated that the direction of the price changes of any one day was independent of the direction of the price changes of any other day. The distribution of directions was found to be based on pure chance, supporting the view that capital markets are weak form efficient. *Filter tests* try to identify significant long-term relationships in security price movements by filtering out short-term price changes. While Alexander (1961) found that filter tests could provide abnormal returns compared to a simple buy and hold strategy, any gains were cancelled out when transaction costs were taken into account.

Semi-strong form tests

Tests for semi-strong form efficiency look at the speed and accuracy of share price movements. In general, such tests provide support to the semi-strong form of the efficient market hypothesis. Fama *et al.* (1969) examined the adjustment of share prices to the publication of information about stock splits and concluded that it was not possible to profit from the information once it was made public. The market seemed to adjust efficiently and effectively to public information.

The famous research study by Ball and Brown (1968) showed that it was not possible to make abnormal returns on the basis of earnings announcements, as the information had already been substantially incorporated into security prices. Similarly, a study by Keown and Pinkerton (1981) showed that it was not possible to make abnormal returns on the basis of announcements concerning mergers. Franks *et al.* (1977) also studied market reaction to the release of information concerning mergers and found that possible benefits were anticipated by the market from up to three months prior to any announcements being made. These studies support the semi-strong form of the efficient market hypothesis by showing that security prices impound new relevant information quickly and accurately.

Strong form tests

Professional analysts, fund managers and other individuals with access to insider information may be able to use that information to make abnormal gains. Because a few people have access to information earlier than other investors and so can make abnormal gains, it could be argued that the market is strong form inefficient. It is hard to test for strong form efficiency directly, that is by conducting empirical studies which examine the market's *use* of information, because of this criticism that insiders can always make abnormal returns. Tests for strong form efficiency must therefore be *indirect* in their approach, examining how the *users* of information perform when compared against a yardstick such as the average return on the market.

Jensen (1968) looked at 115 mutual funds and found that the vast majority did not outperform the market when management costs were taken into consideration. Among many other studies with similar findings, Firth (1972) found that the followers of financial tipsters could not benefit from the investment advice offered due to the speed with which the market factored new information into share prices.

Summary

The empirical evidence suggests that the UK and US stock markets, as well as a large number of other world-class stock markets, respond efficiently to new information, and that only through 'insider dealing' can investors make abnormal gains. Since such cases are small in number when compared with the total value of business in the market as a whole, and since legislation has been introduced to curb the practice of insider dealing, we may conclude that capital markets are efficient.

2.2.5 Implications of the efficient market hypothesis

What are the implications for an investor of the stock market being efficient?

- Paying for investment research serves no purpose.
- Studying published accounts and stock market tips will not generate abnormal returns.
- There are no bargains to be found on efficient stock exchanges.

For a company and its managers, the implications of the stock market being efficient are:

- an efficient market correctly reflects the value of a company and expectations about its future performance and returns. The financial manager should therefore focus on making 'good' financial decisions which increase shareholder wealth, as these decisions will be correctly interpreted by the market and share price will adjust accordingly;
- cosmetic manipulation of accounting information, whether through window dressing of financial statements or by massaging earnings per share, will not mislead the market;
- the timing of new issues and rights issues is not important, since capital market securities are never underpriced.

2.2.6 Technical and fundamental analysis

The efficient market hypothesis suggests that future share prices cannot be predicted by studying past prices and, as we have seen, there is extensive evidence in support of this view. Despite the evidence, investment strategies based on the study of past share prices, or upon the analysis of published information such as annual accounts, are common, and the view held by many investment analysts appears to be that the capital markets are inefficient. Technical analysis involves the use of charts (chartism) and other methods to predict future share prices and share price trends; it clearly predicates, therefore, the existence of a relationship between past and future prices. For technical analysis to lead to abnormal returns on a regular basis, capital markets cannot even be efficient at the weak form level. Fundamental analysis uses public information to calculate a fundamental value for a share, and then offers investment advice by comparing the fundamental value with the current market price. Fundamental analysis is not possible if capital markets are semi-strong form efficient, since security prices will already fully and fairly reflect all publicly available information.

2.2.7 Anomalies in the behaviour of share prices

One of the subjects of empirical research in connection with the efficient market hypothesis has been apparent anomalies in the behaviour of share prices. Many such anomalies have been reported, of which the following are but a few.

Hours of the day effect

It has been reported that trading at particular times of the day can lead to negative or positive returns. For example, it appears that trading during the first 45 minutes on Monday mornings produces negative returns, while share prices tend to rise during the last 15 minutes of trading. While these effects have been reported, no satisfactory explanation has been offered. One suggestion is that investors evaluate their portfolios at weekends and sell on Monday mornings, whereas brokers initiate buy decisions regularly during the week.

Months of the year effect

High returns have been noted in particular months compared with others, e.g. April in the UK. It is possible that these high returns are due to selling strategies designed to crystallise capital losses for tax purposes, as the start of April is the end of the UK tax year. Share prices will be depressed at the start of April by such selling, but will recover as the new tax year gets under way. A trading strategy of buying at the start of the month and selling at the end may produce abnormal returns in April in the UK.

Size anomalies

The returns from investing in smaller companies have been shown, in the long run, to be greater than the average return from the companies of all sizes. For example, research by Dimson and Marsh (1986) found that small firms outperformed large firms by six per cent per year. There have been a number of proposed explanations for the fact that the shares of small companies outperform the market. It has been suggested, for example, that the growth prospects of smaller companies are better because they start from a lower base. However, if all investors are aware of the better growth prospects of small companies, the demand for their shares and hence their market prices would increase and returns would fall. Furthermore, any abnormal returns are likely to be eliminated by the higher dealing costs engendered by the lower liquidity of the shares of smaller companies.

2.3 RATIO ANALYSIS

In the introduction to this chapter, we mentioned that investors, financial managers and the capital markets obtain a great deal of information about companies from their financial statements, from financial databases, from the financial press, and so on. Ratio analysis can be applied to financial statements and similar data in order to assess the performance of a company; to determine whether it is solvent and financially healthy; to assess the risk attached to its financial structure; and to analyse the returns generated for its shareholders and other interested parties. Ratio analysis, then, can provide useful information to inform the decisions of the following user groups.

Investors

Financial institutions and ordinary investors need to make decisions about whether to buy or sell securities relating to particular companies.

Company management

Managers will need to assess and compare the performance of different divisions within the company, and the performance of the company as a whole against its competitors and against previous years.

Financial institutions

Banks and other financial institutions need to make decisions about whether or not to agree to requests for debt finance from companies, and about the terms and conditions under which such finance will be made available.

Information to carry out ratio analysis is primarily derived from company accounts, but financial information is now available through a variety of media. Financial databases are commonly used as a source of information on companies, examples of such databases being Datastream, FAME (Financial Accounting Made Easy), AMADEUS and Extel. Specialist reference books can also be consulted, such as the *Stock Exchange Yearbook*, *Kompass UK*, *Kelly's Business Directory*, the *FT Smaller Companies Handbook* and the *FT European Handbook*. Useful information on significant recent events in the lives of individual companies can be found by searching databases such as the *Financial Times* on CD-Rom and FT McCarthy.

2.3.1 The need for benchmarks

When using ratio analysis, it is important to recognise that ratios in isolation have little or no significance. In order to interpret the significance of particular ratios, they must at the very least be compared to appropriate benchmarks or yardsticks. Ratios may usefully be compared with the following indicators:

- predetermined targets for ratios set by company management, for example a target return on capital employed;

- the ratios of companies of a similar size who are engaged in similar business activities;
- the average ratios for the business sector within which a company operates, i.e. with industrial norms;
- ratios for the company from previous years, with financial data adjusted for inflation if necessary.

The benchmarks selected will naturally depend upon the purpose of the analysis. Comparing calculated ratios with appropriate benchmarks is not an end in itself – the difficult task of interpreting or explaining any differences found must then be undertaken!

2.3.2 Categories of ratios

When using ratios for analytical purposes, computation and interpretation is assisted if the analyst uses some sort of analytical framework. Weetman (1996) suggests that a systematic approach to ratio analysis should initially establish a broad picture, before focusing on areas of concern. A systematic approach to ratio analysis is also facilitated by using ratio pyramids as an analytical aid, but here we shall focus on the division of ratios into groups or categories which are linked to particular areas of concern. There is widespread agreement on the main ratios included in each category, even though the same category is given different names by different authors.

- *Profitability ratios.* Ratios in this category include return on capital employed, net profit margin, net asset turnover and gross profit margin.
- *Activity ratios.* Ratios in this category include debtors' ratio, creditors' ratio, stock turnover, fixed asset turnover and sales/net working capital.
- *Liquidity ratios.* Ratios in this category include the current ratio and the quick ratio.
- *Gearing ratios.* Ratios in this category include capital gearing, debt/equity ratio, interest cover and operating gearing.
- *Investor ratios.* Ratios in this category include return on equity, dividend per share, earnings per share, dividend cover, price/earnings ratio and dividend yield.

Because some ratios can be defined in different ways, it is important when comparing ratios to make sure that they have been calculated on a similar basis. The golden rule in ratio analysis is *always* to compare like with like!

The ratios discussed in the following sections are illustrated by calculations based on the accounts of Boater plc, which are given in Exhibit 2.3.

2.3.3 Profitability ratios

These ratios give a guide to how successful the managers of a company have been in generating profitability. Return on capital employed is often referred to as the 'primary ratio'.

EXHIBIT 2.3

Profit and loss account for the year ended 31 December

	19X7		19X6	
	£000	£000	£000	£000
Turnover		5700		5300
Cost of sales		4330		4000
Gross profit		1370		1300
Administration		735		620
Operating profit		635		680
Interest		220		190
Profit before taxation		415		490
Taxation		175		125
Profit after taxation		240		365
Preference dividends	90		90	
Ordinary dividends	140	230	140	230
Retained profits		10		135

Balance Sheet as at 31 December

		19X7			19X6	
	£000	£000	£000	£000	£000	£000
Fixed assets			5405			4880
Current assets:						
Stock		900			880	
Debtors		460			460	
Cash		5			60	
		1365			1400	
Creditors due within one year:						
Trade creditors	425			190		
Bank	nil			800		
Taxation	155			110		
Dividends	230			230		
		810			1330	
Net current assets			555			70
Total assets less current liabilities			5960			4950
Creditors due after one year:						
Debentures		1100			1100	
Bank loan		1000			0	
			2100			1100
			3860			3850

Financial statements of Boater plc

EXHIBIT 2.3 *(continued)*

		19X7			*19X6*	
	£000	*£000*	*£000*	*£000*	*£000*	*£000*
Capital and reserves:						
Share capital: Ordinary, 100 pence			1500			1500
Preference, 100 pence			1000			1000
Share premium			500			500
Reserves			860			850
			3860			3850

Ordinary share price: 135 pence (19X7) and 220 pence (19X6)

Return on capital employed (ROCE)

$$\frac{\text{profit before interest and tax}}{\text{capital employed}}$$

This relates the overall profitability of a company to the finance used to generate it, and links net profit margin to asset turnover.

$$\text{ROCE} = \text{net profit margin} \times \text{asset turnover}$$

Profit before interest and tax is often called operating profit, as in the Boater plc example. The meaning of 'capital employed' often causes confusion, but for this ratio it is simply 'total assets less current liabilities', a figure that is required to be included in published accounts. An alternative definition of capital employed, with exactly the same meaning, is 'fixed assets plus net working capital'. This ratio is clearly very sensitive to investment in fixed assets, to the age of assets (since older assets will have been depreciated more than young ones), and to when assets were last revalued. For Boater plc:

$$\text{ROCE (19X6)} = 100 \times (680/4950) = 13.74 \text{ per cent}$$
$$\text{ROCE (19X7)} = 100 \times (635/5960) = 10.65 \text{ per cent}$$

Net profit margin

$$\frac{\text{profit before interest and tax} \times 100}{\text{sales or turnover}}$$

This ratio, which is also called operating profit margin, indicates the efficiency with which costs have been controlled in the generation of profit from sales. It does not differentiate between operating costs, administrative costs, distribution costs, and so on. For Boater plc:

$$\text{Net profit margin (19X6)} = 100 \times (680/5300) = 12.8 \text{ per cent}$$
$$\text{Net profit margin (19X7)} = 100 \times (635/5700) = 11.1 \text{ per cent}$$

Asset turnover

$$\frac{\text{sales or turnover}}{\text{capital employed}}$$

Capital employed is defined here in exactly the same way as for ROCE, i.e. 'total assets less current liabilities', and so the asset turnover ratio is also sensitive to fixed asset values. This ratio gives a guide to productive efficiency, i.e. how well assets have been utilised in the generation of sales. For Boater plc:

Asset turnover (19X6) = 5300/4950 = 1.07 times
Asset turnover (19X7) = 5700/5960 = 0.96 times

Gross profit margin

$$\frac{\text{gross profit} \times 100}{\text{sales or turnover}}$$

This ratio shows how well costs of production have been controlled. For Boater plc:

Gross profit margin (19X6) = 100 × (1300/5300) = 24.5 per cent
Gross profit margin (19X7) = 100 × (1370/5700) = 24.0 per cent

2.3.4 Activity ratios

These ratios show how efficiently a company has managed its short-term assets and liabilities, i.e. its working capital, and they are closely linked to the liquidity ratios. With each ratio, the average value for the year should be used, e.g. average level of debtors should be used in calculating the debtors' ratio, but it is usual for the year-end value to be substituted in order to obtain figures for comparative purposes. Activity ratios for a company must be calculated on a consistent basis, however, so either year-end values or average values must be used throughout.

Debtors' ratio or debtor days

$$\frac{\text{debtors} \times 365}{\text{credit sales}}$$

The value of credit sales is usually not available and so sales or turnover is used as a substitute. The debtors' ratio gives the average period of credit being taken by customers and, if compared with a company's allowed credit period, can give an indication of the efficiency of debtor administration. For Boater plc:

Debtors' ratio (19X6) = 365 × (460/5300) = 32 days
Debtors' ratio (19X7) = 365 × (460/5700) = 29 days

Creditors' ratio or creditor days

$$\frac{\text{trade creditors} \times 365}{\text{cost of sales}}$$

Creditors should really be compared with credit purchases, but as this information is not usually available, cost of sales is used instead. The creditors' ratio gives the average time taken for suppliers of goods and services to receive payment. For Boater plc:

Creditors' ratio (19X6) = 365 × (190/4000) = 17 days
Creditors' ratio (19X7) = 365 × (425/4330) = 36 days

Stock turnover

$$\frac{\text{stock or inventory} \times 365}{\text{cost of sales}}$$

This ratio shows how long it takes for a company to turn its stocks or inventory into sales. Several component ratios can be calculated by dividing the total stock figure into its component parts, i.e. raw materials, work in progress and finished goods (*see* Section 10.1.1). The shorter the stock turnover period, the lower will be the costs to the company of holding stock. The general value of this ratio is very dependent upon the need for stock, and so will vary significantly with the nature of a company's business. For Boater plc:

Stock turnover (19X6) = 365 × (880/4000) = 80 days
Stock turnover (19X7) = 365 × (900/4330) = 76 days

Cash conversion cycle

This is found by adding stock turnover and debtor days and then subtracting creditor days. It can be used to indicate the extent of working capital financing needed (*see* Section 10.1.1). For Boater plc:

Cash conversion cycle (19X6) = 31 days + 80 days – 17 days = 94 days
Cash conversion cycle (19X7) = 29 days + 76 days – 36 days = 69 days

Fixed asset turnover

$$\frac{\text{sales or turnover}}{\text{fixed assets}}$$

Net asset turnover is based on capital employed, but a more detailed picture of asset utilisation can be obtained if capital employed is divided into fixed assets and working capital. Fixed asset turnover, then, indicates the sales being generated by the fixed asset base of a company. Like ROCE, it is sensitive to the acquisition, age and valuation of fixed assets. For Boater plc:

Fixed asset turnover (19X6) = 5300/4880 = 1.1 times
Fixed asset turnover (19X7) = 5700/5405 = 1.05 times

Sales/net working capital

$$\frac{\text{sales or turnover}}{\text{net current assets}}$$

This ratio shows the way in which sales are supported by working capital. As sales increase, working capital must increase as well if sales are to be adequately supported. For Boater plc:

Sales/net working capital (19X6) = 5300/(880 + 460 – 190) = 4.6 times
Sales/net working capital (19X7) = 5700/(900 + 460 – 425) = 6.1 times

2.3.5 Liquidity ratios

Current ratio

$$\frac{\text{current assets}}{\text{current liabilities}}$$

This measures a company's ability to meet its financial obligations as they become due. It is often said that the 'normal' current ratio should be around two, but this will vary from industry to industry. For Boater plc:

Current ratio (19X6) = 1400/1330 = 1.05 times
Current ratio (19X7) = 1365/810 = 1.7 times

Quick ratio

$$\frac{\text{current assets less stock}}{\text{current liabilities}}$$

It may be argued that the current ratio overstates a company's ability to meet its financial obligations because of the inclusion of stock in the numerator. This is a valid argument if it takes more than a short time to convert stock into sales, i.e. if stock turnover is not small, and if sales are on credit terms. Where stock is turned over quickly and sales are primarily on a cash or near-cash basis, for example in the retail food trade, the argument is not persuasive. The quick ratio seeks to compare liquid current assets with short-term liabilities and a common rule of thumb is that it should be close to one. In practice, as with the current ratio, the average value will vary from industry to industry. For Boater plc:

Quick ratio (19X6) = (1400 – 880)/1330 = 0.4 times
Quick ratio (19X7) = (1365 – 900)/810 = 0.6 times

2.3.6 Gearing ratios

These ratios reflect how a company is financed with respect to debt and equity and are used to assess the various risks that arise as a result.

Capital gearing ratio

$$\frac{\text{long-term debt capital}}{\text{capital employed}}$$

The purpose of this ratio is to indicate the proportion of debt finance employed by a company. Long-term debt capital includes debentures, loan stock and bank loans. It is important when comparing calculated values to benchmarks to confirm that the method of calculation is the same, since other definitions of this ratio are used. One common alternative replaces long-term debt capital with 'prior charge capital', which includes preference share capital in addition to debt. A company may be considered to be 'highly geared' if capital gearing is greater than 50 per cent, but this is only a rule of thumb. For Boater plc:

Capital gearing (19X6) = 100 × (1100/4950) = 22 per cent
Capital gearing (19X7) = 100 × ((1100 + 1000)/5960) = 35 per cent

Debt/equity ratio

$$\frac{\text{long-term debt}}{\text{share capital and reserves}}$$

This ratio serves a similar purpose to capital gearing. Here, a company would be said to be highly geared if the ratio were greater than 100 per cent, but this is again only a rule of thumb. For Boater plc:

Debt/equity ratio (19X6) = 100 × (1100/3850) = 29 per cent
Debt/equity ratio (19X7) = 100 × ((1100 + 1000)/3860) = 54 per cent

Interest cover

$$\frac{\text{profit before interest and tax}}{\text{interest charges}}$$

This indicates how many times a company can cover its current interest payments out of current profits and so gives an indication of whether servicing its existing debt is becoming a problem. An interest cover of between three and seven times is usually regarded as safe. For Boater plc:

Interest cover (19X6) = 680/190 = 3.6 times
Interest cover (19X7) = 635/220 = 2.9 times

2.3.7 Shareholder ratios

These will primarily be used by investors and analysts in order to decide whether they should buy or sell the shares of particular companies.

Return on equity

$$\frac{\text{earnings after tax and preference dividends}}{\text{shareholders' funds}}$$

While ROCE looks at overall return, return on equity compares the earnings attributable to ordinary shareholders with the funds that they have invested in the business. 'Shareholders' funds' is equal to ordinary share capital plus reserves, but excluding preference share capital. For Boater plc:

Return on equity (19X6) = 100 × ((365 – 90)/(3850 – 1000)) = 9.65 per cent
Return on equity (19X7) = 100 × ((240 – 90)/(3860 – 1000)) = 5.2 per cent

Dividend per share

$$\frac{\text{total dividend paid to ordinary shareholders}}{\text{number of issued ordinary shares}}$$

While the total dividend paid may change from year to year, individual shareholders will usually be concerned that the dividend paid on a per share basis does not decrease. Note that the calculation is based on the number of ordinary shares *issued* by a company, not on the number of ordinary shares it is *authorised* to issue. For Boater plc:

Dividend per share (19X6) = 100 × (140/1500) = 9.3 pence
Dividend per share (19X7) = 100 × (140/1500) = 9.3 pence

Earnings per share ratio

$$\frac{\text{earnings after tax and preference dividends}}{\text{number of issued ordinary shares}}$$

This is regarded as a key ratio by stock market investors. Caution has to be exercised with this ratio though, as there are several methods by which it is calculated. These complications are discussed, for example, by Weetman (1996). Here, we shall calculate earnings per share by simply using earnings attributable to ordinary shareholders, so for Boater plc:

Earnings per share (19X6) = 100 × ((365 – 90)/1500)) = 18.3 pence
Earnings per share (19X7) = 100 × ((240 – 90)/1500)) = 10.0 pence

Dividend cover

$$\frac{\text{earnings per share}}{\text{dividend per share}}$$

This indicates how 'safe' a company's dividend payment is by calculating how many times the current dividend is covered by current earnings. For Boater plc:

Dividend cover (19X6) = 18.3/9.3 = 2.0 times
Dividend cover (19X7) = 10/9.3 = 1.1 times

Price/earnings ratio

$$\frac{\text{market price of share}}{\text{earnings per share}}$$

Like earnings per share, the price/earnings (P/E) ratio is regarded as a key ratio by stock market investors. It shows how much an investor is prepared to pay for a share, given a company's current earnings per share (EPS). It therefore gives an indication of the confidence of investors in the expected future performance of the company, relative to that of other companies. For Boater plc:

Price/earnings ratio (19X6) = 220/18.3 = 12
Price/earnings ratio (19X7) = 135/10 = 13.5

Payout ratio

$$\frac{\text{ordinary dividends} \times 100}{\text{distributable earnings}}$$

This ratio is commonly used in discussions on dividend policy and share valuation. Some companies, for example, may choose to pay out a fixed percentage of earnings every year. For Boater plc:

Payout ratio (19X6) = 100 × (140/(365 – 90)) = 51 per cent
Payout ratio (19X7) = 100 × (140/(240 – 90)) = 93 per cent

Dividend yield

$$\frac{\text{dividend per share} \times 100}{\text{share price}}$$

This ratio gives a measure of how much an investor can expect to receive in exchange for purchasing a given share, although it fails to take into account capital gains due to increasing share prices. It is commonly quoted in the financial press. For Boater plc:

Dividend yield (19X6) = 100 × (9.3/220) = 4.2 per cent
Dividend yield (19X7) = 100 × (9.3/135) = 6.9 per cent

2.3.8 Interpreting financial ratios

The ratios that have been calculated for Boater plc are summarised in Exhibit 2.4. If there had been a particular focus to this analysis, only a selection of ratios would have been calculated. For example, if the focus had been on the efficiency of working capital management, no purpose would have been served by calculating the investor ratios. What is the overall story that is told by Boater's ratios? The following comments are offered as a guide to some of the issues raised in each of the ratio categories, and should be studied in conjunction with Exhibit 2.4.

EXHIBIT 2.4

	19X7	*19X6*
Return on capital employed (per cent)	10.65	13.74
Net profit margin (per cent)	11.1	12.8
Asset turnover (times)	0.96	1.07
Gross profit margin (per cent)	24.0	24.5
Debtors' ratio (days)	29	32
Creditors' ratio (days)	36	17
Stock turnover (days)	76	80
Cash conversion cycle (days)	69	94
Fixed asset turnover (times)	1.05	1.1
Sales/net working capital (per cent)	6.1	4.6
Current ratio (times)	1.7	1.05
Quick ratio (times)	0.6	0.4
Capital gearing (per cent)	35	22
Debt/equity ratio (per cent)	54	29
Interest cover (times)	2.9	3.6
Return on equity (per cent)	5.2	9.65
Dividend per share (pence)	9.3	9.3
Earnings per share (pence)	10	18.3
Dividend cover (times)	1.1	2.0
Price/earnings ratio	13.5	12
Payout ratio (per cent)	93	51
Dividend yield (per cent)	6.9	4.2

Comparative financial ratios for Boater plc

Profitability

Boater's overall profitability has declined, due both to a decline in turnover in relation to capital employed and to a decline in profitability in sales terms. This decline has occurred despite an increase in turnover and seems to be partly due to a substantial increase in administration costs. The decline in ROCE is also linked to the replacement of the overdraft with a bank loan and substantial investment in fixed assets.

Activity and liquidity

The loss of the overdraft has improved both the current ratio and the quick ratio, but cash reserves have fallen. There has been little change in debtor days or stock turnover, but creditor days have more than doubled. The company is more reliant on trade creditors as a source of short-term finance.

Gearing and risk

The new loan has increased gearing and, although this does not seem to be risky, the interest cover is now looking low. This is because operating profit has fallen but interest charges have increased.

Investor interest

Even though earnings have fallen, the dividend has been maintained, and since the share price has fallen, dividend yield has increased as a result. The increase in P/E ratio indicates that investors feel that the company will improve in the future.

2.3.9 Problems with ratio analysis

When using ratio analysis, results must be treated with caution for a number of reasons. One problem is that balance sheet information relates to the company's position on one day of the year. If the balance sheet had been prepared three months earlier, a different picture might have been presented and key ratios might have had different values. Taxation payable and dividends due might not have been included, for example, and the current ratio could have looked much healthier. Should such items be excluded when calculating working capital ratios?

More seriously, it can be quite difficult to find a similar company in order to make inter-company comparisons. No two companies are identical in every respect and so allowance must be made for any differences in commercial activity. For similar reasons, allowance must be made for any differences in accounting policies.

The reliability of ratio analysis is naturally dependent on the reliability of the accounting information on which it is based. Financial statements have become increasingly complex, and it is not easy to determine if 'creative accounting' has taken place. Smith (1992) described company accounting as 'a jungle with many species of animal – some benign, some carnivorous – and its own rules'. Care must be taken to identify any 'off-balance-sheet financing' or use of complex financial instruments which may distort a company's true financial position.

Ratio analysis, in conclusion, should be regarded as only the beginning of financial analysis, serving primarily to raise questions which require deeper investigation before any understanding begins to appear. Investors, financial institutions and company managers will use ratio analysis as one of many sources of information which assist them in making decisions.

2.4 CONCLUSION

In this chapter, we have discussed some of the important aspects of the financing decision in corporate finance – the balance between internal and external finance in capital investment, the different sources of finance available to company management, the importance of the capital markets – and we have also discussed at some length the key topic of efficient capital markets. The debate about market efficiency is a continuing one and it is recommended that you consider carefully the implications for corporate finance theory of markets being efficient as you continue your studies.

The tool of ratio analysis has been introduced in this chapter. Later chapters will discuss particular ratios in more detail, especially those concerned with working capital and gearing.

KEY POINTS

1 An efficient financing policy aims to raise necessary funds at the required time and at the lowest cost.

2 Internal finance is mainly retained earnings, which is not to be confused with retained profit, since only cash can be invested. Most funds for investment come from retained earnings.

3 The split between internal and external finance for capital investment will depend on the amount of finance needed, the profitability of existing operations, the opportunity cost of retained earnings, the cost and availability of external finance, and the company's dividend policy.

4 There are many kinds of external finance available to a company through the capital markets, including ordinary shares, preference shares and debentures, ordinary loan stock and convertibles.

5 The primary market is where new issues of equity and debt are made, while the secondary market is for dealing in securities already in issue. The secondary market provides pricing information and thereby increases the allocational efficiency of the primary market.

6 Smaller companies who are unable or unwilling to seek a full listing can obtain a quotation on the Alternative Investment Market (AIM).

7 An efficient market needs operational efficiency, allocational efficiency and pricing efficiency. A perfect market requires that trading is costless, that information is costless and freely available, and that no one investor is dominant.

8 Operational efficiency means that transaction costs should be as low as possible and sales are quickly effected. Pricing efficiency means that security prices fully and fairly reflect all relevant information so that they are fair prices. Allocational efficiency means that capital markets allocate funds to their most productive use.

9 Markets are weak form efficient if share prices reflect all past price movements. In such a market, abnormal returns cannot be made by studying past share price movements. Empirical evidence suggests capital markets are weak form efficient.

10 Markets are semi-strong form efficient if share prices reflect past information and all publicly available information. In such a market, abnormal returns cannot be made by studying available company information. Empirical evidence suggests that capital markets are semi-strong form efficient.

11 Markets are strong form efficient if share prices reflect *all* information. In such a market, no one can make abnormal returns. While capital markets are not totally strong form efficient, the inefficiency is perhaps limited.

12 The random walk hypothesis suggests that there is no connection between successive share price movements. Empirical evidence supports this view, meaning that capital markets are weak form efficient.

13 Weak form tests have used serial correlation tests, run tests and filter tests.

14 Tests for semi-strong form efficiency look at the speed and accuracy of share price movements, for example in response to news concerning earnings and mergers.

15 Strong form efficiency can only be tested indirectly, for example by comparing the returns of fund managers with the market return.

16 Empirical evidence suggests the UK and US stock markets are efficient.

17 The implications for investors of the efficient market hypothesis are that research is pointless and that no bargains exist on the capital markets.

18 The implications for companies of the efficient market hypothesis are that share prices reflect the true value of a company, that manipulation of accounts is pointless, and that the timing of new issues is irrelevant.

19 Technical analysis seeks to predict share prices through studying their historic movements; fundamental analysis looks for the fundamental value of a share. Neither is worthwhile in a semi-strong form efficient market.

20 A significant body of research has examined apparent anomalies in share price behaviour, such as the day of the week effect and the company size effect.

21 Ratio analysis can provide useful information to investors, company management and financial institutions. Further information is available from financial databases.

22 Ratios on their own mean little. They must be compared with benchmarks, such as target ratios, ratios of similar companies, industrial norms or ratios from previous years.

23 A systematic approach to ratio analysis could look at ratios concerned with profitability, activity, liquidity, gearing and investment, always remembering to compare like with like.

24 Problems with ratio analysis include the following: balance sheet figures are static; similar companies for comparison are hard to find; accounting policies may be different; and creative accounting may have been used together with complex financing methods.

QUESTIONS

Answers to these questions can be found on pages 394–5.

1 Explain the difference between retained earnings and retained profit.

2 Describe the factors that influence the relative proportions of internal and external finance used in capital investment.

3 What is the relevance of the efficient market hypothesis for corporate financial managers?

4 Which of the following statements about the efficient market hypothesis is not correct?
   (a) if the stock market shows weak form efficiency, then chartists cannot make consistently superior returns;
   (b) if the market is strong form efficient, only people with insider information can beat the market;
   (c) if the market is semi-strong form efficient, then fundamental analysis will not bring abnormal returns to analysts;
   (d) if the market is semi-strong form efficient, all past and current publicly available information is reflected in the share price;
   (e) if the market is weak form efficient, then all historic information about a share is embodied in its current market price.

5 Describe the features of a perfect capital market.

6 Explain the difference between allocational efficiency, pricing efficiency and operational efficiency.

7 Why is it difficult to test for strong form efficiency?

8 Describe the different benchmarks that can be used for ratio analysis.

9 Describe the five categories of ratios and list and define the ratios in each category. In each case, without referring to the calculations in the text, calculate the relevant ratio for Boater plc.

10 What are the potential problems associated with using ratio analysis to analyse the financial health and performance of companies?

QUESTIONS FOR REVIEW

Answers to these questions can be found on pages 395–7.

1 Distinguish between the primary and secondary capital markets in the UK and discuss the role played by these markets in financial management. What are the desirable characteristics of primary and secondary capital markets?

2 While there is a large body of evidence in support of the efficient market hypothesis, it has been suggested that this evidence only shows that it is not possible to prove that markets are inefficient. Recent research has explored 'anomalies' in the behaviour of prices of securities. Briefly describe these anomalies and suggest possible explanations.

3 The following financial statements are extracts from the accounts of Hoult plc.

Profit and loss accounts for years ending 31 December

	1995	*1996*	*1997*
	£000	*£000*	*£000*
Sales	960	1080	1220
Cost of sales	670	780	885
Gross profit	290	300	335
Administration expenses	260	270	302
Operating profit	30	30	33
Interest	13	14	18
Profit before taxation	17	16	15
Taxation	2	1	1
Profit after taxation	15	15	14
Dividends	0	0	4
Retained profit	15	15	10

Balance sheets for years to 31 December

	1995		*1996*		*1997*	
	£000	*£000*	*£000*	*£000*	*£000*	*£000*
Net fixed assets		160		120		100
Current assets:						
Stock	200		210		225	
Debtors	160		180		250	
Cash	0		0		0	
	360		390		475	
Current liabilities:						
Trade creditors	75		80		145	
Overdraft	70		80		110	
	145		160		255	
Net current assets		215		230		220
Total assets less current liabilities		375		350		320
8 per cent debentures		120		80		40
		255		270		280
Capital and reserves:						
Ordinary shares		160		160		160
Profit and loss		95		110		120
		255		270		280

The eight per cent debentures are redeemable in instalments and the final instalment is due to be paid in 1998.

The finance director is concerned about the poor liquidity of Hoult plc and has asked you to report on the company's recent performance. After calculating appropriate ratios, comment on the performance and financial health of Hoult plc.

QUESTIONS FOR DISCUSSION

1 You have been approached by Mr Dayton, who is seeking advice about his investment portfolio. He is considering purchasing shares in companies listed on either the Unlisted Securities Market or the Alternative Investment Market. Mr Green, a friend of Mr Dayton, has told him that he should invest only in shares that are listed on markets that are efficient, since otherwise he cannot be sure that he is paying a fair price for them. Mr Dayton has explained to you that he is not sure what an 'efficient' market is.

(a) Explain to Mr Dayton what characteristics are usually required to be present for a market to be described as efficient.

(b) Discuss whether the Alternative Investment Market may be considered to be an efficient market.

(c) Critically discuss the extent to which empirical research has shown capital markets to be efficient.

2 Critically discuss the following statements about stock market efficiency.

(a) The weak form of the efficient market hypothesis implies that it is possible for an investor to generate abnormal returns by analysing changes in past share prices.

(b) The semi-strong form of the efficient market hypothesis implies that it is possible for an investor to earn superior returns by studying company accounts, newspapers and investment journals, or by purchasing reports from market analysts.

(c) The strong form of the efficient market hypothesis implies that since security prices reflect all available information, there is no way that investors can achieve abnormal returns.

3 Discuss the importance of the efficient market hypothesis to the following parties:

(a) shareholders concerned about the maximisation of their wealth;

(b) corporate financial managers making capital investment decisions; and

(c) investors analysing the annual reports of listed companies.

REFERENCES

Alexander, S. (1961) 'Price movements in speculative markets: trends or random walks', *Industrial Management Review*, May, pp. 7–26.

Ball, R. and Brown, P. (1968) 'An empirical evaluation of accounting income numbers', *Journal of Accounting Research*, Autumn, pp. 159–78.

Dimson, E. and Marsh, P. (1986) 'Event study methodologies and the size effect: the case of UK press recommendations', *Journal of Financial Economics*, Sept, Vol. 17, No. 1, pp. 113–42.

Dixon, R. and Holmes, P. (1992) *Financial Markets: An Introduction*, London, Chapman and Hall.

Fama, E. (1965) 'The behaviour of stock market prices', *Journal of Business*, Jan, pp. 34–106.

Fama, E., Fisher, L., Jensen, M. and Roll, R. (1969) 'The adjustment of stock prices to new information', *International Economic Review*, Feb, Vol. 10, pp. 1–21.

Firth, M. (1972) 'The performance of share recommendations made by investment analysts and the effects on market efficiency', *Journal of Business Finance*, Summer, pp. 58–67.

Foley, B. (1991) *Capital Markets*, London, Macmillan.

Franks, J., Broyles, J. and Hecht, M. (1977) 'An industry study of the profitability of mergers in the United Kingdom', *Journal of Finance*, Vol. 32, pp. 1513–25.

Jensen, M. (1968) 'The performance of mutual funds in the period 1945–64', *Journal of Finance*, May, pp. 389–416.

Keane, S. (1983) *Stock Market Efficiency: Theory, evidence, implications*, Philip Allan.

Kendall, R. (1953) 'The analysis of economic time series, part 1: prices', *Journal of the Royal Statistical Society*, Vol. 69, pp. 11–25.

Keown, A. and Pinkerton, J. (1981) 'Merger announcements and insider trading activity', *Journal of Finance*, Sept, pp. 855–70.

Smith, T. (1992) *Accounting for Growth: Stripping the camouflage from company accounts*, Century Business.

Weetman, P. (1996) *Financial and Management Accounting: An Introduction*, London, Pitman Publishing.

RECOMMENDED READING

A very useful source of discussion and analysis on efficient markets is the book by Keane, S. (1983) *Stock Market Efficiency: Theory, evidence, implications*, Philip Allan. A lucid treatment of efficient markets is also found in Samuels, J., Wilkes, F. and Brayshaw, R. (1995) *Management of Company Finance*, Chapman and Hall.

Useful journal articles and other material include the following:

Barberis, N. (1997) 'Markets: the price may not be right', in *Mastering Finance*, issue 7, *Financial Times*.

Fama, E. (1991) 'Efficient capital markets II', *Journal of Finance*, Vol. 46, Dec, pp. 1575–617.

Germain, L. (1997) 'Market efficiency: a mirror for information', in *Mastering Finance*, Issue 1, *Financial Times*.

Lo, A. and MacKinlay, C. (1997) 'Stumbling block for the random walk', in *Mastering Finance*, Issue 7, *Financial Times*.

Musto, D. (1997) 'The end-of-the-year show', in *Mastering Finance*, Issue 7, *Financial Times*.

Naik, N. (1997) 'The many roles of financial markets', in *Mastering Finance*, Issue 1, *Financial Times*.

O'Brien, P. (1997) 'Problems with earnings and cash flow', in *Mastering Finance*, Issue 2, *Financial Times*.

Thaler, R. (1997) 'Giving markets a human dimension', in *Mastering Finance*, Issue 6, *Financial Times*.

CHAPTER 3

AN OVERVIEW OF INVESTMENT APPRAISAL METHODS

INTRODUCTION

Companies need to invest in wealth-creating assets in order to renew, extend or replace the means by which they carry on their business. Capital investment, then, allows companies to continue to generate profits in future periods or to maintain the profitability of existing business activities. Typically, such capital investment projects will require significant cash outflows at the inception of a project, followed by cash inflows over several years. Because significant amounts of cash need to be raised and invested, and because these projects will often determine whether the future of the company is a profitable one, they require careful evaluation.

In order to maximise the return to the shareholders of a company, it is important the best or most profitable investment projects are selected. Because the results of making a bad long-term investment decision can be both financially and strategically devastating, particular care needs to be taken with investment project selection and evaluation. Since capital investment decisions affect a company over a long period of time, it may be helpful to view the balance sheet as the sum total of the previous investment and financing decisions taken by its directors and managers.

LEARNING OBJECTIVES

After studying this chapter, you should have achieved the following learning objectives:

- familiarity with the four main investment appraisal techniques of payback, accounting rate of return, net present value and internal rate of return;
- an understanding of the reasons why discounted cash flow methods are preferred to the traditional techniques of payback and accounting rate of return;
- an understanding of why net present value is considered to be superior to internal rate of return as an investment appraisal method;
- an appreciation of how net present value and internal rate of return can be reconciled in situations where they offer conflicting advice;
- an understanding of the techniques to be employed in order to arrive at the best investment decision if investment capital is rationed.

3.1 THE PAYBACK PERIOD

The payback period is the number of years it will take to recover the original investment from the net cash flows resulting from a capital investment project. If the payback period is equal to or less than a predetermined target value, the investment project is acceptable. It is possible to obtain an estimate of the payback period to several decimal places if cash flows are assumed to occur evenly throughout each year, but a high degree of accuracy in estimating the payback period is not necessarily desirable, since it does not offer information which is especially useful. A figure to the nearest year or half-year is sufficient. While research has shown that payback is the most popular investment appraisal technique, it suffers from such serious shortcomings that it can only really be regarded as a first screening method.

3.1.1 Example of the payback method

Consider an investment project with the cash flows given in Exhibit 3.1.

The cash flows of this project are called 'conventional' cash flows and the project is called a 'conventional project'. A conventional project can be defined as one which requires an initial cash investment at the inception of the project, followed by a series of cash inflows over the life of the project. We can see that, after three years, the project has generated positive cash inflows totalling £400. Within the fourth year, the remaining £50 of the initial investment will be recovered. As the cash inflow in that year is £100 and we have assumed that this occurs evenly during the year, it will take a further six months or 0.5 years for the final sum to be recovered. The payback period, then, is 3.5 years.

Sometimes it can be helpful to draw up a small table of cumulative cash flows for a project as a way of determining its payback period, as shown in Exhibit 3.2.

EXHIBIT 3.1

Year	0	1	2	3	4	5
Cash flow (£)	(450)	100	200	100	100	80

Simple investment project, showing a significant initial investment followed by a series of cash inflows over the life of the project

EXHIBIT 3.2

Year	*Cash flow (£)*	*Cumulative cash flow (£)*
0	(450)	(450)
1	100	(350)
2	200	(150)
3	100	(50)
4	100	50
5	80	130

Table of cumulative cash flows for the conventional project of the previous exhibit, showing that the payback period is between three and four years

3.1.2 The advantages of the payback method

The advantages of the payback method are that it is simple and easy to apply and, as a concept, it is straightforward to understand. The payback period is calculated using cash flows, not accounting profits, and so should not be open to manipulation by managerial preferences for particular accounting policies. If we accept that more distant cash flows are more uncertain and that increasing uncertainty is synonymous with increasing risk, it is possible to argue that another advantage of the payback method is that it takes account of risk, in that it implicitly assumes that a shorter payback period is superior to a longer one.

It has been argued that payback period is a useful investment appraisal method if a company is restricted in the amount of finance that it has available for investment, since the sooner cash is returned by a project, the sooner it can be reinvested into other projects. While there is some truth in this claim, it ignores the fact that there are better investment appraisal methods available to deal with capital rationing, as explained in Section 3.7.

3.1.3 The disadvantages of the payback method

There are a number of difficulties in using the payback method to assess capital investment projects and these are sufficiently serious for it to be generally rejected as a credible method of investment appraisal. One of the major disadvantages is that the payback method ignores the time value of money, so that it gives equal weight to cash flows whenever they occur. The payback method also ignores the size and the timing of cash flows within the payback period. We can illustrate this point by referring back to the example in Exhibit 3.1. We can see that the payback period remains 3.5 years even if the project generates no cash inflows in the first and second years of operation, but then a cash inflow of £400 in the third year. In fact, any combination of cash flows in the first three years which total £400 would have given the same payback period.

The problem of ignoring the time value of money is partly remedied by using the discounted payback method discussed in Section 3.7.

Another serious disadvantage of the payback method is that it ignores all cash flows outside of the payback period and so does not consider the project as a whole. If a company rejected all projects with payback periods greater than three years, it would reject the project given in Exhibit 3.1. Suppose that this project, in Year 4, had been expected to generate a cash inflow of £1000. This expected cash inflow would have been ignored if the sole investment appraisal method being applied was the payback method, and it would still have been rejected. Would this have been a wealth-maximising decision for the company concerned? Hardly! In fact, the choice of the maximum payback period acceptable to a company is an arbitrary one, since it is not possible to say why one payback period is preferable to any other. Why should a project with a payback period of three years be accepted, while a project with a payback period of three-and-a-half years be rejected?

In fairness, we should recognise that when the payback method is used in practice, cash flows outside of the payback period are not ignored, but taken into consideration as part of the exercise of managerial judgement. However, this only serves to reinforce the inadequacy of the payback method as a measure of the acceptability of projects.

The general conclusion that can be drawn from this discussion is that the payback method fails to give any real indication of whether an investment project is a 'good' one for a company to undertake, or not. For this reason, it has been argued that, despite its obvious and well-documented popularity, the payback period is not really an investment appraisal method at all, but rather a means of assessing the effect that acceptance of a project will have on a company's liquidity position.

3.2 THE ACCOUNTING RATE OF RETURN METHOD

There are several different definitions of accounting rate of return (ARR), which is also called return on capital employed (ROCE) or return on investment (ROI) in some books. All of these definitions relate accounting profit to some measure of the capital employed in a capital investment project. One definition that is widely used is:

$$\text{ARR} = \frac{\text{average annual accounting profit}}{\text{average investment}} \times 100$$

The average investment will need to take account of any scrap value:

$$\text{Average investment} = \frac{\text{initial investment + scrap value}}{2}$$

Another common definition, which is similar to the accounting definition of return on capital employed, is:

$$\text{ARR} = \frac{\text{average annual accounting profit}}{\text{initial investment}} \times 100$$

It is important to note that the accounting rate of return is calculated using accounting profits, which are operating cash flows adjusted to take account of depreciation. Accounting profits, then, are not cash flows, since depreciation is an accounting adjustment which does not correspond to a movement of cash. The decision rule here would be to accept an investment project if its accounting rate of return was greater than a target or hurdle rate of return. If only one of two investment projects can be undertaken (i.e. if the projects are mutually exclusive), the project with the highest accounting rate of return should be accepted.

Example Calculation of the accounting rate of return

Carbon plc is considering the purchase of a recycling machine and has found two machines which meet its specification. Each machine has an expected economic life of five years. Machine 1 would generate annual cash flows (receipts less payments) of £210 000 and would cost £570 000. Its scrap value at the end of five years would be £70 000. Machine 2 would generate annual cash flows of £510 000 and would cost £1 616 000. The scrap value of this machine at the end of five years is expected to be £301 000. Carbon plc uses the straight-line method of depreciation.

Calculate the accounting rate of return for both Machine 1 and Machine 2 and state which machine you would recommend, giving reasons.

For Machine 1:	£
Total cash profit = 210 000 × 5 =	1 050 000
Total depreciation = 570 000 – 70 000 =	500 000
Total accounting profit	550 000

Average annual accounting profit = 550 000/5 =	£110 000 per year
Average investment = (570 000 + 70 000)/2 =	£320 000
Accounting rate of return = 100 × (110 000/320 000) =	34.4 per cent

For Machine 2:	£
Total cash profit = 510 000 × 5 =	2 550 000
Total depreciation = 1 616 000 – 301 000 =	1 315 000
Total accounting profit	1 235 000

Average annual accounting profit = 1 235 000/5 =	£247 000 per year
Average investment = (1 616 000 + 301 000)/2 =	£958 500
Accounting rate of return = 100 × (247 000/958 000) =	25.8 per cent

The recommendation is that Machine 1 should be accepted, as it has a higher accounting rate of return than Machine 2 and only one of the machines can be purchased.

3.2.1 Advantages of the accounting rate of return method

There are a number of reasons for the popularity of the accounting rate of return, even though it has no theoretical foundation as a method for securing optimal investment decisions. For example, it gives a value in percentage terms, a familiar measure of return, which can be compared with ROCE, the primary accounting ratio used by accountants and financial analysts to assess company performance. It is also a reasonably simple method to apply and can be used to compare mutually exclusive projects. Unlike the payback method, it considers all cash flows arising during the life of an investment project and can indicate whether a project is a 'good' one by comparing the ARR of the project with a hurdle rate, for example a company's current ROCE or the ROCE of a division.

3.2.2 Disadvantages of the accounting rate of return method

While it can be argued that the accounting rate of return method provides us with useful information about a project, as a method of investment appraisal it has significant drawbacks. For example, it is not based on cash, but based on accounting profit, which is open to manipulation and is not linked to the fundamental objective of maximising shareholder wealth. Because the method uses average profits, it ignores the timing of cash flows.

Consider the two projects A and B in Exhibit 3.3. Both projects have the same average investment:

£45 000/2 = £22 500

Both projects have the same annual accounting profit:

Project A: (–250 + 1000 + 1000 + 20 750)/4 = £5625
Project B: (6000 + 6000 + 5500 + 5000)/4 = £5625

So their accounting rates of return are identical too:

ARR = (100 × 5625)/22 500 = 25 per cent

But Project B has a smooth pattern of returns, whereas Project A offers little in the first three years and a large return in the final year.

We can see that, even though they both have the same ARR, Project B is clearly preferable to Project A by virtue of the pattern of its cash flows.

EXHIBIT 3.3

Year	*0*	*1*	*2*	*3*	*4*
Project A	*£000*	*£000*	*£000*	*£000*	*£000*
cash flows	(45 000)	11 000	12 250	12 250	32 000
depreciation		11 250	11 250	11 250	11 250
accounting profit		(250)	1 000	1 000	20 750
Project B					
cash flows	(45 000)	17 250	17 250	16 750	16 250
depreciation		11 250	11 250	11 250	11 250
accounting profit		6 000	6 000	5 500	5 000

Illustration of how accounting rate of return, which uses average accounting profit, ignores the timing of project cash flows

A more serious drawback is that the accounting rate of return method does not consider the time value of money and so gives equal weight to cash flows whenever they occur. It also fails to take into account the length of the project life and, because it is expressed in percentage terms and is therefore a relative measure, it ignores the size of the investment made. For these reasons, the accounting rate of return method cannot be considered to offer sensible advice about whether a project is wealth-creating or not. In order to obtain such advice, we need to turn to discounted cash flow methods, the most widely accepted of which is the net present value method.

3.3 THE NET PRESENT VALUE METHOD

The net present value (NPV) method of investment appraisal uses discounted cash flows to evaluate capital investment projects. It uses a target rate of return or cost of capital to discount all cash inflows and outflows to their present values, and then compares the present value of all cash inflows with the present value of all cash outflows. A positive net present value indicates that an investment project is expected to give a return in excess of the cost of capital and will therefore lead to an increase in shareholder wealth. We can represent the calculation of NPV algebraically as follows.

$$NPV = -I_0 + \frac{C_1}{(1+r)} + \frac{C_2}{(1+r)^2} + \frac{C_3}{(1+r)^3} + \cdots + \frac{C_n}{(1+r)^n}$$

where: I_0 is the initial investment
$C_1, C_2, \ldots C_n$ are the project cash flows occurring in years 1, 2, . . n
r is the cost of capital or required rate of return.

By convention, in order to avoid continuous discounting, cash flows occurring *during* a time period are assumed to occur at the *end* of that time period. The initial investment occurs at the start of the first time period. The net present value decision rule is then to accept all independent projects with a positive net present value. If two capital investment projects are not independent but mutually exclusive, so that of the two projects available only one project can be undertaken, the project with the highest net present value should be selected.

Example Calculation of the net present value

Carter Ltd is evaluating three investment projects, whose expected cash flows are given in Exhibit 3.4. Calculate the net present value for each project if Carter's cost of capital is 10 per cent. Which project should be selected?

EXHIBIT 3.4

Carter Ltd: cash flows of proposed investment projects

Period	**Project A** *(£000)*	**Project B** *(£000)*	**Project C** *(£000)*
0	(5000)	(5000)	(5000)
1	1100	800	2000
2	1100	900	2000
3	1100	1200	2000
4	1100	1400	100
5	1100	1600	100
6	1100	1300	100
7	1100	1100	100

Three investment projects with different cash flow profiles to illustrate the calculation of net present value

Project A

The cash inflows of this project are identical and so do not need to be discounted separately. Instead, we can use the cumulative present value factor (CPVF) or annuity factor for seven years at 10 per cent ($CPVF_{10,7}$), which is found from annuity tables to have a value of 4.868. We have:

	£000
Initial investment	(5000)
Present value of cash inflows = £1100 × 4.868 =	5355
Net present value	355

Project A has a positive net present value of £355 000.

Project B

Because the cash inflows of this project are all different, it is necessary to discount each one separately. The easiest way to organise this calculation is by using a table, as in Exhibit 3.5.

EXHIBIT 3.5

Year	*Cash flow (£000)*	*10% discount factors*	*Present value (£000)*
0	(5000)	1.000	(5000)
1	800	0.909	727
2	900	0.826	743
3	1200	0.751	901
4	1400	0.683	956
5	1600	0.621	994
6	1300	0.564	733
7	1100	0.513	564
		net present value:	618

Calculation of the net present value of Project B using a tabular approach. This approach organises the calculation and the information used in a clear, easily understood format which helps to avoid errors during the calculation process

Using a table to organise net present value calculations is especially useful when dealing with the more complex cash flows which arise when account is taken of taxation, inflation and a range of costs or project variables. A tabular approach also aids clear thinking and methodical working in examinations. From Exhibit 3.5, we can see that Project B has a positive net present value of £618 000.

Project C

The cash flows for the first three years are identical and can be discounted using the cumulative present value factor for three years at 10 per cent ($CPVF_{10,3}$), which is found from annuity tables to be 2.487. The cash flows for years 4 to 7 are also identical and can be discounted using a cumulative present value factor. To find this, we subtract the cumulative present value factor for three years at 10 per cent from the cumulative present value factor for seven years at 10 per cent. From tables, we have:

$$CPVF_{10,7} - CPVF_{10,3} = 4.868 - 2.487 = 2.381$$

	£000
Initial investment	(5000)
Present value of cash inflows, years 1 to 3 = £2000 × 2.487 =	4974
Present value of cash inflows, years 4 to 7 = £100 × 2.381 =	238
Net present value	212

Project C has a positive net present value of £212 000.

We can now rank the projects in order of decreasing net present value.

Project B	NPV of £618 000
Project A	NPV of £355 000
Project C	NPV of £212 000

Which project should be selected? If the projects are mutually exclusive, then Project B should be undertaken, since it has the highest NPV and will lead to the largest increase in shareholder wealth. If the projects are not mutually exclusive and there is no restriction on capital available for investment, all three projects should be undertaken, since all three have a positive NPV and will increase shareholder wealth. However, the cash flows in years 4 to 7 of Project C should be investigated; while they are not very large, they are critical to the project, since without them it would have a negative NPV and would therefore lead to a decrease in shareholder wealth.

3.3.1 Advantages of the net present value method

The net present value method of investment appraisal, being based on discounted cash flows, takes account of the time value of money, one of the key concepts in corporate finance. Net present value, then, uses cash flows rather than accounting profit, takes account of both the amount and the timing of project cash flows, and takes account of all relevant cash flows over the life of an investment project. For all these reasons, and because it is based on the sound theoretical foundation of the investment–consumption model developed by Hirschleifer (1958), net present value is the academically preferred method of investment appraisal. In all cases where there are no constraints on capital, the net present value decision rule offers sound investment advice.

3.3.2 Disadvantages of the net present value method

It has been argued that the net present value method is conceptually difficult to understand, but this is hardly a realistic criticism. It has also been pointed out that it is difficult to estimate the values of cash inflows and outflows over the life of a project that are required in order to determine its net present value, but this difficulty of forecasting future cash flows is a problem of capital budgeting in general and not one that is specific to any particular investment appraisal technique.

When calculating the NPV of an investment project, we tend to assume not only that the company's cost of capital is known, but also that it remains constant over the life of the project. In practice, the cost of capital of a company may be difficult to estimate (*see* Chapter 8) and the selection of an appropriate discount rate for use in investment appraisal is also far from straightforward (*see* Chapter 9). The cost of capital is also likely to change over the life of the project, since it is influenced by the dynamic economic environment within which all business is conducted. However, if these changes can be forecast the net present value method can accommodate them without difficulty (*see* Section 3.6.3).

3.4 THE INTERNAL RATE OF RETURN METHOD

If the cost of capital used to discount future cash flows is increased, the net present value of a conventional investment project will fall. Eventually, as the cost of capital continues to increase, the net present value will become zero, and then negative. This is illustrated in Exhibit 3.6.

The cost of capital or required rate of return rate which, when used to discount a project's cash flows, produces a net present value of zero is called the internal rate of return (IRR) of that investment project. The internal rate of return method of investment appraisal, also known as the DCF yield method, involves the calculation of the IRR of a project, usually by linear interpolation, and then comparing it with a target rate of return or hurdle rate. The internal rate of return decision rule is to accept all independent investment projects with an IRR greater than the company's target rate of return.

We can restate the expression for net present value in terms of the internal rate of return as follows:

$$\frac{C_1}{(1 + r^*)} + \frac{C_2}{(1 + r^*)^2} + \frac{C_3}{(1 + r^*)^3} + \cdots + \frac{C_n}{(1 + r^*)^n} - I_0 = 0$$

where: I_0 is the initial investment

$C_1, C_2, .. C_n$ are the project cash flows occurring in years 1, 2, . . n
r^* is the internal rate of return.

EXHIBIT 3.6

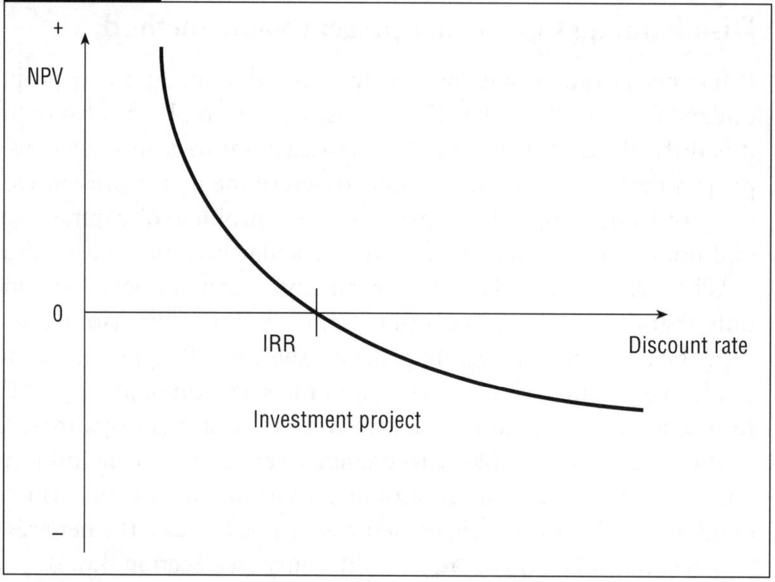

The relationship between the net present values of a conventional project and the discount rate. The internal rate of return produces a net present value of zero

Example Calculation of internal rates of return

Carter Ltd is evaluating three investment projects, whose expected cash flows are given in Exhibit 3.4. Calculate the internal rate of return for each project. If Carter's cost of capital is 10 per cent, which project should be selected?

Project A
On page 59, we found that:

$$(£1100 \times CPVF_{10,7}) - £5000 = (1100 \times 4.868) - 5000 = £355$$

In the case where project cash inflows are identical, we can quickly determine the cumulative present value factor for a period corresponding to the life of the project and a discount rate equal to the internal rate of return. Here, we can represent this by $(CPVF_{r^*,7})$, and from our above expression:

$$(£1100 \times CPVF_{r^*,7}) - £5000 = 0$$

Rearranging:

$$CPVF_{r^*,7} = 5000/1100 = 4.545$$

From annuity tables, looking along the row corresponding to seven years, we find that the discount rate corresponding to this cumulative present value factor is approximately 12 per cent. Project A, then, has an internal rate of return of 12 per cent.

Project B

The cash flows of Project B are all different and so to find its IRR we need to use linear interpolation. This technique relies on the fact that, if we know the location of any two points on a straight line, we can find any other point which also lies on that line. Consider the idealised conventional investment project shown in Exhibit 3.7. It is idealised because we have represented the project as a straight line, when in fact it will be a curve as in Exhibit 3.6.

EXHIBIT 3.7

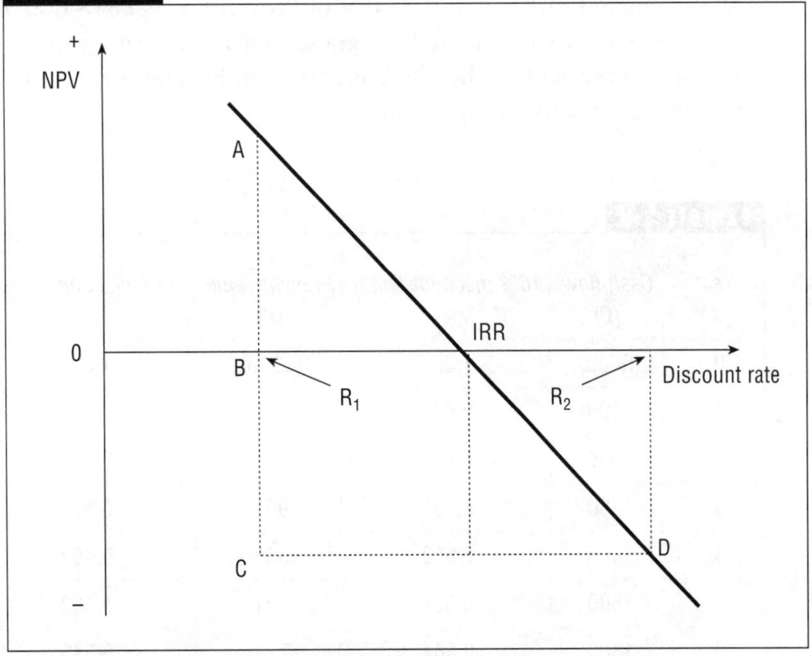

Diagram illustrating the calculation of the internal rate of return of an investment project by linear interpolation

When discounted at the company's cost of capital (R_1), this project gave a positive NPV of AB. We do not know what the internal rate of return of the project is, but let us suppose that we made a guess (R_2) which was too high, giving us a negative NPV (corresponding to the point D on the project line) of BC. We now have two triangles, ABIRR and ACD. Because they are similar triangles, the relationship between their vertical and horizontal sides is the same. We have, then:

$$\frac{IRR - R_1}{AB} = \frac{R_2 - R_1}{AC}$$

Rearranging:

$$IRR = R_1 + \frac{(R_2 - R_1) \times AB}{AC}$$

Since AB is the NPV at R_1, let us call it NPV_1. BC is the NPV at R_2 and we can call it NPV_2. AC is then the total change in NPV in moving from R_1 to R_2. If we remember that NPV_2 is negative, then AC is $(NPV_1 - NPV_2)$. Replacing AB and AC gives the following expression:

$$IRR = R_1 + \frac{(R_2 - R_1) \times NPV_1}{(NPV_1 - NPV_2)}$$

We calculated earlier that the NPV of Project B was £618 000 at a discount rate of 10 per cent. If we now make a guess that the internal rate of return is 20 per cent, we can recalculate the NPV, as shown in Exhibit 3.8. The earlier NPV calculation is included for comparison.

EXHIBIT 3.8

Year	*Cash flow (£)*	*10% discount factor*	*Present value (£)*	*20% discount factor*	*Present value (£)*
0	(5000)	1.000	(5000)	1.000	(5000)
1	800	0.909	727	0.833	666
2	900	0.826	743	0.694	625
3	1200	0.751	901	0.579	695
4	1400	0.683	956	0.482	675
5	1600	0.621	994	0.402	643
6	1300	0.564	733	0.335	436
7	1100	0.513	564	0.279	307
			618		(953)

Computation of the NPV of Project B at discount rates of 10 per cent and 20 per cent as preparation for determining its IRR by linear interpolation

Interpolating, using the method we discussed earlier:

$$\text{IRR} = \frac{10 + (20 - 10) \times 618}{618 - (-953)} = 10 + 3.9 = 13.9 \text{ per cent}$$

The internal rate of return of Project B is approximately 13.9 per cent.

We say approximately since, in using linear interpolation, we have drawn a straight line between two points on a project NPV line that is in fact a curve. As shown in Exhibit 3.9, the straight line will not cut the x-axis at the same place as the project NPV curve, so the value we have obtained by interpolation is not the actual value of the IRR, but only an estimated value. We would have obtained a different value if we had used a different estimate for R_2; for example, if we had used R_1 = 10 per cent and R_2 =15 per cent, we would have obtained a value for IRR of 13.5 per cent. To determine the actual IRR the interpolation calculation must be repeated, feeding successive approximations back into the calculation, until the value produced no longer changes significantly. This can be done easily by a statistical computer package such as Storm or Minitab.

EXHIBIT 3.9

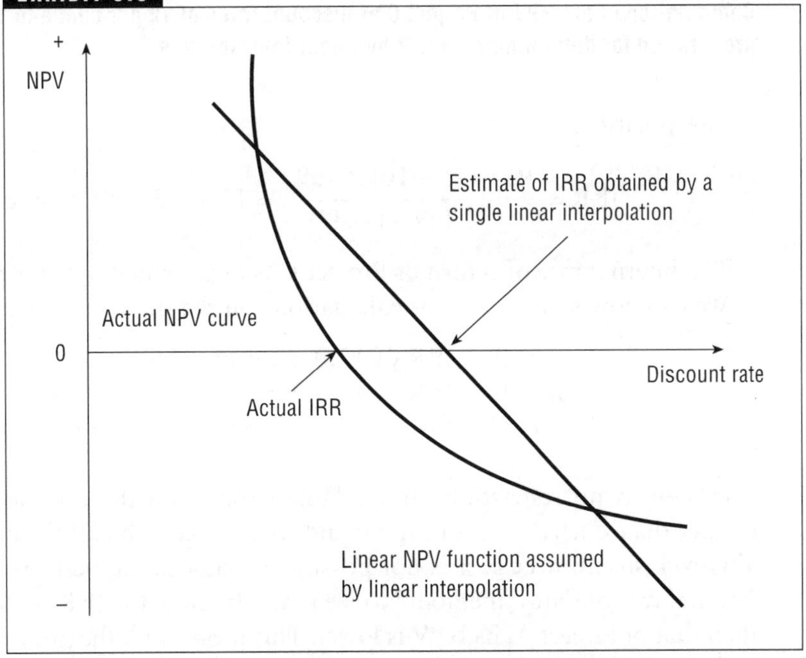

Illustration of why the IRR estimated by a single linear interpolation is only an approximation of the actual IRR of an investment project

Project C

The calculation of the NPV of Project C at Carter's cost of capital of 10 per cent and a first estimate of the project IRR of 15 per cent is given in Exhibit 3.10.

EXHIBIT 3.10

Year	*Cashflow (£)*	*10% discount factor*	*Present value (£)*	*15% discount factor*	*Present value (£)*
0	(5000)	1.000	(5000)	1.000	(5000)
1	2000	0.909	1818	0.870	1740
2	2000	0.826	1652	0.756	1512
3	2000	0.751	1502	0.658	1316
4	100	0.683	68	0.572	57
5	100	0.621	62	0.497	50
6	100	0.564	56	0.432	43
7	100	0.513	51	0.376	38
			209		(244)

Computation of the NPV of Project C at discount rates of 10 per cent and 15 per cent as preparation for determining its IRR by linear interpolation

Interpolating:

$$\text{IRR} = 10 + \frac{(15 - 10) \times 209}{209 - (-244)} = 10 + 2.3 = 12.3 \text{ per cent}$$

The internal rate of return of Project C is approximately 12.3 per cent.
We can now summarise our calculations on the three projects:

Project A	IRR of 12.0 per cent	NPV of £355 000
Project B	IRR of 13.9 per cent	NPV of £618 000
Project C	IRR of 12.3 per cent	NPV of £212 000

If there is no restriction on available capital, all three projects have an IRR greater than Carter's cost of capital and so are acceptable. If the projects are mutually exclusive, however, it is not possible to choose the best project by using the internal rate of return method. Notice that, although the IRR of Project C is higher than that of Project A, its NPV is lower. This means that the projects are ranked differently using IRR than they were using NPV. The problem of mutually exclusive investment projects is discussed later in Section 3.5.1.

3.5 A COMPARISON OF THE NPV AND IRR METHODS

There is no conflict between these two discounted cashflow methods when a *single* investment project with *conventional* cash flows is being evaluated. In the following situations, however, the net present value method may be preferred:

1 where mutually exclusive projects are being compared;
2 where the cash flows of a project are not conventional;
3 where the discount rate changes during the life of the project.

3.5.1 Mutually exclusive projects

Consider the mutually exclusive Projects A and B whose cash flows are given in Exhibit 3.11. The net present value decision rule requires that Project B be preferred, since at a cost of capital of 14 per cent it has the higher NPV. However, if internal rate of return is the basis of comparison, Project A has the higher IRR. If the projects were independent, this conflict between the NPV and IRR decision rules would not be relevant. Since the projects are mutually exclusive, however, which should be accepted?

EXHIBIT 3.11

	Project A	*Project B*
Initial investment (£)	13 000	33 000
Year 1 net cash flow (£)	7 000	15 000
Year 2 net cash flow (£)	6 000	15 000
Year 3 net cash flow (£)	5 000	15 000
Net present value (£)	+1 128	+1 830
Internal rate of return (%)	19.5	17

Table showing the cash flows, net present values at a cost of capital of 14 per cent and internal rates of return of two mutually exclusive projects

In all cases where this conflict occurs, the correct decision is to choose the project with the highest NPV. This can be proved by calculating the IRR of the incremental project whose cash flows are the differences between the cash flows of Project B and Project A. This *incremental yield* approach is illustrated in Exhibit 3.12.

If the internal rate of return method is being used to determine the best investment, Project A will be preferred since it has the highest IRR. However, the IRR of the hypothetical incremental project (B minus A) is 16 per cent, which is greater than the cost of capital of 14 per cent, and so this is also acceptable. Using the internal rate of return method, then, the company should accept the hypothetical incremental project (B minus A) in addition to Project A. But this means that the company should accept Project B rather than Project A, which contradicts the

EXHIBIT 3.12

	Year 0	*Year 1*	*Year 2*	*Year 3*	*IRR (%)*
Project B cash flows (£)	(33 000)	15 000	15 000	15 000	17
Project A cash flows (£)	(13 000)	7 000	6 000	5 000	19.5
Incremental cash flows (£)	(20 000)	8 000	9 000	10 000	16

Determination of the cash flows of the incremental project

result of applying the IRR decision rule in the first place. The conclusion is that Project B should have been favoured, even though it has the lower IRR, which is the decision originally reached by using the net present value method.

If we wish to use the internal rate of return method to choose between mutually exclusive projects, then, we must also calculate the IRR of the incremental project and compare it with the cost of capital. Only if the IRR of the incremental project is less than the cost of capital should the project with the highest IRR be accepted. If the IRR of the incremental project is greater than the cost of capital, the project with the lowest IRR should be selected.

When investment projects are mutually exclusive, then, the net present value method is to be preferred, since in order to use the internal rate of return method we would need to consider not only the IRR of the mutually exclusive projects, but also the IRR of all incremental projects, if a correct decision were to be made.

In order to illustrate the conflict between the two investment appraisal methods in more detail, Exhibit 3.13 shows the NPV of the two projects at different discount rates and Exhibit 3.14 displays the same information in the form of a graph.

From Exhibit 3.14, it can be seen that the two Projects A and B have lines with different slopes. For costs of capital greater than the IRR of the incremental project of 16 per cent, the two methods give the same advice: accept Project A, since it is preferable in terms of both NPV and IRR. For costs of capital less than the IRR of the incremental project of 16 per cent, the advice offered by the two methods is in conflict, and the net present value method is to be preferred.

EXHIBIT 3.13

Discount rate (%)	*12*	*14*	*16*	*18*	*20*	*22*
Project A (£)	1593	1128	697	282	(113)	(473)
Project B (£)	3030	1830	690	(390)	(1410)	(2370)

The net present values of two mutually exclusive projects at different discount rates

EXHIBIT 3.14

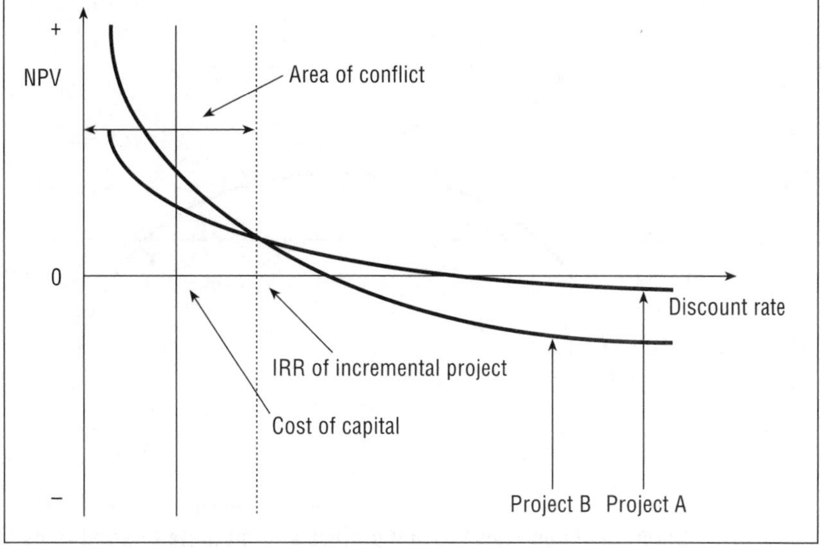

Graph showing the calculated NPV of two mutually exclusive projects and the region of conflict

3.5.2 Non-conventional cash flows

If an investment project has cash flows of different signs in successive periods (e.g. a cash inflow followed by a cash outflow, followed by a further cash inflow), it may have more than one internal rate of return. Such cash flows are called non-conventional cash flows, and the presence of multiple internal rates of return may result in incorrect decisions being taken if the IRR decision rule is applied. The NPV method has no difficulty in accommodating non-conventional cash flows, as can be seen from Exhibit 3.15.

The non-conventional project in Exhibit 3.15 has two internal rates of return, at IRR_1 and IRR_2. This kind of project is not unusual: for example, a mineral extraction project, with heavy initial investment in land, plant and machinery and significant environmental costs towards the end of the project life, might have this kind of NPV profile. Using the internal rate of return method, which IRR should be used to assess the project?

If the cost of capital is R_A, the project would be accepted using the internal rate of return method, since both IRR_1 and IRR_2 are greater than R_A. If the net present value method is used, however, it will be rejected, because at this discount rate it has a negative NPV and would decrease shareholder wealth.

However, if the cost of capital used to assess the project is R_B, it will be accepted using the net present value method, because at this discount rate it has a positive NPV. The internal rate of return method cannot offer any clear advice, since R_B is between IRR_1 and IRR_2.

EXHIBIT 3.15

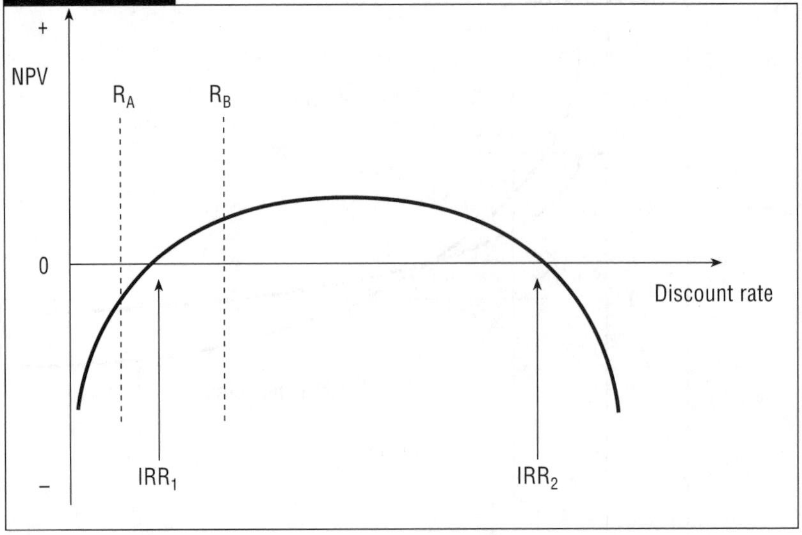

Diagram of non-conventional project with multiple internal rates of return

In each case, the net present value method gives the correct decision and thereby demonstrates its superiority over the internal rate of return method.

3.5.3 Changes in the discount rate

If there are changes in the cost of capital over the life of an investment project, the net present value method can easily accommodate them. Consider the net present value expression described earlier, with the symbols having the same meaning:

$$NPV = -I_0 + \frac{C_1}{(1+r)} + \frac{C_2}{(1+r)^2} + \frac{C_3}{(1+r)^3} + \cdots \frac{C_n}{(1+r)^n}$$

If the discount rates in successive years are r_1, r_2, etc., we have:

$$NPV = -I_0 + \frac{C_1}{(1+r_1)} + \frac{C_2}{(1+r_1)(1+r_2)} + \cdots$$

Consider the investment project in Exhibit 3.16. Here, the discount rate increases from 10 per cent to 15 per cent in Year 3. The discount factor for Year 3 is the discount factor for two years at 10 per cent multiplied by the discount factor for one year at 15 per cent. Using tables, we have:

$$PVF_{10,2} \times PVF_{15,1} = 0.826 \times 0.870 = 0.719$$

The NPV of the project is £1807 while the IRR, calculated by interpolation, is approximately 18.8 per cent. The IRR, however, cannot take into account the fact that the discount rate in Year 3 is different from that in Years 1 and 2.

EXHIBIT 3.16

Year	*0*	*1*	*2*	*3*
Discount rate (%)		10	10	15
Cash flow (£)	(13 000)	7000	5000	6000
Discount factors	1.000	0.909	0.826	0.719
Present value (£)	(13 000)	6363	4130	4314

Investment project in which the discount rate changes during the project life

3.5.4 Reinvestment assumptions

The net present value method assumes that cash flows generated during the life of the project can be reinvested elsewhere at a rate equal to the cost of capital. This seems to be a sensible reinvestment assumption, since the cost of capital represents an opportunity cost, i.e. the best return that could have been obtained on an alternative investment. The internal rate of return method, however, assumes that cash flows generated during the life of the project can be reinvested elsewhere at the internal rate of return. The more the IRR exceeds the cost of capital, the less likely it is that such alternative returns could be realised, and so the reinvestment assumption underlying the internal rate of return method is a doubtful one. The reinvestment assumption underlying the NPV method, however, seems very reasonable.

3.5.5 The superiority of the net present value method

We can now summarise the arguments in favour of the net present value method of investment appraisal:

1 the net present value method gives the correct decision as regards mutually exclusive projects without fuss, whereas the internal rate of return method requires the consideration of incremental yields;

2 the net present value method can accommodate non-conventional cash flows, a situation where the internal rate of return method may offer multiple solutions;

3 the reinvestment assumption underlying the net present value method is reasonable, but that underlying the internal rate of return method is not;

4 the net present value method can easily incorporate changes in the discount rate, whereas the internal rate of return method ignores them.

For these reasons, the net present value method is held to be technically superior to the internal rate of return method.

The internal rate of return method, while technically inferior to the net present value method, enjoys wide popularity (*see* Section 4.6). It is obviously to be preferred to both payback period and accounting rate of return as an investment appraisal method, since it takes account of the time value of money, is based on cash flows and considers the whole of the project. The IRR or 'yield' of a project is also a concept widely understood by financial analysts, investors and managers and offers information on the extent to which a project offers returns in excess of a minimum required level.

This chapter has argued that sophisticated investment appraisal methods (i.e. net present value and internal rate of return) are greatly superior to simplistic investment appraisal methods (i.e. payback and accounting rate of return) and this is widely accepted. Companies using sophisticated investment appraisal methods should therefore perform better than those using simplistic methods. Empirical research on this question has produced mixed results, however, and Haka *et al.* (1985) have shown that there is evidence that adoption of sophisticated investment appraisal methods may not, in itself, necessarily lead to improved performance. While this does not invalidate the academic superiority of NPV and IRR, it does suggest that, in practice, the interaction between capital budgeting decisions and company performance is a complex one.

3.6 THE PROFITABILITY INDEX AND CAPITAL RATIONING

If a company does not have sufficient funds with which to undertake all projects that have a positive net present value, it is in a capital rationing situation. It will need a way of choosing between investment opportunities which maximises the return on the funds invested. Because the net present value method calls for the existence of a perfect market to provide any funds that may be required by a company for investment purposes, absolute NPV cannot be used to rank investment projects if available capital is rationed. This is because a combination of smaller projects may collectively offer a higher NPV than one larger project in return for the available capital, even if, when ranked by NPV, the smaller projects are placed below the larger one.

3.6.1 Soft and hard capital rationing

We can distinguish between 'hard' and 'soft' capital rationing. If there is a limitation on investment funds which is externally imposed, then the capital rationing is described as hard. If the limitation is internally imposed, then the capital rationing is described as soft.

Hard capital rationing

A company may be unable to raise capital for investment because the capital markets are depressed or because investors consider the company to be too risky. If only a small amount of finance is required, for example to satisfy a marginal funding requirement, issue costs might make raising it unacceptably expensive. It is unusual for hard capital rationing to occur, however, and most capital rationing is self-imposed and therefore soft.

Soft capital rationing

Investment funds may be restricted internally by company management for a number of reasons. They may decide against issuing more equity finance, for example, because they wish to avoid possible dilution of control, or because they wish to avoid any potential dilution of earnings per share. They may decide against raising debt finance through a wish to avoid taking on a commitment to further fixed interest payments, perhaps out of concern over their company's existing level of gearing or financial risk. If a company is small or family-owned, its management may limit the funds available for investment as part of a policy of pursuing steady growth via retained earnings, as opposed to a policy of rapid expansion.

It has also been suggested that self-imposed capital rationing, by fostering a competitive internal environment for available investment funds, will result in the weeding out of marginal or borderline investment projects and hence will encourage the generation of better, more robust, investment proposals.

3.6.2 Single-period capital rationing

If available funds are only restricted initially (single-period capital rationing), the company needs to choose the combination of projects which maximises the total net present value. Depending on the circumstances, this can be done either by ranking projects using the profitability index, or by finding the NPV of possible combinations of projects.

Divisible, non-deferrable investment projects

If the available investment projects are divisible, non-deferrable and non-repeatable and capital is rationed in the initial period only, ranking projects by their absolute NPV will not lead to the correct decision since, as pointed out earlier, a project with a large NPV will be favoured over a combination of several smaller projects with a larger collective NPV. Here, 'divisible' means that any portion of a project may be undertaken; 'non-deferrable' means that if a project is not undertaken at the present time, it cannot be undertaken in any subsequent period; 'non-repeatable' means that each project may be undertaken only once. The correct approach here is to calculate a *profitability index* or *benefit to cost ratio* for each project and then to rank them using this measure. The profitability index tells us how much we can expect to receive, in present value terms, for each pound invested in the project.

$$\text{Profitability index} = \frac{\text{Present value of future cash flows}}{\text{Value of initial capital invested}}$$

If there is no restriction on capital, projects with a profitability index greater than one should be accepted (clearly, this corresponds to the NPV decision rule). If capital is restricted, the project with the highest profitability index should be undertaken, then the project with the next highest profitability index should have funds allocated to it, and so on until there is no longer a whole project that can be undertaken. As the projects are divisible, the remaining funds are invested pro rata in the next best project. The total NPV arising from this investment schedule is the sum of the NPV of the complete projects, added to pro rata proportion of the NPV of the partly-undertaken project. This procedure is illustrated in Exhibit 3.17.

EXHIBIT 3.17

Project	*A*	*B*	*C*	*D*
Initial investment (£)	500	650	800	850
Net present value (£)	650	715	800	765
PV of future cash flows (£)	1150	1365	1600	1615
Profitability index	2.3	2.1	2.0	1.9
Ranking by NPV	4	3	1	2
Ranking by profitability index	1	2	3	4

Capital available = £1650

Optimum investment schedule:	*NPV (£)*	*Cumulative investment (£)*
£500 invested in Project A	650	500
£650 invested in Project B	715	1150
£500 invested in Project C	500	1650
Total NPV for £1650 invested:	1865	

Example of the ranking of divisible projects by profitability index in order to derive the optimum investment schedule under single-period capital rationing. Note that the ranking by absolute NPV is quite different to the ranking by profitability index

From Exhibit 3.17 we can see that, if we have £1650 available to invest in the divisible Projects A, B, C and D, the optimum investment is to undertake all of Projects A and B and 62.5 per cent of Project C, giving a total NPV of £1865. This is preferable to investing £1650 in Projects C and D, even though these have the highest NPV, since their total NPV is only £1565. Note that, if Project A had been repeatable, the optimum investment schedule would have been to repeat Project A 3.3 times, giving a total NPV of £2145.

Indivisible, non-deferrable investment projects

If investment projects are not divisible, profitability indices will provide useful information, but the selection of projects can only be achieved by examining the total NPV of all possible combinations of projects. The combination with the highest NPV which does not exceed the available capital will be optimal. Assuming now that the projects in Exhibit 3.17 are indivisible, the best result is found from a combination of Projects C and D.

Projects A and B:	Total NPV = £1365
Projects A and C:	Total NPV = £1450
Projects A and D:	Total NPV = £1415
Projects B and C:	Total NPV = £1515
Projects B and D:	Total NPV = £1480
Projects C and D:	Total NPV = £1565

3.6.3 Multiple-period capital rationing

If the funds available for capital investment are expected to be restricted in more than one period, the decision about which projects to choose cannot be based on a ranking of projects according to a profitability index, or by trying different combinations of projects, since neither of these methods take into account the restriction on finance in future periods. The complexity of the problem calls for the use of techniques such as linear programming. With only two variables, the linear programming problem can be solved graphically, but if there are more than two variables, the simplex method must be used. The solution of multiple-period capital rationing problems is not considered in this text (however, *see*, for example, Drury (1996)).

3.7 DISCOUNTED PAYBACK METHOD

Here, the payback method discussed in Section 3.1 is modified in that the project cash flows are first discounted by the company's cost of capital in order to take account of the time value of money. Consider the example given in Exhibit 3.18 on page 76.

The discounted payback period is approximately 3.5 years, compared with an undiscounted payback period of approximately 2.2 years. The discounted payback method has the same advantages and disadvantages as before, except that the shortcoming of failing to take into account the time value of money has been overcome.

EXHIBIT 3.18

Year	*Cash flow (£)*	*15% discount factor*	*Present value (£)*	*Cumulative NPV (£)*
0	(5000)	1.000	(5000)	(5000)
1	2300	0.870	2001	(2999)
2	2500	0.756	1890	(1109)
3	1200	0.658	790	(319)
4	1000	0.572	572	253
5	1000	0.497	497	750

Table showing how cumulative NPV can be used to determine the discounted payback period for a project

3.8 CONCLUSION

In this chapter, we have considered at an introductory level the methods used by corporate finance to evaluate investment projects. While there are a wide range of techniques that can be used, the net present value method enjoys the support of academics and is regarded as superior to the other methods discussed.

KEY POINTS

1 Payback period is the number of years it takes to get back the original investment from the cash flows resulting from a capital investment project.

2 Payback takes account of risk, if by risk we mean the uncertainty that increases as cash flows become more distant, and is a simple method to apply and understand. However, it ignores the time value of money, the timing of cash flows within the payback period and any cash flows after the payback period. It does not say whether a project is a 'good' one.

3 Accounting rate of return is the ratio of average annual profit to capital invested. It is simple to apply, looks at the whole of an investment project and can be used to compare mutually exclusive projects. A project is acceptable if the ARR exceeds a target value such as current ROCE.

4 Accounting rate of return ignores the time value of money, fails to take account of the size and timing of cash flows and uses accounting profits rather than cash flows.

5 Net present value is the difference between the present value of future benefits and the present value of capital invested, discounted at a company's cost of capital. The NPV decision rule is to accept all projects with a positive net present value.

6 The net present value method takes account of the time value of money and the amount and timing of all relevant cash flows over the life of the project.

7 The net present value method can take account of both conventional and non-conventional cash flows, can accommodate changes in discount rate during the life of a project and gives an absolute rather than a relative measure of project desirability. It can be used to compare all investment projects.

8 Difficulties with using discounted cash flow methods of investment appraisal are: it is difficult to estimate cash inflows and outflows over the life of the project; the cost of capital for a company may be difficult to estimate; and the cost of capital may change over the life of the project.

9 The internal rate of return method involves the calculation of the discount rate which gives a NPV of zero. The IRR decision rule is to accept all projects with an IRR greater than the company's target rate of return.

10 The superiority of the NPV method over the IRR method when comparing mutually exclusive projects can be seen by examining the yield of the incremental cash flows.

11 The NPV method assumes that cash flows can be reinvested at a rate equal to the cost of capital, whereas the IRR method assumes such cash flows are reinvested at the internal rate of return. Only the reinvestment assumption underlying the NPV method is reasonable.

12 Capital rationing can be either hard (externally imposed) or soft (internally imposed).

13 Hard capital rationing may occur because capital markets are depressed or because the company is thought to be too risky.

14 Soft capital rationing may occur because a company wishes to avoid dilution of control, dilution of EPS or any further fixed interest commitments. It may wish to pursue a policy of steady growth, or believe that restricting available funds will encourage better projects.

15 In a single-period capital rationing situation, divisible, non-deferrable and non-repeatable investment projects can be ranked using the profitability index in order to obtain an optimal investment schedule. The profitability index is the ratio of the present value of future benefits to initial capital invested.

16 Multiple-period capital rationing requires the use of linear programming.

QUESTIONS

Answers to these questions can be found on pages 397–400.

1 Explain why the payback method cannot be recommended as the main method used by a company to assess potential investment projects.

2 Calculate the ARR for the following projects based on the average investment, and show which ones would be selected if the target rate of return is 12 per cent. Assume straight-line depreciation over the life of the project, with zero scrap value.

	Project A (£)	*Project B (£)*	*Project C (£)*
Initial investment	10 000	15 000	20 000
Net cash inflows:			
Year 1	5 000	5 000	10 000
Year 2	5 000	5 000	8 000
Year 3	2 000	5 000	4 000
Year 4	1 000	10 000	2 000
Year 5		5 000	

3 Explain the shortcomings of accounting rate of return as an investment appraisal method and the reasons for its popularity.

4 Three investment projects have the following net cash flows. Decide which of them should be accepted using the NPV decision rule if the discount rate to be applied is 12 per cent.

Year	*Project A (£)*	*Project B (£)*	*Project C (£)*
0	(10 000)	(15 000)	(20 000)
1	5 000	5 000	10 000
2	5 000	5 000	10 000
3	2 000	5 000	4 000
4	1 000	10 000	2 000
5		5 000	

5 List the advantages of the net present value method of investment appraisal.

6 Explain how NPV and IRR deal with non-conventional cash flows.

7 Discuss the problem of selecting between mutually exclusive projects with respect to their net present values and internal rates of return.

8 Explain how linear interpolation can be used to determine the internal rate of return of a project.

9 Explain the distinction between hard and soft capital rationing and the reasons why such conditions might occur.

10 What techniques can be used to determine the optimum investment schedule for a company under conditions of capital rationing?

QUESTIONS FOR REVIEW

Answers to these questions can be found on pages 400–5.

1 The expected cash flows of three projects are given below. The cost of capital is 10 per cent.

(a) Calculate the payback period, accounting rate of return, internal rate of return and net present value of each project.

(b) Show the rankings of the projects by each of the four methods.

Period	*Project A (£)*	*Project B (£)*	*Project C (£)*
0	(5000)	(5000)	(5000)
1	900	700	2000
2	900	800	2000
3	900	900	2000
4	900	1000	1000
5	900	1100	
6	900	1200	
7	900	1300	
8	900	1400	
9	900	1500	
10	900	1600	

2 Tarragon Ltd needs to choose between two mutually exclusive investment projects lasting for five years. The company uses the straight-line method of depreciation and its cost of capital is 15 per cent.

Project Alpha would generate annual cash inflows of £200 000 after the purchase of machinery costing £556 000 with a scrap value of £56 000.

Project Beta would generate annual cash inflows of £500 000 after the purchase of machinery costing £1 616 000 with a scrap value of £301 000.

Calculate, for each project:

(a) the accounting rate of return (ARR);

(b) the net present value (NPV);

(c) the internal rate of return (IRR);

(d) the payback period;

and state which project, if any, you would recommend, giving reasons.

3 Martan Ltd is considering buying a new machine which would have a useful economic life of five years, a cost of £100 000 and a scrap value of £5000. The machine would produce 50 000 units per annum of a new product with an estimated selling price of £3 per unit. Direct costs would be £1.75 per unit and annual fixed costs, including depreciation calculated on a straight-line basis, would be £40 000 per annum.

In Years 1 and 2, special sales promotion expenditure, not included in the above costs, would be incurred, amounting to £10 000 and £15 000 respectively. As a consequence of this particular project, investment by the company in debtors and stocks would increase, during Year 1, by £15 000 and £20 000 respectively, and creditors would also increase by £10 000. At the end of the machine's life, debtors, stocks and creditors would revert to their previous levels.

Evaluate the project using the NPV method of investment appraisal, assuming the company's cost of capital is 10 per cent.

4 A company with a cost of capital of 10 per cent has non-postponable investment opportunities with the estimated cash flows shown below.

Year	*Project A (£)*	*Project B (£)*	*Project C (£)*	*Project D (£)*	*Project E (£)*
0	(1000)	(800)	(750)	(500)	(800)
1		200	300	150	
2		300	300	150	350
3		400	300	150	350
4		400	300	150	350
5		300	300	150	350
6		200		150	350
7		(100)		150	350
8	3000				

Decide which projects should be accepted in the following circumstances:

(a) the company is not in a capital rationing situation;

(b) the company is in a capital rationing position, the projects are divisible, and only £2500 is available;

(c) the company is in a capital rationing position, the projects are not divisible, and only £2500 is available.

QUESTIONS FOR DISCUSSION

1 The finance manager of Yates plc is preparing a report for the next board meeting on the proposed construction of a new factory at an estimated cost of £5m. The factory will produce the Turbojet Printer Mark 4, a state-of-the-art laserjet printer for business use. This project was sanctioned by the management of Yates plc prior to the take-over of the company by Smith Holdings plc and it appears that little in the way of financial analysis of the project was carried out before that decision was taken. The land needed for the new factory, costing £2.2m, has already been purchased. The factory cost, while additional to the cost of the land, does include £4m for the cost of plant, equipment and computerised control systems.

Net cash sales of £2m per year for three years are expected, with a decline to £1m in the fourth year due to increasing competition from more technologically advanced substitutes. The Turbojet Printer Mark 4 will be replaced in the fifth year by the more advanced Mark 5 model.

No decision has yet been taken as to where the Mark 5 model will be made, but it is likely that the site used to manufacture the Mark 4 model will be redeveloped. At the end of four years, the plant and equipment used to manufacture the Mark 4 model will have negligible value. The value of the factory at that time is uncertain, but it is anticipated that if manufacture of the Mark 5 model takes place on the same site, the factory used for the Mark 4 will require demolition and replacement.

Smith Holdings plc requires its subsidiaries to evaluate new projects using its own overall required rate of return, which is 10 per cent. Taxation may be ignored.

(a) For the Turbojet Printer Mark 4 Project, calculate the following, and for each investment appraisal method discuss whether your calculations show the project to be acceptable or not:

(i) the accounting rate of return, based on the average investment;

(ii) the net present value;

(iii) the internal rate of return.

(b) Discuss what other information might assist the board on reaching a decision as regards the Turbojet Printer Mark 4 Project.

(c) Discuss the reasons why net present value is regarded as superior to internal rate of return as a method of investment appraisal.

2 The finance director of Rosad Meerhay plc is considering several investment projects and has collected the following information about them.

Project	*Estimated initial outlay (£)*	*Cash inflow Year 1 (£)*	*Cash inflow Year 2 (£)*	*Cash inflow Year 3 (£)*
A	200 000	150 000	150 000	150 000
B	450 000	357 000	357 000	357 000
C	550 000	863 000	853 000	853 000
D	170 000	278 000	278 000	nil
E	200 000	250 000	250 000	250 000
F	330 000	332 000	332 000	nil

Projects D and E are mutually exclusive. The capital available for investment in these new projects is limited to £1 000 000 in the first year. All projects are divisible and none may be postponed or repeated. The cost of capital of Rosad Meerhay plc is 15 per cent.

(a) Discuss the possible reasons why Rosad Meerhay plc may be limited as to the amount of capital available for investment in its projects.

(b) Determine which investment projects the finance director of Rosad Meerhay plc should choose in order to maximise the return on the capital available for investment. If the projects were not divisible, would you change your advice to the finance director?

(c) Critically discuss the reasons why net present value is the method of investment appraisal preferred by academics. Has the internal rate of return method now been made redundant?

REFERENCES

Haka, S., Gordon, L. and Pinches, G. (1985) 'Sophisticated capital budgeting selection techniques and firm performance', *The Accounting Review*, Vol. 60, No. 4, pp. 651–69.

Hirschleifer, J. (1958) 'On the theory of optimal investment decisions', *Journal of Political Economy*, Vol. 66, pp. 329–52.

RECOMMENDED READING

Many textbooks offer the opportunity to read further on the topic of investment appraisal techniques. Especially useful is Weston, J. F. and Copeland, T. E. (1988) *Managerial Finance*, Cassell.

For further consideration of the solutions of multiple-period capital rationing problems *see* Drury, C. (1996) *Management and Cost Accounting*, London, Thomson, pp. 743–5.

CHAPTER 4

INVESTMENT APPRAISAL

APPLICATIONS AND RISK

INTRODUCTION

In order to make optimal capital investment decisions with respect to real world investment projects, the investment appraisal process needs to take account of the effects on project cash flows and the required return of taxation and inflation, since in the real world both of these influences are inescapable. In the real world, too, the expected future cash flows are subject to both risk and uncertainty, and in this chapter we shall consider some of the different ways that have been suggested for the investment appraisal process to take them into account. Another real world problem that we shall consider is that of unequal project lives, for example in the case where we wish to determine the best time to replace one fixed asset with another identical asset. Finally, we shall consider what empirical research has to say about the way in which investment appraisal is conducted in the real world. Do companies in the real world take the advice of academics about the best investment appraisal methods to use, or do they have their own ideas about the way to evaluate capital investment projects?

LEARNING OBJECTIVES

After studying this chapter, you should have achieved the following learning objectives:

- an understanding of the influence of taxation on investment decisions and a familiarity with the calculation of tax liabilities and benefits;
- an understanding of the influence of general and specific inflation on investment decisions;
- a familiarity with both the real-terms and nominal-terms approaches to investment appraisal under conditions of inflation;
- an understanding of the distinction between risk and uncertainty;
- a familiarity with the application of sensitivity analysis to investment projects;
- a general understanding of the ways in which risk can be incorporated into the investment appraisal process;
- an understanding of the problem of unequal project lives and a familiarity with the methods available for its solution, including the determination of equivalent annual cost;
- an appreciation of the general results of empirical research into the capital investment decision-making process.

4.1 RELEVANT PROJECT CASH FLOWS

In Chapter 3, we gave little thought to which costs and revenues should be included in the appraisal of an investment project, beyond emphasising that cash flows rather than accounting profits should be considered. The key concept to grasp is that only *relevant* cash flows should be included. The test of the relevance of a cash flow is simply to ask whether the cash flow comes about as a result of undertaking the project. If the answer is no, then the cash flow is not a relevant one. It is useful to think in terms of *incremental* cash flows, which are the changes in a company's cash flows that arise as a direct result of undertaking an investment project. These are the only cash flows that should be included in the investment appraisal. There are several cash flows, however, that are worthy of careful consideration.

4.1.1 Sunk costs

Costs which were incurred prior to the inception of an investment project are termed 'sunk costs' and are not relevant to its appraisal, since they will be incurred regardless of whether it is undertaken or not. Examples of such costs which are commonly met are market research, the cost of machinery already owned, and research and development expenditure.

4.1.2 Apportioned fixed costs

Costs which will be incurred over the life of a project regardless of whether it is undertaken or not, such as apportioned fixed costs (e.g. rent and building insurance) or apportioned head office charges, are not relevant to the evaluation of the project and should be excluded. Only *incremental* fixed costs which arise as a result of a project should be included as a relevant project cash flow.

4.1.3 Opportunity costs

An opportunity cost is the benefit foregone by using an asset for one purpose rather than another. If an asset is used for an investment project, then, it is important to ask what benefit has thereby been lost, since this lost benefit or opportunity cost is the relevant cost as far as the project is concerned. An example using raw materials will serve to illustrate this point.

Suppose that we have in stock 1000 kg of raw material A, which cost £2000 when purchased six months ago from our regular supplier. This bill has just been settled and the supplier is now quoting a price of £2.20 per kg for material A. The existing stocks could be sold on the second-hand market for £1.90 per kg, the lower price being due to slight deterioration in storage. Two-thirds of the stock of material A is required for a new project which begins in three weeks' time. What is the relevant cost of material A to the project?

Since material A has already been paid for, the original price of the stock of £2.00 per kg is irrelevant, as it is a sunk cost. If there is no other use for material A, the benefit of reselling it on the second-hand market is lost and the relevant cost is the resale price of £1.90 per kg. If material A is regularly used in production activities, any quantity of the material used will have to be replaced, and so the relevant cost is the repurchase price of £2.20 per kg.

4.1.4 Incremental working capital

As activity levels rise as a result of investment in fixed assets, levels of stocks of raw materials and finished goods and of debtors will also increase, financed in part by increases in trade creditors. The incremental increase in working capital will represent a cash outflow for the company, and is a relevant cash flow which must be included in the investment appraisal process. Further investment in working capital may be needed, as sales levels continue to rise, if the problem of undercapitalisation or 'overtrading' is to be avoided (*see* Section 10.2). At the end of the project, however, levels of debtors, stocks and trade creditors will fall and so any investment in working capital will be recovered. By convention, the recovery of working capital will be a cash inflow either in the final year of the project or in the year immediately following the end of the project.

4.2 TAXATION AND CAPITAL INVESTMENT DECISIONS

At the start of this chapter, it was pointed out that the influence of taxation on capital investment decisions could not be ignored. In order to determine the net cash benefits accruing to a company as a result of an investment project, an estimate must be made of the benefits or liabilities that arise as a result of a corporate taxation system. There are a number of factors to consider when estimating these benefits or liabilities, which will now be discussed.

4.2.1 Capital allowances

In financial accounting, capital expenditure is passed through the profit and loss account in the form of annual depreciation charges which are determined by company management, subject to adherence to relevant accounting standards. For taxation purposes, capital expenditure is written off against taxable profits in a manner laid down by government and enforced by the tax authorities. Under this system, companies write off capital expenditure by means of capital allowances, also known as writing down allowances and, in some countries, as tax-allowable depreciation. Until 1984, 100 per cent of first-year capital allowances were available for plant and machinery, but since 1986 capital allowances on these items have mainly only been available on a 25 per cent reducing balance basis. The latter are clearly less attractive in present value terms, but the value consumed by the business (capital expenditure minus scrap value) is still eventually written off in full against profits.

Capital allowances are very much a matter of government policy: in recent years, for example, a 100 per cent first-year capital allowance has been available in Enterprise Zones in the UK and, for one year only in order to encourage investment, a 40 per cent first-year allowance followed by reversion to 25 per cent on a reducing balance basis. Since July 1997, small businesses (those with profits up to £300 000) have been able to claim a 50 per cent first-year capital allowance followed by reversion to 25 per cent on a reducing balance basis. The capital allowances on offer also depend upon the type of asset for which capital expenditure is being claimed; on industrial buildings, for example, the allowance is limited to four per cent per year on a straight-line basis. Balancing allowances or charges, which are needed in addition to writing down allowances to ensure that the capital value consumed by the business over the life of the project (capital cost minus scrap value) has been deducted in full in calculating taxable profits, will also need to be determined.

It is useful to calculate taxable profits and tax liabilities separately before attempting to calculate the net present value of a project. Performing the two calculations at the same time can lead to confusion. In July 1997, the corporation tax rate for small businesses was cut from 23 per cent to 21 per cent, while the main corporation tax rate, which had been 33 per cent for many years, was cut to 31 per cent. Since a worked example makes these concepts easier to grasp, an example of the calculation of capital allowances on a 25 per cent reducing balance basis, together with the associated tax benefits at a corporation tax rate of 31 per cent, is given in Exhibit 4.1.

EXHIBIT 4.1

Calculation of capital allowances:	£	£
Year 1: 200 000 × 0.25 =		50 000
Year 2: (200 000 – 50 000) × 0.25 =		37 500
Year 3: (200 000 – 50 000 – 37 500) × 0.25 =		28 125
Year 4: (200 000 – 50 000 – 37 500 – 28 125) × 0.25 =		21 094
Initial value	200 000	
Scrap value	50 000	
Value consumed by the business over 4 years =	150 000	
Sum of capital allowances to end of Year 4 =	136 719	
Year 4 balancing allowance		13 281
Total capital allowances over 4 years		150 000

Taxation benefits:		£
Year 1 (taken in Year 2):	50 000 × 0.31 =	15 500
Year 2 (taken in Year 3):	37 500 × 0.31 =	11 625
Year 3 (taken in Year 4):	28 125 × 0.31 =	8 719
Year 4 (taken in Year 5):	(21 094 + 13 281) × 0.31 =	10 656
Total benefits (should equal 150 000 × 0.31 = 49 500)		46 500

Capital allowances on a 25 per cent reducing balance basis are available on a machine costing £200 000 which is purchased at Year 0. The expected life of the machine is 4 years and its scrap value after 4 years is £50 000. Corporation tax is 31 per cent

4.2.2 Tax allowable deductions and relevant costs

Tax liability will arise on taxable profits generated by an investment project. Liability to taxation is reduced, however, to the extent that expenses are allowed to be deducted from annual revenue in the calculation of taxable profits for a given year. Relief for capital expenditure is given by means of capital allowances, as already discussed. Relief for revenue expenditure is given by allowing relevant expenses to be deducted in full. Such expenses include the costs of materials, components, wages and salaries, production overheads, insurance, maintenance, hire charges, and so on.

4.2.3 Tax relief on interest payments

While interest payments on debt are an allowable deduction for the purpose of determining taxable profit, it is a mistake to include interest payments as a relevant cash flow in the appraisal of a capital investment project. The reason for excluding interest payments is that the required return on any debt finance used in an investment project is already accounted for as a part of the cost of capital used to discount the project cash flows. Here, if a company is not tax exhausted, the tax allowability of interest payments is accommodated by using the after-tax weighted average cost of capital (*see* Section 8.1.3) to discount after-tax net cash flows.

4.2.4 The timing of tax liabilities and benefits

Corporation tax on taxable profits in the UK is payable nine months after the end of the relevant accounting year. It follows, from the convention that cash flows arising in a period are taken as occurring at the end of that period, that tax liabilities are paid one year in arrears of the corresponding taxable profits. Any benefits arising from the tax system, for example from capital allowances, are also received one year in arrears. While there is some variation in the way that different authors include the benefits arising from capital allowances in investment appraisal calculations, the method used here is as follows:

- capital investment occurs in Year 0;
- the first capital allowance affects cash flows arising in Year 1;
- the benefit from the first capital allowance arises in Year 2;
- the number of capital allowances is the same as the number of years in the life of the project.

Example NPV calculation involving taxation

Lark plc is considering buying a new machine costing £200 000 which would generate the following pre-tax profits from the sale of goods produced.

Year	*Profit before tax*
1	55 000
2	65 000
3	75 000
4	65 000

Lark plc pays corporation tax of 31 per cent one year in arrears and also receives capital allowances on a 25 per cent reducing balance basis. The machine will be sold after four years for £50 000. If Lark plc's after-tax cost of capital is 10 per cent, should the company buy the machine in the first place?

The capital allowances were calculated in Exhibit 4.1. The tax liabilities arising from the taxable profits, which are found by subtracting the capital allowances from the pre-tax profits, are as follows:

		£
Year 1 (taken in Year 2):	(55 000 – 50 000) × 0.31 =	1 550
Year 2 (taken in Year 3):	(65 000 – 37 500) × 0.31 =	8 525
Year 3 (taken in Year 4):	(75 000 – 28 125) × 0.31 =	14 531
Year 4 (taken in Year 5):	(65 000 – 34 375) × 0.31 =	9 494

The calculation of the net cash flows and the net present value of the proposed investment are shown in Exhibit 4.2. Since the NPV is a positive value of £15 052, the purchase of the machine by Lark plc can be recommended on financial grounds.

EXHIBIT 4.2

Year	*Capital (£)*	*Operating cash flows (£)*	*Taxation (£)*	*Net cash flows (£)*
0	(200 000)			(200 000)
1		55 000		55 000
2		65 000	(1 550)	63 450
3		75 000	(8 525)	66 475
4	50 000	65 000	(14 531)	100 469
5			(9 494)	(9 494)

Year	*Net cash flows (£)*	*10% discount factor*	*Present value (£)*
0	(200 000)	1.000	(200 000)
1	55 000	0.909	49 995
2	63 450	0.826	52 410
3	66 475	0.751	49 923
4	100 469	0.683	68 620
5	(9 494)	0.621	(5 896)
Net present value			15 052

Calculation of net cash flows and net present value for Lark plc

4.2.5 Can taxation be ignored?

Scarlett (1993, 1995) has shown that, if a simple project is determined to be viable using the net present value method, the introduction of corporate taxation is unlikely to change the decision and that this remains true even when tax payments are paid one year in arrears. Where taxation can make a difference to project viability, however, is where the profit upon which tax liability is calculated is different from the cash flows generated by an investment project. This situation arises when capital allowances are introduced into the evaluation, although it has to be said that the effect on project viability is still only a small one. It is amplified, however, under conditions of inflation, since capital allowances are based on the historical cost of investment and their real value will therefore decline over the life of the project. This decline in the real value of capital allowances is to some extent counteracted, at least in the case of plant and machinery, by the use of the 25 per cent reducing balance method of calculation.

We may conclude, then, that while the introduction of the effects of taxation into investment appraisal calculations makes them both more accurate and more complex, it does not necessarily lead, in all cases, to better investment decisions.

4.3 INFLATION AND CAPITAL INVESTMENT DECISIONS

Inflation can have a serious effect on capital investment decisions, both by reducing the real value of future cash flows and by increasing the uncertainty associated with the values of those cash flows. Future cash flows must be adjusted to take account of any expected inflation in the prices of individual goods and services in order to express them in 'nominal' (or money) terms, that is, in terms of the actual amounts of cash to be received or paid on a future date. These nominal cash flows can then be discounted by a nominal cost of capital using the net present value method of investment appraisal.

As an alternative to the nominal approach to dealing with inflation in investment appraisal, it is possible to deflate nominal cash flows by the general rate of inflation in order to obtain cash flows expressed in real terms, that is, with inflation stripped out. These 'real' cash flows can then be discounted by a real cost of capital to determine the net present value of the investment project. Whichever method is used, whether nominal terms or real terms, care must be taken to determine and apply the correct rates of inflation to the correct cash flows.

4.3.1 Real and nominal costs of capital

The real cost of capital is obtained from the nominal (or money) cost of capital by making an adjustment to the nominal cost of capital to allow for inflation. Rearranging the expression for the Fischer effect:

$$(1 + \text{nominal cost of capital}) = (1 + \text{real cost of capital}) \times (1 + \text{inflation rate})$$

gives

$$(1 + \text{real cost of capital}) = \frac{(1 + \text{nominal cost of capital})}{(1 + \text{inflation rate})}$$

For example, if the nominal cost of capital is 15 per cent and inflation is nine per cent, the real cost of capital will be 5.5 per cent:

$$(1 + 0.15)/(1 + 0.09) = 1.055$$

4.3.2 General and specific inflation

It is very likely that individual costs and prices will inflate at different rates and so individual cash flows will need to be inflated by *specific* rates of inflation. These specific rates will need to be forecast as part of the investment appraisal process. There will also be an expected *general* rate of inflation, calculated perhaps by reference to a basket of goods and services in a similar manner to changes in the retail price index (RPI), which represents the average increase in prices. The general rate of inflation can be used to deflate a nominal cost of capital to a real cost of capital and to deflate nominal cash flows to real cash flows.

4.3.3 The golden rule for dealing with inflation in investment appraisal

The golden rule is to discount real cash flows with real costs of capital, and to discount nominal cash flows with nominal costs of capital. Cash flows which have been inflated using either specific or general rates of inflation are nominal cash flows and so should be discounted with a nominal cost of capital. Such inflated cash flows may, if it is desired, be discounted with a general rate of inflation to produce real cash flows, which should then be discounted with a real cost of capital. A little thought will show that, as a result of this approach to incorporating inflation into investment appraisal, the net present value obtained by discounting real cash flows with real costs of capital is identical to the net present value obtained by discounting nominal cash flows with nominal costs of capital. After all, the real cost of capital is obtained by deflating the nominal cost of capital by the general rate of inflation and the same rate of inflation is also used to deflate the nominal cash flows to real cash flows.

Example NPV calculation involving inflation

Wren plc is planning to sell a new Gamebox. Fixed assets costing £750 000 would be needed, with two-thirds payable at once and the balance payable after one year. An investment of £330 000 in working capital would be made at the start of the project. Wren plc expects that, after four years, the Gamebox will be obsolete and the disposal value of the fixed assets will be zero. The project would incur attributable fixed costs of £550 000 per year at current prices, including annual depreciation of £180 000. Expected sales of Gameboxes are 120 000 per year at a selling price of £22 per unit and a variable cost of £16 per unit, both in current price terms. Wren plc expects the following annual increases because of inflation:

Fixed costs:	4 per cent
Selling price:	5 per cent
Variable costs:	7 per cent
General prices:	6 per cent

If Wren's real cost of capital is 7.5 per cent and the issue of taxation is ignored, is the project viable?

Fixed costs per year (minus depreciation) = 550 000 – 180 000 = £370 000

Inflating by four per cent per year:

Year 1 fixed costs = 370 000 × 1.04 = £384 800
Year 2 fixed costs = 384 800 × 1.04 = £400 192
Year 3 fixed costs = 400 192 × 1.04 = £416 200
Year 4 fixed costs = 416 200 × 1.04 = £432 848

The contribution per unit is the difference between the sales price and the variable cost per unit, inflated by their respective inflation rates. The nominal net operating cash flow for each year is then the difference between the total contribution and the inflated fixed costs for that year, as shown in Exhibit 4.3.

The investment in fixed assets in Year 0 is 750 000 × 2/3 = £500 000
The investment in fixed assets in Year 1 is 750 000 × 1/3 = £250 000
£330 000 is invested in working capital in Year 0.
The investment in working capital is recovered at the end of Year 4.

We could deflate the nominal cash flows by the general rate of inflation to obtain real cash flows and then discount them by Wren's real cost of capital. It is simpler and quicker to inflate Wren's real cost of capital into nominal terms and use it to discount the nominal cash flows that we have calculated. Wren's nominal cost of capital is $1.075 \times 1.06 = 1.1395 \approx 14$ per cent.

The calculation of the net present value, using a nominal (money terms) approach, is given in Exhibit 4.3.

Since the NPV is positive, the project can be recommended on financial grounds. Since the NPV is not very large, however, care must be taken to ensure that the forecasts and estimates are as accurate as possible. In particular, a small increase in inflation during the life of the project might make it uneconomical.

4.4 INVESTMENT APPRAISAL AND RISK

While the words 'risk' and 'uncertainty' are often used interchangeably, they do have different meanings. 'Risk' refers to a set of circumstances regarding a given decision which can be assigned probabilities. 'Uncertainty', as pointed out by Grayson (1967), implies that it is not possible to assign probabilities to different sets of circumstances: the probabilities of future events are either not meaningful or unknown. In the context of investment appraisal, suggested Marek (1991), risk refers to the business risk of an investment, which will increase with the variability of expected returns, rather than to financial risk, which relates to the capital

EXHIBIT 4.3

Year	*1*	*2*	*3*	*4*
Selling price per unit (£)	23.10	24.25	25.45	26.74
Variable cost per unit (£)	17.12	18.32	19.60	20.97
Contribution per unit (£)	5.98	5.93	5.85	5.77
Contribution per year (£)	717 600	711 600	702 000	692 000
Fixed costs per year (£)	384 800	400 192	416 200	432 848
Net operating cash flow (£)	332 800	311 408	285 800	259 152

Year	*0*	*1*	*2*	*3*	*4*
Capital (£)	(500 000)	(250 000)			
Working capital (£)	(330 000)				330 000
Operating profits (£)		332 800	311 408	285 800	259 152
Net cash flow (£)	(830 000)	82 800	311 408	285 800	589 152
14% discount factors	1.000	0.877	0.769	0.675	0.592
Present value (£)	(830 000)	72 616	239 473	192 915	348 778

NPV = 72 616 + 239 473 + 192 915 + 348 778 – 830 000 = £23 782

Net operating cash flows and net present value for Wren plc

structure of the company. Risk is thus distinct from uncertainty, which will increase as the lives of investment projects become longer. The distinction between the two terms has little significance in the context of real world business decisions, suggested Grayson (1967), since managers are neither completely ignorant nor completely certain about the probabilities of future events, although they may be able to assign probabilities with varying degrees of confidence. For this reason, the distinction between risk and uncertainty is usually neglected in the context of investment appraisal.

A risk-averse company is concerned with the likelihood of receiving a return less than expected, i.e. with 'downside risk', and can turn to a number of different methods of incorporating risk into investment appraisal. These methods are concerned with assessing the risk of an investment project and with ways of incorporating risk preferences into the decision-making process.

4.4.1 Sensitivity analysis

Sensitivity analysis is a method of assessing the risk of an investment project by evaluating how sensitive the viability of the project is to changes in the various factors which affect it. As a technique, it examines how responsive the NPV of the project is to changes in the variables from which it has been calculated. There are a number of ways that this can be measured. In the first method, variables are changed by a set amount, say 10 per cent, and the NPV is recalculated. Only one variable is changed at a time. Since we are more concerned with the downside risk, the 10 per cent change is made so as to adversely affect the NPV calculation. In the second method, the amounts by which individual variables would have to change to make the NPV of the project become zero are determined. Again, only one variable is changed at a time.

Both methods of sensitivity analysis give an indication of the *key variables* associated with an investment project. Key variables are those variables where only a small relative change can have an adverse effect on project viability. These variables may merit further investigation, for example to determine the extent to which their values can be relied upon, and their identification will also serve to indicate where management should focus its attention in order to ensure the success of the proposed investment project.

Both methods suffer from the disadvantage that only one variable at a time can be changed. This implies that all of the variables in the investment project are independent, which is clearly unrealistic. A more fundamental problem is that sensitivity analysis is not really a method of assessing the risk of an investment project at all. This may seem surprising, since sensitivity analysis is always included in discussions of investment appraisal and risk, but the method does nothing more than give an indication of *which* are the key variables. It gives no information as to the *probability of changes* in key variables, which is the information that would be needed if the risk of the project were to be estimated. If the values of all variables used in the appraisal of a project are certain, then it will have zero risk, even if a sensitivity analysis has identified the project's key variables. In such a case, however, knowledge of the key variables is still useful in assisting managers in the task of monitoring and controlling the project in order to ensure that the desired objectives are achieved from a financial point of view.

Example Application of sensitivity analysis

Swift Ltd, which has a cost of capital of 12 per cent, is considering the investment of £7m in an improved moulding machine project with a life of four years. The garden ornaments produced will retail at £9.20 each and cost £6 each to make. It is expected that 800 000 ornaments will be sold each year. What are the key variables for the project?

The net present value of the project can be expressed in terms of the project variables as follows:

$$NPV = ((S - VC) \times N \times CPVF_{12,4}) - I_0$$

where: S = selling price per unit
VC = variable cost per unit
N = number of units sold per year or sales volume

$CPVF_{12,4}$ = cumulative present value factor for four years at 12 per cent
I_0 = initial investment.

Inserting the information given in the question and finding the cumulative present value factor from annuity tables, we have:

$$NPV = ((9.20 - 6.00) \times 800\,000 \times 3.037) - 7\,000\,000 = £774\,720$$

We can now calculate the change needed in each variable to make the NPV zero. Reformulating our original expression gives:

$$((S - VC) \times N \times CPVF_{12,4}) - I_0 = \text{zero}$$

Initial investment. We need to find the value of the initial investment that makes the NPV zero.

We have $((9.20 - 6.00) \times 800\,000 \times 3.037) - I_0 = \text{zero}$
and so $I_0 = ((9.20 - 6.00) \times 800\,000 \times 3.037) = £7\,774\,720$

This is an increase of £774 720 or 11.1 per cent on the planned initial investment.

Sales price. We need to find the value of the sales price that makes the NPV zero.

We have $((S - 6.00) \times 800\,000 \times 3.037) - 7\,000\,000 = \text{zero}$
and so $S = 6.00 + (7\,000\,000/(800\,000 \times 3.037)) = £8.88$

This is a decrease of 32 pence or 3.5 per cent on the planned sales price.

Variable cost. As a decrease of 32 pence in sales price makes the NPV zero, an increase of 32 pence or 5.3 per cent in variable cost will have the same effect.

Sales volume. We need to find the value of the sales volume that makes the NPV zero.

We have $((9.20 - 6.00) \times N \times 3.037) - 7\,000\,000 = \text{zero}$
and so $N = 7\,000\,000/((9.20 - 6.00) \times 3.037)) = 720\,283$

This is a decrease of 79 717 units or 10 per cent on the planned sales volume.

Project discount rate. What is the cumulative present value factor that makes the NPV zero?

We have $((9.20 - 6.00) \times 800\,000 \times CPVF) - 7\,000\,000 = \text{zero}$
and so $CPVF = 7\,000\,000/(9.20 - 6.00) \times 800\,000) = 2.734$

Using annuity tables, and looking along the row of values for a life of four years (so that the project life remains constant), we find that 2.734 corresponds to a discount rate of almost exactly 17 per cent, an increase of 5 per cent in absolute terms or 42 per cent on the current project discount rate. This is the method for finding the IRR described in the example on page 62.

The results of our sensitivity analysis are summarised in Exhibit 4.4. The project appears to be most sensitive to changes in sales price and variable cost per unit. These are, then, the key variables for the project.

EXHIBIT 4.4

Variable	*Change to make NPV zero*		*Sensitivity*
Sales price	– 32p	– 3.5 per cent	high
Sales volume	– 79 717 units	– 10.0 per cent	low
Variable cost	+ 32p	+ 5.3 per cent	high
Initial investment	+ £774 720	+ 11.1 per cent	low
Project discount rate	+ 5 per cent	+ 33.3 per cent	very low

Sensitivity analysis of the proposed investment by Swift Ltd

4.4.2 Payback

The payback method discussed in Section 3.1 is the oldest and most widely used method of explicitly recognising uncertainty in the capital investment decision. It recognises uncertainty by focusing on the near future and thereby emphasising company liquidity, and by promoting short-term projects over longer-term (and therefore perhaps riskier) ones. While it has been rightly criticised for its shortcomings as an investment method, it is harder to criticise shortening payback as a way of dealing with risk. After all, since the future cash flows on which both payback and net present value are based are only estimates, it may be sensible to question whether the advice offered by the use of discounted cash flow methods to incorporate risk offer any real advantage. Furthermore, the effect of investment on company liquidity cannot be ignored, especially by small firms. However, payback has such serious shortcomings as a method of investment appraisal that its use as a method of adjusting for risk cannot be recommended.

4.4.3 Conservative forecasts

This traditional method of dealing with uncertainty, where estimated future cash flows are reduced to a more conservative figure 'just to be on the safe side', cannot be recommended. First, such reductions are subjective and may be applied differently between projects. Second, reductions may be anticipated and cash flows increased in compensation before investment projects are submitted for consideration. Finally, attractive investment opportunities may be rejected due to the focus on pessimistic cash flows, especially if further methods of adjusting for risk are subsequently applied.

4.4.4 Risk-adjusted discount rates

It is widely accepted that investors require a return in excess of the risk-free rate as compensation for taking on a risky investment; this concept is used in both portfolio theory and the capital asset pricing model, for example (*see* Chapter 9). The greater the uncertainty attached to future returns, the greater the risk and so the greater the risk premium called for. Grayson (1967) wrote that, when using discount cash flow (DCF) investment appraisal methods, the discount rate can be regarded as having two components, one allowing for time preference and the other for risk preference. While this approach is intuitively appealing, there are serious difficulties in deciding on the size of the risk premium to be applied to particular investment projects.

One solution is to assign investment projects to particular risk classes and then to discount them using the discount rate selected as appropriate for that class. This solution clearly gives rise to problems with both the assessment of project risk and with the determination of appropriate discount rates for the different risk classes. Another solution is to assume that the average risk of the investment projects of a company will be similar to the average risk of its current business. In these circumstances a single overall discount rate – typically the company's weighted average cost of capital – can be applied.

The application of a risk-adjusted discount rate assumes that project risk increases at a constant rate with project life. If this assumption reflects the risk profile of an investment project, all well and good. If, however, a risk-adjusted discount rate is applied without considering whether the assumption is appropriate, incorrect decisions may result. There are situations where the use of a constant risk allowance could be appropriate, in which case the risk-adjusted discount rate should decline over time. With the launch of a new project, a higher risk premium may be appropriate in the initial years of the project, with progressive reduction as the product becomes established.

4.4.5 Probability analysis

So far, we have discussed investment projects with single-point estimates of future cash flows. If, instead, a probability distribution of expected cash flows can be estimated, even only in simple terms, it can be used to obtain an expected net present value. If a more detailed probability analysis is available, the risk of an investment project can be examined in more detail by calculating the probability of the worst case and the probability of failing to achieve a positive NPV.

In its simplest form, a probability distribution may consist of estimates of the probabilities of the best, most likely and worst cases, as follows.

Forecast	*Probability*	*Net present value*
Optimistic	0.2	£30 000
Most likely	0.7	£20 000
Worst case	0.1	£10 000

The expected net present value can then be determined:

$$(0.2 \times £30\ 000) + (0.7 \times £20\ 000) + (0.1 \times £10\ 000) = £21\ 000$$

This approach, it is argued, gives more useful information than can be provided by single-point estimates. The calculations of the probability of the worst case and of the probability of failing to achieve a positive NPV are illustrated in Exhibit 4.5.

EXHIBIT 4.5

Star plc, which has a cost of capital of 12 per cent, is evaluating an investment with an initial capital outlay of £375 000. The estimated net cash flows and their respective probabilities over the life of the project are as follows.

Net cash flows for Year 1		
Economic conditions	*Probability*	*Cash flow (£)*
Weak	0.2	100 000
Moderate	0.5	200 000
Good	0.3	300 000

Net cash flows for Year 2		
Economic conditions	*Probability*	*Cash flow (£)*
Moderate	0.7	250 000
Good	0.3	350 000

If the economic conditions in Year 2 are not dependent on the economic conditions in Year 1, what is the expected value of the project's NPV? What is the risk that the NPV will be negative?

Suggested answer
The first step is to calculate the present values of the cash flows.

Year	*Cash flow (£000)*	*12% discount factor*	*Present value (£000)*
1	100	0.893	89.3
1	200	0.893	178.6
1	300	0.893	267.9
2	250	0.797	199.2
2	350	0.797	279.0

EXHIBIT 4.5 *(continued)*

The next step is to calculate the total present value of the cash flows under different sets of economic circumstances.

Year 1		*Year 2*		
Economic conditions	*Present value of cash flow (£000)*	*Economic conditions*	*Present value of cash flow (£000)*	*Total present value of cash flow (£000)*
Weak	89.3	Moderate	199.2	288.5
Weak	89.3	Good	279.0	368.3
Moderate	178.6	Moderate	199.2	377.8
Moderate	178.6	Good	279.0	457.6
Good	267.9	Moderate	199.2	467.1
Good	267.9	Good	279.0	546.9

Total present value of cash flow (£000)	*Year 1 probability*	*Year 2 probability*	*Joint probability*	*Expected present value of cash flow (£000)*
A	B	C	D = B × C	A × D
288.5	0.2	0.7	0.14	40.4
368.3	0.2	0.3	0.06	22.1
377.8	0.5	0.7	0.35	132.2
457.6	0.5	0.3	0.15	68.6
467.1	0.3	0.7	0.21	98.1
546.9	0.3	0.3	0.09	49.2
				410.6

	£
Expected value of net cash inflows	410 600
Less project cost	375 000
Expected value (EV) of NPV	35 600

The probability that the project will have a negative NPV is the probability that the total PV of the cash flows is less than £375 000. Using the column in the table headed 'Total present value of cash flow' and picking out values less than £375 000, we can see that the probability that the project will have a negative NPV is 0.14 + 0.06 = 0.20 or 20 per cent.

The probabilities being discussed here are the probability estimates which are made by managers as a result of reflecting on the objective data available to them. While such estimates are subjective, this is not grounds for their rejection, since they only make explicit the assessments of the likelihood of future events which are made by managers in the normal course of business.

4.4.6 Simulation models

In order to improve the decision-making process involving the calculation of NPV, it may be possible to estimate probability distributions for each of the variables. However, some of the variables may well be interdependent, for example costs and market share, and a simulation model can be used to determine by repeated analysis how these variables may influence the expected net present value. The procedure is as follows. Random numbers are assigned to the individual probabilities in the probability distributions and a computer then uses the random numbers to select values from each distribution. The NPV of that set of values is then calculated. The computer then repeats the process many times and builds up a frequency distribution of the NPV. From this frequency distribution, the expected NPV and its standard deviation can be determined.

This sophisticated simulation technique, usually referred to as the Monte Carlo method, does not give clear investment advice. From a corporate finance point of view, the manager must still decide whether an investment is acceptable or not, or whether it is preferable to a mutually exclusive alternative, having regard to both its return (the expected NPV) and its risk (the standard deviation of the expected NPV). The rational investment decision would be to prefer the investment project with the highest return for a given level of risk, or with the lowest risk for a given level of return.

4.5 THE PROBLEM OF UNEQUAL PROJECT LIVES

If two machines can do the same job for a company, but have different operating costs and purchase prices and will last for different periods of time, it would be a mistake for the company to choose between them by applying the net present value method and then selecting the machine with the lowest present value of costs. A wrong decision could be made because the machine with the lowest present value cost might need to be replaced earlier than the more expensive machine. When choosing between mutually exclusive investment projects with different project lives, the evaluation must be made using an equivalent time horizon; that is, the evaluation must consider any future replacement decisions. After considering the methods that can be used to choose between mutually exclusive investments with unequal lives, we shall look at how these methods can be applied to the more complex problem of determining the optimum replacement cycle for an individual asset.

4.5.1 Matching replacement cycles

Sprog Ltd needs to choose a new mechanical mower and has selected two machines which meet its specifications. Machine A costs £600 and lasts for three years, while Machine B costs £750 and lasts for four years. Operating costs, to be paid at the end of each year, are £150 per year for Machine A and £100 per year for Machine B. Neither Machine A nor Machine B has any resale value at the end of its life. If Sprog Ltd has a cost of capital of 12 per cent, which mower should be chosen?

The cash outflows and the present value of the costs of each machine are shown in Exhibit 4.6. We can see that the present value of the costs of Machine A (£960.3) is lower than that of Machine B (£1053.7).

EXHIBIT 4.6

	Cash flows (£)	
Year	*Machine A*	*Machine B*
0	(600)	(750)
1	(150)	(100)
2	(150)	(100)
3	(150)	(100)
4		(100)
Present value of costs (£)	(960.3)	(1053.7)

Cash flows and present values of costs for Sprog's mower

However, since Machine B has a longer life, its cost per year may actually be lower. One way to check this is by matching the replacement cycles. If we extend the time horizon to 12 years, Machine A will have four complete cycles and Machine B will have three complete cycles. When Machine A is replaced at the end of Year 3, an identical machine will be purchased for £600 with annual operating costs of £150 payable at the end of Years 4, 5 and 6. Machine A will then be replaced again for £600 at the end of Year 6, with annual operating costs of £150 being payable at the end of Years 7, 8 and 9, and replaced again for £600 at the end of Year 9 with annual operating costs of £150 being payable in Years 10, 11 and 12.

Since the present value of the costs of Machine A over its three-year cycle is £960.3, the same present value cost of £960.3 will arise at Year 3 for the second replacement cycle, at Year 6 for the third replacement cycle and at Year 9 for the fourth replacement cycle. Each of these present value costs at Years 3, 6 and 9 can be discounted back to Year 0 to give the present value of the costs of Machine A over the full 12 years, as follows:

$$960.3 + \frac{960.3}{(1.12)^3} + \frac{960.3}{(1.12)^6} + \frac{960.3}{(1.12)^9} = £2477.6$$

When Machine B is replaced at the end of Year 4, an identical machine will be purchased for £750 with annual operating costs of £100 payable at the end of Years 5, 6, 7 and 8. Machine B will then be replaced again for £750 at the end of Year 8, with annual operating costs of £100 being payable at the end of Years 9, 10, 11 and 12. The present value of the costs of the three cycles for Machine B over the full 12 years is as follows:

$$1053.7 + \frac{1053.7}{(1.12)^4} + \frac{1053.7}{(1.12)^8} = £2149.5$$

When compared over a common time horizon, then, Machine B has the lowest present value cost (£2149.5 compared with £2477.6) and will be preferred to Machine A.

4.5.2 The lowest common multiple method

If we consider mutually exclusive assets with identical uses which can be replaced after two, three or four years, the shortest time period which can incorporate a whole number of replacements for each asset is 12 years. In mathematical terms, 12 is the lowest common multiple of two, three and four. For this reason, comparing the present value costs of assets over a common time horizon is usually referred to as the lowest common multiple (LCM) method. As the number of asset choices increases and as asset lives are extended beyond four years, the LCM method becomes more and more difficult to use in computational terms. The LCM of 3, 4 and 5, for example, is 60, while the LCM of 3, 4, 5 and 7 is 420.

One solution to this problem is to impose an arbitrary time limit on the number of years considered in the LCM computations. While this approach, termed the *finite horizon method*, reduces the amount of computation, it gives an answer which is only approximately correct and cannot be recommended.

4.5.3 The equivalent annual cost method

A more straightforward solution to the problem of unequal asset lives can be found if we consider the example of Machine A from Exhibit 4.1, and note that the cash outflows of £600 at Year 0 and £150 at each of Years 1, 2 and 3 are equivalent to a discounted cash outflow of £960.3 at Year 0. We can then determine the value of a three-year annuity which, when discounted at the company's cost of capital of 12 per cent, gives an identical discounted Year 0 cash outflow, as follows:

$$£960.3 = C \times CPVF_{12,3}$$

From tables, $CPVF_{12,3} = 2.402$ and so the value of C, the annuity payment per year which equates with a discounted cash outflow of £960.3, can be found:

$$C = 960.3/2.402 = £399.8$$

If we continue to use and replace Machine A, its use is still equivalent to annual payments of £399.8. For this reason, £399.8 is called the *equivalent annual cost* for Machine A. In general, this can be calculated as follows:

$$\text{Equivalent annual cost} = \frac{\text{Present value cost over one replacement cycle}}{\text{Cumulative present value factor for that cycle}}$$

For Machine B in our example from Exhibit 4.6:

$$\text{Equivalent annual cost} = 1053.7/\text{CPVF}_{12,4} = 1053.7/3.037 = £347.0$$

The decision rule for the equivalent annual cost (EAC) method is that the machine with the lowest EAC should be chosen. In our example, as the EAC of Machine B is £347.0 and that of Machine A is £399.8, the preferred option is the purchase of Machine B. Here, we arrive at the same advice as that offered by the LCM method, which is only to be expected, as the two methods are merely different ways of presenting the same information.

4.5.4 Optimum replacement cycle decisions

As assets get older, it is reasonable to expect that their residual values will decrease and that their maintenance and operating costs will increase. Both the LCM method and the EAC method can be used to determine the optimum replacement cycle, which is the replacement cycle with the lowest present value cost, taking into account the changes in cost and residual value.

Example Calculation of an optimum replacement cycle

Slag Ltd is trying to determine the optimum replacement cycle of a new Waste Recycler. It has obtained the financial data given in Exhibit 4.7 for a recently developed machine which could replace its existing unit. Slag Ltd believes that 12 per cent is an appropriate discount rate to use in evaluating its investment decisions, and it expects this rate to be unchanged for the foreseeable future. The new machine can be replaced after one, two, three or four years. How often, using the information given, should Slag replace the machine in order to minimise its costs?

The LCM method requires, as a first step, the calculation of the shortest time period which can incorporate a whole number of replacements for each replacement cycle. For Slag Ltd, this is 12 years (i.e. 3 × 4). The cash flows for each replacement cycle can then be carefully compiled and the present values of the costs for each cycle calculated. We can see from Exhibit 4.8 that these present value costs are £3662, £5660, £8265 and £10 563 for cycles of one, two, three and four years, respectively. Using the method outlined earlier, the present value costs of each replacement cycle over the 12-year LCM period can then be calculated. For example, considering three replacement cycles of four years, we have:

$$10\,563 + \frac{10\,563}{(1.12)^4} + \frac{10\,563}{(1.12)^8} = £21\,543$$

EXHIBIT 4.7

Year	*0*	*1*	*2*	*3*	*4*
Initial investment (£)	(5000)				
Operating costs (£)		(1400)	(1400)	(1500)	(1600)
Maintenance costs (£)		(500)	(300)	(600)	(1000)
Scrap value (£)		3400	3000	1800	1000

Financial data for the new Waste Recycler for Slag Ltd

The present value costs of replacement cycles of one, two and three years over the 12-year LCM period are £25 397, £20 745 and £21 316, respectively, as shown in Exhibit 4.8.

EXHIBIT 4.8

The first step is to compile the cash flows, as shown in the following table.

Year	*Replace in 1 year (£)*	*Replace in 2 years (£)*	*Replace in 3 years (£)*	*Replace in 4 years (£)*
0	(5000)	(5000)	(5000)	(5000)
1	(1400) (500) 3400	(1400) (500)	(1400) (500)	(1400) (500)
2		(1400) (300) 3000	(1400) (300)	(1400) (300)
3			(1500) (600) 1800	(1500) (600)
4				(1600) (1000) 1000

EXHIBIT 4.8 *(continued)*

The next step is to express the cash flows in present value terms, as shown in the table below.

Number of years in cycle	*1*	*2*	*3*	*4*
Initial cost	(5000)	(5000)	(5000)	(5 000)
Year 1 operating costs	(1250)	(1250)	(1250)	(1 250)
Year 1 maintenance costs	(446)	(446)	(446)	(446)
Year 1 scrap value	3036			
Year 2 operating costs		(1116)	(1116)	(1 116)
Year 2 maintenance costs		(239)	(239)	(239)
Year 2 scrap value		2392		
Year 3 operating costs			(1068)	(1 068)
Year 3 maintenance costs			(427)	(427)
Year 3 scrap value			1281	
Year 4 operating costs				(1 017)
Year 4 maintenance costs				(636)
Year 4 scrap value				636
Present cost of one cycle (£)	(3660)	(5659)	(8265)	(10 563)

The present cost using the LCM method and the equivalent annual cost can now be calculated, as follows.

Number of years in cycle	*1*	*2*	*3*	*4*
Present cost over 12 years using the LCM method (£)	(25 397)	(20 745)	(21 316)	(21 543)
Present cost of one cycle (£)	(3 660)	(5 660)	(8 265)	(10 563)
Cumulative present value factors	0.893	1.690	2.402	3.037
Equivalent annual cost (£)	(4 098)	(3 349)	(3 441)	(3 478)

Calculation of the optimum replacement cycle for Slag Ltd and its Waste Recycler using both the lowest common multiple method and the equivalent annual cost method

Replacement every two years has the lowest cost using the LCM method and therefore should be chosen by Slag Ltd.

The equivalent annual cost also requires, as a first step, the calculation of the present value of the costs of each replacement cycle. The equivalent annual cost of each cycle is then calculated by dividing the present value cost for a cycle by the cumulative present factor for that cycle. Referring to Exhibit 4.8, we can see that, for the Waste Recycler, the lowest equivalent annual cost of £3349 is that of the two-year cycle. The recommendation, then, using both the LCM method and the EAC method, is that the Waste Recycler should be replaced every two years.

4.5.5 Non-identical asset replacement decisions

If an existing asset is to be replaced by a non-identical asset, the optimum replacement cycle of the new asset must first be calculated. The equivalent annual cost of this optimum replacement cycle can then be converted into the present value of an annuity, equal in size to the equivalent annual cost, paid every year from Year 1 hence for ever. This is easily achieved by dividing the equivalent annual cost by the required rate of return, as follows:

$$\text{Present value of perpetual costs} = \frac{\text{Equivalent annual cost}}{\text{Required rate of return}}$$

The best time to replace the existing asset can then be found by comparing the present value of its costs for various replacement cycles, including in each cycle the present value of the perpetual costs of the new asset as occurring in the year of replacement.

Example Optimum replacement with a non-identical asset

Slag Ltd is still looking at the replacement of its existing Waste Recycler with the new model which was evaluated in Exhibit 4.8. There, it was found that the optimum replacement cycle of the new model was two years at an EAC of £3349. Using the cost of capital of 12 per cent, the present value of £3349 paid in perpetuity is:

$$£3349/0.12 = £27\ 908$$

This is the present value cost of purchasing the new machine and then replacing it every two years for ever. Given the financial data on Slag's existing machine in Exhibit 4.9, when should it be replaced so as to minimise costs?

We can build up a table of the cash flows for replacing the existing machine after different periods, inserting the present value cost of perpetual replacement of £27 908 in the final year of each cycle. This has been done in Exhibit 4.10.

Having determined the cash flows for the different replacement periods, the present value costs of the different cash flows in each year and the present value cost

EXHIBIT 4.9

Year	*0*	*1*	*2*	*3*	*4*
Resale value (£)	3000	2500	2000	1250	200
Operating costs (£)		(2250)	(2500)	(3000)	(4000)

Financial data on Slag's existing machine

EXHIBIT 4.10

Year	*Replace now (£)*	*Replace in 1 year (£)*	*Replace in 2 years (£)*	*Replace in 3 years (£)*	*Replace in 4 years (£)*
0	(27 908) 3 000				
1		(27 908) (2 250) 2 500	(2 250)	(2 250)	(2 250)
2			(27 908) (2 500) 2 000	(2 500)	(2 500)
3				(27 908) (3 000) 1 250	(3 000)
4					(27 908) (4 000) 200

Table of cash flows associated with replacing Slag's existing machine after different time periods

of each replacement option can be calculated. These calculations are shown in Exhibit 4.11.

The lowest present value cost occurs with the replacement of the existing machine after two years, so the existing machine should be replaced in two years in order to minimise costs.

EXHIBIT 4.11

Years to replacement	*0*	*1*	*2*	*3*	*4*
Year 0 scrap value	3 000				
Year 0 new machine perpetuity	(27 908)				
Year 1 operating costs		(2 009)	(2 009)	(2 009)	(2 009)
Year 1 scrap value		2 232			
Year 1 new machine perpetuity		(24 918)			
Year 2 operating costs			(1 993)	(1 993)	(1 993)
Year 2 scrap value			1 594		
Year 2 new machine perpetuity			(22 248)		
Year 3 operating costs				(2 135)	(2 135)
Year 3 scrap value				890	
Year 3 new machine perpetuity				(19 864)	
Year 4 operating costs					(2 542)
Year 4 scrap value					127
Year 4 new machine perpetuity					(17 736)
Present cost of option	(24 908)	(24 695)	(24 656)	(25 112)	(26 288)

Calculation of the present cost of each replacement option

4.6 EMPIRICAL INVESTIGATIONS OF INVESTMENT APPRAISAL

Over the past few decades there have been a number of studies that have sought to build up a picture of the investment appraisal methods that companies actually employ, as exemplified by Pike (1983), McIntyre and Coulthurst (1986), Lapsley (1986), and Drury *et al.* (1993), and whose findings can be briefly summarised as follows:

1 the payback method is the most commonly used technique;
2 in large organisations, payback is used in conjunction with other methods. In smaller organisations, payback is often used on its own;
3 internal rate of return is used in preference to net present value;
4 the use of past experience and qualitative judgement is an important complement to quantitative methods;
5 accounting rate of return is very popular, despite its theoretical drawbacks and limitations;

6 companies tend not to use sophisticated methods to account for project risk and the impact of inflation on the investment appraisal process;

7 where companies do take account of risk, sensitivity analysis is most often used.

We have noted that the academically preferred investment appraisal methods are discounted cash flow (DCF) methods, with net present value being regarded as superior to internal rate of return. This conclusion was rooted in the fact that DCF techniques take account of both the time value of money and corporate risk preferences. On this analysis, cash flows earlier in the life of a project are discounted less heavily than more distant ones, while risk can be brought into the picture by applying a higher discount rate to more risky projects. There are a number of drawbacks with the payback and accounting rate of return, as discussed earlier in Chapter 3.

In the following sections we shall focus on the survey by Drury *et al.* (1993). The findings of this questionnaire-based survey, which elicited approximately 280 positive replies, are generally consistent with those of earlier surveys.

4.6.1 Investment appraisal techniques used

Companies were asked which financial appraisal techniques they used when appraising new capital investment projects. The results are summarised in Exhibit 4.12.

EXHIBIT 4.12

Method	*Never (%)*	*Rarely (%)*	*Sometimes (%)*	*Often (%)*	*Always (%)*
Payback	14	9	14	27	36
Discounted payback	28	13	18	20	22
Accounting rate of return	23	16	21	21	20
Internal rate of return	20	12	11	23	34
Net present value	9	13	16	21	22

Use of investment appraisal methods by all companies

From Exhibit 4.12 it can be seen that payback is more frequently used than net present value, which is also less popular than internal rate of return. In fact, the popularity of net present value is on a par with that of accounting rate of return.

If the 'always' and 'often' responses from companies are added together and if the responses from small and larger organisations are distinguished, we have the findings summarised in Exhibit 4.13. It is clear from this exhibit that unadjusted payback period is more frequently used by smaller companies, while larger companies tend to favour discounted cash flow techniques. Further analysis by Drury *et al.* found that 90 per cent of larger companies use at least one discounted cash flow technique compared to 35 per cent of smaller companies.

EXHIBIT 4.13

Method	*Companies*		
	All (N=278) (%)	*Smaller (N=43) (%)*	*Larger (N=46) (%)*
Payback	63	56	55
Discounted payback	42	30	48
Accounting rate of return	41	35	53
Internal rate of return	57	30	85
Net present value	43	23	80

Investment appraisal methods used by smaller and larger companies

The survey shows that only 23 per cent of all companies using payback period did not use a discounted cash flow technique in tandem, i.e. only 14 per cent of all companies use payback on its own. This suggests that, after using payback as an initial screening device to select suitable projects, companies then subject them to a more thorough screening using net present value or internal rate of return. Why should companies do this? One possible explanation is that using a first screening device may eliminate expenditure of resources on marginal projects, encouraging the submission of more robust and worthy projects in a similar way to internal capital rationing. Another possible explanation, suggested by Kennedy and Sugden (1986), is that using multiple evaluation techniques may reinforce the justification for the decision and increase the feeling of security or comfort derived from the use of analytical investment appraisal methods.

4.6.2 The treatment of inflation

Since the high inflation experienced in the 1970s, it has been important to account for inflation in the investment appraisal process in order to prevent sub-optimal decisions being made. The techniques to deal with the problem of inflation that have been discussed earlier (*see* Section 4.3) are:

1 the use of nominal discount rates to discount nominal cash flows that have been adjusted to take into account expected future inflation;
2 the use of real discount rates to discount real cash flows.

Earlier surveys had found that companies either ignored inflation or else accommodated it incorrectly in the investment appraisal process. The findings of Drury *et al.* on how inflation is dealt with are shown in Exhibit 4.14.

EXHIBIT 4.14

Cash flow adjustment	*Real discount rate (%)*	*Nominal discount rate (%)*
By anticipated inflation	36	29
No adjustment	41	63
Expressed in real terms	23	8

How inflation is accommodated in investment appraisal

From Exhibit 4.14, we can see that only 23 per cent of companies which used real discount rates and only 29 per cent of companies which used nominal discount rates allowed correctly for inflation. The majority of companies applied a nominal discount rate to unadjusted cash flows. As a whole, only 27 per cent of all companies allowed for inflation using a theoretically correct method. The findings of this survey were thus consistent with those of previous surveys, in that the majority of companies did not account for inflation in the investment appraisal process in an appropriate manner.

4.6.3 Risk analysis

The next area to consider is how companies take into account the risk of projects. It is generally agreed (*see* Section 4.4) that risk should be taken into account in the capital investment process and that higher risk projects should have a correspondingly higher discount rate applied to them. Prior to the 1970s, companies took account of risk by shortening the payback period or by the use of conservative cash flows, although this period also saw the advent of probability analysis and the Monte Carlo method. These models, while addressing the risk attached to future cash flows, gave no guidance on the selection of an appropriate discount rate. This problem was addressed by the capital asset pricing model (*see* Chapter 9), which enabled the systematic risk of a project to be measured and reflected in an appropriate discount rate.

Drury *et al.*'s survey also investigated how companies allowed for risk in their investment appraisal process. They found that 63 per cent of companies were either very unlikely to use probability analysis, or had never used it at all. Monte Carlo simulation and the use of the capital asset pricing model were even less popular, being rejected by 95 per cent and 97 per cent of companies respectively. This indicates a very low level of use of the more sophisticated methods of allowing for risk.

EXHIBIT 4.15

Risk adjustment technique	*Organisations* *All (%)*	*Smaller (%)*	*Larger (%)*
Sensitivity analysis	51	30	82
Discounted payback	37	42	33
Conservative cash flow forecast	32	24	43
Adjusting the discount rate	18	9	31

Use of sophisticated risk adjustment techniques

The comparative usage of other, more popular techniques is summarised in Exhibit 4.15, which analyses the 'always' and 'often' responses received. We can see that the most widely used techniques were sensitivity analysis, adjustment of the payback period and the use of conservative cash flow estimates. It can also be seen from Exhibit 4.15 that larger companies are more likely to use sensitivity analysis than smaller companies, while smaller companies are more likely to use adjusted payback period. The survey also found that, of the companies using adjusted payback period, 64 per cent varied the payback period from project to project, while the other 36 per cent of companies kept the payback period constant. The payback period most commonly applied was between two and three years, while the most commonly applied discount rates fell in the range of 15 to 19 per cent.

4.6.4 Conclusions of empirical surveys

We can conclude that the majority of companies use a combination of investment appraisal techniques. In Drury *et al.*'s survey, 80 per cent of companies were found to use payback combined with either of the discounted cash flow methods. They also found a significant difference between the replies of smaller and larger companies, a finding of many earlier surveys summarised by Mills (1988). Larger companies were more likely to use discounted cash flow methods and preferred IRR to NPV. A large number of companies were found to be dealing with inflation incorrectly, resulting in possible distortions in NPV and IRR calculations and perhaps resulting in sub-optimal investment decisions. With respect to the treatment of risk, companies were found to be more likely to use simplistic methods than theoretically correct techniques such as the capital asset pricing model.

4.7 CONCLUSION

In this chapter, we have considered some of the problems which arise when we evaluate 'real world' investment projects, including the difficulties associated with allowing for the effects of taxation and inflation. We have also considered the power of the equivalent annual cost approach to the solution of the problem of unequal asset lives. We have considered the need to take account of project risk in the investment appraisal process, and examined a number of the different ways by which this has been attempted. Some of these methods were found to be more successful than others. We concluded our discussion by examining the investment appraisal methods used by companies in the real world, as revealed by a number of empirical surveys that focused on the question, and noted the distance that exists between the academically preferred methods of investment appraisal and the methods used in the real world.

KEY POINTS

1 Only relevant cash flows, which are the incremental cash flows arising as the result of an investment decision, should be included in investment appraisal. Relevant cash flows include opportunity costs and incremental working capital.

2 Non-relevant cash flows, including sunk costs and apportioned fixed costs, must be excluded from the investment appraisal.

3 Relief for capital expenditure from a tax point of view is given through capital allowances, which are a matter of government policy and depend upon the type of asset for which capital expenditure is being claimed.

4 Tax liability is reduced to the extent that expenses can be deducted from revenue in working out taxable profits. Relief for revenue expenses is given by allowing them to be deducted in full.

5 Tax liabilities are paid nine months after the end of the year in which taxable profits arise.

6 It can be shown that the introduction of corporate taxation does not alter the viability of simple projects unless the profit upon which tax liability is calculated is different from the cash flows generated by the project.

7 Inflation can have a serious effect on investment decisions by reducing the real value of future cash flows and by increasing their uncertainty.

8 Inflation can be accommodated in the investment appraisal process by discounting nominal cash flows by a nominal cost of capital or by discounting real cash flows by a real cost of capital.

9 The real cost of capital can be obtained from the nominal cost of capital by adjusting the nominal cost of capital to allow for inflation.

10 Both specific and general inflation need to be considered in investment appraisal.

11 Risk refers to situations where the probabilities of future events are known. Uncertainty refers to circumstances where the probabilities of future events are either not meaningful or unknown.

12 Sensitivity analysis examines how responsive the NPV of a project is to changes in the variables from which it has been calculated.

13 One problem with sensitivity analysis is that only one variable at a time can be changed, but project variables are unlikely to be independent in reality.

14 While sensitivity analysis gives an indication of the key project variables, it gives no indication of the probability of changes in them occurring. For this reason, it is not really a method of assessing project risk at all.

15 Payback recognises risk and uncertainty by focusing on the near future and by promoting short-term projects.

16 Conservative forecasts can be criticised because they are subjective, because they may be applied inconsistently, because cash flow reductions may be anticipated, and because attractive investments may be rejected.

17 Despite difficulties in assessing project risk and determining risk premiums, risk-adjusted discounted rates are a favoured way of incorporating risk into investment appraisal.

18 Probability analysis can be used to obtain the expected NPV of a project, the probability of the worst case and the probability of a negative NPV.

19 The Monte Carlo method can be used to obtain a frequency distribution of the NPV, the expected NPV and its standard deviation.

20 When choosing between mutually exclusive investment projects with unequal lives, any future replacement decisions must be considered.

21 The problem of unequal lives can be solved by matching cycles, by using the LCM method, and by using EAC. The investment advice offered by the lowest common multiple method and the equivalent annual cost method is identical.

22 Non-identical asset replacement decisions can be solved by converting the equivalent annual cost of the replacing asset into a perpetuity and incorporating this perpetuity into the analysis of the existing asset.

23 Empirical investigation has shown that payback is the most commonly used technique, usually in conjunction with other methods, that IRR is preferred to NPV, and that ARR is very popular.

24 Companies tend to use simple methods of taking account of risk, such as sensitivity analysis, rather than sophisticated methods.

25 The majority of companies do not account for inflation in investment appraisal correctly.

QUESTIONS

Answers to these questions can be found on pages 405–6.

1 Discuss which cash flows are relevant to investment appraisal calculations.

2 Explain, with the aid of a short example, how 25 per cent reducing balance capital allowances are calculated.

3 Explain the difference between the nominal (or money) terms approach and the real terms approach to dealing with inflation in the context of investment appraisal.

4 Explain whether general or specific inflation should be taken into account in investment appraisal.

5 Explain the difference between risk and uncertainty.

6 Discuss how sensitivity analysis can help management to assess the risk of an investment project.

7 Why is payback commonly used as a way of dealing with risk in investment projects?

8 Discuss the use of risk-adjusted discount rates in the evaluation of investment projects.

9 Explain the meaning of the term 'Monte Carlo simulation'.

10 Explain the difference between the lowest common multiple (LCM) and the equivalent annual cost (EAC) methods of deciding when to replace identical assets.

QUESTIONS FOR REVIEW

Answers to these questions can be found on pages 406–11.

1 A machine is to be purchased by Blake Ltd for £100 000. The expected life of the machine is four years, at the end of which it will have zero value and will be scrapped. Blake Ltd pays corporation tax at a rate of 33 per cent and its discount rate for investment purposes is eight per cent. What are the present values of the tax benefits arising to Blake Ltd from the purchase of the machine in the following circumstances:

(a) first year capital allowances of 100 per cent are available;

(b) capital allowances are available on a straight-line basis over the asset's life;

(c) capital allowances are available on a 25 per cent reducing balance basis?

2 The financial manager of Logar plc is considering the purchase of a finishing machine which will improve the appearance of the company's range of decorated fudges. She expects that the improved output will lead to increased sales of £110 000 per year for a period of five years. At the end of the five-year period, the machine will be scrapped. Two machines are being considered and the relevant financial information on the capital investment proposal form is as follows:

	Machine A	*Machine B*
Initial cost (£)	200 000	250 000
Labour cost (£ per year)	10 000	7 000
Power cost (£ per year)	9 000	4 000
Scrap value (£)	nil	25 000

The following forecasts of average annual rates of inflation have been prepared by the planning department of Logar plc:

Sales prices:	6 per cent per year
Labour costs:	5 per cent per year
Power costs:	3 per cent per year

Logar plc pays corporation tax of 31 per cent one year in arrears and has a nominal after-tax cost of capital of 15 per cent. Capital allowances are available on a 25 per cent reducing balance basis.

Advise the financial manager of Logar plc on her choice of machine.

3 Mr Smart has £75 000 invested in relatively risk-free assets returning 10 per cent per year. He has been approached by a friend with a 'really good idea' for a business venture. This would take the whole of the £75 000. Market research has revealed that it is not possible to be exact about the returns of the project, but that the following can be inferred from the study:

(a) there is a 20 per cent chance that returns will be £10 000 per year;

(b) there is a 60 per cent chance that returns will be £30 000 per year;

(c) there is a 20 per cent chance that returns will be £50 000 per year.

(i) if returns are £10 000 per year, there is a 60 per cent chance that the life of the project will be five years and a 40 per cent chance that it will be seven years;

(ii) if returns are £30 000 per year, there is a 50 per cent chance that the life of the project will be five years and a 50 per cent chance that it will be seven years;

(iii) if returns are £50 000 per year, there is a 40 per cent chance that the life of the project will be five years and a 60 per cent chance that it will be seven years.

Assume that cash flows happen at the end of each year.

(a) Calculate the worst likely return and the best likely return on the project, along with the probabilities of these events happening.

(b) Calculate the expected value of the investment.

4 Buddington Ltd is evaluating the purchase of a new machine and has the following information:

Initial investment:	£350 000
Residual value:	nil
Expected life:	10 years
Sales volume:	20 000 units per year
Sales price:	£8.50 per unit
Variable cost:	£3.50 per unit
Fixed costs:	£24 875 per year
Cost of capital:	15%

(a) Calculate the internal rate of return of the project.

(b) Assess the sensitivity of the purchase to a change in project life.

(c) Assess the sensitivity of the purchase to a change in sales price.

5 Nodil Ltd wishes to determine the optimal replacement cycle for its capping machine. The finance department has estimated the following costs and resale values for the next four years.

Year	*0*	*1*	*2*	*3*	*4*
Initial investment (£)	(50 000)				
Operating costs (£)		(14 000)	(17 000)	(20 000)	(24 000)
Maintenance costs (£)			(3 000)	(4 500)	(7 000)
Scrap value (£)		(30 000)	(18 000)	(11 000)	(6 000)

If the cost of capital of Nodil Ltd is 12 per cent, determine the optimum replacement cycle using:

(a) the equivalent annual cost method;

(b) the lowest common multiple method.

QUESTIONS FOR DISCUSSION

1 Rosad Meerhay Ltd, a manufacturer of fizzy drinks whose cost of capital is 11 per cent, is looking at the problem of how often to replace its canning machine. The machine costs £220 000 and has a resale value which diminishes as its age increases. Operating and maintenance costs of the machine also increase with age, as follows:

Year	*1*	*2*	*3*	*4*
Operating costs (£)	60 000	64 800	70 000	76 000
Maintenance costs (£)	12 000	14 400	17 280	20 700
Resale value (£)	165 000	125 000	85 000	40 000

(a) Calculate the canning machine's optimum replacement cycle using the equivalent annual cost method. Ignore taxation.

(b) Discuss the reasons why the equivalent annual cost method is preferred to other ways of solving the 'asset replacement problem'.

2 Darla Kinsett plc is evaluating the purchase of a freeze dryer, which will allow it to move from the supply of raw food to local supermarkets into the more lucrative frozen foods market. Packets of frozen food will be sold in boxes of eight and the following information applies to each box:

	£ per box
Selling price	9.70
Packaging and labour	2.20
Frozen food and processing	4.80

The selling price and cost of the frozen food are expected to increase by six per cent per year, while packaging and labour costs are expected to increase by five per cent per year. Investment in working capital will increase by £90 000 during the first year. The freeze dryer will have a useful life of five years before being scrapped, the net cost of disposal being £18 000. Sales in the first year are expected to be 80 000 boxes but sales in the second and subsequent years will be 110 000 boxes.

The manufacturer of the freeze dryer, in order to encourage Darla Kinsett to go ahead with the deal, has offered to defer payment of part of the purchase price. The total cost of the freeze dryer is £1 000 000 and the offer is for 60 per cent to be paid initially, with the remaining 40 per cent to be paid one year later. The company's nominal cost of capital is 14 per cent. Ignore taxation.

(a) Assess whether Darla Kinsett plc should invest in the freeze dryer.

(b) Explain your choice of discount rate in your answer to part (a) above.

3 Critically discuss the use of the following techniques as methods of dealing with risk in the appraisal of capital investment projects:

(a) sensitivity analysis;

(b) risk-adjusted discount rates;

(c) adjusted payback;

(d) Monte Carlo methods.

4 Cryptic plc has recently completed a strategic evaluation of its products and has concluded that excellent prospects exist for an updated version of an existing product, the 'BookWorm', an electronic pocket-sized crossword solver. The development director feels that with more powerful software, a redesigned shell and sophisticated marketing, sales could be quite healthy for a few more years until technological developments make the product relatively uncompetitive.

The software could be used under a licensing agreement requiring an initial fee of £250 000 and annual payments at the end of each year of five per cent of sales. The Inland Revenue has ruled that lump sum initial payments on such licensing agreements are of a capital nature, attracting 25 per cent reducing balance capital allowances, although it has indicated that the annual payments are allowable against tax on a revenue basis only.

Sales of the BookWorm are expected to be £800 000 per year initially, with sales growth of five per cent per year expected over five years. At the end of five years, it is expected that technological obsolescence will cause sales to decline by 50 per cent per year. After three years of declining sales, the product will have to be withdrawn.

Redesign of the shell containing the electronics and the display screen will cost £200 000. The development director expects that working capital needs will increase by £68 000 during the first year, and that this additional amount will grow by five per cent per year in line with sales. Once sales start to decline, this additional working capital will be released proportionately with the decline in sales.

Marketing the BookWorm will cost £300 000 spread evenly over the first three years of the project. Direct costs of production, including raw materials, are expected to be 65 per cent of sales. In order to maintain growth in sales, it is expected that further redesign will be needed in Year 4, at a cost of £200 000. The Inland Revenue has ruled that redesign costs may be capitalised and will attract capital allowances at a rate of 25 per cent on a reducing balance basis. Corporation tax is to be levied at a rate of 31 per cent.

(a) Calculate the internal rate of return of the BookWorm project.

(b) Discuss what other information might be useful in reaching a decision on whether to proceed with the project.

REFERENCES

Drury, C., Braund, S., Osborn, P. and Tayles, M. (1993) 'A survey of management accounting practices in UK manufacturing companies', *Certified Research Report 32*, ACCA.

Grayson, C. (1967) 'The use of statistical techniques in capital budgeting', in Robicheck, A. (ed.) *Financial Research and Management Decisions*, New York, Wiley & Sons, pp. 90–132.

Kennedy, A. and Sugden, K. (1986) 'Ritual and reality in capital budgeting', *Management Accounting*, Feb, pp. 34–7.

Lapsley, I. (1986) 'Investment appraisal in UK non-trading organisations', *Financial Accountability and Management*, Summer, pp. 135–51.

Marek, S. (1991) 'Risk and capital investment', *ACCA Students Newsletter*, Dec, pp. 38–41.

McIntyre, A. and Coulthurst, N. (1986) 'Capital budgeting in medium-sized businesses', *CIMA Research Report*.

Mills, R. (1988) 'Capital budgeting – the state of the art', *Long Range Planning*, Vol. 21, No. 4, pp. 76–81.

Pike, R. (1983) 'A review of recent trends in formal capital budgeting processes', *Accounting and Business Research*, Summer, pp. 201–8.

Scarlett, R. (1993) 'The impact of corporate taxation on the viability of investment', *Management Accounting*, Nov, p. 30.

Scarlett, R. (1995) 'Further aspects of the impact of taxation on the viability of investment', *Management Accounting*, May, p. 54.

RECOMMENDED READING

A more detailed analysis of risk and uncertainty in the context of investment appraisal can be found in: Levy, H. and Sarnat, M. (1994) *Capital Investment and Financing Decisions*, Prentice-Hall.

Other useful articles include:

Emery, G. (1982) 'Some guidelines for evaluating capital investment alternatives with unequal lives', *Financial Management*, Vol. 11, Spring, pp. 14–19.

Pike, R. (1989) 'Do sophisticated capital budgeting techniques improve investment decision-making effectiveness?', *The Engineering Economist*, Vol. 34, No. 2, Winter, pp. 149–61.

CHAPTER 5

SOURCES OF LONG-TERM FINANCE

EQUITY FINANCE

INTRODUCTION

Ordinary share capital or equity finance is the foundation of the financial structure of a company and should be the source of most of its long-term finance. Since a company is owned by its ordinary shareholders, raising additional finance by issuing new ordinary shares has ownership and control implications which merit careful consideration.

In this chapter, we shall look at a number of the key areas for corporate finance as far as ordinary share capital is concerned. Among the areas covered are the various ways in which a company can raise finance through issuing new shares, as well as the implications for a company of obtaining a stock market quotation. Rights issues (the issuing of new shares to existing shareholders) are discussed, together with their impact on shareholder wealth. We examine some of the ways in which a company can increase or decrease the number of ordinary shares in issue, and their implications for both companies and investors. We also include in this chapter a discussion of preference shares, which have features in common with both equity and debt, and consider the relative merits of preference shares and equity.

LEARNING OBJECTIVES

After studying this chapter, you should have achieved the following learning objectives:

- a knowledge of the key characteristics of equity finance;
- an understanding of the different ways that a company can issue new equity finance and the reasons why a stock market quotation may be desirable;
- an understanding of rights issues, their importance to companies and their effect on shareholder wealth;
- the ability to estimate the effect of rights issues on share prices;
- an appreciation of the difference between stock splits, bonus issues, scrip dividends and share repurchases and their importance to companies;
- an understanding of preference shares as a source of finance for a company.

5.1 EQUITY FINANCE

Equity finance is provided by the sale of ordinary shares to investors. This may be a sale of shares to new owners, perhaps through the stock market as part of a company seeking a quotation, or it may be a sale of shares to existing shareholders, for example by means of a rights issue. In addition, ordinary shares are bought and sold on a regular basis on stock exchanges all over the world. Ordinary shareholders, as the owners of a company, will wish to have a satisfactory return on their investment. This is true whether they are the original purchasers of the shares or they are investors who have bought them subsequently on a secondary market.

By law, the ordinary shares of a company must have a nominal, or par, value and cannot be issued for less than this amount. The nominal value of a share, usually 25p, 50p or £1, bears no relation to its market value: ordinary shares with a nominal value of 25p may have a market price of several pounds. New shares, whether issued at the foundation of a company or subsequently, are almost always issued at a premium to their nominal value. This gives rise in the balance sheet to a share premium account; the nominal value of shares issued is represented by the ordinary share account.

5.1.1 The rights of ordinary shareholders

Ownership of ordinary shares confers rights on ordinary shareholders on both an individual and a collective basis. From a corporate finance perspective, some of the most important rights available to shareholders are as follows:

- the right to attend general meetings of their company;
- the right to vote on the election of the directors of their company;

- the right to vote on the appointment, remuneration and removal of auditors;
- the right to receive the annual accounts of their company and the report of its auditors;
- the right to receive a share of any dividend distributed;
- the right to vote on important matters such as a change in their company's authorised share capital, the repurchase of its shares, or a take-over bid;
- the right to receive a share of any assets remaining after their company has been liquidated;
- the right to participate in a new issue of shares in their company (the pre-emptive right).

5.1.2 Equity finance, risk and return

Ordinary shareholders are the ultimate bearers of the risk associated with the business activities of the companies they own. This is because, in the event of the company going into liquidation, there is an order of precedence governing the way in which the proceeds of liquidation are distributed. The first claims to be settled are those of secured creditors, such as debenture holders and banks, who are entitled to receive in full both unpaid interest and the outstanding principal. The next claims to be settled are those of unsecured creditors, such as suppliers of goods and services. Ordinary shareholders are not entitled to receive any of the proceeds of liquidation until the amounts owing to creditors, both secured and unsecured, have been satisfied in full. This placing of ordinary shareholders at the bottom of the 'creditor hierarchy' means that they carry the very real risk of receiving nothing at all in the event of liquidation. This is especially true when it is recognised that liquidation is likely to be the consequence of a protracted period of unprofitable trading. However, it is possible, because the claims of creditors are fixed in nature, that ordinary shareholders have the possibility of making substantial gains from the proceeds of liquidation.

Since ordinary shareholders carry the greatest risk of any of the providers of long-term finance to a company, they will expect in compensation the highest return. In terms of regular returns on capital provided, this means that ordinary shareholders will expect the return they receive, through dividends and capital gains, to be higher than interest payments on debt. In terms of the cost of capital (*see* Chapter 8), it means that the cost of equity will invariably be higher than the cost of debt.

5.2 THE NEW ISSUES MARKET

The regulations governing a new issue of equity onto the capital markets, whether laid down by the government or by the Stock Exchange, are not only complex but also subject to frequent revision and change. In order to help it to meet and abide by these regulations, a company wishing to raise finance through a new equity issue will employ the services of an issuing house. The issuing house, usually a merchant bank, will try to make the new issue a successful one by advising on the steps to be taken as part of the issuing process, by determining an appropriate issue price for the new shares, and by marketing the issue to institutional and other investors. The issuing house will arrange for advertisements, often taking the form of a prospectus, to appear in the national press and, if a Stock Exchange listing is being applied for, will arrange for the appointment of a sponsor.

The sponsor, which may also be the issuing house, has the responsibility of ensuring that a company seeking a listing satisfies the requirements and carries out the procedures laid down in the Stock Exchange's *Yellow Book*, which contains a substantial number of detailed regulations covering the admission of companies to its Official List.

5.2.1 New issue methods

A company may issue shares and/or obtain a quotation or listing on the Stock Exchange by several methods.

Placing

There are two main methods of issuing shares in the UK and the one used most frequently is called a placing. Here, the shares are issued at a fixed price to a number of institutional investors, who are sounded out by the issuing bank before the issue takes place. The issue is underwritten by the issuing company's sponsor, who is usually a merchant bank. This issue method carries very little risk, since it is essentially just a way of distributing a company's shares to institutional investors, and so it has a low cost when compared to other issue methods.

Offer for sale at fixed price

The other main method of raising funds by issuing shares or obtaining a quotation is called an offer for sale, which is usually made at a fixed price. It is usually used for a large issue when a company is coming to the market (seeking a quotation) for the first time. In an offer for sale at fixed price, the shares are offered to the public with the help of the sponsoring merchant bank, who will help the company to decide on an issue price. The issue price should be low enough to be attractive to potential investors, but high enough to allow the required finance to be raised without the issue of more shares than necessary. The issue is underwritten, usually by institutional investors, so that the issuing company is guaranteed to receive the finance it needs. Any shares on offer which are not taken up will be bought by the underwriters at an agreed price.

Offer for sale by tender

An alternative to an offer for sale at fixed price is an offer for sale by tender or 'tender issue'. Here, the public is invited to bid for the available shares at prices in excess of a minimum decided by the issuing company. The price which ensures that all the shares on offer are sold is called the striking price. The available shares are then allocated pro rata to investors who have bid at or above the striking price. All investors who receive shares will pay the striking price: excess money is returned to investors who are receiving fewer shares than they bid for, or who bid at a price greater than the striking price. While tender issues were common in the early 1980s, no private sector offer for sale by tender has occurred since 1986.

Intermediaries offer

Since 1991, medium-sized issues onto the London Stock Exchange have been allowed to be sold either by an offer for sale or by an 'intermediaries offer'. In an intermediaries offer, all member firms of the Stock Exchange can apply for shares, which they can subsequently pass on to their clients. This method, while quicker and cheaper than an offer for sale at fixed price, still ensures that the shares of a company are widely distributed.

Introduction

A Stock Exchange quotation may also be gained via an introduction. This is where a listing is granted to the existing shares of a company which are already widely held. It does not involve the offering of any new shares and so no new finance is raised. A company may choose an introduction in order to increase the marketability of its shares, to obtain access to capital markets, or simply to determine the value of its shares.

Example Tender issue

Falcon plc is issuing 2 500 000 shares by tender (minimum tender price £2.00 per share) and has received the following tenders:

Tender price per share	*Shares applied for at this price*
£4.00	100 000
£3.50	300 000
£3.00	600 000
£2.50	1 200 000
£2.00	1 500 000

The cumulative total of shares applied for and the funds raised as the striking price is progressively lowered are as follows:

Striking price	*Total shares applied for*	*Total amount raised*
£4.00	100 000	£400 000
£3.50	400 000	£1 400 000
£3.00	1 000 000	£3 000 000
£2.50	2 200 000	£5 500 000
£2.00	2 500 000	£5 000 000

Note that, when the striking price is lowered to £2.00, there were bids for a total of 3 700 000 shares, but the issue is limited to 2 500 000 shares. At this striking price, each applicant will receive only 67.5 per cent of the shares applied for. If Falcon plc issues exactly 2 500 000 shares at a striking price of £2.00, the company raises £5m (ignoring issue costs). If Falcon wishes to maximise the amount raised, it should select an issue price of £2.50, since this raises £5.5m. At this striking price the number of shares exceeds the number of applications, so all applicants will receive the number of shares they asked for. Where a bid was at a higher price, excess application money is returned. An investor bidding for 1000 shares at £4 each, for example, would receive 1000 shares and have (£4 – £2.50) × 1000 = £1500 returned.

5.2.2 Stock exchange regulations

Some of the important requirements covered by the regulations in the *Yellow Book*, which seek to protect investors, are as follows:

- audited accounts must have been published, usually for at least three years prior to admission;
- at least 25 per cent of the company's shares must be in public hands when trading in its shares begins;
- the company must agree to abide by the regulations contained in the *Yellow Book*;
- the company must publish a prospectus, as required by the Companies Act, containing a forecast of expected performance and other detailed information to assist investors in making an assessment of its prospects;
- the company must meet the minimum market capitalisation requirements in force at the time.

From September 1993, the rules of the Stock Exchange allowed issues up to £25m to be made entirely by a placing, while issues greater than £50m had to be made through an offer for sale. Between these limits, the Stock Exchange allowed issues to be made partly by a placing and partly by an offer for sale or intermediaries offer. Since January 1996, these limits have been removed, so that any issue method meeting listing requirements can be employed.

5.2.3 Relative importance of placing and offer for sale

Although placings are the most common method of obtaining a stock market quotation in the UK, they have not accounted for the majority of finance raised because they have been subject to limits on the maximum size of issues that can be placed. Most of the new finance raised is by means of offers for sale at fixed price, which tend to be much larger than placings. Of the £12.2bn raised by private sector new issues on the London Stock Exchange between 1984 and 1991, Byrne and Rees (1994) found that 79 per cent was raised by fixed price offers for sale, eight per cent by tender issues and 13 per cent by placings.

The relative importance of offers for sale at fixed price and placings varies between markets. Essentially, placings are used much more frequently in smaller markets, where the amounts raised cannot usually justify the additional costs incurred by an offer for sale, such as marketing, advertising and underwriting. Between 1984 and 1991, 49 per cent of non-introduction new issues on the London Stock Exchange were by offers for sale, while 51 per cent were by placings. In contrast, over the same period on the now defunct Unlisted Securities Market (USM), only 10 per cent of new issues were by offers for sale while 90 per cent were placed. The dominant position of placings has been maintained in the successor to the USM, the Alternative Investment Market (AIM), since Corbett (1996) reports that most AIM companies obtain a market listing by means of a placing. Offers for sale, though, still accounted for most of the funds raised. This data reflects the limitation of placings to smaller offers and the smaller size of USM and AIM offers.

5.2.4 Underwriting

In the period of time between the announcement of a new equity issue and its completion, there is the possibility of adverse price fluctuations which may lead to the issue being unsuccessful. An unsuccessful issue is one where a company fails to raise the finance that it is seeking, or where it is left with shares that investors did not wish to purchase. A company will wish to avoid an unsuccessful issue because of the damage that may be caused to its reputation, because it is likely to make raising further finance more expensive, and because it still has to bear the costs of the unsuccessful issue. For these reasons, companies insure against the possibility of a new issue being unsuccessful by having it underwritten.

For each new issue, one or more main underwriters will be appointed, who will further spread the risk by appointing a number of sub-underwriters. While the main underwriter is usually the issuing house or merchant bank organising the issue, most underwriters are financial institutions such as insurance companies and pension funds. In return for a fee of about 1.25 per cent of the proceeds of the new issue (the total underwriting fee is about two per cent of proceeds), underwriters will accept the shares not taken up by the market, each underwriter taking shares in proportion to the amount of fee income received. Through underwriting, then, a company can be sure of raising the finance that it needs.

A new equity issue would still be regarded as unsuccessful, however, if most of the shares were taken up by underwriters rather than by the market. This has not been the case in recent years, as most new issues have been over- rather than under-subscribed. In consequence, it has been suggested that the cost of underwriting could be reduced by making underwriters compete openly for new issue business.

5.2.5 Advantages of obtaining a stock exchange quotation

There are a number of benefits that may be obtained by a company through becoming quoted on a stock exchange and any one of them may encourage the directors of a company to decide to seek a listing. Broadly speaking, these benefits include the raising of finance by coming to market, easier access to finance, and the uses to which quoted shares can be put.

Raising finance through coming to market

The owners of a private company may decide to seek a stock market quotation so that, as part of the process of coming to market, they can sell some of their shares and thereby realise some of the investment they have made in the company. An unquoted company whose growth has been due in part to an investment of venture capital may decide to seek a stock market listing in order to give the venture capitalists an 'exit route' by which to realise their investment. In both of these situations, some or all of the funds raised by selling shares pass to a third party rather than to the company obtaining a stock market listing. But a company may also decide to seek a stock market quotation primarily to raise funds for its own use, for example in order to fund an expansion of business activities.

Access to finance

By being listed on a recognised stock exchange, a company will have easier access to external sources of equity capital, whether through the new issues market or by rights issues, since a listed company is more likely to be attractive to institutional investors. This means that a listed company can more easily obtain any long-term equity funds it needs for expansion. Unquoted companies, in contrast, may find their growth limited because of difficulties in raising the finance they need: this is a gap which is filled to some extent by venture capitalists, who usually take an equity stake in companies they invest in. As far as debt finance is concerned, lenders tend to look on quoted companies more favourably, since both credibility and reputation are enhanced by a listing, which increases a company's security and lowers its perceived risk. This may result in a lower cost of debt.

Uses of shares

Taking over another company can be a relatively easy way to achieve corporate growth and a common way of financing a take-over is by issuing new shares. The shares of a company that is quoted are more likely to be accepted by the shareholders in a target company, in part or whole exchange for their existing shares, than shares in a private company. This is partly because the shares of a quoted company will be easier to sell: a ready market exists in them since, in satisfying the listing requirements, 25 per cent of a company's shares must be placed in public hands. There may not be a ready market in the shares of a private company. Marketability will also increase the value of the shares and hence the value of the company.

5.2.6 Disadvantages of obtaining a stock market quotation

Naturally, the benefits that can be derived from obtaining a quotation are not without their price, and the disadvantages associated with being listed must be considered if a balanced view is to be presented. There are, after all, many other ways to obtain funds or to establish a reputation: seeking a stock market quotation will not be the best option for all companies.

Costs of a quotation

Obtaining and maintaining a stock exchange quotation is a costly business. The costs of obtaining a listing will reduce the amount of finance raised by a new issue. The Bank of England (1990) found that these costs were between six per cent and 14 per cent for an offer for sale, and between six per cent and 11.5 per cent for a placing. A breakdown of the costs of obtaining a listing is given in Exhibit 5.1. On an annual basis, the costs of satisfying listing requirements must also be met. One of these costs is the cost of increased financial disclosure, since stock exchange disclosure requirements are more demanding than those of company law. This will lead to increased public scrutiny of the company and its performance.

EXHIBIT 5.1

Fee or charge	£	*% of sum raised*
Capital duty	70 000	1.0
Stock Exchange listing fee	7 340	0.1
Accountant's fees	93 500	1.3
Legal fees	98 000	1.4
Advertising costs	98 000	1.4
Printing costs	30 000	0.4
Extel fees	1 500	0.0
Receiving bank's charges	10 000	0.1
Issue house fee (underwriting etc.)	140 000	2.0
Additional advisers' fees	14 000	0.2
Total	562 340	8.0

Analysis of the costs of obtaining a listing, based on a £7m offer for sale at fixed price

Source: *Bank of England Quarterly Bulletin*, December 1986. Reproduced with kind permission of the Bank of England

Shareholder expectations

The directors of a listed company need to take account of the expectations of their shareholders. The directors of a private company may have been used to satisfying their own needs but, once the company becomes listed, they will need to consider the expectations of new shareholders. These will include the expectations of institutional shareholders, which may well include a focus on short-term profitability and dividend income. The possibility of being taken over is increased if the company fails to meet such expectations, since dissatisfied shareholders are likely to be more willing to sell their shares to a predator company. The stock exchange is thus seen as providing a market for corporate control, in the sense that poor performance by a listed company may be corrected by removing its incumbent management in a take-over. The increased financial transparency resulting from the stock exchange requirement to produce regular reports and accounts means that predator firms are more easily able to select likely acquisition targets, whose shares they can then seek to acquire on the open market.

5.3 RIGHTS ISSUES

If a company wishes to issue new shares, it is required by law to offer them first to its existing shareholders, unless those shareholders have already agreed in a meeting of the company to waive the right for a period. Because of this legal right to be offered the shares before new investors, such an issue of new shares is called a *rights issue*. In order to preserve existing patterns of ownership and control, a rights issue is offered on a pro rata basis, such as one new share for every four existing shares (referred to as a '1 for 4' issue).

As a way of raising finance, rights issues have the advantage of being cheaper than an offer for sale to the general public. In addition, if the rights offered are fully taken up, there is no dilution of ownership and control. But they are not appropriate if the amount of finance needed to be raised is large, since the funds available to individual shareholders are likely to be limited.

Rights issues are offered at a discount to the current market price, commonly in the region of 15 per cent to 20 per cent. This discount makes the new shares more attractive to shareholders and also allows for any adverse movements in the share price prior to the issue. The current market price will normally be quoted 'ex-div', which means that purchase of the share will not convey the right to receive a dividend about to be paid. The price of shares already issued will increase to reflect the value of the right to receive new shares at a discount; this new price is called the 'cum rights' price. When purchase of shares on the open market no longer gives the purchaser the right to take part in the rights issue because the list of shareholders has closed, the share price will fall as it goes 'ex-rights'.

5.3.1 The theoretical ex-rights price

After the issue, both old and new shares will trade at the theoretical ex-rights price (P_e), which is a weighted average of the cum rights price and the rights issue price. We have:

$$P_e = P_P \frac{N_o}{N} + P_N \frac{N_N}{N}$$

where: P_P is the cum rights price
P_N is the rights issue price

N_O is the number of old shares
N_N is the number of new shares
N is the total number of shares.

Consider the case of Nolig plc, a company with 2 000 000 ordinary shares of par value £1 in issue, currently trading at £2.20 per share. The company decides to raise new equity funds for an investment project by offering its existing shareholders the right to subscribe for one new share at £1.85 each for every four shares already held. After the announcement of the issue, the ordinary share price falls to £2.10 and remains at this level until the time of the rights issue. Here:

Cum rights price, P_P =	£2.10
New issue price, P_N =	£1.85
Number of old shares, N_O =	2.0 million
Number of new shares, N_N =	0.5 million
Total number of shares, N =	2.5 million

and so:

$$\text{Theoretical ex-rights price, } P_e = \frac{(2 \times 2.10) + (0.5 \times 1.85)}{2.5} = £2.05$$

Alternatively, using simply the terms of the 1 for 4 rights issue:

$$\text{Theoretical ex-rights price, } P_e = \frac{(4 \times 2.10) + (1 \times 1.85)}{5} = £2.05$$

5.3.2 The value of the rights

An ordinary shareholder can detach the rights from the shares and sell them to other investors; there is an active market in rights, with prices quoted regularly in the financial press. The value of the rights, the price that a buyer is prepared to pay for them, is the theoretical gain that the buyer could make by exercising them. It is the difference between the theoretical ex-rights price and the rights issue price. Continuing the example of Nolig plc, the value of the rights attached to four Nolig shares is £2.05 – £1.85 = £0.20 or 20p. This is the amount that an investor would be prepared to pay in exchange for the rights attached to the four shares, as he could then subscribe £1.85 for a share which would in fact be worth £2.05. The value of the rights can also be expressed in terms of the existing shares held, i.e. here it would be 20p/4 = 5p per existing share.

5.3.3 Rights issues and shareholder wealth

If we regard cash in a shareholder's bank account to be equivalent in wealth terms to the ordinary shares that could be obtained in exchange for it, then there is no need for the wealth of the shareholder to be affected by a rights issue. If shareholders subscribe for their full entitlement of new shares or if they sell all the rights attached to their existing shares (or any combination of these two alternatives), their wealth position will be unchanged. If they do nothing and allow their rights to lapse, however, their wealth will fall. We can show this with a simple example.

Earlier, we considered the example of Nolig plc, which has 2 000 000 ordinary shares of par value £1 in issue. The company decided to make a 1 for 4 rights issue at £1.85 per new share and the cum rights share price was £2.10. The theoretical ex-rights price was found to be £2.05 and the value of the rights was found to be 5p per existing share.

If Sarah, a shareholder, owns 1000 shares in Nolig plc, she has the right to subscribe for 250 new shares, and so we have:

	£
1000 shares cum rights @ £2.10 =	2100.00
Cash for 250 new shares @ £1.85 =	462.50
1250 shares ex-rights @ £2.05 =	2562.50

If Sarah sells her rights, we have:

	£
1000 shares ex-rights @ £2.05 =	2050.00
Sale of rights, 1000 @ 5 pence =	50.00
Cash not subscribed for shares =	462.50
Comparable wealth position	2562.50

Sarah's wealth position is unchanged if she sells her rights. If she does nothing and allows her rights to lapse, we have:

	£
Initial position, 1000 shares @ £2.10 =	2100.00
Final position, 1000 shares @ £2.05 =	2050.00
Decline in wealth by doing nothing	50.00

Sarah's wealth has declined because the price of her shares has fallen from the cum rights value to the ex-rights value. Choosing neither to subscribe for new shares offered, nor to sell the rights attached to existing shares held, will lead to a decrease in shareholder wealth, as this example shows. If appropriate action is taken, however, the effect on shareholder wealth is, theoretically at least, a neutral one. This will be true no matter how great a discount is attached to the new shares.

5.3.4 Market price after a rights issue

The ex-rights price is likely to be different in practice to the price predicted by theory. This is primarily due to the different expectations that investors have, which will influence their buying and selling preferences and hence market prices.

Investors will have expectations about the future state of the economy: they may be expecting interest rates or inflation to increase, for example, or may be anticipating a downturn in economic activity. Investors may also have formed opinions about the proposed use of the new funds by the company. If these opinions are favourable, the share price will increase accordingly.

As far as earnings are concerned, if these are expected to be maintained or increased after the new issue then, in spite of there being more shares in circulation, the share price may be unchanged or even increase. This points to the need to consider the effect of a proposed rights issue not only on earnings per share, but also on earnings yield, which is the relationship between the earnings per share and the share price. If the earnings yield on existing funds remains unchanged, the key variable affecting the ex-rights price will be the expected earnings yield on the funds raised.

We can modify our original expression for the theoretical ex-rights price, given earlier in Section 5.3.1, to enable it to take into account the expected earnings yield on the new funds raised (γ_N), compared with the earnings yield on existing funds (γ_O). We have:

$$P_e = P_P \frac{N_o}{N} + P_N \frac{N_N \gamma_N}{N \gamma_O}$$

where: P_P = cum rights price
P_N = rights issue price
N_O = number of old shares
N_N = number of new shares
N = total number of shares
γ_N/γ_O = ratio of the yield on new capital to the yield on old capital.

If γ_N/γ_O is greater than one, the ex-rights share price will be greater than the price predicted by the simple weighted average considered in Section 5.3.1, corresponding to the situation where investors expect earnings to be increased after the rights issue. If the issue is not seen as a positive move by the market, so that overall earnings are expected to fall, then γ_N/γ_O is less than one and the ex-rights share price will be less than a simple weighted average.

Returning to the earlier example of Nolig plc, you will recall that the theoretical ex-rights price was found to be £2.05. If we now assume that the earnings yield on existing funds is 18 per cent, but that the expected earnings yield on the funds raised by the rights issue is 25 per cent, we have:

$$\text{Ex-rights price, } P_e = \frac{(2 \times 2.10)}{2.5} + \frac{(0.5 \times 1.85) \times 25}{(2.5 \times 18)} = £2.19$$

The increased earnings expected from the new funds have led to a higher predicted ex-rights share price.

The ex-rights share price will also be affected by the expected level of dividends: if dividends are expected to fall, the share price will decline. While earnings from the new investment may take some time to come on stream, the decision on how much to pay out as dividends rests with the directors of the company. In order to reassure shareholders, who are being asked to subscribe further funds to the company, an announcement about the expected level of dividends often accompanies the announcement of a rights issue.

Empirical evidence suggests that the market assumes that companies will be able to maintain their level of dividend payments and that the formula for determining the theoretical ex-rights price is a reasonably accurate reflection of the true state of affairs.

5.3.5 Underwriting and deep discount rights issues

Theoretically shareholder wealth is not affected by a rights issue since the value of the rights is equivalent to the difference between the value of the original shares held and the theoretical ex-rights price. We have also noted that one of the reasons why a rights issue is issued at a discount to the current market price is in order to make it attractive to existing shareholders and thereby help to ensure the issue's success. Why, in that case, is it common for a company to seek a further guarantee of the success of a rights issue by having it underwritten? Since the size of the discount is irrelevant, the cost of underwriting could be avoided and the success of a rights issue could be assured by increasing the size of the discount, i.e. by offering the new shares at a 'deep discount' to the current share price. Deep discount rights issues, however, are seldom encountered.

An explanation of the rarity of deep discount rights issues has been sought in the role played by underwriters. It has been suggested that underwriting may act as a signalling device, giving assurance to shareholders that the risk associated with a rights issue is seen as an acceptable one by the underwriters and hence by institutional investors. On this analysis, underwriting will have a positive effect on both the rights issue and on the company's market price. It has also been suggested, perhaps cynically, that there is little incentive for major corporate sector shareholders to press for deep discount rights issues in view of the decrease in fee income derived from underwriting that they would suffer as a consequence.

5.4 SCRIP ISSUES, STOCK SPLITS, SCRIP DIVIDENDS AND SHARE REPURCHASES

5.4.1 Scrip issues and stock splits

Scrip issues and stock splits are both ways in which a company can increase the number of shares in issue, without raising any additional finance. A scrip issue (which is also known as a bonus issue) is a conversion of existing capital reserves or retained earnings into additional shares, which are then distributed pro rata to existing shareholders. It is essentially a balance sheet transfer from reserves to the ordinary share account. A stock split (which is also known as a share split) involves simultaneously reducing the nominal value of each share and increasing the number of shares in issue, so that the total book value of the shares is unchanged. For example, a company with one million shares of par value 50p could, as a result of a stock split, have two million ordinary shares of par value 25p.

A number of possible explanations for stock splits have been advanced. One common theory is that stock splits increase the ease with which ordinary shares can be traded on the secondary market by moving them into a more favourable price range. More investors will be willing to buy shares trading at £5, it is argued, than shares trading at £10. Under this theory, stock splits increase liquidity. Research by Copeland (1979), however, suggests that liquidity actually declines following a stock split, since trading volume is proportionately lower and transactions costs are proportionately higher.

Another common theory about why stock splits occur is that they have, in some unexplained way, a positive effect on shareholder wealth. The effect of stock splits on shareholder wealth has been the subject of much research, but the results are not conclusive. Some researchers, such as Firth (1973), have found that stock splits do not have any beneficial effects resulting from share price movements. Other researchers, such as Grinblatt *et al.* (1984), have detected a positive effect on shareholder wealth and suggest that the announcement of a stock split might be interpreted by investors as a favourable signal concerning a company's future cash flows. Grinblatt *et al.* (1984) also found that positive effects on shareholder wealth appeared to occur as a result of scrip issue announcements.

5.4.2 Scrip dividends

Another method of issuing new equity which does not result in the raising of additional finance is the issuing of a scrip dividend (also known as a share dividend). Here, a shareholder accepts more ordinary shares in a company as a partial or total alternative to a cash dividend.

There are definite cash flow advantages to the company in offering a scrip dividend, for two reasons. First, if investors choose to take up the scrip dividend there will be less cash paid out by the company as dividends. Second, scrip dividends do not give rise to a need to make an early payment of corporation tax (i.e. advance corporation tax). A further benefit to the company is that, as a result of the increase in equity, there will be a small decrease in gearing. Since the scrip dividend replaces a cash dividend that would have been paid anyway, there is no reason why, in an efficient capital market, a scrip dividend should cause a fall in the share price.

If ordinary shareholders wish to increase their shareholdings, a scrip dividend allows them to do so cheaply, without incurring dealing costs. For a tax-paying ordinary shareholder, there is no difference in the UK between a scrip dividend and a cash dividend, since a scrip dividend is taxed as though it were income. For tax-exempt ordinary shareholders, however, there is a difference. With a cash dividend, tax-exempt shareholders can benefit by reclaiming the tax paid by the company on the profits distributed. With a scrip dividend, this benefit is lost, since no advance corporation tax liability arises when a scrip dividend is issued. As a cash dividend and any scrip dividend alternative offered by a company are required by regulation to be similar in value, there is a financial disincentive for tax-exempt ordinary shareholders to accept scrip dividends.

5.4.3 Share repurchases

Share repurchases are becoming increasingly accepted as a way of returning value to ordinary shareholders in the UK, following their adoption by a number of leading companies such as Reuters and Boots. Prior to 1981, however, companies were not allowed to purchase their own shares unless they were redeemable preference shares. As a result of changes introduced by the Companies Act 1981, a company can now purchase its own shares provided that permission has been given by shareholders in a general meeting of the company. To protect the interests of creditors and the remaining shareholders, though, share repurchases are carefully regulated. By law, payment for repurchased shares can only be made from distributable profits. In the UK, repurchased shares must be cancelled: in the US and under the EU Second Directive, however, repurchased shares can be held for reissue at a later date. Companies listed on the Stock Exchange must obtain the prior approval of the Stock Exchange Takeover Panel.

There are several reasons for returning surplus capital to shareholders. One rationale is that shareholders will be able to invest the cash more effectively than the company. Another is that the value of the remaining shares will be enhanced after shares have been repurchased. Since the capital employed by a company is reduced by repurchasing shares, return on capital employed (ROCE) will increase. The number of shares will fall, resulting in an increase in earnings per share. While share repurchases also lead to an increase in gearing, it is argued that any increase in financial risk is negligible and so, if the cost of equity is unaltered, the value of both shares and company will be increased.

5.5 PREFERENCE SHARES

Preference shares differ from ordinary shares in giving the holder preferential rights to receive a share of annual profits. An ordinary dividend cannot be paid unless preference dividends due have been paid in full. Preference shares are also higher up in the creditor hierarchy than ordinary shares, and will have a preferential right to receive the proceeds of disposal of the assets of a company in the event of a winding-up. They are therefore less risky than ordinary shares, even though they are legally share capital as well. Like ordinary shares, preference shares are normally undated, but unlike ordinary shares, they do not in normal circumstances carry voting rights. However, preference shares carry a higher risk than debt, for several reasons:

- preference shares, unlike debt, are not secured on company assets;
- preference dividends cannot be paid until interest payments on debt have been covered;

- in the event of liquidation, preference shareholders will not be paid off until the claims of debt holders have been satisfied.

Preference shares may be either 'cumulative' or 'non-cumulative' with respect to preference dividends, which like ordinary dividends are a distribution of taxed profits and not a payment of interest. With non-cumulative preference shares, if distributable profits are insufficient to pay the preference dividend, it is lost; with cumulative preference shares, if distributable profits are not sufficient to pay the preference dividend, the right to receive it is carried forward and unpaid preference dividends must be settled before any ordinary dividend can be paid in subsequent years. If preference shares are 'non-participating', the preference dividend represents the sole return to the holders of the shares, irrespective of the company's success in terms of earnings growth or increase in share price. 'Participating' preference shares, in addition to paying a fixed preference dividend, offer the right to receive an additional dividend if profits in the year exceed an agreed amount.

5.5.1 Variable rate preference shares

Preference shares commonly pay investors a fixed rate dividend, but preference shares paying a variable rate dividend have become more common in recent years. Two distinct methods of periodically resetting the preference dividend rate are used. With the first method, the preference dividend rate is a floating rate or an adjustable rate determined by adding a fixed percentage to a market rate such as the London Interbank Offered Rate (LIBOR). With the second method, the preference dividend rate is adjusted periodically to the rate which allows the preference shares to trade at a constant stated value on the capital markets. An example of the second method of resetting the dividend rate is given by auction market preferred stock (AMPS).

5.5.2 Convertible preference shares

Other features may be added to preference shares to make them attractive or to satisfy particular company financing needs. Convertible preference shares, for example, give the holder the option to convert them into ordinary shares on prescribed terms in prescribed circumstances.

5.5.3 The popularity of preference shares

The cost disadvantage of preference shares relative to debt has led to a decline in their popularity in the UK. It is unlikely that the dividend rate on preference shares would be less than the after-tax interest cost of a debenture issue, due to the relative risks associated with the two securities. Convertible redeemable preference shares have proved to be a popular investment vehicle with providers of venture capital, however. If the company supported by the venture finance is doing well, the preference shares can be converted into ordinary shares, leading to higher returns;

if the company is not doing well, the preference shares can be redeemed. The 1980s saw preference shares growing in popularity with banks issuers, while AMPS proved attractive to corporate issuers.

5.5.4 The advantages and disadvantages of preference shares

One of the main advantages of preference shares compared to debt, an advantage that is shared with ordinary equity, is that the dividend need not be paid if there are insufficient profits to cover it. This is not so much of a problem for holders of cumulative preference shares – although the real value of unpaid preference dividends is likely to suffer a decline – but owners of non-cumulative preference shares are unlikely to be happy about not receiving a dividend. For this reason, holders of non-cumulative preference shares are likely to demand a higher return in compensation.

Unlike ordinary equity, preference shares do not carry general voting rights and so will not dilute existing patterns of ownership and control. When compared to debt, preference shares offer on the one hand the advantage of preserving debt capacity, since they are not secured, and on the other hand the advantage of protection from legal action for default, since non-payment of preference dividends does not give holders of preference shares the right to appoint a receiver.

The major disadvantage of preference shares is their cost relative to, say, the cost of debentures. Due to the higher risk associated with preference shares the percentage dividend may, for example, be 12 per cent while the interest coupon on debentures stands at 10 per cent. This difference is further exacerbated when the favourable tax position of the interest paid on debentures is taken into consideration. Assuming that a company is not in a tax-exhausted position, its after-tax cost of debt with a corporation tax rate of 31 per cent and an interest coupon rate of 10 per cent will be $10 \times (1 - 0.31)$ or 6.9 per cent. Given these relative costs, companies will choose debenture finance rather than preference shares.

5.6 CONCLUSION

In this chapter we have discussed a number of the important issues in connection with equity finance and preference shares. Equity finance gives a company a solid financial foundation, since it is truly permanent capital which does not normally need to be repaid. Ordinary shareholders, as the owners of the company and the carriers of the largest slice of risk, expect the highest returns. Their position and rights as owners are protected by both government and stock market regulations and any new issue of shares must take these into account.

KEY POINTS

1 Ordinary shares have a nominal value which is different from their market value, and are usually issued at a premium. They confer individual and collective rights on their owners.

2 Ordinary shareholders are the ultimate bearers of risk because, being at the base of the creditor hierarchy, they stand to lose everything in the event of liquidation. They therefore expect the greatest return.

3 To help it to satisfy the regulations on new equity issues and to advise it on procedure, a company will employ an issuing house, which is usually a merchant bank. A sponsor is needed to help in obtaining a listing.

4 A placing involves issuing blocks of new shares at a fixed price to institutional investors. It is a low-cost issue method involving little risk.

5 An offer for sale at fixed price is usually used for large issues of new equity and involves offering shares to the public through an issuing house or sponsoring merchant bank.

6 A tender issue involves inviting the public to bid for the new equity shares on offer. The available shares are then allocated at the striking price pro rata to successful investors.

7 An intermediaries offer involves the sale of new equity shares to Stock Exchange member firms for subsequent sale to their clients.

8 An introduction is the granting of a listing to the existing shares of a company, and does not involve the issuing of new shares.

9 The Stock Exchange's *Yellow Book* contains detailed regulations which are designed to protect investors and screen companies seeking a quotation.

10 Placings are the most common method of obtaining a stock market quotation, but most of the new finance raised is by offers for sale.

11 Companies insure against the failure of a new equity issue through underwriting. The main underwriter is usually the issuing house and most underwriters are financial institutions.

12 The benefits arising from obtaining a listing are: raising finance by coming to market, easier access to equity and other finance, and uses to which quoted shares can be put, including payment in a take-over bid.

13 The disadvantages of being listed include the costs of obtaining and maintaining a listing, increased financial transparency, the need to meet shareholder expectations, the need to maintain dividends and the risk of take-over.

14 A rights issue involves the issue of new shares to existing shareholders, pro rata to their existing holdings. It can preserve existing patterns of ownership and

control and is cheaper than an offer for sale, but is unsuitable for raising large amounts of finance.

15 Rights issue shares are usually offered at a 15 per cent to 20 per cent discount to the current market price, making them more attractive to shareholders and allowing for any adverse share price movements.

16 After a rights issue, shares should trade at the theoretical ex-rights price.

17 Rights can be sold to investors: the value of rights is the difference between the theoretical ex-rights price and the rights issue price. If shareholders either buy the offered shares or sell their rights, there is no effect on their wealth.

18 The actual ex-rights price will be different from the theoretical ex-rights price due to market expectations about the economy, the company and dividends. In particular, the share price will reflect the expected yield on existing and new funds.

19 A scrip issue is a conversion of existing reserves into additional shares. A stock split involves reducing the nominal value of shares while at the same time increasing the number of shares in issue, so that total book value is unchanged.

20 It has been suggested that stock splits increase liquidity, but research has not supported this view. It has also been suggested that stock splits increase shareholder wealth, but the evidence is inconclusive.

21 A scrip dividend involves offering ordinary shares as an alternative to a cash dividend. It has cash flow advantages for a company, but tax effects make it an imperfect substitute for some shareholders.

22 Share repurchases are a way of returning cash to shareholders that is becoming increasingly common. They are carefully regulated in order to protect creditors.

23 Preference shares give a right to receive a dividend before ordinary shareholders, which may not need to be paid if profits are low. They are less risky than ordinary shares but are riskier than debt. They do not normally give voting rights and are unsecured. They preserve debt capacity, but are not tax efficient.

24 Preference shares may be either cumulative or non-cumulative with respect to preference dividends. It is also possible to issue variable rate preference shares, participating and non-participating preference shares, and convertible preference shares.

25 Ordinary preference shares are less attractive than debt. Convertible redeemable preference shares have been used by venture capitalists. Auction market preferred stock has proved attractive to US companies.

QUESTIONS

Answers to these questions can be found on pages 411–13.

1 Explain the reason why the return required by ordinary shareholders is different from the return required by debenture holders.

2 Briefly outline some of the important rights of shareholders.

3 Briefly explain the various ways in which a company may obtain a quotation for its ordinary shares on the London Stock Exchange.

4 Outline the advantages and disadvantages which should be considered by a currently unquoted company which is considering obtaining a listing on a recognised stock exchange.

5 What are pre-emptive rights and why are they important to shareholders?

6 Discuss the advantages and disadvantages of a rights issue to a company.

7 XTC is planning a 1 for 4 rights issue at a 20 per cent discount to the current market price of £2.50. If an investor is to sell their 'rights per share' how much should they sell it for?

(a) 10p (b) 20p (c) 30p (d) 40p (e) 50p

8 'A conversion of existing capital reserves into ordinary shares, which are then distributed pro rata to existing shareholders'. This statement best defines:

(a) scrip dividends;
(b) a rights issue;
(c) bonus bonds;
(d) scrip issues;
(e) stock splits?

9 Explain why preference shares do not enjoy great popularity as a source of finance for companies.

10 Which one of the following statements best describes a cumulative preference share?

(a) It has the right to be converted into ordinary shares at a future date.
(b) It entitles the shareholder to a share of residual profits.
(c) It carries forward the right to receive unpaid dividends to the next year.
(d) It entitles the shareholder to a fixed rate of dividend.
(e) It gives its holder voting rights at a company's annual general meeting.

QUESTIONS FOR REVIEW

Answers to these questions can be found on pages 413–14.

1 Brand plc generates profit after taxation of 15 per cent on shareholders' funds. Its current capital structure is as follows:

	£
Ordinary shares of 50p each	200 000
Share premium	87 500
Reserves	312 500
	600 000

The board of Brand plc wishes to raise £160 000 from a rights issue in order to expand existing operations. Its return on shareholders' funds will be unchanged. The current ex-div market price of Brand plc is £1.90. Three different rights issue prices have been suggested by the finance director: £1.80, £1.60 and £1.40.

Determine the number of shares to be issued, the theoretical ex-rights price, the expected earnings per share and the form of the issue for each rights issue price. Comment on your results.

2 Maltby plc, a company quoted on the London Stock Exchange, has been making regular annual after-tax profits of £7 000 000 for some years and has the following long-term capital structure.

	£000
Ordinary shares, 50p each	4 000
16 per cent debentures	9 000
	13 000

The debenture issue is not due to be redeemed for some time and the company has become increasingly concerned about the need to continue paying interest at 16 per cent when the interest rate on newly issued government stock of a similar maturity is only seven per cent.

A proposal has been made to issue 2 000 000 new shares in a rights issue, at a discount of 20 per cent to the current share price of Maltby plc, and to use the funds raised to pay off part of the debenture issue. The current share price of Maltby plc is £3.50 and the current market price of the debentures is £112 per £100 block.

Alternatively, the funds raised by the rights issue could be invested in a new project giving an annual after-tax return of 20 per cent. Whichever option is undertaken, the stock market view of the company's prospects will be unchanged and its P/E ratio will remain unchanged. Maltby plc pays corporation tax at a rate of 31 per cent.

By considering the effect on the share price of the two alternative proposals, discuss whether the proposed rights issue can be recommended as being in the best interests of the ordinary shareholders of Maltby plc. Your answer should include all relevant calculations.

3 It has become increasingly common for companies to offer their shareholders a choice between a cash dividend or an equivalent scrip issue of shares. Briefly consider the advantages of scrip dividends from the point of view of:

(a) the company;

(b) the shareholders.

QUESTIONS FOR DISCUSSION

1 Hanging Valley plc has issued share capital of 2m ordinary shares, par value £1. The board of the company, in order to finance a new product, has announced its intention to raise £1m net of issue costs.

(a) It has been suggested that the additional finance be raised by means of a 1 for 4 rights issue. The issue price will be at a 20 per cent discount to the current market price of £2.75 and issue costs are expected to be £50 000. Calculate and explain the following:

(i) the theoretical ex-rights price per share;

(ii) the net cash raised;

(iii) the value of the rights.

(b) Is the underwriting of rights issues an unnecessary expense?

(c) An alternative suggestion, to raise the finance by means of an offer for sale by tender, was adopted. Hanging Valley plc has offered 500 000 shares for sale and has received the following applications:

Application price (£)	*Shares applied for at this price*
3.25	50 000
3.00	100 000
2.75	150 000
2.50	180 000
2.25	240 000

Issue costs are eight per cent of cash raised. Mr Glacier has applied for 5000 shares at a price of £3.00 per share. How many shares would be issued, and how much cash would be raised, if Hanging Valley plc chooses to:

(i) maximise the amount raised;

(ii) issue exactly 500 000 shares?

In each case, how many shares will Mr Glacier receive, and how much of his application money will be returned to him?

REFERENCES

Bank of England (1990) 'New equity issues in the UK', *Bank of England Quarterly Bulletin*, May, pp. 243–52.

Byrne, A. and Rees, W. (1994) 'Initial public offerings in the United Kingdom', *Certified Research Report 36*, ACCA.

Copeland, T. (1979) 'Liquidity changes following stock splits', *Journal of Finance*, Vol. 34, March, pp. 115–41.

Corbett, P. (1996) 'Share ownership', *AIM News*, Issue 5, July.

Firth, M. (1973) 'Shareholder wealth attendant upon capitalisation issues', *Accounting and Business Research*, Vol. 4, No. 13, Winter, pp. 23–32.

Grinblatt, M., Masulis, R. and Titman, S. (1984) 'The valuation effects of stock splits and stock dividends', *Journal of Financial Economics*, Dec, pp. 461–90.

RECOMMENDED READING

A useful discussion of equity finance, new issue methods and preference shares can be found in Samuels, J., Wilkes, F. and Brayshaw, R. (1995) *Management of Company Finance* (6th edn), Chapman and Hall, Chapter 12. It is interesting to contrast the treatment of equity in the UK and the US, for example by studying Ross, S., Westerfield, R. and Jaffe, J. (1996) *Corporate Finance*, Irwin, Chapters 14 and 19.

Useful articles include the following:

Blume, M. (1997) 'Stock exchanges: forces of change', in *Mastering Finance*, Issue 9, *Financial Times*.

Brealey, R. and Nyborg, K. (1997) 'New equity issues and raising cash', in *Mastering Finance*, Issue 4, *Financial Times*.

CHAPTER 6

SOURCES OF LONG-TERM FINANCE

DEBT FINANCE, HYBRID FINANCE, AND LEASING

INTRODUCTION

Long-term debt finance, for example fixed interest securities such as loan stock or debentures, has significant differences from equity finance. The interest received on long-term debt finance is a charge against pre-tax profit and not an appropriation of after-tax profits, as is the case with the dividends paid to ordinary and preference shareholders. Furthermore, the interest paid is an allowable deduction from profits chargeable to tax, whereas equity and preference dividends are not. Interest must be paid before dividends and, in the event of liquidation, debt holders are paid off before shareholders because they rank higher in the creditor hierarchy. Shareholders may receive only a part payment, or perhaps in some cases nothing at all. Long-term debt finance, then, carries less risk than equity finance and this is reflected in a lower relative required return. The required return of the providers of debt finance can be applied to the interest and capital payments to be received from a debt security in order to gain an estimate of its fair price.

Debt can be engineered to suit the requirements of companies and investors. For example, debt can be made more attractive to investors by the attachment of warrants, which give the holder the right to subscribe for ordinary shares at an attractive price in the future. Alternatively, the debt may be convertible at a future date into ordinary shares, in which case it may pay a lower interest rate because of the higher capital and dividend returns that may be available following conversion.

A further source of finance discussed in this chapter is lease finance, which can be regarded as a substitute for debt finance and which represents an increasingly popular method of gaining access to a wide range of assets. We compare leasing with borrowing to buy and examine recent trends in lease finance.

LEARNING OBJECTIVES

After studying this chapter, you should have achieved the following learning objectives:

- a knowledge of the key features of long-term debt finance;
- an appreciation of the range of long-term debt finance available to a company, including bank debt, ordinary loan stock, debentures, deep discount and zero coupon bonds, convertible debentures and Eurobonds;
- a familiarity with the valuation of redeemable and irredeemable debt, warrants and convertible debentures;
- an understanding of the relative attractions of different kinds of long-term debt finance to a company, together with an appreciation of the relative attractions of debt and equity finance;
- an ability to compare leasing with borrowing to buy as a source of finance for a company and an appreciation of the way in which the financing decision can interact with the investment decision;
- an understanding of the reasons for the popularity of leasing as a source of finance in recent years.

6.1 LOAN STOCK AND DEBENTURES

Loan stock and debentures are, generally speaking, long-term debt securities with a par value of £100. Interest, based on the par value, is paid once or twice each year. For example, a fixed interest 10 per cent debenture will pay the holder £10 per year in interest, although this might be in the form of £5 paid twice each year. Interest is an allowable deduction in the calculation of taxable profits and so the effective servicing cost of debt to a company is lower than the coupon rate. On a fixed interest 10 per cent debenture, with corporation tax at 31 per cent, the servicing cost is reduced to 6.9 per cent per year. In corporate finance, this is referred to as the *tax efficiency* of debt. If the loan stock or debenture is redeemable, the principal will need to be repaid on the redemption date.

While the terms 'debenture' and 'loan stock' can be used interchangeably, since a debenture is simply a written acknowledgement of indebtedness, debentures are usually taken to signify loan stock that is secured by a trust deed, while loan stock is usually taken to refer to unsecured debt securities. The debenture trust deed will cover in detail such matters as any charges on the assets of the issuing company; the way in which interest is paid; the procedures for redemption of the issue; the production of regular reports on the position of the issuing company; the power of trustees to appoint a receiver; and any restrictive covenants intended to protect the investors of debt finance.

The debenture may be secured against assets of the company by either a fixed or a floating charge. A fixed charge will be on all assets of a company or only on specified assets. In either case the assets cannot be disposed of, whereas with a floating charge disposal of some assets is permitted. In the event of default, for example the non-payment of interest, a floating charge will crystallise into a fixed charge on the assets of the company.

6.1.1 Restrictive covenants

Restrictive covenants are attached to loan stock and debentures as a means by which the providers of long-term debt finance can try to stop the managers of the issuing company from changing significantly the risk profile of the company which existed when the long-term debt was first issued. This was the risk profile which was taken into account by the cost of debt (i.e. the required return) at the time of issue. For example, the covenant could limit the amount of additional debt that can be issued by the company, or it may require maintenance of a target gearing ratio between debt and equity. In order to help to guard against insolvency and liquidity difficulties, it is possible for a restrictive covenant to specify a target range for the ratio of current assets to current liabilities, thereby hoping to encourage good working capital management. If the terms agreed in the restrictive covenant are breached, then disposal of assets may be needed in order to satisfy the debenture holders, although the actual course of events following such a breach will be determined by negotiation.

6.1.2 Redemption

The redemption of loan stock or debentures represents a significant demand on the cash flow of a company and calls for careful financial planning. Because of the amount of finance needed, some companies may choose to invest regularly in a fund which has the sole purpose of providing for redemption. The intention of such a 'sinking fund' is that the amounts invested, together with accrued interest, will be sufficient to enable the company to face redemption without placing undue strain on liquidity. Alternatively, a company may seek to replace an issue of long-term debt which is due for redemption with a new issue of long-term debt; this choice has the advantage that the relationship between long-term assets and long-term liabilities is maintained, i.e. the matching principle is upheld (*see* Section 10.4.2).

The cash flow demands arising from the need to redeem can also be eased by providing in the trust deed for redemption over a period of time, rather than redemption on a specific date. This 'redemption window' will allow the company to choose for itself the best time for redemption in the light of prevailing conditions. A choice about when to redeem can also be gained by attaching a call option to the debenture issue, as this gives the company the right, but not the obligation, to redeem the issue before maturity. Early redemption might be secured in exchange for the payment of a premium over par value, in order to compensate investors for any interest foregone.

Redemption at a premium can also be used as a means of obtaining a lower coupon (interest rate) on a loan stock or debenture, thereby lowering the cost of servicing the debt issue during its life. It is even possible for loan stock or debentures to be irredeemable, in the sense that they have no specified redemption date, although it must be said that such issues are rare.

6.1.3 Floating interest rates

While it is usual to think of debentures as fixed interest securities, they may be offered with a floating rate linked to a current market interest rate, for example at three per cent over the three-month London Interbank Offered Rate (LIBOR). A floating rate coupon may be attractive to investors who want to obtain a return which is consistently comparable with prevailing market rates, or to investors who want a way of protecting themselves against unanticipated inflation. A company may also issue floating rate debt as a way of hedging against falls in market interest rates (*see* Chapter 12).

6.1.4 Deep discount and zero coupon bonds

There is clearly a relationship between the terms of redemption, the coupon rate and the issue price of loan stock or debentures. This relationship is explored in more detail in Section 6.5, which deals with the valuation of debt securities. One possibility which is open to a company is to offer loan stock at a price well below its par value, in exchange for a lower coupon rate coupled with redemption at par or at a premium on maturity. Such a security, referred to as a deep discount bond, will be attractive to investors who prefer to receive a higher proportion of their return in the form of capital gains, as opposed to interest income. If the personal taxation treatment of interest income and capital gains is different, this will also be a factor which will influence the preferences of individual investors.

From a company point of view, the lower servicing cost of deep discount bonds may be attractive if cash flow problems are being experienced or are anticipated, for example if the cash raised by the new issue is to be used in a capital investment project whose returns are expected to be low in the initial years.

If no interest at all is paid on a bond issued at a deep discount, so that all of the return to investors will be in the form of capital appreciation, it is called a zero coupon bond. The general attractions of zero coupon bonds are similar to those of deep discount bonds: depending on their circumstances, companies will find the absence of interest attractive, as well as the removal of the risk of liquidation due to non-payment of interest. These advantages must be weighed against the high cost of redemption compared with the amount of finance raised.

6.2 BANK AND INSTITUTIONAL DEBT

Long-term loans are available from banks and other financial institutions with both fixed and floating rates, provided that the issuing bank can be convinced that the purpose of the loan is a good one. The cost of bank loans is usually a floating rate of three per cent to six per cent above bank base rate, depending on the perceived risk of the borrowing company. An arrangement fee is charged by the issuing bank on such loans, which are usually secured by a fixed or floating charge, the nature of which will depend upon the availability of assets of good quality to act as security. The repayment schedule agreed between the bank and the borrowing company will be structured to accommodate the specific needs of the borrower, to the extent that these are compatible with the lending policies of the bank.

Long-term bank loans cannot be sold on by the bank to a third party. The growth of securitisation, however, means that banks, financial institutions and large companies can, in some circumstances, parcel up debts and sell them on the securitised debt market.

The problems faced by small businesses in raising non-equity finance can be partially mitigated by government assistance, for example, the current Loan Guarantee Scheme operated by the UK government. This allows smaller companies to obtain bank loans without offering security. Repayments on long-term bank loans may include both interest and capital components.

6.3 INTERNATIONAL DEBT FINANCE

The international operations of companies directly influence their financing needs. For example, a company may choose to borrow in the currency of a particular country in order to finance business activities there and so hedge against exchange rate losses (*see* Chapter 12). It may choose to borrow in a foreign currency because of comparatively lower interest rates (although it is likely that exchange rate movements will eliminate these). Foreign currency borrowing can also allow companies to get round any domestic restrictions on currency exchange. One way of obtaining long-term foreign currency debt finance is through the issuing of Eurobonds.

6.3.1 Eurobonds

Eurobonds are long-term debt finance raised in different countries at the same time by companies or governments and are usually denominated in a different currency to that of the country of issue. The maturities of Eurobonds are typically five to 15 years, and interest on them, which is payable gross, may be either at a fixed or floating rate. Because the Eurobond market is not as tightly regulated as domestic capital markets, Eurobond interest rates tend to be lower than those on comparable domestic securities. Floating rate Eurobonds which have a minimum coupon rate payable are known as *drop lock* bonds.

Eurobonds are bearer securities, since the owner is unregistered, and so offer investors the attraction of anonymity. Because Eurobonds are unsecured, companies who issue Eurobonds must be internationally known and have an excellent credit rating. Common Eurobond issue currencies are US dollars, yen, deutschmarks and Swiss francs.

Companies may find Eurobond issues useful for long-term purposes, for example in international capital investment, or as a way of balancing their long-term asset and liability structures in terms of exposure to exchange rate movements. Investors, for their part, may be attracted to Eurobonds because they offer both security and anonymity, but will be concerned about achieving an adequate return, especially as the secondary market for Eurobonds has been criticised for poor liquidity in recent years.

6.4 HYBRID FINANCE

6.4.1 Convertible loan stock

Convertible loan stocks are fixed interest debt securities which can be converted, on predetermined dates and at a predetermined rate, at the option of the holder, into ordinary shares of the company. The conversion rate is stated either as a conversion *price* (the nominal value of loan stock that can be converted into one ordinary share) or as a conversion *ratio* (the number of ordinary shares that will be obtained from one unit of loan stock). Conversion terms may possibly vary over time, with the conversion ratio decreasing in line with the expected increase in the value of ordinary shares. For example, the conversion terms on 1 January 2005 may be that one unit of stock can be converted into 35 ordinary shares, while later, on 1 January 2006, one unit of stock can only be converted into 30 ordinary shares.

Conversion *value* is the market value of ordinary shares into which a unit of stock may be converted, and is equal to the conversion ratio multiplied by the market price per ordinary share. When the convertible loan stock is first issued, the conversion value will be less than the issue value of the stock. It is expected that, as the conversion date approaches, the conversion value will increase in line with the growth of the ordinary share price, so that conversion becomes attractive to investors. The conversion *premium* is the difference between the market price of the convertible loan stock and its conversion value. In Exhibit 6.1 (on page 157), the conversion premium is represented by the vertical distance between the lines MM′ and CM′. The conversion premium is proportional to the time remaining before conversion takes place and, as conversion approaches, the market value and the conversion value converge and the conversion premium becomes negligible. The conversion premium is often expressed on a per share basis. The difference between the market value of convertible loan stock and its value as straight debt is called the *rights premium*. In Exhibit 6.1, the rights premium is represented by the vertical distance between the lines MM′ and LR.

Consider a 12 per cent convertible debenture, redeemable at par in six years' time, which can be converted at any time in the next three years into 30 ordinary shares. The debenture is currently trading ex-interest at £118.20 and the current ordinary share price is £3.20. The ex-interest market value of ordinary loan stock of a similar risk class is £108.70.

Current conversion value:	30 × 3.20 = £96.00
Current conversion premium:	118.20 – 96.00 = £22.20 or 74p per share
Current rights premium:	118.20 – 108.70 = £9.50 or 32p per share

The interest on convertible loan stock is less than that on straight or 'vanilla' debentures because of the value to the investor of the conversion rights. The minimum price of a convertible loan stock is equivalent to its value as a straight debenture with the same coupon rate and maturity. The actual market value of convertible loan stock will depend upon:

- the current conversion value;
- the time to conversion;
- market expectations as to the size and risk of equity returns.

We consider the valuation of convertible loan stock in Section 6.6.

6.4.2 The attractions of convertible loan stock to companies

Companies tend to view convertible loan stock as delayed equity. Issuing such debt securities may be attractive when, in the directors' opinion, the company's ordinary share price is depressed and so does not reflect the true worth of the company. Alternatively, the directors may turn to convertible loan stock as a way of raising finance because they feel that an immediate issue of new equity would cause an unacceptably large fall in earnings per share.

Convertible loan stock is also attractive because, like ordinary loan stock, it pays fixed interest, making financial forecasting and planning somewhat easier. In addition, the use of convertibles allows a company to pay a lower rate of interest than it would otherwise have to pay if it were to issue straight debentures of a similar maturity, therefore helping its cash flow situation. As interest payments on loan stock are tax deductible, the issue of convertibles will, other things being equal, lead to a decrease in the overall cost of capital. Convertible loan stock also allows companies to push their debt capacity beyond what is normally considered acceptable by creditors, due to the expectation that future conversion, with a consequent reduction in gearing, is likely to occur. One of the main attractions of convertible loan stock is that it can be self-liquidating, if the conditions governing conversion were assessed correctly at the time of issue, whereas straight debentures must be redeemed at maturity.

As far as disadvantages are concerned, while convertible loan stock remains unconverted, gearing will be increased, which may affect the overall risk profile of the company. Also, on conversion, dilution of earnings per share will occur, as well as some dilution of the control of existing shareholders.

6.4.3 The attractions of convertibles to investors

The convertible loan stock combination of fixed interest in the short term and the option to convert into equity in the long term may be attractive to some investors, giving as it does a lower risk investment in the short term with the possibility of greater gains in the long term. This may be seen as a distinct advantage compared with ordinary debentures, since convertibles thereby offer investors the opportunity to participate in the growth of the company. An advantage over ordinary equity is that holders of convertible loan stock can evaluate the performance of a company and its shares before deciding whether to become ordinary shareholders by converting. Management may thus be able to use convertibility to increase the chances of a new issue of debt being taken up.

There is no certainty, however, that bond holders will exercise their option to convert. They are under no obligation to do so if conversion is unattractive, for example if the expected growth in share price has failed to materialise. This lack of growth may be due entirely to factors which are outside of the control of the company, for example a general downturn in overall economic conditions. If conversion does not occur, the stock will run its full term and will need to be redeemed at maturity.

6.4.4 Warrants

A warrant is the right to buy new ordinary shares in a company at a future date, at a fixed, predetermined price, known as the *exercise price*. Warrants are usually issued as part of a package with loan stock as an 'equity sweetener', a phrase which signifies that the attachment of warrants to the issue of loan stock will make the issue more attractive to investors. Warrants can be separated from the underlying loan stock, however, and so are tradable in their own right, both before or during the specified exercise period. The intrinsic value of a warrant (V_w) is the current ordinary share price (P) less the exercise price (E), multiplied by the number of shares which are obtained for each warrant exercised (N):

$$V_w = (P - E) \times N$$

As an example, if a warrant entitles the holder to purchase five ordinary shares at an exercise price of £1 and the current ordinary share price is £1.35, the intrinsic value is:

$$V_w = (1.35 - 1.00) \times 5 = £1.75$$

During the exercise period, the warrant price should not fall below the intrinsic value. If the share has good prospects for growth, the warrant price will be above the theoretical price and the warrant will have a conversion premium.

Continuing our example, suppose that, over a six-month period, the ordinary share price increases from £1.35 to £2.70. The intrinsic value of the warrant has now increased to:

$$V_w = (2.70 - 1.00) \times 5 = £8.50$$

The value of the underlying ordinary share has increased by 100 per cent, but the value of the warrant has increased by 386 per cent. This means that a greater gain, proportionately, has been obtained by holding the warrant than by holding the ordinary share. If the share price had fallen over the period, however, then a greater loss, proportionately, would have been sustained through holding the warrant than would have been sustained by holding the ordinary share. This phenomenon is known as the *gearing effect* of warrants.

For investors, the attractions of warrants include a low initial outlay, a lower downside potential than that entailed by the purchase of the underlying share, and a high profit potential due to the gearing effect of warrants.

From a company point of view, the interest rate on 'sweetened' loan stock will be lower than that on a vanilla issue of debt securities of similar maturity, while the inclusion of warrants will make the issue more attractive to investors. Warrants may even make an issue of loan stock possible when the available security is insufficient. Unlike the issue of convertible loan stock, however, the issue of warrants will, providing that satisfactory share price growth is achieved, lead to the subscription of additional equity funds in the future.

6.5 THE VALUATION OF FIXED INTEREST DEBT SECURITIES

6.5.1 Irredeemable loan stock

The valuation of irredeemable debt, where the principal is never repaid, is quite straightforward and represents the sum to infinity of the discounted future interest payments, as follows:

$$P_0 = \frac{I}{K_d}$$

where: P_0 = ex-interest market value
I = annual interest paid
K_d = rate of return required by debt investors.

For example, if we consider the case of eight per cent irredeemable loan stock when debt investors require a return of 11 per cent, the predicted market value will be:

$$P_0 = I/K_d = £8/0.11 = £72.73$$

It is important to remember that this formula gives the *ex-interest* market price of irredeemable loan stock, since it represents the present value of *future* cash flows. The formula does not include in the valuation any interest which is shortly to be paid. The rate of return (K_d) on debt securities required by investors is the cost of debt (*see* Chapter 8) and is also known as the 'yield' of the loan stock. If the current market value (P_0) is known, therefore, the formula can be used to calculate the current yield.

6.5.2 Redeemable loan stock and debentures

Redeemable loan stock and debentures can be valued by discounting the future interest payments and the future redemption value by the debt holders' required rate of return (K_d). Interest payments, as mentioned earlier, are usually made on an annual or semi-annual basis, while redemption value is, more often than not, at the par value of £100.

$$P_0 = \frac{I}{(1 + K_d)} + \frac{I}{(1 + K_d)^2} + \frac{I}{(1 + K_d)^3} + \ldots + \frac{I + RV}{(1 + K_d)^n}$$

where: P_0 = ex-interest market value
n = number of years to maturity
RV = redemption value
I = interest paid
K_d = rate of return required by debt investors.

Consider the example of a 10 per cent debenture, redeemable at par in four years' time, and let us suppose that investors in this type of debt security require a return of 12 per cent. Because the security is redeemed at par and the required rate of return is greater than its coupon rate, we would expect its market value to be less than its par value. We can calculate the current market value as follows:

$$P_0 = \frac{10}{(1.12)} + \frac{10}{(1.12)^2} + \frac{10}{(1.12)^3} + \frac{(10 + 100)}{(1.12)^4} = £93.93$$

If the interest on the security is paid semi-annually the formula above can be modified by dividing both the annual discount rate and the annual coupon rate by two, while leaving the treatment of the redemption value unchanged. While not mathematically accurate, this approximation is good enough for most purposes. We can see this by repeating our earlier calculation, but now including in our calculations interest payments of £5 paid semi-annually and discounted at a six-monthly required rate of return of six per cent. The current market value is now expected to be:

$$P_0 = \frac{5}{(1.06)} + \frac{5}{(1.06)^2} + \ldots + \frac{5}{(1.06)^8} + \frac{(100)}{(1.12)^4} = £94.60$$

The increase in expected market value of 67p occurs because half of each year's interest payment is received sooner and therefore has a higher present value.

6.6 THE VALUATION OF CONVERTIBLE LOAN STOCK

Because convertible loan stock or debentures give the holder the option to convert them into ordinary equity at some point in time, their valuation is a more complex process than the valuation of ordinary loan stock. It is important to recognise that the valuation can be carried out from two different perspectives:

1 convertible loan stock can be valued as ordinary loan stock, if conversion at some future date appears unlikely. The market value will be the present value of the interest payments to be received and the principal to be repaid on maturity;
2 alternatively, convertible loan stock can be valued on the assumption that it will be converted into ordinary equity. The market value will be the sum of the present value of the interest payments to be received up to the date of conversion and the present value of the shares into which the debenture is converted.

Which valuation is reflected in the current market value of the loan stock will depend upon the expectations of investors with respect to the future price of the underlying share, which is a function of the current market value of the underlying share and its expected growth rate. If growth in the share price is expected to be great enough to make conversion attractive when the opportunity to convert becomes available, the market value of the convertible loan stock will reflect this conversion value. If growth in the share price is not expected to be sufficient to make conversion attractive, the convertible loan stock will be valued as straight debt.

6.6.1 Conversion value

If investors expect the company's share price to increase at an average annual rate which will be sufficient to make future conversion into ordinary equity an attractive option, the current market value of a convertible loan stock or debenture will depend primarily upon its future conversion value. The conversion value, which will depend upon the estimated share price on the conversion date, can be estimated as follows:

$$CV_t = P_0(1 + g)^n R$$

where: CV_t = conversion value of the convertible loan stock at time t
P_0 = current ex-div ordinary share price
g = expected annual growth rate of ordinary share price
n = number of years to conversion
R = number of shares received on conversion.

6.6.2 Current market value

The current market value of a convertible loan stock will be the sum of the present value of the interest payments to be received and the present value of the conversion value of the loan stock, as follows:

$$V_0 = \frac{I}{(1 + K_d)} + \frac{I}{(1 + K_d)^2} + \frac{I}{(1 + K_d)^3} + \ldots + \frac{I + CV_t}{(1 + K_d)^n}$$

where: V_0 = ex-interest market value
n = number of years to maturity
CV_t = conversion value of the convertible loan stock at time t
I = interest paid
K_d = rate of return required by investors.

This can also be expressed as follows:

$$V_0 = \sum_{i=1}^{i=n} \frac{I}{(1 + K_d)^i} + \frac{P_0(1 + g)^n R}{(1 + K_d)^n}$$

Example Valuation of a convertible loan stock

How much would an investor be prepared to pay for a 10 per cent convertible loan stock, if it could be converted in four years' time into 25 ordinary shares and if his required return is 11 per cent? The current market price of the underlying share is £3.35 and it is expected to grow by five per cent per year.

From discount tables, the cumulative present value factor for four years at 11 per cent is 3.102 and the discount factor for four years at 11 per cent is 0.659. Using our valuation model, we have:

$$\begin{aligned} V_0 &= (I \times CPVF_{11,4}) + (P_0 \times (1 + g)^4 \times R \times PVF_{11,4}) \\ &= (10 \times 3.102) + (3.35 \times 1.05^4 \times 25 \times 0.659) \\ &= 31.02 + 67.1 \\ &= £98.10 \end{aligned}$$

6.6.3 Factors influencing the market price of convertible loan stock

The factors that influence the market value of a convertible loan stock are represented diagramatically in Exhibit 6.1. The market value is shown by the dotted line MM′. Initially, the floor price of the convertible loan stock will be its redemption value. As the ordinary share price rises over time, however, the conversion value (CM′) will become greater than the redemption value, and the conversion value will then become the floor price. The actual market value (MM′) is greater than the conversion value (CM′) because of the expectation of investors that the share price will increase even further in the future, therefore increasing the future conversion value.

The conversion premium is represented by the vertical distance between the curve MM′ and the line CM′, while the rights premium is represented by the vertical distance between the curves MM′ and LR. Conversion should only take place after M′, since conversion before this point will result in a loss in potential profit to the investor.

EXHIBIT 6.1

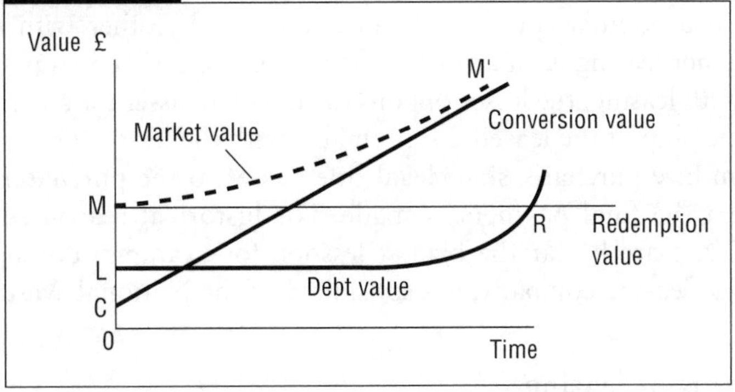

Factors influencing the market value of a convertible security

6.6.4 Debt value

If the underlying share price rises slowly or falls and conversion is not anticipated, the convertible loan stock will have value only as debt and its market value will fall to that of an ordinary loan stock, where it will remain until redemption at point R, as shown in Exhibit 6.2. At point A, the right to convert has ceased to have any value and the convertible loan stock is valued thereafter as ordinary loan stock.

EXHIBIT 6.2

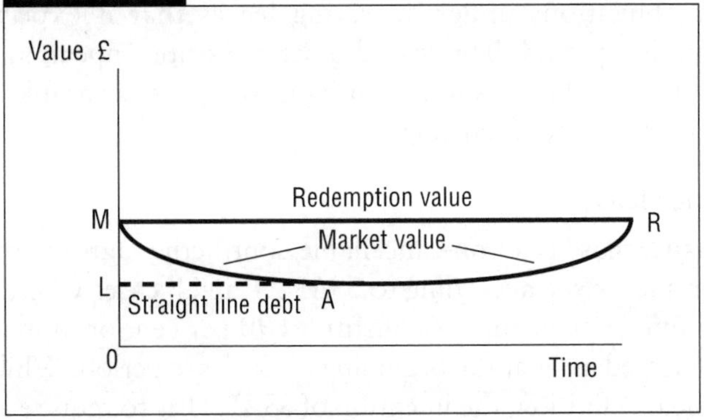

The debt value of a convertible

6.7 LEASING

Leasing is a form of short- to medium-term financing which essentially refers to the hire of an asset under an agreed contract. The company hiring the asset is called the *lessee*, while the company owning the asset is called the *lessor*. From a corporate finance point of view, we are concerned on the one hand with the reasons why leasing is a popular source of finance, and on the other with how we can evaluate whether leasing is an attractive financing alternative in a particular case.

With leasing, the lessee obtains the use of an asset for a period of time while legal ownership of the leased asset remains with the lessor. This is where leasing differs from hire purchase, since legal title passes to the purchaser under hire purchase when the final payment is made. For historical reasons, banks and their subsidiaries are by far the biggest lessors; for example, Lombard North Central, a major leasing company, is a subsidiary of the National Westminster Bank.

6.7.1 Forms of leasing

Leases can be divided into two broad categories, namely *operating leases* and *finance leases*. The distinction between the two is clarified by Statement of Standard Accounting Practice 21 (SSAP 21).

Operating leases

Operating leases are essentially rental agreements between a lessor and a lessee in which the lessor tends to be responsible for servicing and maintaining the leased asset. The lease period is substantially less than the expected economic life of the leased asset, so assets leased under operating leases can be leased to a number of different parties before they cease to have any further use. The type of assets commonly available under operating leases include cars, computers and photocopiers. Under SSAP 21, a company is only required to disclose in its balance sheet the payment obligations under operating leases that it expects to meet in the next accounting period. The leased asset does not appear in the company's balance sheet and for this reason operating leases are an example of what is referred to as 'off-balance-sheet financing'.

Finance leases

A finance lease is a non-cancellable contractual agreement between a lessee and a lessor and exists, according to SSAP 21, in all cases where the present value of the minimum lease payments constitutes 90 per cent or more of the fair market value of the leased asset at the beginning of the lease period. While this may seem a rather technical definition, the intention of SSAP 21 is to require accounting statements to recognise that the lessee owns the leased asset in everything but name. The substance of the finance lease agreement, in other words, is one of ownership, even though under its legal form, title to the leased asset remains with the lessor. In consequence, SSAP 21 requires that finance leases be 'capitalised' in the balance sheet of a company. The present value of the capital part of future lease payments becomes an asset under the fixed assets heading, while the obligations to make future lease payments appear under the headings of both current and long-term liabilities.

One example of the way in which the lessee enjoys 'substantially all the risks and rewards of ownership', in the words of the accounting standard, is that the lessee tends to be responsible under finance lease agreements for the servicing and maintenance of the leased asset.

A finance lease usually has a primary period and a secondary period. The primary lease period covers most, if not all, of the expected economic life of the leased asset. Within this primary period, the lessor recovers the capital cost of the leased asset, together with their required return, from the primary lease payments. Within the secondary period, the lessee may be able to lease the asset for a nominal or 'peppercorn' rent.

6.7.2 Trends in leasing

The most significant economic factor in the growth of leasing before 1984 was taxation. If a company is not producing sufficient taxable profits at the time that a decision to acquire an asset is taken, it will not be able to take immediate advantage of available capital allowances. Leasing would be an attractive alternative to buying for a company in such circumstances, especially if a lessor with adequate profitability were able to pass on the benefit of capital allowances in the form of lower lease payments. This was the situation that arose in the late 1960s and early 1970s when leasing first experienced a rapid rise in popularity. Many clearing banks set up leasing subsidiaries to improve profitability by taking advantage of capital allowances. This early growth of leasing was stimulated by relatively high levels of corporation tax and by the introduction in 1972 of 100 per cent first-year capital allowances, leaving many companies in the position of being tax-exhausted.

EXHIBIT 6.3

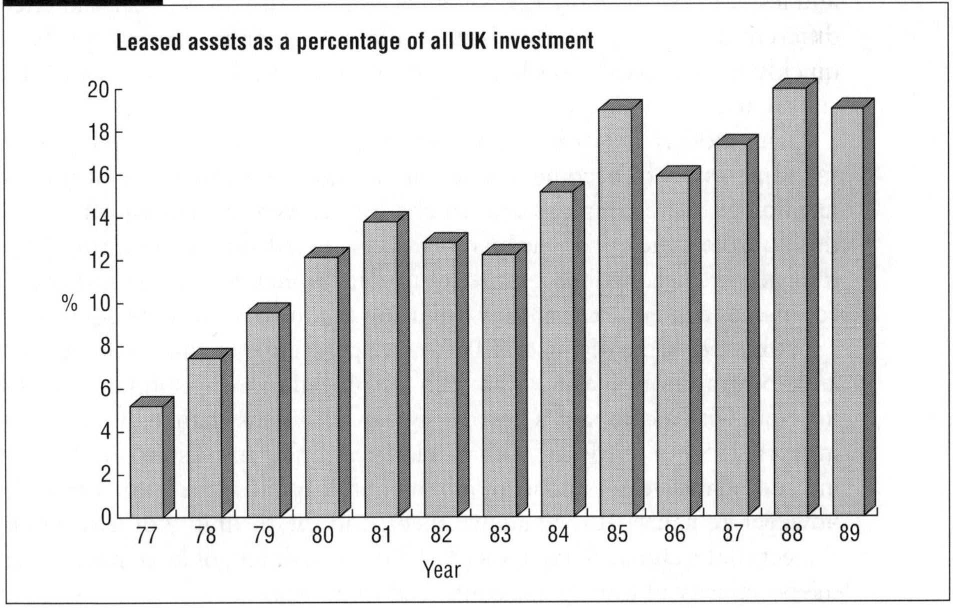

Illustration of the popularity of leasing in the UK
Source: Central Statistics Office

The Finance Act 1984 paved the way for the introduction over two years of 25 per cent capital allowances on a reducing balance basis as a replacement for 100 per cent first-year allowances, and a reduction in the corporation tax rate over the same period from 50 per cent to 35 per cent. These changes reduced the taxation incentives to lease, since they led directly to fewer companies being in a tax exhausted position and to more companies being in a position to take full advantage of capital allowances. Despite these changes to the tax system, though, leasing continued to grow in popularity, as illustrated in Exhibit 6.3. The reasons for this continued growth in popularity are explored in the next section.

6.7.3 Non-tax reasons for leasing

Drury and Braund (1990) have suggested a number of possible explanations why companies choose to lease assets rather than buy them outright. It has been pointed out that leasing provides a source of finance if a company is short of liquidity. If a company has difficulty in borrowing to finance the acquisition of an asset due to a lack of good quality assets to offer as security, leasing can be used instead since title to the leased asset never passes to the lessee, leaving the lessor with no need for security. For this reason, leasing provides an attractive source of finance for small companies.

It should not be thought that all tax advantages disappeared after 1984, since there is still the possibility of tax advantages due to the different tax-paying positions of the lessor and lessee. For example, a lessor in a tax-paying position could buy an asset, use the capital allowance, and then lease the asset to the lessee in a non-tax-paying situation, setting the lease payments at a level where both lessor and lessee derive benefit. Tax benefits can also arise due to year-end effects, in that different accounting year ends may allow a lessor to capture tax benefits more quickly than a lessee. This benefit can be enhanced by lessors having a number of subsidiaries with different year ends.

In our modern era of fast-changing technology and rapid development, it is easy for some assets to become obsolete in a relatively short space of time. Computer technology, for example, seems to change every year. Leasing offers a solution to this 'obsolescence problem', since assets leased under operating leases can be returned in exchange for a more up-to-date model. By leasing rather than buying, companies can ensure that they are using the most up-to-date equipment.

Before 1984, the distinction between operating and finance leases did not exist and, by tradition, leasing was seen as off-balance-sheet finance which did not interfere with a company's borrowing capacity. This changed with the publication in April 1984 of SSAP 21, with its clarification of the distinction between operating and finance leases and its requirement to capitalise the latter. Operating leasing, however, remains off the balance sheet, and the flexibility of lease contracts with respect to the choice of equipment and the scheduling of lease payment means that the popularity of leasing has continued to increase.

6.7.4 Evaluating leasing as a source of finance

It is important to recognise that the evaluation of leasing as a source of finance may involve both an investment decision and a finance decision. The optimal overall decision can be reached in several ways, as follows:

1 make the investment decision first, then optimise the financing method;

2 make the financing decision first, then evaluate the investment decision;

3 combine the investment and financing decisions.

If the investment decision is taken first, it may happen that an investment project is rejected which would have been accepted if the lowest cost financing method had been taken into account. Combining the investment and financing decision involves investment appraisal methods which have not been considered in this book. For these reasons, the second method, where the lowest cost financing method is determined before the investment decision is evaluated, is now recommended. This means that the financing decision can be divorced from the investment decision, and we need consider the investment decision no further in this section.

If we assume that the debt capacity of a company is not unlimited and if we recognise that the commitment to a series of regular payments arises under both leasing and borrowing, then we can regard leasing as being equivalent to borrowing as a way of acquiring the use of an asset, as proposed by Myers *et al.* (1976). Discounted cash flow methods can then be used to compare the relative economic costs of the two alternatives. In order to perform this comparison, we need first of all to identify the relevant cash flows, as follows.

- *Taxation.* As far as taxation is concerned, capital allowances are available to the buyer if an asset is purchased, while if an asset is leased, the lessee can set lease payments against taxable profits. The relevant cash flows are therefore the tax benefits arising from capital allowances and lease payments, taken one year in arrears.
- *Maintenance costs.* Maintenance costs, which are an allowable deduction against profits for tax purposes, may be payable by the lessor under an operating lease, but by the lessee if the asset is leased under a finance lease, or by the owner if the asset is purchased.
- *Lease payments.* Lease payments may be payable in advance or in arrears, and their amount and timing is clearly important.
- *Purchase price and disposal value.* If the asset is purchased through borrowing, the purchase price is equivalent to the present value cost of the loan and must be considered, together with any disposal value. The taxation balancing allowance or charge will be affected by any disposal value that is expected to arise at the end of the useful life of the purchased asset.

Before these cash flows can be discounted, an appropriate discount rate must be selected. Since, as a source of finance, leasing is being considered as a direct substitute for borrowing, an appropriate discount rate to use is the cost of borrowing of the company, or alternatively the gross interest rate on the loan that the company would need to take out in order to purchase the required asset. If, as is generally the case, the company is not in a tax exhausted position, then the discount rate to use is the after-tax borrowing rate of the company.

If the net present value method is used to compare leasing with buying through borrowing, then cash flows can be discounted by the after-tax cost of borrowing. If the internal rate of return method is used, the IRR of leasing can be compared with the cost of borrowing, as demonstrated by Tan (1992). Here, we shall consider only the net present value method.

Example Evaluation of leasing *vs* buying

Dadd Ltd is trying to decide whether to lease or to buy a machine which is expected to have a useful economic life of six years. The machine will cost £90 000 to buy, a sum which Dadd Ltd would have to borrow, or it could be leased for lease payments of £20 000 per year for six years, payable at the start of each year. If the machine is bought, maintenance costs of £1000 per year will be incurred. These costs will not be incurred if the machine is leased. Dadd Ltd pays corporation tax at a rate of 31 per cent and can claim capital allowances on a 25 per cent reducing balance basis. The company's cost of capital is 21 per cent and its pre-tax cost of debt is 17.4 per cent. Should Dadd Ltd lease or buy the machine?

Since leasing is being seen as an alternative to borrowing, the relevant cash flows of the two alternatives should be compared using the after-tax cost of borrowing. This is 17.4 × (1 – 0.31) = 12 per cent.

The capital allowances are calculated as follows:

Year		£
1	90 000 × 0.25 =	22 500
2	67 500 × 0.25 =	16 875
3	50 625 × 0.25 =	12 656
4	37 969 × 0.25 =	9 492
5	28 476 × 0.25 =	7 119
6	(by difference)	21 358
		90 000

The tax benefits of borrowing to buy are calculated in Exhibit 6.4. Notice that the maintenance costs give rise to tax relief, a factor that is often overlooked.

We can now calculate the present costs of leasing and of borrowing to buy, as shown in Exhibit 6.5.

From Exhibit 6.5, we can see that the present cost of leasing (£69 340) is less than the present cost of borrowing (£75 416), and so on financial grounds the recommendation is that the machine should be leased. The present cost of leasing can now be included in the evaluation of the investment decision using the net present value method as described in Chapter 3.

EXHIBIT 6.4

Year	Capital allowances (£)	Operating costs (£)	Total deductions (£)	31% tax relief (£)	Taken in year
1	22 500	1000	23 500	7285	2
2	16 875	1000	17 875	5541	3
3	12 656	1000	13 656	4233	4
4	9 492	1000	10 492	3252	5
5	7 119	1000	8 119	2517	6
6	21 358	1000	22 358	6931	7

Tax relief computation for Dadd Ltd if buying is used

EXHIBIT 6.5

Present cost of leasing

Years	Cash flow	(£)	12% discount factors	Present value (£)
0–5	lease payments	(20 000)	4.605	(92 100)
2–7	tax relief	6 200	3.671	22 760
				(69 340)

Present cost of borrowing

Year	Capital (£)	Operating costs (£)	Tax relief (£)	Net cash flow (£)	12% discount factors	Present value (£)
0	(90 000)			(90 000)	1.000	(90 000)
1		(1000)		(1 000)	0.893	(893)
2		(1000)	7285	6 285	0.797	5 009
3		(1000)	5541	4 541	0.712	3 233
4		(1000)	4233	3 233	0.636	2 056
5		(1000)	3252	2 252	0.567	1 277
6		(1000)	2517	1 517	0.507	769
7			6931	6 931	0.452	3 133
						(75 416)

The present costs of leasing and borrowing for Dadd Ltd

6.7.5 The distribution of financial benefits

For a leasing contract to go ahead, both parties to the lease must benefit. If both lessee and lessor pay taxes at the same rate, then, from a taxation perspective, there are no overall financial benefits to be distributed, and leasing, as Drury and Braund (1990) pointed out, appears to be what is called a *zero sum game*. For taxation benefits to arise, lessee and lessor must be faced to some extent with differences in their respective cash flow situations, arising as a result of some or all of the following factors:

1 different costs of capital for the lessor and lessee;

2 different tax rates between the lessor and lessee;

3 different abilities to utilise the available capital allowances.

Different costs of capital may arise because the cost of equity and the cost of borrowing of a large leasing company are likely to be lower than those of a small company wishing to lease an asset from it. Different tax rates may arise because the UK tax system differentiates between small and large companies. Different abilities to utilise capital allowances can arise, for example, if a lessor sets up multiple subsidiaries with different year ends. One non-tax financial benefit that can lead to lower lease payments is any discount given to a lessor making bulk purchases of assets to lease.

The distribution of financial benefits will depend on the size and timing of lease payments. The lessor will have a minimum amount that it wishes to receive, while the lessee will have a maximum amount that it is prepared to pay. The actual lease payments are likely to be between these limits, and arrived at according to the relative bargaining power of the two parties.

6.8 CONCLUSION

We have seen in this chapter that debt, hybrid finance and leasing can all be useful ways for a company to obtain the financing it needs to acquire assets for use in its business. Each of these financing methods has advantages and disadvantages which must be considered carefully by a company before a final decision is reached as to the most suitable method to use. It should be possible, given the wide range of methods available, for a company to be able to satisfy its individual financing requirements.

KEY POINTS

1 Loan stock and debentures are interest-paying debt securities which must be redeemed on maturity unless irredeemable. Interest paid is tax deductible, which reduces the cost of debt finance. Debentures are usually secured on assets of the company.

2 Restrictive covenants are a way of protecting providers of debt finance and may, for example, limit how much further debt can be raised, set a target gearing ratio or set a target current ratio.

3 Redemption of loan stock requires careful financial planning, and can be over a period of time rather than on a specific date. Companies may use a debenture sinking fund or a new issue of long-term debt to aid redemption. The latter choice upholds the matching principle.

4 A deep discount bond is issued at a price well below par value in exchange for a lower coupon rate. It may be attractive to investors who prefer capital growth to revenue returns, and to companies who prefer lower servicing costs to match expected returns on capital investment.

5 A zero coupon bond pays no interest at all, but is issued at a deep discount to its par value.

6 Fixed and floating rate long-term loans are available from banks and other financial institutions, secured by either a fixed or a floating charge on the assets of a company.

7 Debt finance may be raised in a particular currency to hedge exchange rate risk, to exploit interest rate differentials or to circumvent restrictions on currency movements.

8 Eurobonds are long-term international debt finance issued as bearer securities, with fixed or floating rate interest that can be lower than domestic rates.

9 Eurobonds can be used to finance international capital investment or to hedge exchange rate risk. Investors may find them attractive because they offer both security and anonymity.

10 Convertible loan stocks can be converted, on predetermined dates and at a predetermined rate, at the option of the holder, into ordinary shares of the company.

11 Conversion value is the market value of shares into which a unit of stock can be converted. Conversion premium is the difference between a convertible's market price and its conversion value. Rights premium is the difference between a convertible's market value and its value as straight debt.

12 Convertible loan stock interest can be less than that on ordinary loan stock.

13 The floor value of convertible loan stock is its value as ordinary loan stock. Its actual value depends upon its current conversion value, the time to conversion and market expectations.

14 Issuing convertible loan stock can be attractive if a company's share price is depressed or if dilution of EPS by new equity is unacceptable. It will also decrease the overall cost of capital. A major attraction of convertible loan stock is that it can be self-liquidating.

15 Convertible loan stock offers a lower risk short-term investment coupled with the possibility of greater long-term gains. Unlike ordinary debentures, it offers the opportunity to participate in company growth.

16 A warrant is the right to buy new shares at a future date, at a fixed, predetermined price. Warrants are often issued as an equity sweetener.

17 The gearing effect of warrants means that a greater proportionate gain can be obtained by holding the warrant than by holding the ordinary share. The initial outlay is also lower.

18 The interest rate on 'sweetened' loan stock will be lower than on ordinary stock, while the attached warrants may make it easier to sell.

19 The expected market value of fixed interest loan stock can be found by discounting interest payments and redemption value by the cost of debt.

20 Convertible loan stock is valued in the same way as ordinary loan stock, except that its expected value is the greater of two possible values: its value as ordinary redeemable stock and its value if converted into equity.

21 Leasing is a source of financing where the lessee obtains use of an asset for a period of time, while legal title of the asset remains with the lessor.

22 SSAP 21 distinguishes operating leases from finance leases. Operating leases are essentially rental agreements. With a finance lease, the lessee has most of the risks and rewards of ownership and the leased asset must be capitalised in the balance sheet.

23 Taxation-related reasons were primarily responsible for the growth of leasing before the Finance Act 1984, which introduced 25 per cent reducing balance capital allowances and progressively cut corporation tax from 50 per cent to 35 per cent, making other reasons for the growth of leasing more important.

24 Post-1984 reasons for leasing include:

(a) leases can represent an off-balance-sheet source of finance;

(b) leasing is a source of finance if a company is short of liquidity;

(c) leasing allows small companies access to expensive assets;

(d) leasing allows a company to avoid obsolescence of some assets;

(e) the lessor may be able to borrow at a cheaper rate than the lessee;

(f) leases offer flexibility of payment and choice of equipment;

(g) year-end tax effects.

25 Leasing can be regarded as being equivalent to borrowing as a way of acquiring assets. The two alternatives can be compared in present value terms by discounting using the after-tax cost of borrowing.

26 For tax benefits to arise, the cash flows of lessee and lessor must be different due to different costs of capital, different tax rates, or different abilities to use capital allowances.

QUESTIONS

Answers to these questions can be found on pages 414–16.

1 Discuss briefly the key features of debentures and ordinary loan stock.

2 Briefly explain what is meant by the following terms that refer to fixed interest debt securities:
   (a) restrictive covenant;
   (b) debenture sinking fund;
   (c) redemption window.

3 Explain the meaning of the following terms and state the circumstances under which their issue would be beneficial to lenders and borrowers:
   (a) deep discount bonds;
   (b) zero coupon bonds;
   (c) warrants;
   (d) convertible loan stock.

4 What are the advantages and disadvantages of raising finance by issuing Eurobonds?

5 Explain the difference between a conversion premium and a rights premium with respect to a convertible debenture.

6 A company has in issue a 10 per cent debenture, redeemable at the option of the company between one and five years from now. What factors do you think will be considered by the company in reaching a decision on when to redeem the debenture?

7 Briefly outline the advantages and disadvantages to a company of issuing convertible loan stock.

8 What is the gearing effect of warrants?

9 A company has in issue some nine per cent debentures, which are redeemable at par in three years' time. Investors now require an interest yield of 10 per cent. What will be the current ex-interest market value of £100 worth of debentures? What would the current ex-interest market value be if the issue had been one of irredeemable loan stock?

10 Explain the difference between a finance lease and an operating lease, and discuss the importance of the distinction for corporate finance.

QUESTIONS FOR REVIEW

Answers to these questions can be found on pages 416–18.

1 Bugle plc has some surplus funds that it wishes to invest in corporate bonds. The company requires a return of 15 per cent on such bonds, and you have been asked to advise on whether it should invest in either of the following stocks which have been offered to it.

(a) *Stock 1*: 12 per cent debentures redeemable at par at the end of two more years, current market value per £100 block is £95.

(b) *Stock 2*: 8 per cent debentures redeemable at £110 at the end of two more years, current market value per £100 block is also £95.

2 Discuss, with the aid of a diagram, the relationship between the conversion premium, the rights premium and the market value of a convertible debenture.

3 Laursen plc has in issue 10 per cent convertible loan stock which will be redeemed in 10 years' time and is currently selling at £93 per £100 block. Interest on the loan stock is paid annually and each £100 block is convertible into 25 shares at any time over the next two years. The current market price of Laursen plc's ordinary shares is £3.20 per share and it is expected that this will increase by 14 per cent per year for the foreseeable future. Loan stock of a similar risk class is currently yielding 12 per cent.

(a) Advise an investor who holds some of Laursen plc's convertible loan stock as to which of the following courses of action to take:

(i) sell the convertible loan stock now;

(ii) convert it now or within the next two years;

(iii) hold the loan stock to maturity.

(b) Explain the importance to an investor of the distinction between convertible debentures and loan stock with warrants attached.

4 Discuss the reasons for the growth in popularity of leasing during the last 15 years. What significant changes affecting leasing occurred in 1984?

5 Turner plc is considering whether to buy a machine costing £1000 through a three-year loan with interest at 14 per cent per year. The machine would have zero scrap value at the end of its three-year life. Alternatively, the machine could be leased for £320 per year, payable in advance. Corporation tax is payable at 33 per cent and capital allowances are available over the life of the machine on a 25 per cent reducing balance basis. Calculate whether Turner should lease or buy the machine.

QUESTIONS FOR DISCUSSION

1 At 31 July 19X4, Tetney plc and Habrough plc both have in issue five million ordinary shares. In addition, Tetney plc has in issue £500 000 of convertible debentures, carrying an annual coupon rate of 11 per cent and convertible into 40 ordinary shares at any time up to 31 July 19X9. Habrough plc has in issue 800 000 warrants, each with a

subscription price of £2.50 for one ordinary share in Habrough plc. The warrants can be exercised at any time until 31 July 19X9. The redemption price of the convertible debentures is £105.

(a) Explain under what circumstances you would advise a company to issue convertible debentures or warrants.

(b) Calculate the value of each convertible debenture and each warrant on 30 July 19X9, for the following situations:

(i) the share price of both companies is £2;

(ii) the share price of both companies is £3.

(c) For each situation, advise holders of the securities whether to exercise their respective conversion and/or warrant rights.

(d) Estimate what the market price should have been on 31 July 19X4 for each convertible debenture if the ordinary share price on that date was either £2 or £3, given the yield on ordinary debentures with equivalent risk to Tetney plc was eight per cent per annum.

2 (a) Discuss the factors which determine the market price of convertible loan stock.

(b) Marlowe plc has in issue loan stock which is convertible in three years' time into 25 ordinary shares per £100 unit. If not converted, it will be redeemed in six years' time at par. The stock has a coupon rate of nine per cent and a current market price of £90.01 per unit. Marlowe's current share price is £3.24. If holders of ordinary loan stock of a similar risk class require a return of 13 per cent per annum:

(i) what is the minimum expected annual growth in Marlowe's share price that would be needed to ensure that conversion takes place in three years' time?

(ii) what is the implicit conversion premium?

3 Utterby Ltd was formed four years ago to manufacture decorative tableware, and has relied upon trained artists to carry out the detailed finishing work on its handpainted range of dinner sets, which sell at a premium to its budget product lines. The market for tableware is very competitive and Utterby Ltd's rivals have been cutting costs by investing in automated production methods. The finance director is therefore considering the purchase of the AutoDec, a recently developed machine which can reproduce the work of experienced finishing artists after scanning in a detailed original template. This would enable the company to reduce the number of trained artists in its employment, cutting its salaries bill by £130 000 per year.

The machine would cost £480 000 if purchased from the manufacturers, Fotherby plc. Annual service costs, mainly the wages of a service engineer employed by Utterby Ltd, would be £14 500. The machine would need to be replaced after five years, but at that time could be sold on by Utterby Ltd for breaking up into spare parts. It is expected this sale for spare parts would realise 2.5 per cent of the purchase price of the AutoDec.

Fotherby plc has offered to lease the AutoDec to Utterby Ltd for a lease payment of £98 000 per year, payable in advance at the start of each year. This lease payment would also cover service costs, with the lease contract renewable on an annual basis.

Utterby Ltd could finance the purchase of the AutoDec by a medium-term bank loan from Laceby Bank plc at an interest rate of 11 per cent per year.

Utterby Ltd pays corporation tax at a rate of 31 per cent per year, one year in arrears, and has been making a small profit after taxation in each of the last two years. Current legislation allows the company to claim 25 per cent capital allowances on plant and machinery on a reducing balance basis.

(a) The finance director of Utterby Ltd is not sure, because of the low profitability of the company, whether the tax benefits of leasing or buying would be significant or not. Using the net present value method, determine whether Utterby Ltd should buy through borrowing or lease the AutoDec, considering:

(i) the case where tax benefits are utilised; and

(ii) the case where tax benefits are ignored.

(b) Critically discuss the reasons why leasing has proved a popular source of finance in recent years, illustrating your answer where appropriate by referring to the information provided about Utterby Ltd.

REFERENCES

Drury, C. and Braund, S. (1990) 'The leasing decision: a comparison of theory and practice', *Accounting and Business Research*, Vol. 20, No. 79, pp. 179–91.

Myers, S.C., Dill, D.A. and Bautista, A.J. (1976) 'Valuation of financial lease contracts', *Journal of Finance*, June, pp. 799–819.

Tan, C. (1992) 'Lease or buy?', *Accountancy*, Dec, pp. 58–9.

RECOMMENDED READING

Ross, S.A., Westerfield, R.W. and Jaffe, J. (1996) *Corporate Finance*, Irwin, offers a useful discussion of leasing and adds an international perspective.

CHAPTER 7

DIVIDEND POLICY

INTRODUCTION

Traditionally, corporate finance was seen to involve two distinct areas of decision making: the investment decision, where investment projects are appraised and suitable projects selected; and the finance decision, where finance is raised to enable the selected projects to be executed. The dividend decision, which considers the amount of funds to be retained by the company and the amount to be distributed to shareholders, is closely linked to both the investment and financing decisions. For example, a company with few suitable projects should return unutilised funds to shareholders via increased dividends. A company with several suitable projects that maintains high dividends will have to find finance from external sources.

In recent years, the decision on the amount of money to retain and the amount to pay out has become an increasingly important decision in its own right, to the extent that it is now usual to talk about the three decision areas of corporate finance, as we did in Chapter 1. Management needs to take into account the views and expectations of shareholders and other providers of capital when making dividend decisions. The attitude of the company's shareholders to changes in dividend level must be balanced with the availability and cost of external sources of finance. Retained earnings are often preferred by companies as a source of investment because:

- retained earnings are seen as a ready source of cash;
- the decision on what to pay shareholders is an internal one and does not require management to argue a case for funding with third parties;
- retained earnings have no issue costs;
- the use of retained earnings as a source of finance avoids the dilution of control associated with issuing new equity shares or any restrictions on business operations that might arise with a new issue of debt.

LEARNING OBJECTIVES

The key question this chapter sets out to answer is whether or not the dividend policy adopted by a company affects its share price and the value of the company, and hence which factors determine a company's optimal payout ratio. After studying this chapter, you should have achieved the following learning objectives:

- an understanding of the arguments put forward by the 'dividend irrelevance' school;
- a general understanding of the arguments put forward by those who believe that dividends are relevant to share valuation due to their informational, liquidity and taxation implications;
- the ability to discuss the reasons why a financial manager disregards the importance of the dividend decision at his peril;
- an appreciation of the alternative dividend policies that companies can operate and their significance to investors;
- the ability to describe alternatives to cash dividends such as share repurchases, scrip dividends and non-pecuniary benefits.

7.1 DIVIDENDS: OPERATIONAL AND PRACTICAL ISSUES

A dividend is a cash payment made on a quarterly or semi-annual basis by a company to its shareholders after the deduction of tax at the standard personal income tax rate. The majority of UK companies pay dividends semi-annually, while their US counterparts pay them on a quarterly basis. The interim dividend, paid mid-way through the company's financial year (and after the publication of the interim results), tends to be smaller than the final dividend, which requires shareholder approval at the company's annual general meeting (AGM) and is therefore paid after the end of the financial year after the annual accounts have been published. The size of the interim relative to the final dividend can be explained in part by two factors. First, leaving the larger payment until the final dividend allows the company to defer the need to pay advanced corporation tax (*see* Section 7.3.3 for further implications of dividends from a taxation point of view). Second, at the end of the financial year the company is in a far better position to assess the level of dividend it can afford to pay.

The delay between the announcement of a dividend and the actual discharging of the cash payment gives rise to the terms *cum dividend* and *ex-dividend* when quoting share prices. When a dividend is announced, a company's share price will change. This change will reflect the market's attitude to the dividend that has just been declared. The share price will then continue to be cum dividend for a short period of time. This means that anyone purchasing the share during this period is entitled to receive the dividend when it is paid. When the share price goes ex-dividend, anyone purchasing the share on or after this date will not be entitled to the dividend payment, even though the payment has yet to be made. The entitlement to the dividend will remain with the previous owner of the share. The share price will change on the ex-dividend date – the price falling by the value of the dividend to be paid – reflecting an intrinsic change in the value of the share. For example, if a share is currently trading at a cum dividend price of £3.45 and the recently announced dividend is 23p, then if the share were to go ex-dividend tomorrow, the share price would fall by 23p to £3.22.

EXHIBIT 7.1

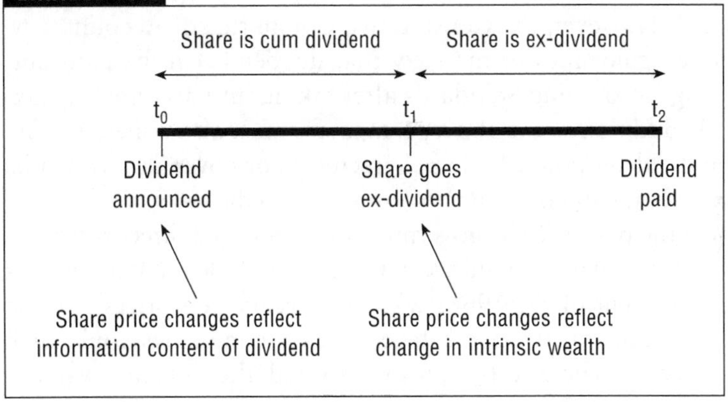

Diagram showing the relationship between cum dividend and ex-dividend share prices

EXHIBIT 7.2

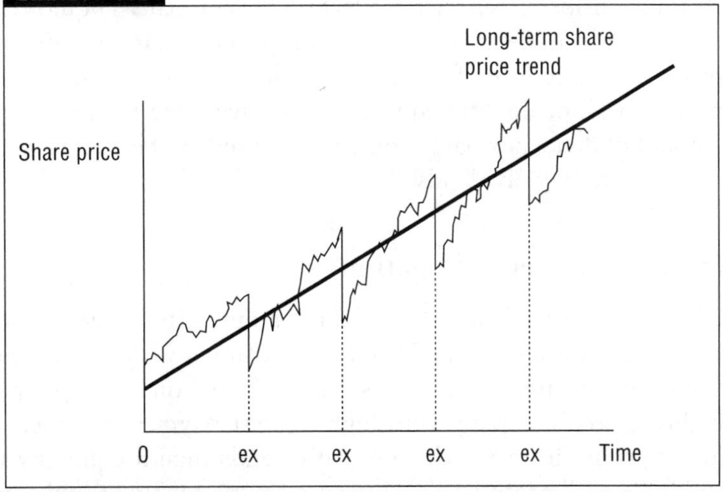

Diagram showing how a company's share price changes over time. The long-term upward trend is punctuated by falls in the share price on the company's ex-dividend dates

The timing of dividend announcement and payment and the corresponding cum dividend and ex-dividend periods are illustrated in Exhibits 7.1 and 7.2.

There are a number of practical constraints that companies have to consider when paying out dividends to shareholders. These are as follows.

7.1.1 Legal constraints

Companies are bound by the Companies Act 1985 to pay dividends solely out of 'accumulated net realised profits'. This includes profits that have been realised in the current year and those that have been realised historically. Unfortunately, the Act fails to define clearly how 'accumulated net realised profit' should be calculated. However, the Consultative Committee of Accountancy Bodies (CCAB) has issued guidelines of the view that dividends can be paid out of profit calculated using Accounting Standards after taking into account any accumulated losses.

In addition to the above, companies must also adhere to any restrictions imposed on dividend policy by loan agreements or covenants which have been included to protect the interests of the company's creditors.

In the past, the UK government has imposed direct restrictions on the amount of dividends that companies can pay to shareholders. One such example is the Labour government of the 1960s who, as part of their prices and incomes policy, placed restrictions on the percentage increase companies could make on their dividend payments. These restrictions were lifted after a Conservative government came to power in 1979.

7.1.2 Liquidity

Since dividends and their associated tax liabilities are cash transactions, managers need to consider carefully the effect on the company's liquidity position of any proposed dividends. A common misconception is that a company with high levels of profits can therefore afford to pay high dividends. As stressed in the first chapter, profit does not directly equate to cash available to the company and hence the amount of dividends paid should not just reflect the company's profit level but also its ability to pay dividends.

7.1.3 Interest payment obligations

Dividends are paid out of profits remaining after interest and taxation liabilities have been accounted for. Therefore, a company's level of gearing and its interest commitments are a major constraining factor on a company's dividend policy. A highly geared company with high interest payments to meet will have relatively lower profits from which to pay dividends than a company with low gearing at similar overall profit levels. However, since a highly geared company may be operating with a smaller shareholder base than a low geared company of similar profitability, the highly geared company may actually pay the higher dividend per share.

7.1.4 Investment opportunities

Retained earnings are a major source of finance for companies in the UK. Hence, when companies are faced with a number of attractive projects, there is a pressure for them to reduce dividends in order that such projects can be financed as much as possible from retained earnings. Whether a company will reduce dividend payments to finance new projects will depend on a number of factors. These will include:

- the attitude of shareholders and investors to a reduction in dividends;
- the availability and cost of external sources of finance;
- the amount of funds required relative to the available distributable profits.

7.1.5 The effect of paying dividends on shareholders' wealth

The objectives of a company's dividend policy should be consistent with the overall objective of maximisation of shareholders' wealth. Therefore, a dividend should only be paid by a company if it leads to an increase in the wealth of its shareholders. A simple model for analysing dividend payments was put forward by Porterfield (1965), who suggested that paying a dividend will only increase shareholders' wealth when:

$$d_1 + P_1 > P_0$$

where d_1 represents the cash value of the dividend paid to shareholders, P_1 is the expected ex-dividend share price and P_0 is the market price before the dividend was announced. It is important to consider the factors that will influence these variables. For example, d_1 will be influenced by the marginal income tax rate of individual shareholders, while P_0 will reflect market expectations of the company's performance before the dividend is paid. P_1 will be influenced by any new information about the future prospects of the company which the market perceives as being conveyed by the dividend. Porterfield's equation is consistent with the dividend relevance school of thought which is considered in Section 7.3. If the equation is modified to:

$$d_1 + P_1 = P_0$$

it implies that dividends do not affect shareholders' wealth and hence are irrelevant. This school of thought is discussed in the next section.

7.2 DIVIDEND IRRELEVANCE

The question of the effect of dividends on share prices has been a controversial one for a number of years. The dividend irrelevance school originated with a paper published by Modigliani and Miller (1961). They argued that share valuation is a function of the level of corporate earnings, which reflects a company's investment policy, rather than a function of the proportion of a company's earnings that are paid out as dividends. They further argued that the investment decisions responsible for a company's future profitability are the only determinants of its market value. For Modigliani and Miller, then, share valuation is *independent* of the level of dividend paid by a company.

Modigliani and Miller pointed out that investors who are rational, in the sense that they always make the choice that maximises their utility, are indifferent to receiving capital gains or dividends on their shares. What does matter however, from the perspective of maximising shareholder utility, is that a company maximises its market value by adopting an optimal investment policy. Such a policy is represented by a company which invests in all projects that yield a positive net present value and hence maximises the net present value of the company as a whole. If we assume that capital markets are efficient, then capital rationing is no longer a hindrance to such an investment policy. A company with insufficient internal funds can raise funds on the capital markets, allowing it to finance all desirable projects.

Alternatively, after the optimal investment policy has been implemented and a company has invested in all projects available to it that yield a positive net present value, it may not have needed to raise funds externally and may have some internal funds (retained earnings) left over. These surplus funds can then be paid out as dividends. This means that, for Modigliani and Miller, dividends are a residual payment. If no dividends are paid, because all earnings have been consumed by the company's optimum investment schedule, the market value of the company will increase to reflect the expected future dividend payments or increasing share prices resulting from the investment returns. A graphical representation of dividends as a residual payment is given in Exhibit 7.3. Here, a company is faced with six projects. Only the first three are attractive to the company, i.e. they have an internal rate of return greater than the cost of equity. The amount of reinvestment required therefore is OA. If the company has profits OP then OA is retained and AP paid as a residual dividend. If the profits are only OP*, however, OP* is retained, no dividend is paid and P*A is raised from the capital markets.

Hence, according to Modigliani and Miller, the investment decision is divorced from the dividend decision. Or, more precisely, a company's choice of dividend policy, given its investment policy, is really a choice of financing strategy.

Modigliani and Miller did not argue, as is often assumed, that investors were not concerned whether they received a dividend or not. Rather, they argued that shareholders were indifferent to the *timing* of dividend payments. Shareholders who wanted cash when no dividend had been paid could, it was argued, generate a 'home-made' dividend by selling part of their shareholding.

Modigliani and Miller's argument rests on a number of assumptions. The first assumption is that capital markets are perfect. The requirements that have to be satisfied for a capital market to be considered perfect were discussed in Chapter 2. They also assumed that no taxes exist at either a corporate or a personal level and that the issue of securities is costless.

EXHIBIT 7.3

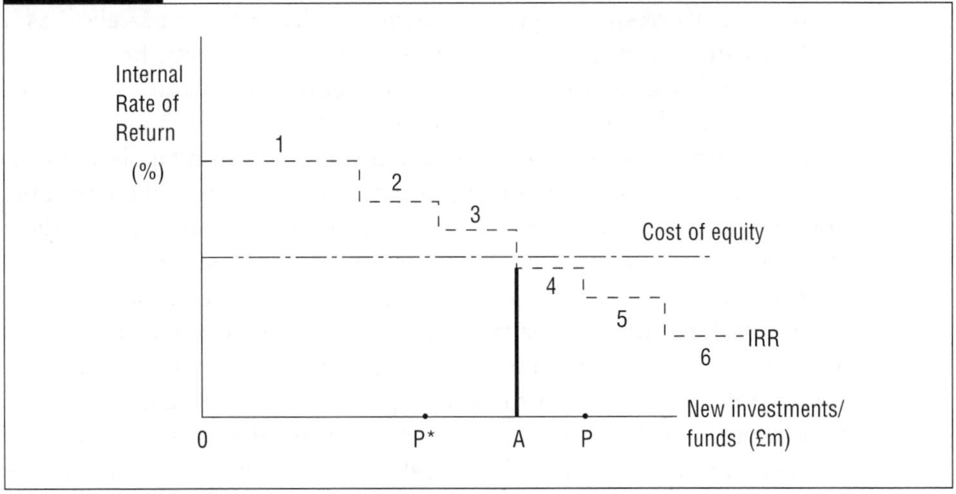

A graphical representation of dividends as a residual payment

7.3 DIVIDEND RELEVANCE

In contrast to the theory advanced by Modigliani and Miller, there is a school of thought which argues for the relevance of dividend policy to share valuation. This was, in fact, the conventional wisdom at the time that Modigliani and Miller published their paper, with the case for the relevance school being put forward by Lintner (1956) and Gordon (1959). They argued that dividends are preferred to capital gains due to their certainty. This is often called the 'bird in the hand' argument and means that the investor will prefer to receive a certain dividend payment now rather than leaving the equivalent amount in an investment whose future value is uncertain. Current dividends, on this analysis, represent a more reliable return than future capital gains.

Since dividends are preferred to capital gains by investors, dividend policy has a vital role to play in the determination of the market value of a company. Companies that pay out low dividends may experience a fall in share price as investors exchange their shares for those of a different company with a more liberal dividend policy.

There are a number of other arguments that have been put forward in support of the case of dividend relevancy. These are now considered in turn.

7.3.1 Dividends are signals to investors

In support of the dividend relevance school, it has also been argued that investors, due to the asymmetry of information that exists between themselves and company management, consider dividends to convey new information about the company and its prospects. Usually an increase in a dividend is perceived by the market to convey 'good news' and to mean that the future prospects for the company are favourable. Correspondingly, a reduction in dividends is perceived as 'bad news' and indicates that the future for the company looks gloomy. In practice, though, an increase in dividends could be due to the fact that few attractive investments exist, implying that the prospects for growth of the company and its dividends in the future are poor. Likewise, a decrease in dividends may in fact be a positive sign for investors, indicating an abundance of attractive projects and hence good prospects for growth with respect to future dividend payments. Unfortunately, the market has become rather blinkered in its perception of dividend changes, taking dividend increases to be 'good news' and dividend decreases to be 'bad news'. It becomes vital, therefore, for a company considering cutting its dividends for the purpose of reinvestment to communicate clearly to the market the reason behind the proposed cut, in order to prevent any market misperceptions and resultant falls in share price. Companies will also face problems when they want to cut dividends for reasons of financial prudence. In the UK in 1991, for example, both British Steel plc and Trafalgar House plc experienced significant decreases in their share prices when they suggested that they might have to cut their final dividend payments due to their financial positions. A similar dilemma faced Barclays Bank in March 1993, which is the subject of Vignette 7.1.

Miller (1986) argued that it was not so much the direction of a dividend change that mattered, but more the level of the actual dividend payment in relation to the market's expectations of what the dividend will be. The market, for instance, may be expecting a drop in a company's dividend payment. If the actual drop turns out

VIGNETTE 7.1

Dividend dilemma

FT

The moment of truth has arrived for Barclays Bank this week when it must decide on its dividend for 1992. The stock market assumes the payout will be maintained despite large property lending losses. But should Barclays blithely pay a dividend out of reserves as if nothing had occurred? The question, if the bank and its shareholders are being honest, is far from easy.

A bad reason for doing so would be to save the skin of Mr Andrew Buxton the bank's executive chairman, who was managing director for a period from 1988 when much of the bad property lending was approved. A cut dividend would almost certainly set the City baying for blood. It might no longer be possible for Mr Buxton to satisfy his critics simply by splitting the functions of chairman and chief executive.

Yet a cut dividend could also imply the bank was gloomy about its own prospects despite the succession of interest rate cuts since last September. The signal would be seriously misleading if the real reason was to atone for past mistakes. Barclays would have some justification for maintaining its dividend if it felt confident of continued growth in operating income – provided the cost to its reserves did not impair its ability to finance higher lending in the recovery. Having squandered the proceeds of its 1988 rights issue, it can scarcely ask shareholders for more.

Source: Lex Column, *Financial Times*, 1 March 1993

to be higher than that expected by the market, this will lead to a fall in the company's share price.

7.3.2 The clientele effect

It has been argued that a company's investors are not indifferent as to whether they receive dividends or capital gains. Preferences for one or the other can arise for two main reasons. First, some types of investor require dividends as a source of regular income. This is true of small shareholders such as pensioners and also true of institutional investors such as pension funds and insurance companies who all have regular liabilities to meet. This is balanced by dealers on the stock exchange, who over a small holding period prefer capital gains to dividend payments. Second, preferences may arise due to the different tax treatment of dividends and capital gains. In the past, in the UK, capital gains were taxed at 35 per cent while the two major income tax bands were at 25 per cent and 40 per cent. This led investors paying tax at a marginal rate of 25 per cent to prefer dividends and investors paying tax at a marginal rate of 40 per cent to prefer capital gains. Currently though, capital gains tax is equal to the marginal income tax rate in the UK. For smaller individual investors who have used up their income tax allowance, capital gains will be relatively more attractive than dividends due to an annual capital gains allowance which currently stands at £6300. Tax-exempt investors will have a preference for dividends since they can reclaim the tax paid by the company. Pension funds and charities, while tax-exempt, had the ability to reclaim the dividend tax credit removed by the budget of June 1997. The blow was softened for charities by allowing them to continue to claim the tax credits until April 1999, when a five-year transition period will begin. Clearly, the relative tax treatment of dividends and capital gains is, and remains, a matter of government policy.

The existence of preferences for either dividends or capital gains will mean that investors will be attracted to companies whose dividend policies satisfy their requirements. The implication for companies is that significant changes in dividend policy could give rise to dissatisfaction among their shareholders and result in downward pressure on the share prices.

The empirical evidence with respect to both dividends as signals to investors and the clientele effect will be considered in Section 7.7.

7.3.3 Dividends and taxation

The taxation implications of dividend payments are felt on two levels. As we have seen in Section 7.3.2, the different treatment of dividends and capital gains from a personal taxation point of view means that investors are not indifferent as to which they receive. Dividends also have important tax implications at a corporate level since they trigger a liability to advance corporation tax (ACT), which is payable on the next quarterly accounting date after a net dividend has been paid. Companies pay their total corporation tax liability in two ways: through ACT, which is currently charged at 20 per cent of the total dividend payment, and through mainstream corporation tax (MCT), which is paid nine months after the end of a company's financial year. ACT already paid will reduce the amount of MCT to be paid, so together MCT and ACT will represent a company's total corporation tax liability (unless some of the ACT is unrelieved, as discussed later). Paying high dividends doesn't change the physical amount of corporation tax paid, but affects the timing of tax payments, i.e. the company will pay more of its overall tax liability sooner in terms of ACT and less later on through MCT. Therefore, from a company's point of view, the most tax efficient distribution policy is to pay no dividends at all and to pay all of its corporation tax liability as MCT, rather than a combination of ACT and MCT.

ACT paid cannot be set off against MCT at a greater rate than the current ACT rate. Since the 20 per cent ACT rate is less than the current corporation tax rate (21 per cent for small companies, rising to 31 per cent for large companies), a company paying high dividends may not be able to relieve all of the ACT paid against its MCT liability, leading to what is called 'unrelieved' ACT. Surplus ACT can be carried back for a maximum of six years or carried forward as a tax credit into future years – further increasing the amount of corporation tax a company is paying in present value terms. The problem of companies and unrelieved ACT led to the government tapering the rate at which ACT is charged from 25 per cent in 1992 down to 20 per cent by 1994. While benefiting companies, this ACT reduction had a less favourable effect on tax-exempt shareholders, as illustrated by Vignette 7.2.

7.3.4 The Gordon growth model

The Gordon growth model is a theoretical model used to value ordinary equity shares. The model puts forward the proposition that the value of a share reflects the value of the future dividend payments accruing to that share, hence lending support to the dividend relevance school of thought. The model holds that a share's market price is equal to the sum of that share's discounted future dividend payments. Algebraically, we have:

$$P_0 = \frac{D_1}{(1+r)} + \frac{D_1(1+g)}{(1+r)^2} + \frac{D_1(1+g)^2}{(1+r)^3} + \cdots + \frac{D_1(1+g)^{n-1}}{(1+r)^n}$$

where: P_0 = current ex-dividend market price of the share
r = shareholders' required rate of return
g = expected future growth rate of dividends
D_1 = declared dividend at time t_1
n = number of years the share is held for.

The equation above can be simplified if it is assumed that the share is held, since as 'n' tends towards infinity we have:

$$P_0 = \frac{D_0(1+g)}{(r-g)}$$

VIGNETTE 7.2

Worse off at the end of the day

FT

A look at the effect on companies and shareholders of Budget changes to ACT

One might imagine that a Budget which reduced the tax burden on UK companies would be good news for shareholders. However, the largest blocks of shares are owned by tax-exempt pension funds which have suffered a significant blow from the changes in advance corporation tax.

In time, this will adversely affect those companies which have set up pension funds for their employees; for these companies usually promise to make up any shortfall between contributions and the cost of providing pensions promised by the scheme. The extra pensions burden will offset the corporate gain from the easing of the costs imposed by ACT.

ACT is a percentage of a company's dividends which is levied as a down-payment on its ultimate 'mainstream' corporation tax. Tax-exempt shareholders, along with pension funds, can reclaim the ACT the company has paid on their dividends.

The Budget reduced the rate of ACT from 25 per cent to 20 per cent and trimmed the amount tax-exempt shareholders can claim by the same amount. The effect is to cut the value of the total payments received by 6.25 per cent. Although there are offsetting benefits for companies, the government's tax take from companies and their shareholders will rise by £1bn a year.

How will these forces affect pension funds? Much depends on exactly how UK companies react to the ACT changes. In the past, companies have raised dividends, to protect shareholders from the impact of tax changes. Between 1986 and 1988, ACT was reduced to 25 per cent from 30 per cent in line with a general reduction in tax rates.

But that reduction, says Mr Andrew Wilson, research partner at consulting actuaries R Watson and Co., was phased in gradually, falling to 29 per cent in 1986, 27 per cent in 1987 and 25 per cent in 1988. More important, UK companies were doing so well that they could afford double-digit increases in their dividend rises.

This time, although at least two companies – Rentokil and Unilever – have increased dividends with the specific aim of compensating investors for the tax changes, others are unlikely to follow suit.

They cannot afford it. Dividend cover – the ratio of current earnings to dividend expense – is now low by historical standards. Companies usually feel they need earnings of at least 2.5 times dividend expense to be able to increase payouts. On average, earnings cover on the FT-Actuaries All-Share index is only 1.7 times dividend expense.

Far from rising, payouts are under pressure. Dividends of the 800 or so companies making up the All-Share shrank 0.5 per cent in 1992 and have shrunk a further 1 percentage point in the first two months of this year. Mr Wilson estimates that it will take companies two years to make up the income lost to pension schemes.

The drop in dividend income is of crucial importance to pension schemes, which rely on these to pay contributions. Mr Wilson estimates that a 6.25 per cent reduction in pension funds' UK dividend income will reduce it by £500m per year. And because actuaries value assets based on dividend stream rather than cash flow, the change will cut some £10bn off the value of UK pension funds.

Source: Norma Cohen, *Financial Times*, 5 April 1993

This expression is often called the Gordon growth model. Here D_0 represents the current year's dividend. The shareholders' required rate of return, r, can be calculated by using the capital asset pricing model (*see* Chapter 9). The expected future growth rate of dividends can be estimated by looking at historic dividend growth rates. We can illustrate the use of the Gordon model as follows.

Shareholders require a 15 per cent return on their shares and a company has just paid a dividend of 80p. Over the last four years, the company has paid dividends of 68p, 73p, 74p and 77p. What is a fair price for the share using the Gordon growth model?

First, we need to make an estimate of g. Since, over the four-year period, dividends have grown from 68p to 80p:

$$68\,(1 + g)^4 = 80$$

Rearranging, $$g = \sqrt[4]{\frac{80}{68}} - 1$$

hence $$g = 4.1 \text{ per cent}$$

Inserting D_0, g and r into the Gordon growth model:

$$P_0 = \frac{80\,(1 + 0.041)}{(0.15 - 0.041)} = £7.64$$

A number of problems are commonly mentioned in connection with the use of the Gordon growth model to value shares. These include the following.

- It has been pointed out that dividends do not grow smoothly in reality and so g is only an approximation of future dividend growth. This is a valid point, and care must be taken, when estimating g, that the sample of dividend payments used shows an approximately stable trend. Drawing a graph may help to show this.
- The model implies that if D_0 is zero, the share is worthless. This is not really a problem, though, since presumably dividend payments will be resumed in the future. The model can therefore be applied at a future date.
- It is often said that the Gordon model does not take into account capital gains, i.e. that it assumes investors buy shares and hold them for an infinite period of time. Again this is not really a problem, either, since if a share is sold, the price will be the present value of its future dividends on the selling date.
- It has been recognised that the Gordon model makes no allowance for personal or other taxation. While this is true, it is possible to modify it.

In the model's favour, though, if dividends have followed a particular growth path over the years, there is no reason to assume it will change in the future, especially if companies have a declared dividend policy which they are following. As dividends become distant (especially when the discount rate is high), small errors in dividend estimation become less significant due to the progressively higher rate of discount that is being applied.

7.4 DIVIDEND RELEVANCE OR IRRELEVANCE?

Who is right? It is possible to criticise a number of the assumptions made by Modigliani and Miller as being unrealistic. First, transaction costs are not zero and so there is a price to be paid by investors who try to sell their share to create a 'home-made' dividend. This will mean that capital gains are not a perfect substitute for dividends in cash flow terms. Second, taxation exists in the real world, at both the corporate and the personal level, further distorting the equivalence of capital gains and dividends. Third, securities are not costless to float, but will incur issue costs. Finally, information is not necessarily freely available and the investor will have to expend time and money in acquiring it.

While these shortcomings undermine Modigliani and Miller's argument, they do not totally invalidate it. In fact, empirical research since Modigliani and Miller published their paper has tended to support the dividend irrelevance school, for example the research by Black and Scholes (1974) and by Miller and Scholes (1978). Further empirical evidence with respect to dividend policy will be looked at later in Section 7.7.

Ultimately, it is the attitude of a company's investors that will determine whether or not the dividends paid and hence its dividend policy are important. Certainly in the current climate, where roughly two-thirds of all ordinary shares are owned by institutional investors, the reactions of these investors to proposed cuts in dividends by companies indicates that they consider dividend payments to be very important. Because of the need for a constant stream of dividends from their shares, institutional investors have on a number of occasions been accused of putting pressure on companies to maintain dividends when they can ill afford to pay. The irony here is that institutional investors might, potentially, be restricting future dividends through limiting the amount of retained earnings available to companies for reinvestment.

7.5 DIVIDEND PAYOUT STRATEGIES

There are a number of different payout strategies that companies can adopt in practice. These will be considered in turn, as will the relative merits and demerits of each policy.

7.5.1 Fixed percentage payout ratio

Here the company annually pays out a fixed percentage of its profits as dividends. The advantages of this policy are that, from the company's point of view, it is easy to operate and sends a clear signal to investors of the level of the company's performance. The disadvantage is that it imposes a straitjacket on the amount of funds a company is able to retain for reinvestment. It will prove totally unsuitable for companies experiencing volatile profits who have shareholders who require a relatively stable dividend payment.

7.5.2 Zero dividend payout

A company could decide to pay no dividend at all. Such an extreme policy, though, is likely to be highly beneficial to a small number of investors while being totally unacceptable for the majority. Again, such a policy is easy to operate and will not incur the administration costs associated with paying dividends. The tax implications of paying a zero dividend are also important. As indicated in Section 7.3.3, from a corporation tax perspective a zero distribution policy is optimal as it results in a company paying its corporation tax liability later via MCT rather than sooner through ACT. In addition, a zero dividend policy will allow the company to reinvest all of its profits and so will be attractive to investors who, from a personal tax perspective, prefer capital gains to dividends. Given that the majority of ordinary shareholders are institutional investors, who rely on dividend payments for income, a zero dividend policy is hardly likely to be acceptable. A zero payout policy, however, is often adopted by new companies who require large amounts of reinvestment in the first few years of their existence. Eurotunnel plc, for instance, which floated in 1987, has indicated that a payment of dividends is not likely to occur before the year 2005, although this is to a large extent due to the high level of interest payments arising out of inaccurate cost and revenue projections.

7.5.3 Constant or steadily increasing dividend

Here the company changes its payout ratio in order either to stabilise dividends or to increase them gradually to preserve the dividend level, so that in real terms dividend payments are kept in line with long-term sustainable earnings. As mentioned earlier in Section 7.3.2, it is important for companies to avoid volatility in dividends payments so as to maintain a stable share price. Cuts in dividends, however well signalled or justified to the markets, are usually taken to signify financial weakness and result in downward pressure on the company's share price. The drawback of keeping dividends constant or steadily increasing them is that it may lead to investor expectations that dividend payments will continue on this trend indefinitely. This can cause major problems when companies want to reduce dividend payments, either to fund reinvestment or in the name of financial prudence. Because of the reaction of the market to dividend cuts, companies experiencing increases in profit tend to tread cautiously when increasing dividends. Rarely will a 20 per cent increase in profits lead to a 20 per cent increase in dividends. Companies tend to increase dividends slowly over time, to reflect the new profit level, when they are confident that the new level is sustainable.

7.5.4 Dividend payout strategies in practice

The dividend policies adopted by companies will tend in practice to be influenced by a number of factors. The first factor is the industry or commercial sector within which a company operates. Companies in industries that require large amounts of long-term reinvestment are usually found to have lower payout ratios in order to facilitate such reinvestment. Companies that operate in industries associated with high business risk, or that are susceptible to large cyclical swings in profit, tend to pay lower dividends and hence have lower payout ratios to avoid the risk of having to reduce dividend payments in the future. This view was supported by Rozeff

(1986) in a paper that examined how companies determined their payout ratios. The wide fluctuations in payout ratios between different industries can clearly be seen in Exhibit 7.4.

EXHIBIT 7.4

Industry	*Payout ratio in 1997 (%)*
Transport	79
Textiles and apparel	78
Property	75
Chemicals	70
Building materials	62
Building and construction	53
Leisure and hotels	50
Breweries and pubs	48
Household goods	44
Utilities: water	43
Retailers (food)	43
Diversified industrials	39
Extractive industries	37
Banks retail	36

Average dividend payout ratios for a selection of UK industries: 1997
Source: *Financial Times*, October 1997

The second factor that affects companies' dividend policies is the nature of the company and its individual characteristics. For example, a company which has reached the mature stage in its life cycle may choose to adopt a high payout ratio due to its minimal reinvestment requirement. Alternatively, a company which has a high level of bank borrowings relative to the rest of the companies in its sector may, in response to an increase in interest rates, choose to decrease its level of dividend payout in order to meet its interest commitments.

These two factors will combine to influence what a company decides to pay out in dividends. An example of an individual company's dividend policy is given in Exhibit 7.5. Here we can see that Sainsbury plc, between the years 1987 and 1991, kept its annual dividend rising steadily by keeping its payout ratio at a reasonably constant level. Since 1991, however, the company has had progressively to increase

EXHIBIT 7.5

	1987	*1988*	*1989*	*1990*	*1991*	*1992*	*1993*	*1994*	*1995*	*1996*
Dividend (pence)	3.46	4.15	4.99	6.03	7.27	8.75	10.0	10.6	11.7	12.1
Payout ratio (%)	31.3	30.9	30.1	29.3	31.5	34.0	35.1	37.9	39.3	45.1

Dividend policy of Sainsbury plc 1987–96
Source: Sainsbury plc annual report

its payout ratio in order to maintain its dividend increases, albeit at a decreasing rate.

As can be seen from the example in Exhibit 7.5, companies tend to change their dividend policies over time in accordance with changes in their situation – as well as to accommodate changes in the environment in which they operate.

7.6 ALTERNATIVES TO CASH DIVIDENDS

In addition to paying cash dividends, there are a number of other ways in which companies can reward their shareholders. These are now considered in turn.

7.6.1 Scrip dividends

Scrip dividends involve the offer of additional ordinary shares to equity investors, in proportion to their existing shareholding (1 for every 20 shares held, for example), as a partial or total alternative to a cash dividend. Usually shareholders are given the choice of taking either the declared cash dividend or the scrip alternative, allowing them to take the alternative that best suits their liquidity and tax position. The major advantage associated with paying a scrip dividend is that it allows the retention of cash by the company. In addition, the payment of scrip dividends does not give rise to the need to pay ACT and hence to the early payment of UK corporate tax liability. From a personal taxation point of view, the scrip share received is treated as income, with tax deemed to have been paid at the basic rate of personal income tax. Unfortunately though, scrip dividends will be unattractive to investors who are exempt from paying tax on dividends as they will be unable to reclaim ACT which is only 'deemed' to have been paid. Sometimes a scrip issue may be 'enhanced', meaning that the value of the scrip share is in excess of the cash dividend foregone, as a way of making it more attractive to shareholders. If the enhancement is more than 15 per cent of the cash alternative, though, shareholders may be liable to pay additional income tax.

Another possible advantage associated with paying a scrip dividend is that it allows a company to decrease its gearing ratio slightly. In addition, if the capital markets are efficient, the share price will not be depressed, since the scrip dividend merely replaces a cash dividend which would have caused the price to fall anyway.

Cadbury plc's 1995 bid for Dr Pepper/7-UP, the US soft drinks manufacturer, is the subject of Vignette 7.3. Here, Cadbury proposed the use of an enhanced scrip dividend to allow it to retain cash to finance its proposed take-over.

VIGNETTE 7.3

Cadbury defends the bid price

FT

Funding for Dr Pepper buy to come in part from £395m rights issue

Cadbury went to great lengths yesterday to try to reassure shareholders it could afford the deal, stressing the combined group's interest cover of more than 4.5 times in the current year and strong cash flow.

It also sought to enlist shareholders' support not only for the 1-for-7 two-part rights issue but also for an innovative underwritten enhanced scrip dividend. The first tranche of the rights will raise £280m if it is completed.

The scrip dividend will improve cash flow by up to £111m in the first half of 1995, thanks to Cadbury saving on cash dividends and unrelieved advance corporation tax. The less desirable alternative was a large rights issue, but that would have required dividend payments on the new shares and exacerbated unrelieved ACT.

'This buys us time to manage our way through the long-term ACT problem', Mr Kappler, Cadbury Schweppes finance director, said.

For the second interim dividend, shareholders can choose either an 11p cash payment per share or 0.0432432 of a new Cadbury share, worth about 16.5p. The enhanced scrip also carries a cash alternative of not less than 14.7p underwritten by Kleinwort Benson, Cadbury's advisor.

Source: Roderick Oram, *Financial Times*, 27 January 1995

7.6.2 Share repurchases

Share repurchases are becoming an increasingly accepted way of returning value to ordinary shareholders in the UK, following their adoption by a number of leading companies. Recent examples include Reuters plc, who repurchased £350m of their shares in 1993, representing nearly six per cent of their total ordinary share capital; a £500m share repurchase by Boots plc in 1994; and a £463m share repurchase by Guinness in 1996 (*see* Vignette 7.4). Share repurchases had been commonplace in the US a long time before the 1981 Companies Act was introduced allowing, by law, companies to repurchase their own shares in the UK. Before any repurchase takes place, however, a company is required to obtain approval from both its current shareholders and any warrant, option and convertible holders it may have.

The main benefits for companies repurchasing their shares are, first, it enables them to return surplus funds to shareholders who can use the funds more effectively than the company and, second, the value of the remaining shares will be enhanced following the repurchase. Since capital employed is reduced by repurchasing shares, return on capital employed (ROCE) will increase, as will earnings per share. While this has to be balanced against an increase in gearing, it is argued that the increase

VIGNETTE 7.4

Corporate cashpoints

FT

In the UK, share buy-backs have traditionally been considered a mark of defeat by managements. But in the current environment of low inflation and low interest rates, they are an increasingly attractive option. Guinness's £463m share buy-back yesterday will enhance earnings by only one per cent this year. But by gearing up the balance sheet it will increase longer-term returns to shareholders. It has more than enough cash flow to support higher debt, and its tax-exempt shareholders get the benefits of a tax credit. Besides, the poor performance of its last significant investment, Cruzcampo, amply demonstrates the wisdom of returning cash to shareholders when there is no obvious alternative.

Buy-backs were a feature of the US market last year, with around $21bn of repurchases completed. By comparison, a total of £1.4bn of buy-backs in the UK looks miserly. In the US there are significant tax incentives for pursuing buy-backs rather than special dividends.

Furthermore, the benefits of consolidation in sectors such as pharmaceuticals has meant that take-overs have been a far more significant means of spending surplus cash.

Nonetheless, corporate cash flow after dividends and capital expenditure is expected to grow from £12bn to £18bn in the UK this year, excluding the financial sector. So buy-backs could really catch on.

Consumer-oriented sectors such as general retailers and supermarket groups have little incentive to build new capacity in a gloomy retail environment, and little scope for deals. Share repurchases look an easier and safer source of earnings growth.

Source: Lex Column, *Financial Times*, 23 March 1996

in financial risk associated with a share repurchase is negligible and so, since the cost of equity is unaltered, the value of shares and the company will increase.

There are three ways for a company to repurchase its shares. A tender offer to all shareholders is where shareholders are invited to offer their shares to be sold back at the price set by the company. The main advantage with this method is that it allows all shareholders to participate in the repurchase. Alternatively, a company can buy back its shares by purchasing them on the stock exchange. This is more flexible than a tender offer, as there is no one unique price at which the shares have to be repurchased and, in addition, less documentation is required. Finally, a company may repurchase its shares by arrangement with individual shareholders. Often companies employ a broker as an agent to organise the repurchase of its shares from institutional shareholders who are clients of the broker. Hence, this method of repurchase is sometimes known as an 'agency buy-back'.

As with scrip dividends, share repurchases have tax implications for both companies and investors. In the case of tender offers and repurchases by private arrangement, the capital amount (equivalent to the current market price of the shares) is taxed as capital gains. Any payment in excess of the current market price of the share is treated as a net dividend payment and therefore carries an ACT credit which tax-exempt shareholders may be able to reclaim from the Inland Revenue. With stock market repurchases the whole payment is treated as a capital gain and taxed accordingly. Hence we can conclude that investors, due to their differing tax situations, will have different preferences for how a company should go about repurchasing its shares.

7.6.3 Special dividends

Occasionally companies return surplus funds to shareholders by making what is known as a special dividend payment. A special dividend represents a cash payout that is far in excess of the dividend payments usually made by a company. If a company has funds surplus to its investment requirements then by paying out these funds via a special dividend it enables shareholders to reinvest them accordingly. A special dividend scheme was used by East Midlands Electricity plc in October 1994 to return a £186.5m surplus of funds to its shareholders. Special dividends may also be paid to make a company less attractive as a take-over target.

7.6.4 Non-pecuniary benefits

These can take the form of discounts on a company's goods and services and/or the offer of complimentary goods and services. House of Fraser, for example, distributed shareholder vouchers worth about £40 with its 1995 annual report. To qualify for non-pecuniary benefits, shareholders will usually have to hold a specified minimum number of the company's shares.

7.7 EMPIRICAL EVIDENCE ON DIVIDENDS

Dividend policy is an area of corporate finance that has been the subject of empirical research from early days of the subject's infancy. This is due in no small part to both the continuing debate on whether dividend payments are relevant and to the readily available supply of data on companies' dividend payments.

Before Miller and Modigliani's paper in 1961, the generally held belief of both academics and practitioners was that dividends were preferred by investors to capital gains due to their certainty, and that companies could therefore increase share prices by generous distribution policies. Lintner (1956) surveyed the financial managers of 28 US companies and concluded that the dividend decision was an important one, with dividend payments being determined independently from companies' investment decisions. He found that companies changed dividend payments gradually towards their desired payout ratio as earnings increased, in order to reduce the need for subsequent dividend reductions in the future should earnings decrease. A later study by Fama and Babiak (1968) of 201 US companies came to similar conclusions as those reached by Lintner. Gordon (1959) found that companies with high payout ratios also had high P/E ratios, implying that investors valued companies with high payouts more highly than companies with low payout ratios.

However, this research has now been thoroughly discredited. First, P/E and payout ratios tend to move together as earnings fluctuate due to both ratios having earnings per share as a denominator. Second, the relationship between P/E and payout ratios may be explained, not by shareholder preference for high payouts, but by the level of risk of companies. Companies whose earnings are volatile and hence normally have lower P/E ratios as a consequence, usually pay out a lower proportion of their earnings as dividends to reflect the instability of their earnings.

After the publishing of Miller and Modigliani's paper on dividend policy in 1961 a large amount of empirical investigation focused on dividends and the tax implications of their payment. Seminal work carried out by Brennan (1970) in the US put forward the proposition that the market price of a company's shares would change in order to give the same after-tax rate of return regardless of its dividend policy. For instance, if a company were to start distributing a higher level of earnings, hence increasing the amount of taxes paid by its investors, the company's share price would fall to reflect this. The implication of Brennan's proposition was that companies could increase their share price by adopting lower levels of earnings distribution. Black and Scholes (1974) tested Brennan's proposition by testing to see if companies with high dividend yields gave greater before-tax security returns to compensate investors for the undesirable tax implications of high dividend distribution. Their results were inconclusive and they failed to find any positive relationship between dividend yields and before-tax security returns. In contrast to Black and Scholes' findings, though, were those of Litzenberger and Ramaswamy (1979), who found a statistically significant relationship between before-tax security returns and dividend yields. The findings of Litzenberger and Ramaswamy were later discredited by Miller and Scholes (1982), who repeated Litzenberger and Ramaswamy's tests and concluded that the relationship between high before-tax security returns and high dividend yields could be explained away by dividend information effects rather than by dividend tax effects.

Elton and Gruber (1970) investigated the existence of tax clienteles by examining share price falls at the time when shares went ex-dividend. By looking at the magnitude of the share price fall they inferred the average marginal rate of income tax that a company's shareholders were paying. They concluded that high dividend shares were associated with lower marginal rates of income tax, hence supporting the proposition of the existence of a tax clientele. Subsequent investigations by Pettit (1972) in the US and by Crossland *et al.* (1991) in the UK has given further support to the existence of a clientele effect.

Miller and Scholes (1978) showed that US investors could negate less preferential tax rates on dividends compared with capital gains by the appropriate use of tax planning, hence lending support to the applicability of Miller and Modigliani's dividend irrelevancy theory. Feenberg (1981), however, concluded that very few investors had taken advantage of the tax planning suggested by Miller and Scholes. This was in some part due to the transaction costs associated with such a course of action.

Research into the effect on share prices of the information content of dividends has been carried out by Pettit (1972), Watts (1973), Aharony and Swary (1980) and Kwan (1981). All of these studies, apart from that of Watts, concluded that dividend changes do convey new information to shareholders.

7.8 CONCLUSION

In recent years corporate dividend policies have become an important decision area in their own right. A large number of factors influence the dividend decision of a company; these include the levels of personal and corporate taxation, the amount of reinvestment opportunities available to the company relative to its distributable earnings and the company's liquidity position. Broadly speaking, companies have the choice of three types of dividend policy: paying no dividend at all, paying a constant or slightly increasing dividend, and paying out a fixed proportion of earnings. In addition to cash dividends, companies are also able to use scrip dividends, share repurchases and non-pecuniary benefits as ways of rewarding shareholders.

The debate over whether dividend policy affects the value of a company has been raging for some time. While Miller and Modigliani's argument for dividend irrelevance is logical within the restrictive assumptions they made, recent trends in corporate dividend policies lend more support to the relevance school. Given that two-thirds of ordinary shares are now owned by large institutional investors looking for a regular income stream, only a naive financial manager would fail to appreciate the practical importance of the dividend decision of his company.

KEY POINTS

1 A company's dividend decision has important implications for both its investment and financing decisions.

2 Dividends in the UK are paid on a semi-annual basis, net of deduction of tax at the standard personal income tax rate.

3 Generally speaking, interim dividends tend to be smaller than final dividends due to cash flow, taxation and financial planning considerations.

4 When a share passes from being cum dividend to ex-dividend, its price will fall by the value of the net dividend foregone to reflect a change in intrinsic value of the share.

5 Legal constraints on the payment of dividends include the Companies Act 1985, which states dividends must be paid out of 'accumulated net realised profits', and any restrictive loan agreements or covenants.

6 Other restrictions on a company's dividend policy include the company's liquidity situation, its interest payment obligations and the level of attractive investment opportunities available.

7 A dividend should only be paid if it increases the wealth of the company's shareholders, i.e. if $d_1 + P_1 > P_0$.

8 Miller and Modigliani argued that dividend payments were irrelevant and should only be paid as a residual after all attractive investment projects have

been accepted. Shareholders who require dividends but did not receive them could make 'home-made' ones by selling shares.

9 While it is agreed that the Miller and Modigliani model is academically sound, the assumptions that underpin it are not applicable to the real world.

10 Dividend relevance, as argued by Lintner and Gordon, put forward the theory that investors preferred dividends to capital gains due to their certainty.

11 Dividend relevance was further supported by the argument that dividends were seen by investors as signals of a company's future profitability.

12 The existence of taxation at both a personal and corporate level further undermines Miller and Modigliani's dividend irrelevance theory – leading to the existence of 'tax clienteles'.

13 Companies have a number of choices when selecting a dividend payout strategy. The choices include: adopting a fixed payout ratio, paying zero dividends or maintaining a constant or steadily increasing dividend.

14 In practice companies try to keep dividends rising smoothly by accommodating temporary drops in earnings and by only increasing dividends gradually in response to an increase in earnings.

15 Payout ratios vary from industry to industry depending on their associated risk and the level of required reinvestment.

16 Scrip dividends, where new shares are offered as an alternative to cash dividends, allow companies to retain money for reinvestment.

17 Share repurchases and special dividends are sometimes used by companies to return surplus cash to shareholders.

18 Empirical research on the importance of dividends is by no means clear cut. While Miller and Modigliani's model has not been totally discredited, there is substantial evidence to support the existence of tax clienteles and to support the view that dividends are seen by investors as signalling new information about a company's future prospects.

QUESTIONS

Answers to these questions can be found on pages 418–19.

1 Which of the following statements about tax and dividend payments in the UK are correct?

(a) Taxation at a personal level makes capital gains slightly more attractive than dividend payments for smaller investors.

(b) Investors receive dividends net of tax but have to make further payments to the Inland Revenue if they are in the 40 per cent tax bracket.

(c) The current regime of ACT means that from a tax efficiency point of view it is optimal for companies to pay no dividend at all.

2 Which of the following statements lends support to dividend irrelevance rather than to the dividend relevance theory?

(a) Investors prefer the certainty of dividends to the uncertainty of capital gains.

(b) Certain companies may build up a clientele of shareholders due to their dividend policy.

(c) Dividends are believed by many investors to signal information about the company.

(d) The existence of taxes distorts the desirability of dividends relative to capital gains.

(e) Shareholders can manufacture their own dividends by selling off part of their shareholding.

3 XYZ's current cum dividend share price is £3.45 and the company has just announced a dividend of 20p. At what rate do investors expect dividends to grow in the future given that the current share price is considered to be a fair price and that investors require a 15 per cent rate of return from their shares?

4 The ordinary shares of Chock-stock plc are currently quoted at 200p per share and the company has been paying a dividend of 30p for the past 10 years. The company is planning to retain the next three years' dividends to invest in a new project. The increased cash flows will begin in Year 4, allowing the company to pay an inflated dividend of 40p for the foreseeable future from that year onwards. What is the increase in wealth for the shareholders?

(a) –24.6p;

(b) –14.2p;

(c) 5.8p;

(d) 10.2p;

(e) 17.6p.

5 Which of the following statements best sums up recent trends in corporate dividend payments?

(a) Nominal dividends have remained constant or slightly increased.

(b) Companies have made large increases in real dividends.

(c) Companies have decreased payout ratios to stabilise nominal dividends.

(d) Nominal dividends have been decreased on the whole.

(e) Nominal dividends have been slightly increased to increase companies' dividend cover.

6 Given the assumptions that Miller and Modigliani's 'dividend irrelevance' theory makes, do you consider their conclusions to be logical?

7 Discuss how the assumptions that Miller and Modigliani's 'dividend irrelevance' theory make do not mirror the real world. If you agree that it doesn't mirror the real world, does that totally invalidate the usefulness of their theory?

8 How do you consider the increased ownership of shares by institutional shareholders has affected the dividend policies of British public limited companies?

9 Explain the following terms:
(a) residual theory of dividends;
(b) clientele effect;
(c) signalling properties of dividends;
(d) the 'bird-in-the-hand' argument.

QUESTIONS FOR REVIEW

Answers to these questions can be found on pages 420–1.

1 The decision about how much of earnings to retain and how much to return to the ordinary shareholders as a dividend is one of the key decision areas of financial management. Discuss some of the key factors that should be considered by the senior management of a listed company in making a decision on the size of the annual dividend to be paid to its equity investors.

2 (a) Stant plc has just announced a dividend of 20p on its ordinary shares. Given that the past four years' dividends have been 13p, 14p, 17p and 18p and that Stant's shareholders have a required rate of return of 14 per cent, use the Gordon model to calculate a fair price for Stant plc's equity shares.
(b) Stant now decides to increase its debt level, thereby increasing the financial risk associated with its equity shares. As a consequence of this, Stant's shareholders increase their required rate of return up to 15.4 per cent. Calculate a new fair price for Stant's shares.
(c) Given your above answer, outline major problems with using the Gordon model as a method of share valuation.

3 It has become increasingly common for companies to offer their shareholders a choice between a cash dividend or an equivalent scrip issue of shares. Briefly consider the advantages of scrip dividends from the points of view of both the company and the shareholders.

4 The managing directors of three profitable companies were discussing their companies' dividend policies over lunch. Each managing director is certain that their company's policy is maximising shareholder wealth.

- Company A has deliberately paid no dividends for the last five years.
- Company B always pays a dividend of 50 per cent of earnings after taxation.
- Company C maintains a low but constant dividend per share and offers regular scrip issues and shareholder concessions.

(a) What are the advantages and disadvantages of the alternative dividend policies of the three companies?
(b) Discuss the circumstances under which each managing director might be correct in

their belief that the company's dividend policy is maximising shareholder wealth. State clearly any assumptions that you make.

(ACCA 1987)

QUESTIONS FOR DISCUSSION

1 Zim-zam-zom plc's shares are currently trading at 80p. The last dividend paid was 15p and dividends have been constant for the past 10 years. The firm is considering a new investment project – financed out of retained earnings – hence for the next two years dividends will drop to 10p. Benefits will be reaped from the project after three years and hence the firm will raise dividends to 18p thereafter. Using the Gordon model and assuming that shareholders have all the above information, what would be a fair price for the share?

2 (a) It is said that financial management is concerned with investment decisions, dividend decisions, and financing decisions. Critically discuss why financial management theorists have claimed that only investment decisions have any importance and that decisions about financing and dividends depend upon a firm's optimal investment schedule.

(b) In the context of dividend policy, discuss the meaning of the following terms:

(i) asymmetric information;

(ii) scrip dividends;

(iii) shareholder perks.

(c) Discuss whether a policy of paying out zero dividends means that a firm has no value.

3 Pavlon plc has recently obtained a listing on the Stock Exchange. Previously, 90 per cent of the firm's shares were owned by members of one family, but since the listing about 60 per cent of the issued shares have been owned by other investors. Pavlon's earnings and dividends for the five years prior to the listing are detailed below:

Years prior to listing	*Profit after tax (£)*	*Dividend per share (pence)*
5	1 800 000	3.60
4	2 400 000	4.80
3	3 850 000	6.16
2	4 100 000	6.56
1	4 450 000	7.12
Current year	5 500 000 (estimate)	

The number of issued ordinary shares was increased by 25 per cent three years prior to the listing and by 50 per cent at the time of listing. The company's authorised capital is currently £25m in 25p ordinary shares, of which 40m have been issued. The market value of the company's equity is £78m.

The board of directors is discussing future dividend policy. An interim dividend of 3.16p per ordinary share was paid immediately prior to the listing and the finance director has suggested a final dividend of 2.34p per share. The company's declared objective is to maximise shareholder wealth.

(a) Comment upon Pavlon's dividend policy prior to listing and discuss whether such a policy is likely to be suitable for a listed company.

(b) Discuss whether the proposed final dividend of 2.34p is likely to be an appropriate dividend if:

(i) the majority of the shares are owned by institutional investors;

(ii) the majority of shares are owned by wealthy individuals.

(c) Pavlon's profit after tax is expected to grow by 15 per cent per year for three years, and by eight per cent per year after that. Pavlon's cost of equity is estimated to be 12 per cent per year. Dividends may be assumed to grow at the same rate as profits.

(i) Using the dividend valuation model, calculate whether Pavlon's shares are currently undervalued or overvalued.

(ii) Briefly outline the weaknesses of the dividend valuation model.

(ACCA 1986)

REFERENCES

Aharony, J. and Swary, I. (1980) 'Quarterly dividend and earnings announcements and stock holders returns: an empirical analysis', *Journal of Finance*, March, pp. 1–12.

Black, F. and Scholes, M. (1974) 'The effects of dividend yield and dividend policy on common stock prices and returns', *Journal of Financial Economics*, Vol. 1, pp. 1–22.

Brennan, M. (1970) 'Taxes, market valuation and corporate financial policy', *National Tax Journal*, Vol. 23, pp. 417–27.

Crossland, M., Dempsey, M. and Mozier, P. (1991) 'The effect of cum and ex dividend changes on UK share prices', *Accounting and Business Research*, Vol. 22, No. 85, pp. 47–50.

Elton, E. and Gruber, M. (1970) 'Marginal stockholder tax rates and the clientele effect', *Review of Economics and Statistics*, Vol. 52, pp. 68–74.

Fama, E. and Babiak, H. (1968) 'Dividend policy: an empirical analysis', *Journal of the American Statistical Association*, Vol. 63, pp. 1132–61.

Feenberg, D. (1981) 'Does the investment interest limitation explain the existence of dividends?' *Journal of Financial Economics*, pp. 265–9.

Gordon, M. (1959) 'Dividends, earnings and stock prices', *Review of Economics and Statistics*, Vol. 41, pp. 99–105.

Kwan, C. (1981) 'Efficient market tests of the information content of dividend announcements; critique and extension', *Journal of Financial and Quantitative Analysis*, June, pp. 193–206.

Lintner, J. (1956) 'Distribution of incomes of corporations among dividends, retained earnings and taxes', *American Economic Review*, Vol. 46, pp. 97–113.

Litzenberger, R. and Ramaswamy, K. (1979) 'The effect of personal taxes and dividends on common stock prices and returns', *Journal of Financial Economics*, June, pp. 163–95.

Miller, M. (1986) 'Behavioural rationality in finance: the case of dividends', *Journal of Business*, Vol. 59, pp. 451–68.

Miller, M. and Modigliani, F. (1961) 'Dividend policy, growth and the valuation of shares', *Journal of Business*, Vol. 34, pp. 411–33.

Miller, M. and Scholes, M. (1978) 'Dividends and taxes', *Journal of Financial Economics*, Vol. 6, Dec, pp. 333–64.

Miller, M. and Scholes, M. (1982) 'Dividends and taxes: some empirical evidence', *Journal of Political Economy*, Vol. 90, pp. 1118–41.

Pettit, R. (1972) 'Dividend announcements, security performance and capital market efficiency', *Journal of Finance*, Vol. 27, pp. 993–1007.

Pettit, R. (1977) 'Taxes, transaction cost and clientele effects of dividends', *Journal of Financial Economics*, Dec, pp. 419–36.

Porterfield, J. (1965) *Investment Decisions and Capital Costs*, Englewood Cliffs, NJ, Prentice-Hall.

Rozeff, M. (1986) 'How companies set their dividend payout ratios'. Reprinted in Stern, J. and Chew, D. (eds) *The Revolution in Corporate Finance*, Basil Blackwell.

Watts, R. (1973) 'The information content of dividends', *Journal of Business*, Vol. 46, pp. 191–211.

RECOMMENDED READING

Puxty, G. and Dodds J. (1991) *Financial Management: Method and* Meaning (2nd edn), Chapman and Hall. This title has a very well written and comprehensive chapter on dividend policy.

Stern, J. and Chew, D. (eds) (1986) *The Revolution in Corporate Finance*, Basil Blackwell; and Ward, K. (ed.) (1994) *Strategic Issues in Finance*, Butterworth-Heinemann; collect together a number of very readable and interesting articles on dividend policy.

Important and informative papers and articles recommended for further reading on the subject of dividend policy include:

Bank of England (1988) 'Share repurchase by quoted companies', *Bank of England Quarterly Bulletin*, Aug, pp. 382–8.

Barker, R. (1993) 'The future of dividends', *Professional Investor*, Sept, pp. 37–9.

Goodhart, W. (1991) 'Dividend dilemma', *Corporate Finance*, March, pp. 17–21.

Shaw, A. (1995) 'Share repurchases – a new fashion in corporate finance?' *The Treasurer*, Jan, pp. 35–6.

CHAPTER 8

THE COST OF CAPITAL AND CAPITAL STRUCTURE

INTRODUCTION

The concept of the cost of capital has a very important role to play within corporate finance theory and practice. It is a company's cost of capital that is (or should be) used as the discount rate in the investment appraisal process when using such techniques as net present value and internal rate of return. If we assume that a company is a rational agent, it will seek to raise capital by the cheapest and most efficient methods, hence minimising its cost of capital. This will have the effect of increasing the net present value of the company's projects and ultimately will have an upward effect on its market value. In order for a company to try to minimise its cost of capital, it first requires information on the costs associated with the different ways of raising finance. Second, it needs to know how to combine the different sources of finance in order to reach its optimal capital structure.

The importance of a company's capital structure, like the importance of dividend policy, has been the subject of heated academic debate. As with dividends, Miller and Modigliani argued, somewhat against the grain of academic thought at the time, that a company's capital structure was irrelevant. They later revised their paper to take account of the taxation implications of debt finance and, if market imperfections are also considered, it can be argued that capital structure does have relevance. In practice, however, the calculation of a company's cost of capital turns out to be both extremely difficult and time consuming, while the existence of an optimal financing mix for a given company is hard either to identify or to prove.

LEARNING OBJECTIVES

After studying this chapter, you should have achieved the following learning objectives:

- a firm understanding of how to calculate a company's cost of capital and how to apply it appropriately in the investment appraisal process;
- the ability to calculate the costs of the different sources of finance used by a company and to weight them according to their relative importance;
- an appreciation of why, when calculating the weighted average cost of capital, it is better to use market values in preference to book values;
- the ability to discuss critically whether or not a company can, by adopting a particular capital structure, influence its cost of capital.

8.1 CALCULATING THE COST OF INDIVIDUAL SOURCES OF FINANCE

The first step in calculating a company's weighted average cost of capital (WACC) is to calculate the cost of the individual components of its capital. In this section we consider, in turn, the different sources of long-term finance available to a company and how to calculate the cost of using the source.

8.1.1 Equity capital

Equity finance can be raised either through issuing new securities or through the utilisation of retained earnings. To find the cost of equity (K_e) we can adapt the Gordon growth model for the valuation of equity capital which was considered in Chapter 7:

$$K_e = \frac{D_0(1 + g)}{P_0} + g$$

where: K_e = cost of equity
P_0 = ex-dividend share price
g = expected annual increase in dividends
D_0 = dividend to be paid shortly.

A common misconception is that retained earnings are a costless source of finance. Although retained earnings do not have any servicing costs, they have an opportunity cost equivalent to the ongoing cost of equity, since if these funds were returned to investors they could have achieved an equivalent return through re-investment at a personal level.

An alternative and arguably more reliable method of calculating the cost of equity finance is to use the capital asset pricing model (CAPM), which is the subject of the next chapter. This model allows investors to work out their required return on the equity finance of a company, based on the rate of return earned on risk-free investments plus a risk premium. The risk premium reflects both the systematic risk of the company and the excess generated by the market relative to the risk-free rate.

Using the CAPM, the cost of equity finance is given by the following linear relationship:

$$R_j = R_f + \beta_j \times (R_m - R_f)$$

where: R_j = the rate of return of security j predicted by the model
R_f = the risk-free rate of return
β_j = the 'beta' coefficient of security j
R_m = the return of the market.

8.1.2 Preference shares

Calculating the cost of a company's preference shares is considerably easier than calculating the cost of ordinary equity. This is due in no small part to the fact that the dividends paid on preference shares are usually stable. Preference shares are, generally speaking, irredeemable and, since preference dividends are a distribution of after-tax profits, they are not tax deductible. The cost of irredeemable preference shares (K_{ps}) can be calculated from the ex-dividend market price and the dividend payable using the following model:

$$K_{ps} = \frac{\text{Dividend payable}}{\text{Market value (ex-dividend)}}$$

If calculating the cost of raising new preference shares, the above equation can be modified, as can the Gordon model, to take into account issue costs.

8.1.3 Securitised debt: debentures and loan stock

There are two major types of securitised debt: irredeemable bonds and redeemable bonds. The cost of irredeemable bonds is calculated in a similar manner to that of irredeemable preference shares. In both cases, the model being used is one that values a perpetual stream of cash flows. Since the interest payments made on irredeemable bonds are tax deductible it will have both a before- and an after-tax cost of debt. The before-tax cost of irredeemable debt (K_{id}) can be calculated as follows:

$$K_{id} = \frac{\text{Interest rate payable}}{\text{Market value of bond}}$$

The after-tax cost of debt is then easily obtained if the company taxation rate (C_T) is assumed to be constant:

$$K_{id}\text{ (after tax)} = K_{id}(1 - C_T)$$

To find the cost of redeemable bonds we need to find the overall required return of the providers of debt finance, which combines both revenue (interest) and capital (principal) returns. This is equivalent to the internal rate of return (K_d) of the following valuation model:

$$P_0 = \frac{I}{(1 + K_d)} + \frac{I}{(1 + K_d)^2} + \frac{I}{(1 + K_d)^3} + \ldots + \frac{I + RV}{(1 + K_d)^n}$$

where: I = annual interest payment
RV = redemption value
K_d = cost of debt before tax
P_0 = current market price of bond
n = number of years to redemption.

In order to estimate K_d interpolation can be used. This was dealt with earlier in Chapter 3.

Alternatively, to save the trouble of doing an interpolation calculation, K_d can be estimated using the yield approximation method developed by Hawanini and Vora (1982). This is given by the following equation:

$$K_d = \frac{I + \left[\frac{P - NPD}{n}\right]}{P + 0.6(NPD - P)}$$

where: P = par value or face value
NPD = net proceeds from sale or market value
I, n = as above.

Again the after-tax cost of debt can be easily obtained using the company taxation rate (C_T):

$$K_d \text{ (after tax)} = K_d(1 - C_T)$$

More accurately, the determination of the after-tax cost of debt should take account of the way in which interest payments and principal repayments are treated from a taxation perspective. This may vary between different taxation systems.

8.1.4 Bank borrowings

The sources of finance considered so far have all been in security form and have a market price with which to relate interest and dividend payments to in order to calculate their cost. This is not true of bank borrowings. Therefore, to approximate the cost of bank borrowings the interest rate paid on the loan should be taken, making the appropriate calculation to allow for the tax deductibility of the interest payments.

It has to be noted that, in both Section 8.1.3 and 8.1.4 above, an after-tax cost of debt was calculated. It must be remembered, however, that this is only appropriate if the company is in a non-tax-exhausted position, that is, it has taxable profits against which to set its interest payments.

8.1.5 The relationship between the costs of different sources of finance

When calculating the cost of the different sources of finance used by a company, a logical relationship should emerge between the different sources and their cost on the one hand and the level of risk faced by the supplier of funds on the other. Equity finance represents the highest risk category of finance to investors. This is due both to the uncertainty surrounding dividend payments and capital gains and to the fact that equity finance ranks at the bottom of the creditor hierarchy should a company go into liquidation. Hence new equity issues will represent the most expensive source of finance, with retained earnings working out slightly cheaper due to the savings on issue costs over a new issue. The cost of preference shares will be less than the cost of equity finance for two reasons. First, preference dividends must be paid before those on ordinary equity shares and, second, preference shares rank higher up the creditor hierarchy than equity shares.

There are no uncertainties with respect to the interest payments on debt unless a company is likely to be declared bankrupt. Debts are also further up the creditor hierarchy than both preference shares and equity finance, implying that debt finance has a lower cost of capital than both. Whether bank borrowings are cheaper than bonds will depend upon the relative costs associated with issuing bonds and obtaining a bank loan, as well as the amount of debt being raised. Generally speaking, the longer the period over which debt is being raised, the larger the cost, due to lenders requiring higher rewards for giving up their purchasing power for a longer period of time. The cost of debt will also be lowered for a company if it is secured rather than unsecured.

The relationships discussed above are evident in the worked example of a WACC calculation in Section 8.2.

8.2 CALCULATING THE WEIGHTED AVERAGE COST OF CAPITAL

Once the costs of a company's individual sources of finance have been calculated, the overall weighted average cost of capital (WACC) can be determined. In order to calculate the WACC, the costs of the individual sources of finance are weighted according to their relative importance as a source of finance. WACC can be calculated either for the existing capital structure (average basis) or for additional incremental finance packages (marginal basis). The problem of average versus marginal basis WACC will be further discussed in Section 8.3.

The WACC equation for a company financed solely by debt and equity finance is represented by:

$$\text{WACC} = \frac{K_e \times E}{(D + E)} + \frac{K_d(1 - C_T) \times D}{(D + E)}$$

where: E = value of equity
D = value of debt.

Clearly this equation will expand according to the number of different sources that a company draws its capital from. For instance, for a company using equity finance, preference shares and both redeemable and irredeemable debt, the equation will become:

$$\text{WACC} = \frac{K_e \times E}{E + P + D_i + D_r} + \frac{K_{ps} \times P}{E + P + D_i + D_r} + \frac{K_{id}(1 - C_T)D_i}{E + P + D_i + D_r} + \frac{K_{rd}(1 - C_T)D_r}{E + P + D_i + D_r}$$

where P, D_i and D_r are the value of preference shares, irredeemable debt and redeemable debt respectively.

8.2.1 Market or book value weightings?

The next question that needs to be answered is how the different costs of finance are weighted. Here we are faced with two choices: book values or market values. Book values are easily obtained from a company's accounts while market values are obtainable from the financial press and from various financial databases. While book values are easy to access, their use to determine the WACC cannot be recommended. Book values are based on historic costs and rarely reflect the current required return of providers of finance, whether equity or debt. The nominal value of equity, for example, is usually only a fraction of its market value. In our example below, a share with a nominal value of 25p has a market value of £1.76. The use of book values, then, will seriously understate the impact of the cost of equity finance on the average cost of capital, and since the cost of equity is always greater than the cost of debt, this will lead to the WACC being understated. This can clearly be seen in the following example, when comparing the WACC calculated using market values with the WACC using book values. If the WACC is understated, unprofitable projects will be accepted.

Example Calculation of WACC

Dasterdly plc is currently trying to work out its weighted average cost of capital. As the company's financial director, you have been asked to perform the necessary calculations, using both book values and market values, and you have at your disposal the following information:

Balance sheet as at 31 December 1997

	£000
Fixed assets	445
Current assets	185
Current liabilities	(110)
	520
Ordinary share capital (25p shares)	90
9 per cent preference shares (£1 shares)	50
Reserves	145
11 per cent loan stock (redeemable 2002)	80
10 per cent irredeemable loan stock	95
Bank loans	60
	520

1 The current dividend, shortly to be paid, is 20p per share. Dividends in the future are expected to grow at a rate of five per cent per year.

2 Corporation tax currently stands at 35 per cent.

3 The interest rate on bank borrowings currently stands at 12.5 per cent.

4 Stock market prices as at 31 December 1997 (all ex-div or ex-interest):

Ordinary shares:	£1.76p
Preference shares:	£0.67p
11 per cent loan stock:	£95 per £100 block
10 per cent irredeemable loan stock:	£72 per £100 block

First, calculate the costs of the individual sources of finance:

1 *Cost of equity*: using the Gordon model and ignoring issue costs.

$$\begin{aligned} K_e &= D_0 (1 + g)/P_0 + g \\ &= 20 (1 + 0.05)/176 + 0.05 \\ &= 16.9 \text{ per cent} \end{aligned}$$

2 *Cost of preference shares*:

$$K_{ps} = 9/67 = 13.4 \text{ per cent}$$

3 *Cost of redeemable bonds (after tax)*: using the Hawanini and Vora yield approximation method.

$$K_{rd} = \frac{11 + \left(\dfrac{100 - 95}{5}\right)}{100 + 0.6(95 - 100)}$$

K_{rd} = 12.4 per cent

K_{rd} (after tax) = 12.4 per cent (1 – 0.35) = 8.1 per cent

4 *Cost of irredeemable bonds (after tax)*:

$$K_{id} = 10\ (1 - 0.35)/72 = 9.0 \text{ per cent}$$

5 *Cost of bank loans (after tax)*:

$$K_{bl} = 12.5\ (1 - 0.35) = 8.1 \text{ per cent}$$

Source of finance	*Book value (£000)*	*Market value (£000)*
Equity	90 + 145 = 235	90 × 4 × 1.76 = 633.6
Preference shares	50	50 × 0.67 = 33.5
Redeemable debt	80	80 × 0.95 = 76
Irredeemable debt	95	95 × 0.72 = 68.4
Bank loans	60	60
Total	520	871.5

WACC (book values)
= (16.9 per cent × 235/520) + (13.4 per cent × 50/520)
+ (8.1 per cent × 80/520) + (9.0 per cent × 95/520)
+ (8.1 per cent × 60/520)
= 12.75 per cent

WACC(market values)
= (16.9 per cent × 633.6/871.5) + (13.4 per cent × 33.5/871.5)
+ (8.1 per cent × 76/871.5) + (9.0 per cent × 68.4/871.5)
+ (8.1 per cent × 60/871.5)
= 14.8 per cent

Note that in the above example issue costs have been ignored.

8.3 AVERAGE *VS* MARGINAL COST OF CAPITAL

As mentioned earlier, the cost of capital can be calculated in two ways. If it is calculated using a company's balance sheet, as in the example above, i.e. on an average basis, it will represent the cost of the capital currently employed. This represents financial decisions taken in previous periods. Alternatively, the cost of raising the next increment of capital can be determined – this is what we term the *marginal* cost of capital. The relationship between marginal (MC) and average (AC) cost of capital can be represented graphically, as indicated in Exhibit 8.1.

The relationship between the AC and MC curves can be explained as follows. While the marginal cost is less than the average cost of capital, the average cost of capital will fall. Once the marginal cost rises above the average cost of capital, however, the marginal cost of capital will pull up the average cost of capital, albeit at a slower rate than that at which marginal cost is rising.

Should we use the marginal or the average cost of capital when appraising investment projects? Well, strictly speaking the costs associated with raising the marginal capital to finance a project should be used rather than an average cost of capital. The problem with calculating the marginal cost of capital, though, is that

EXHIBIT 8.1

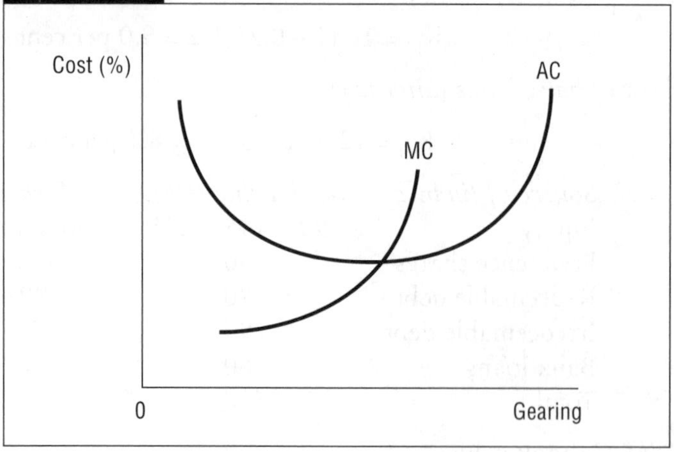

The marginal cost and average cost of capital

it is often difficult to allocate particular funding to a specific project. Furthermore, companies who have a target capital structure will often raise marginal finance by utilising only one source of finance at a time. For example, suppose that a company aims to finance itself equally with equity and debt. If the company requires £10m, it might prefer to raise this as debt finance, and incur one issue fee, rather than split the finance equally between debt and equity. The next year, the company will then raise £10m by equity finance to restore its desired financing mix. The problem here is that the marginal cost of capital will fluctuate from low levels when debt financing is used at the margin to high levels when equity financing is used. Therefore, it could be argued that a rolling average marginal cost of capital is more appropriate than a 'straight' marginal cost of capital.

Using an average cost of capital as the discount rate to appraise new projects can sometimes be appropriate, but only if several restrictive assumptions are satisfied. These restrictive assumptions are:

- the business risk of proposed projects is similar to the business risk of the company's current activities;
- incremental finance is raised in proportions which preserve the existing capital structure of the company;
- incremental investment projects do not disturb the existing risk/return relationships between providers of finance, whether by synergy, scale economies or other effects.

If these restrictive assumptions are not satisfied, a cost of capital calculated on a marginal basis may be more appropriate, but any effect on the existing average cost structure must be reflected in the marginal cost of capital.

8.4 THE PRACTICAL APPLICATION OF WACC

In addition to the problems of deciding whether an average or marginal cost of capital is appropriate, there are a number of practical difficulties associated with the calculation of a company's WACC. These are now considered in turn.

8.4.1 Problems with calculating the cost of sources of finance

Calculating the cost of a particular source of finance is not always straightforward. Certain securities may not be traded on a regular basis and therefore do not have a market price. This is particularly true for the shares of private companies. One way to overcome this problem is to calculate the cost of equity for a public limited company in a similar line of business and then add on a premium to reflect the higher level of risk of the private limited company. Similar problems may be experienced with obtaining the market value of bonds. A possible solution here is to find the market value of a bond with similar maturity, risk and coupon of another company and use this value as a surrogate or proxy.

The cost of convertibles can prove very difficult to calculate due to the complex nature of these securities. Convertibles start life as debt and therefore initially have a cost in line with bonds of a similar coupon and maturity. Later in their life, however, they are likely to convert into equity shares and hence receive an equity-related return. Problems arise if convertible securities are likely to convert in the near future, since the current market value will reflect the value of the shares on conversion; if this current market value is used to calculate the cost of capital of the securities as straight debt rather than as a security shortly to be converted, the cost of debt will be understated.

Leasing can also provide problems when we are seeking to calculate its cost. Many leases provide finance on a medium- to long-term basis and therefore should be included in the cost of capital calculations. While it may be relatively easy to identify the lease payments, which should be taken after tax due to their tax deductibility, the capital value to which these payments should be related is more difficult to determine. As leasing is seen as an alternative to debt finance, however, it may be appropriate to treat the cost of leasing as similar to that of debt finance.

Another complication with respect to the cost of sources of finance relates to borrowings where the interest payments have been subject to swap agreements. The main issue here revolves around whether the cost of the loan should reflect the initial interest rate, when the loan was first raised, or the post-swap interest rate. There is no clear answer to this problem.

Finally, with respect to calculating the cost of equity, the accuracy of the cost obtained will depend very heavily upon the reliability and applicability of the models used. For example, if a company increases its dividends at a very low but constant rate, perhaps as a result of a high retentions policy, the cost of equity calculated using the Gordon growth model is likely to be greatly understated. Alternatively, if a company's beta, which is used within the capital asset pricing model, is unstable and unreliable, then so will be the resulting cost of equity. The authors recommend the use of the CAPM for the calculation of the cost of equity, not only because it is theoretically sounder than the Gordon growth model but also because it does not depend upon an estimate of a company's dividend growth rate. It is very difficult to establish a growth trend for an individual company's dividends which has real credibility.

8.4.2 Which sources of finance should be included in WACC?

A major issue is which sources of finance should be included in the calculation and which should not. The rule of thumb to apply is that, if finance is being used to fund the long-term investments of a company, it should be included in the cost of capital calculation. Therefore, equity finance and medium- to long-term debt and leasing finance should all be included. Generally speaking, though, short-term trade creditors should not be included in the calculation, as they are connected with the financing of a company's working capital rather than its long-term assets. However, if a short-term source of finance, say for instance a bank overdraft, is used on an ongoing basis, it could be argued that it is being used to finance the long-term assets of the company and hence it should be included in the WACC calculation.

8.4.3 Problems associated with weighting the sources

Difficulties in finding the market values of securities will also have an impact on cost of capital through the weightings that are applied to the costs of the different sources of finance. Ideally it is better to use market values in preference to book values, as discussed in Section 8.2.1. However, market values may be hard to find or, in the case of bank borrowings, may simply not exist. Therefore, in practice, the weightings applied will be made up of a mixture of book and market values.

Additional problems will be experienced by companies that have raised capital denominated in foreign currencies. These amounts will have to be translated into sterling in order to include them in the WACC calculation. Two problems arise here. First, at which exchange rate should they be converted into sterling? Second, as exchange rates move, the weightings in terms of sterling will also move.

8.4.4 WACC will change over time

WACC is not a static concept. As the market values of securities change, so will a company's cost of capital. Not only will the weightings change, but the costs of the different sources of finance will also change as macro-economic conditions and the preferences and attitudes of investors change. Therefore, it is both advisable and necessary for companies to recalculate their cost of capital frequently in order to reflect such changes.

One thing that should become apparent after reading this section is that the concept of weighted average cost of capital is, in practice, both hard to calculate and difficult to apply to the investment appraisal process.

8.5 GEARING: ITS MEASUREMENT AND IMPLICATIONS

The term *gearing* in a financial context refers to the amount of debt finance a company uses relative to its equity finance. A company with a high level of debt finance relative to equity finance is referred to as highly geared and vice-versa. The gearing of a company can be measured or quantified using a number of financial ratios. These include:

- debt/equity ratio (long-term debt/shareholders' funds);
- capital gearing ratio (long-term debt/capital employed).

Debt/equity ratio and capital gearing ratio are both examples of balance sheet gearing ratios, as opposed to income gearing ratios such as operating gearing and interest cover (*see* Section 2.4.6). It is possible to include short-term debt as well as long-term debt in the calculation of balance sheet gearing ratios, especially if it is an overdraft which is persistent. Both debt/equity ratio and capital gearing ratio, with the weighted average cost of capital, can be calculated using market or book values. A common argument put forward for the use of book values is that they are less volatile than market values. The problem, though, is that in most cases book values for securities, for example ordinary shares, are significantly different from their true or market value. Hence, as with weighted average cost of capital, market values must be considered to be more appropriate than book values when calculating a company's gearing ratio.

A major determining factor of what the market considers an appropriate level of gearing for a company will be the industry within which that particular company is operating. Industries with lower levels of business risk, such as utilities, typically have higher levels of gearing than industries associated with high levels of business risk, for example the luxury goods sector. The difference in gearing levels between industries is apparent from Exhibit 8.2. Something else that must be appreciated is that gearing levels within a particular industry are not static over time. In fact gearing levels change in response to changing economic conditions.

There are a number of problems associated with companies having excessively high levels of gearing. These include the following.

8.5.1 Increased volatility of equity returns

The higher a company's level of gearing, the more sensitive are its profitability and earnings to changes in interest rates. This sensitivity will be accentuated if the company has predominantly floating interest rate debt.

If a company is partly financed by debt, then profits and distributable earnings will be at risk to changes in the interest rate charged on the company's debt. This risk will be borne by shareholders, as the company may have to reduce dividend payments in order to meet its interest payments as they fall due. This kind of risk is referred to as financial risk. The more debt that a company has in its capital structure, the higher will be its financial risk from its shareholders' point of view.

EXHIBIT 8.2

Industry	*Capital gearing ratio (%)*
Transport	58
Distributors	46
Oil exploration and production	45
Food producers	36
Textiles and apparel	32
Chemicals	31
Gas distribution	27
Food retailers	26
Building and construction	24
Tobacco	10

How the gearing ratio varies between industries
Source: Datastream, 1997

8.5.2 Increased possibility of bankruptcy

At very high levels of gearing, shareholders will start to face what is known as *bankruptcy risk*. This is defined as the risk of interest rate charges actually putting the company into liquidation. From the shareholders' point of view, this is the risk that they might lose the value of their initial investment, due to the position they occupy in the creditors' hierarchy.

8.5.3 Reduced credibility on the Stock Exchange

Because of the extensive informational requirements that accompany Stock Exchange membership it will be relatively straightforward for investors to calculate a company's level of gearing. Investors having made this calculation may feel that a company has too high a level of gearing, resulting in what they perceive as unacceptable levels of financial or bankruptcy risk. This may result in them being reluctant either to purchase the company's shares or to offer the company further debt and, in consequence, downward pressure will be exerted on the company's share price.

8.5.4 The encouragement of short-termist behaviour

If a company has a high level of gearing its primary objective may shift from that of maximising long-term shareholder wealth to that of generating enough cash flow to meet its interest commitments and thereby staving off possible bankruptcy.

8.6 THE CONCEPT OF AN OPTIMAL CAPITAL STRUCTURE

Earlier in the chapter we looked at how a company can determine its cost of capital by calculating the costs of the various sources of finance it utilises and then weighting them according to their relative importance. Clearly the market value of a company will depend upon its weighted average cost of capital. The lower a company's WACC, the higher will be the net present value of its future cash flows and therefore its market value.

One thing that we have not considered so far is whether financing decisions can have an effect on investment decisions and thereby affect the value of the company. Put another way, will the way in which a company finances its assets (i.e. how much debt a company uses relative to equity) affect the company's overall cost of capital and hence the company's value? If an optimum financing mix does in fact exist, then it would be in a company's best interests to locate it and move towards this *optimal capital structure*. There has been a large amount of academic literature on the subject of whether or not an optimal capital structure exists for individual companies. Before we go on to evaluate these differing approaches to capital structure, we shall first consider the factors that will determine the level of return required by shareholders and debt holders.

8.6.1 Gearing and the required return of shareholders and debt holders

The level of return required by shareholders and debt holders will reflect the risk they are facing. One thing that should be clear from our earlier discussions is that the required rate of return of shareholders will always be higher than that of debt holders, due to the former facing higher levels of risk. What does need further consideration, though, are the factors that determine the shape of the cost of debt and the cost of equity curves faced by a company, that is, the relationship between those costs of capital and the level of gearing.

First, let us consider the cost of equity curve. Exhibit 8.3 summarises the factors which contribute to the determination of shareholders' required rate of return. As a starting point, shareholders will require at least the risk-free rate of return, which can be approximated by the interest yield on short-dated government Treasury bills. In addition to this, they will require a premium for commercial or business risk, which is the risk associated with a company's profits and earnings varying due to systematic influences on that company's sector. Clearly, the level of business risk faced by shareholders will vary from company to company, as will the required premium. The combination of the risk-free rate and the business risk premium will represent the cost of equity that a company will have if it is all equity financed.

As a company starts to gear up by taking on debt finance, its distributable profits will be reduced by the interest payments it is required to make, although this reduction in profitability is lessened by the tax shield on debt. Any volatility in operating profits will be accentuated by the need to meet interest payments, since these payments represent an additional cost. Further volatility in distributable profits arises if some or all of the interest payments are on floating rate rather than fixed rate debt, since the size of such payments will be determined by prevailing market interest rates. The volatility of distributable profits arising from the need to meet interest payments, which is called financial risk, will get progressively higher as a company's gearing level increases. In income gearing terms, this risk is measured by financial gearing, defined as the ratio of the percentage change in earnings available to shareholders to the percentage change in profit before interest and tax (*see* Section 2.4.4).

Shareholders will require a premium for facing financial risk and this premium will increase with the level of a company's gearing. Finally, at very high levels of gearing, the possibility of the company going into liquidation increases due to its potential inability to meet its interest payments. At high gearing levels, shareholders will require compensation for facing bankruptcy risk in addition to their compensation for facing financial risk, and this results in a further steepening in the cost of equity curve.

EXHIBIT 8.3

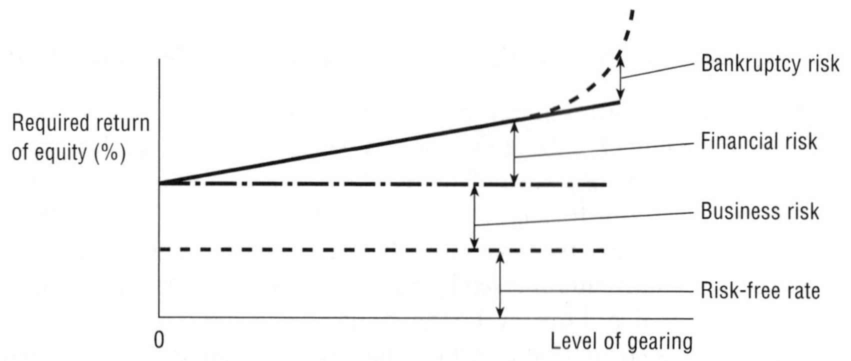

The determinants of a company's cost of equity finance

Now let us turn to the shape of the cost of debt curve. The situation from the debt holders' point of view is different to that of equity holders. The returns of the debt holders are fixed and cannot vary with changes in a company's profit level. Therefore, by definition, they do not face financial risk. They do, however, face bankruptcy risk at very high levels of gearing, albeit at a lower level than shareholders due to debt holders' preferential position in the creditor hierarchy and to their ability to secure debts against corporate assets.

8.7 THE TRADITIONAL APPROACH TO CAPITAL STRUCTURE

The first of the models that we are going to consider is usually called the traditional approach to capital structure. This model, like those that follow it, relies on a number of simplifying assumptions which are:

- no taxes exist, either at a personal or a corporate level;
- companies have two choices of finance: perpetual debt finance or ordinary equity shares;
- companies can simultaneously change their capital structure without issue or redemption costs, i.e. if a company increases its debt finance by 10 per cent this is accompanied by a 10 per cent decrease in the company's equity finance;
- companies pay out all distributable earnings as dividends;
- the business risk associated with a company is constant over time;
- companies' earnings and hence dividends do not grow over time.

The proposition of the traditional approach is that an optimal capital structure does exist and therefore that a company can increase its total value by the sensible use of debt finance within its capital structure. A diagrammatic representation of the traditional approach is given in Exhibit 8.4.

EXHIBIT 8.4

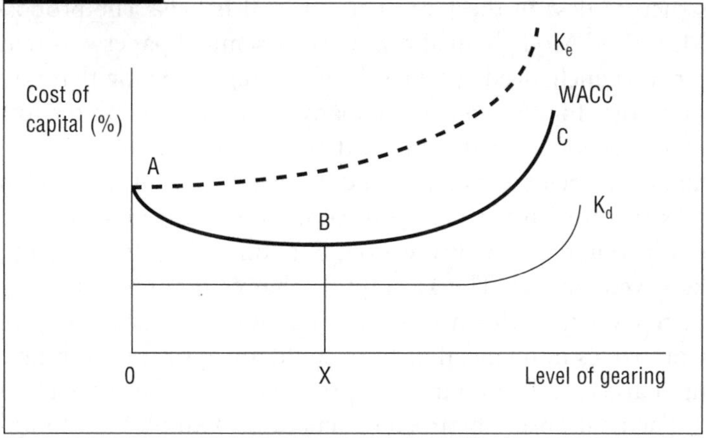

The traditional approach to capital structure

Exhibit 8.4 can be explained as follows. The cost of equity curve (K_e) rises initially with increased gearing due to the increasing level of financial risk being faced by shareholders. The curve rises at a steeper rate at high gearing levels due to the risk of bankruptcy threatening the value of shareholders' investments. The cost of debt curve (K_d) will only rise at high levels of gearing, where bankruptcy risk threatens the value of debt holders' investments. An all-equity financed company will be located at point A in Exhibit 8.4. As this company starts to replace more expensive equity with cheaper debt finance, its WACC will fall due to the benefit of the cheaper debt finance outweighing the increases in the cost of the company's remaining equity finance. Hence the company's WACC will fall to B, to give an optimal capital structure represented by the point X. If the company then increases its gearing level past X the benefits associated with the use of cheaper debt finance will be out-weighed by the increase in the company's cost of equity finance. Therefore, the company's WACC curve will start to rise. At very high levels of gearing the risk of bankruptcy will cause the cost of equity curve to rise at an even steeper rate and, for similar reasons, the company's cost of debt will also start to rise. At very high levels of gearing, then, the company's WACC curve will rise at an even faster rate.

The conclusion of the traditional approach to capital structure, then, is that an optimal capital structure *does* exist for individual companies, who will have to locate the combination of debt and equity finance that minimises their overall cost of capital. This is in sharp contrast to the view put forward by Miller and Modigliani, which we will now consider in the next section.

8.8 MILLER AND MODIGLIANI (I) – NET INCOME APPROACH

As with their views on the importance of dividend policy, which were considered in Chapter 7, the opinions of Miller and Modigliani on the importance of capital structure flew in the face of traditional beliefs. The proposition put forward by Miller and Modigliani (1958) in their seminal paper was that a company's WACC remains unchanged at all levels of gearing, implying that no optimal capital structure exists for a particular company. They argued that the total value of a company was dependent on its expected performance and commercial risk and that the market value of a company and its cost of capital were independent from its capital structure. They came to this conclusion using a model based on the assumptions outlined in the previous section, but added the extra assumption that capital markets were perfect. The assumption that capital markets are perfect was central to their model, as this assumption implies that bankruptcy risk could be ignored. Companies in financial distress could always raise fresh finance in a perfect capital market. A diagrammatic representation of their model is show in Exhibit 8.5.

The relationship between the curves in Exhibit 8.5 can be explained as follows. The cost of equity curve (K_e) increases at a constant rate in order to reflect the higher financial risk faced by shareholders at higher levels of gearing. As debt holders do not face bankruptcy risk, the cost of debt curve (K_d) is horizontal and does not start to steepen at high levels of gearing. An all-equity financed company will be represented by point A in Exhibit 8.5. As the company increases it level of gearing and moves to the right of point A, the benefit of using an increased level of cheaper debt finance is exactly offset by the company's equity finance becoming more expensive, therefore keeping the company's WACC at a constant level.

EXHIBIT 8.5

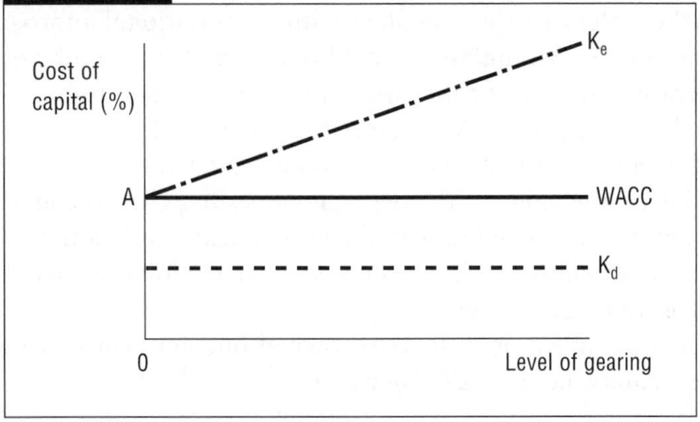

Miller and Modigliani's net operating income approach to capital structure

According to Miller and Modigliani, the weighted average cost of capital of a geared company is identical to the cost of equity the company would have if it were financed entirely by equity, which in turn is determined by the risk-free rate of return and the business risk of the company.

Miller and Modigliani supported the argument that capital structure was irrelevant in determining the market value of a company by using arbitrage theory.

8.8.1 The arbitrage approach to capital structure

Arbitrage theory excludes the possibility of perfect substitutes from selling at different prices in the same market. Miller and Modigliani argued that two companies identical in every way except for their gearing levels should not have different costs of capital and hence different valuations. This argument is best illustrated with an example. Consider two firms, Company A and Company B, identical in every respect (i.e. both companies have similar net operating incomes and levels of business risk) except that Company A is not geared, while Company B is partly financed by £3000 of debt with an associated interest rate of five per cent. Data for the two companies is as follows:

	Company A	*Company B*
Net operating income (£)	1000	1000
Interest on debt (5 per cent × £3000)	nil	150
Earnings available to shareholders (£)	1000	850
Cost of equity	10%	11%
Market value of equity (£)	10 000	7727
Market value of debt (£)	nil	3000
Total value of company (£)	10 000	10 727
WACC	10%	9.3%

Company B has a higher cost of equity but a lower overall WACC, and a higher market value. This is consistent with the traditional approach to the capital structure debate. Modigliani and Miller, however, would argue that since the net operating incomes of the two companies are the same, they must have the same market values and WACC. Since this is not the case, Miller and Modigliani would consider Company A to be undervalued and Company B overvalued, and arbitrage will drive the value of the two companies together. Using Miller and Modigliani's assumptions, which imply that companies and individuals can borrow at the same rate, we can illustrate how an investor can exploit the misvaluation of the two companies to make a profit.

Suppose a 'rational' investor owned one per cent of Company B's (the geared firm) equity, i.e. £77.27. They could:

- sell their shares in Company B for £77.27;
- borrow £30 at five per cent. Here the investor is making their personal gearing equal to the corporate gearing – thus emulating Company B's level of financial risk;
- buy one per cent of the shares in Company A (ungeared firm) for £100 thus leaving a surplus of £7.27.

If we compare the investor's income streams, we get the following results:

Original situation		
Holding Company B shares:	return = 11 per cent × 77.27 =	£8.50
New situation		
Holding Company A shares:	return = 10 per cent × £100 =	£10.00
Less interest on debt:	5 per cent × £30 =	(£1.50)
Net return:		£8.50

Here we see that, although the annual incomes are the same, by selling shares in Company B and buying shares in Company A the investor has generated a £7.27 surplus. A rational investor would keep repeating this process until the opportunity to create a profit disappears. The consequence of this would be the following sequence of events:

- Company B's share price will fall, due to pressure to sell its shares;
- since returns to its shareholders remain the same, its cost of equity will rise;
- since its cost of equity increases, its WACC will increase and its market value fall.

For Company A the scenario would be exactly the opposite. This process of arbitrage would stop when the companies' WACCs and market values were equalised.

However, there are serious flaws in Miller and Modigliani's arbitrage argument, due mainly to the unrealistic nature of their assumptions. First, the assumption that individuals can borrow at the same rate as companies can be challenged. The costs of personal debt and corporate debt cannot be the same, because companies have a higher credit rating than the majority of individuals. Personal borrowing is therefore seen as riskier, and hence more costly, than corporate borrowing. Second, their assumption that there are no transaction costs associated with the buying and selling of shares is clearly untrue. The fact that personal borrowing rates are higher than corporate borrowing rates and the existence of transaction costs both undermine the ability of investors to make abnormal gains from arbitrage, therefore creating the possibility of identical companies being overvalued and undervalued. Miller and Modigliani (1958) acknowledged the rather unrealistic nature of their assumptions in their paper, stating that: 'These and other drastic simplifications have been necessary in order to come to grips with the problem at all. Having served their purpose they can now be relaxed in the direction of greater realism and relevance . . .'

Another simplification made by Miller and Modigliani was to ignore the existence of taxation. They amended their model to take into account corporation tax in a later paper, which is the subject of the next section.

8.9 MILLER AND MODIGLIANI (II) AND MARKET IMPERFECTIONS

In their second paper on capital structure, Miller and Modigliani (1963) amended their earlier model by recognising the existence of corporate tax. Their acknowledgement of the existence of corporate tax and of the tax deductibility of interest payments implies that the more debt companies take on, the more of their profits they will shield from corporate tax. The tax advantage enjoyed by debt finance over equity finance suggests, therefore, that the optimal capital structure for companies to adopt is one of 100 per cent debt finance, since a company's WACC will decrease as gearing increases. This is represented in Exhibit 8.6.

EXHIBIT 8.6

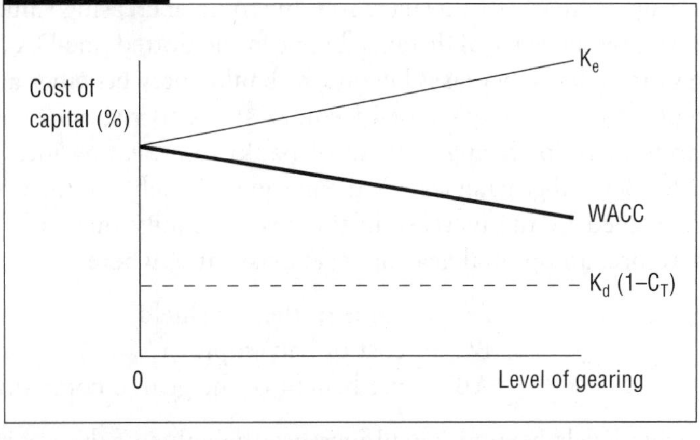

Miller and Modigliani (II), incorporating corporate taxation

Clearly, there is a problem with the model proposed in Miller and Modigliani's second paper, since in practice companies do not adopt an all-debt capital structure. This indicates the existence of factors which undermine the tax advantages of debt finance and which Miller and Modigliani failed to take into account. These will now be considered in turn.

8.9.1 Bankruptcy costs

The obvious omission from their second model is their failure to take into account bankruptcy costs. This stems from their assumption that capital markets are perfect. In perfect capital markets, companies will always be able to raise finance and thereby prevent bankruptcy. In practice, while capital markets are considered to be efficient, they cannot be considered to be perfect. In reality, at high levels of gearing, there is a significant possibility of a company defaulting on its interest commitments and hence being declared bankrupt. At higher levels of gearing, then, where bankruptcy becomes a possibility, shareholders will require a higher rate of return on their equity to compensate them for facing such risk. The concept of bankruptcy risk was earlier introduced in Section 8.5.2. The costs of bankruptcy can be classified in two ways:

- *direct costs*, including the costs of paying lenders higher rates of interest to compensate them for higher risk and, if forced into liquidation, the cost of employing lawyers and accountants to manage the liquidation process;
- *indirect costs*, which include the loss of sales and goodwill as a consequence of the company operating at levels of extreme financial distress and, if forced into liquidation, the cost of having to sell assets off below their market value.

If we now combine the tax shield advantage of increasing gearing with the bankruptcy costs associated with very high levels of gearing (effectively Miller and Modigliani's 1963 paper modified to take into account bankruptcy risk) we again see an optimal capital structure emerging. This is demonstrated in Exhibit 8.7.

Exhibit 8.7 can be explained in the following manner. As an all-equity company gears up, its market value increases due to the increasing value of its tax shield. This is given by the vertical distance between the dotted line DA and the line DC. After the gearing level increases beyond X, bankruptcy becomes a possibility and consequently the company's cost of equity starts to rise more steeply to compensate shareholders for facing the risk of bankruptcy, eating into the benefit of the tax shield. Beyond gearing level Y the marginal benefits of the tax shield are more than outweighed by the increase in the cost of equity due to higher bankruptcy risk. Therefore, an optimal gearing level exists at Y where:

AC = value of the tax shield
BC = cost of bankruptcy risk
AB = net benefit of the geared company.

Gearing levels beyond Y will increase the value of the tax shield but this is more

EXHIBIT 8.7

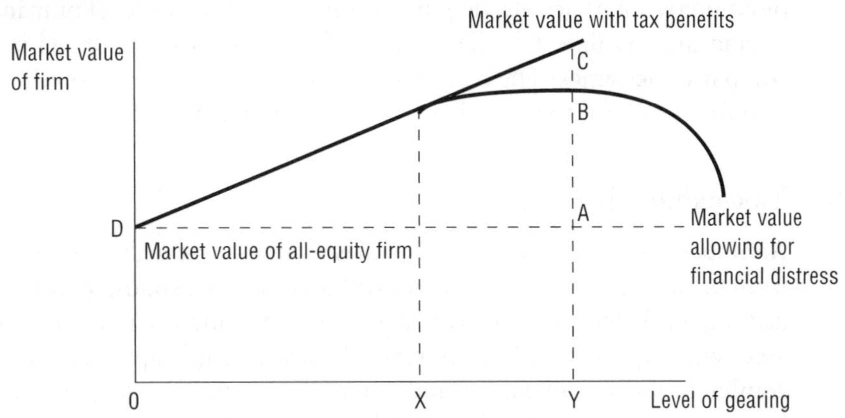

Miller and Modigliani (II), incorporating bankruptcy risk

than cancelled out by increasingly higher bankruptcy costs, leading to a decline in the value of the company.

While there is little doubt about the existence of bankruptcy costs at high gearing levels, the level of gearing at which such costs become relevant (indicated by point X in Exhibit 8.7) and the size of such costs is less clear. Very little research has been done in the area of bankruptcy costs. Baxter (1967), in his US study on individual and small company liquidations, found bankruptcy costs to be of sufficient magnitude to warrant their consideration. Warner (1977) considered the bankruptcy of large public limited companies and found that direct bankruptcy costs were insignificant. More recent research by Altman (1984) into the bankruptcy of industrial companies found that the combined direct and indirect costs at the time of filing for bankruptcy averaged 16.7 per cent of a company's value. This figure is clearly significant, even after allowing for the probability of bankruptcy occurring and its time of occurrence.

8.9.2 Agency costs

At higher levels of gearing, in addition to bankruptcy costs, there are costs associated with the problem of agency. If gearing levels are high, shareholders have a lower stake in a company and have less funds at risk if the company fails. They will therefore prefer the company to invest in high risk/high return projects, since they will enjoy the benefit of the higher returns that arise. Providers of debt finance, however, will not share in the higher returns from such high-risk projects, since their returns are not dependent on company performance. They will take steps, then, to prevent the company from undertaking high-risk projects which might put their investment at risk. They may, for example, impose restrictive covenants on the management. Such covenants could restrict future dividend payments, place restrictions on ways of raising finance, or impose minimum levels of liquidity. Alternatively, debt holders may increase the level of management monitoring and require a higher level of financial information with respect to the company's activities. The costs associated with the agency problem will further eat into the beneficial tax shield associated with increasing gearing levels.

8.9.3 Tax-exhaustion

Another explanation of why companies do not adopt higher levels of gearing arises from the fact that many companies will become tax-exhausted as they increase their gearing level. This will prevent them from enjoying the tax-shield benefits associated with high gearing but still leave them with bankruptcy and agency costs. The combination of bankruptcy and agency costs and the fact that companies may become tax-exhausted at high levels of gearing explains why companies, in contradiction to Miller and Modigliani's second paper, do not adopt 100 per cent debt capital structures.

8.10 MILLER AND PERSONAL TAXATION

Although Miller and Modigliani amended their earlier paper to take into account the effects of corporate tax in 1963, it was left to Miller (1977) to integrate the effects of personal taxes into their model. Miller's model, which considers the relationship that exists between gearing levels, corporate tax, the rate of personal taxation of debt and equity returns and the amount of debt and equity available for investors to invest in, is a very complex one. The following explanation represents a simplification of his model.

Given a company's capital structure and the level of debt finance and equity finance that it and other companies have issued, investors will choose investments in companies that suit their personal taxation situation. For instance, investors who are in an income-tax-paying situation will be inclined to invest in equity shares, in preference to debt, due to the delay of capital gains tax and capital gains allowances associated with equity shares. Hence, when the economy is in equilibrium, all investors will be holding investments that suit their personal tax situation. In order for a company to increase its debt finance and take advantage of the associated tax benefits, it will have to persuade equity holders to swap their equity shares for debt securities. Because this will involve investors moving to a less favourable personal tax position they will have to be 'bribed' by the company through a higher, more attractive interest rate on the new debt. This, according to Miller's model, will have the effect of cancelling out the tax benefits of the extra debt, therefore leaving the company's cost of capital unchanged. The result is a horizontal WACC curve similar to that in Miller and Modigliani's first model, which was illustrated earlier in Exhibit 8.5. As with both Miller and Modigliani's previous models, Miller's 1977 paper did not take into account bankruptcy risk. If his model is modified to take into account the bankruptcy costs which exist at high levels of gearing, then we arrive at a WACC curve of the shape indicated in Exhibit 8.8.

EXHIBIT 8.8

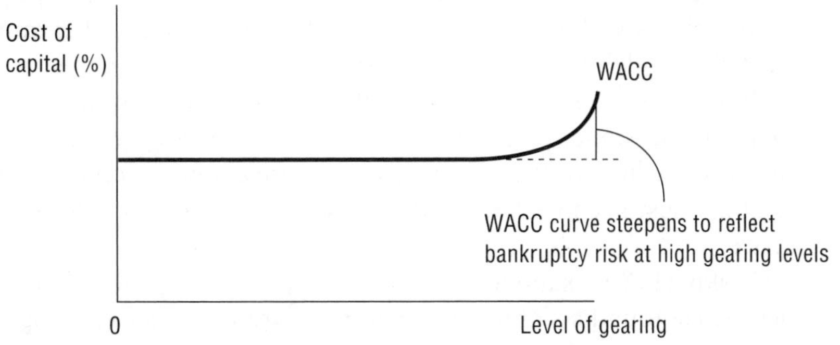

Miller's 1977 model, incorporating bankruptcy risk

Miller's paper was applicable to the tax regime that was prevalent in the US during the 1970s. Since then, as in the UK, the US tax regime has changed so that there is now only a small difference in the personal tax treatment of debt and equity returns. This implies that, overall, the introduction of personal tax into the capital structure debate reduces, but does not eradicate, the corporate tax savings associated with an increase in gearing level.

8.11 PECKING ORDER THEORY

The concept of pecking order theory, which was first introduced by Donaldson (1961), goes against the idea of companies having a unique combination of debt and equity finance which minimises their cost of capital. The theory suggests that when a company is looking to finance its long-term investments, it has a well-defined order of preference with respect to the sources of finance it uses. The first preference is to use internal or retained earnings over external sources of finance. If these prove insufficient the most preferred source of external source of finance is bank borrowings and corporate bonds. After exhausting both of these possibilities, the final and least preferred source of finance is to issue new equity capital.

The initial explanation put forward to explain such preferences involves issue costs and the ease at which the sources are accessed. With retained earnings there are no issue costs, dealings or negotiations with third parties such as banks. As for the choice between new debt and issuing shares, the issue costs associated with debt are much smaller than those of issuing equity.

A more sophisticated explanation for the existence of the pecking order was put forward by Myers (1984). He suggested that the order of preference stemmed from the existence of asymmetry of information between the company and the markets. For example, suppose that a company is wanting to raise finance for a new project and the market has underestimated the benefit of it. The management, with their inside information, will consider the company to be undervalued by the market. Therefore, they will want to finance the project through retained earnings so that, when the market finally sees the true value of the project, the existing shareholders will benefit. If there are insufficient retained earnings, the company will choose debt finance in preference to issuing new shares, as the management will not want to issue new shares if they consider them to be undervalued by the market. The opposite is true if the company considers the market to be overvaluing it in the light of the new project they are about to accept. In this situation they will be most keen to issue new shares at what they consider to be an overvalued price.

Baskin (1989) examined the relationship between profits and companies' gearing levels. He found a significant negative relationship between high profits and high gearing levels, in sharp contradiction to the idea of the existence of an optimal capital structure. His findings, then, gave support to the existence of pecking order theory.

8.12 DOES AN OPTIMAL CAPITAL STRUCTURE EXIST? A CONCLUSION

In this chapter we have shown that gearing is an important consideration for companies. Some academic theories support the existence of an optimal capital structure (i.e. the traditional approach, and Miller and Modigliani (II) with bankruptcy costs). Others argue that one capital structure is as good as another (Miller and Modigliani (I), and Miller). When considering the market imperfections that exist, such as corporate and personal taxation and bankruptcy and agency costs, we tend towards accepting the existence of an optimal capital structure. In practice, though, it is more likely that there exists a range of capital structures with which a company can minimise its WACC (i.e. between P and Q in Exhibit 8.9) rather than one particular combination of debt and equity financing (i.e. optimal capital structure) that such academic theories as the traditional approach suggest. This implies that the WACC curve will be flatter in practice when compared with the U-shaped curve academic theories put forward.

In conclusion, it appears that by integrating sensible levels of debt into its capital structure a company can enjoy the tax advantages arising from debt finance and reduce the level of its weighted average cost of capital, as long as it does not increase its gearing to levels that give rise to concern among its investors about its possible bankruptcy.

EXHIBIT 8.9

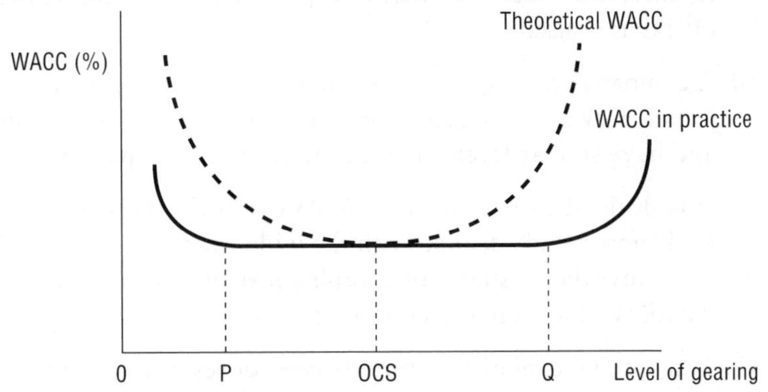

The relationship between the academic approach to optimal capital structure and weighted average cost of capital in practice

KEY POINTS

1 A company's cost of capital is a fundamental determinant of its market value, since its cost of capital is used as the discount rate in investment appraisal methods such as net present value and internal rate of return.

2 A major determinant of a company's cost of capital is its cost of equity finance, which can be calculated using either the Gordon growth model or the capital asset pricing model.

3 The calculation of the cost of preference shares and irredeemable bonds is straightforward. The dividend or interest payment is divided by the security's market value.

4 Calculating the cost of redeemable bonds is more difficult, as their cost of capital is found by using an internal rate of return calculation or a bond approximation formula.

5 The cost of bank loans, which have no market value, is approximated by the interest rate paid on them.

6 If a company is in a tax-paying position, the cost of debt finance must be adjusted to take into account the tax-deductibility of interest payments.

7 The costs of the individual sources of finance must be weighted according to their relative importance, using either market or book values.

8 While book values are easier to find and more stable, it is better to use market values as they reflect the true value of a company's securities.

9 A company can calculate its average cost of capital, which represents existing finance, or its marginal cost of capital, which represents the cost of incremental capital raised.

10 A company's average cost of capital is only appropriate for appraising new projects if they are financed in similar proportions to its existing capital structure and have similar levels of risk to that of the company as a whole.

11 It is difficult in practice to calculate a company's cost of capital or WACC. Problems include dealing with the wide variety of sources of finance used by a company; the existence of complex instruments such as convertibles; and the volatility of a company's cost of capital.

12 The optimal capital structure debate addresses the question of whether or not a company can minimise its cost of capital by adopting a particular combination of debt and equity finance.

13 Many academic papers have addressed the optimal capital structure question. The traditional approach argued that an optimal capital structure did exist for companies.

14 Miller and Modigliani's first paper argued that a company's value was solely determined by its investment decisions and therefore independent of its financing policy, supporting their argument with arbitrage theory. While academically sound, their model was based on a number of restrictive and unrealistic assumptions.

15 Miller and Modigliani later modified their earlier model to take account of corporate taxes and argued that companies should gear up in order to take advantage of the tax shield of debt. If this later model is modified to take into account the existence of bankruptcy and agency costs at high levels of gearing, then an optimal capital structure emerges.

16 Miller amended their earlier model to take into account the differences in the personal tax treatment of equity and debt returns. He argued that the need to 'bribe' investors into holding more debt cancelled out the tax benefits to companies of issuing extra debt finance, and concluded that all combinations of debt and equity finance were optimal.

17 Pecking order theory suggests that companies, rather than seeking an optimal capital structure, have a preference for retained over external funds and a preference for new debt rather than new equity.

18 In practice it seems plausible that companies can reduce their cost of capital by integrating sensible levels of debt finance into their balance sheet. Whether a company can accurately locate its range of optimal capital structures is open to debate.

QUESTIONS

Answers to these questions can be found on pages 421–2.

1 Gorky plc has in issue 500 000 £1 ordinary shares whose current ex-dividend market price is £1.50 per share. The company has just paid a dividend of 27p per share, and dividends are expected to continue at this level for some time. If the company has no debt capital, what is the weighted average cost of capital?

2 Five years ago, Eranio plc issued 12 per cent irredeemable debentures at £103, a £3 premium to their par value of £100. The current market price of these debentures is £94. If the company pays corporation tax at a rate of 35 per cent what is its current cost of debenture capital?

3 Pollock plc has a capital structure consisting of one million ordinary shares, par value 25p and £100 000 of 10 per cent irredeemable debentures. The current ex-dividend market price of the ordinary shares is 49p per share, and the current ex-interest market price of the debentures is £72 per £100 block. The company has just paid a dividend of 9p per share and dividends are expected to continue at this level indefinitely. If the company pays corporation tax at a rate of 33 per cent, what is its weighted average cost of capital?

4 Should companies use their weighted average cost of capital as the discount rate when assessing the acceptability of new projects?

5 A company incorporates increasing amounts of debt finance into its capital structure while leaving its operating risk unchanged. Assuming that a perfect capital market exists with no taxation, will the company's weighted average cost of capital:

(a) fall slowly;

(b) fall quickly;

(c) remain the same;

(d) fall to a minimum and then rise;

(e) rise steadily?

6 One-third of the total market value of Johnson plc consists of loan stock, which has a cost of 10 per cent. Another company, York, is identical in every respect to Johnson plc, except that its capital structure is all-equity, and its cost of equity is 16 per cent. According to Modigliani and Miller, if we ignored taxation and tax relief on debt capital, what would be the cost of equity of Johnson plc?

7 Which of the following statements concerning capital structure is incorrect?

(a) Bankruptcy risk is ignored in Miller and Modigliani's first model.

(b) Debt holders are not subject to the effects of financial risk.

(c) The traditional approach assumes that capital markets are perfect.

(d) Miller and Modigliani's second paper takes into account the effects of corporate taxation.

(e) Miller and Modigliani's first model argues that no optimal capital structure exists and supports this proposition with arbitrage theory.

8 If a company finds that its cost of capital has changed does this affect the profitability of the company?

9 Briefly explain the traditional view that an optimal capital structure exists.

10 What is the significance of the arbitrage proof for Miller and Modigliani's first paper on the cost of capital?

QUESTIONS FOR REVIEW

Answers to these questions can be found on pages 422–4.

1 Calet plc, which pays corporation tax at 33 per cent, has the following capital structure:

Ordinary shares: 1 000 000 ordinary shares of nominal value 25p per share. The market value of the shares is 49p per share. A dividend of 7p per share has just been paid, and dividends are expected to grow by eight per cent per year for the foreseeable future.

Preference shares: 250 000 preference shares of nominal value 50p per share. The market value of the shares is 32p per share and the annual net dividend of 7.5 per cent has just been paid.

Debentures: £100 000 of irredeemable debentures with a market price of £92 per £100 block. These debentures have a coupon rate of 10 per cent and the annual interest payment has just been made.

Calculate the weighted average after-tax cost of capital of Calet plc.

2 Smith plc, a quoted company, has the following long-term capital structure:

	£000
Ordinary shares, 50p each	4 000
16 per cent debentures	9 000
	13 000

The current share price of Smith plc is £3.50 and the current market price of the debentures is £112 per £100 block. Smith plc pays corporation tax at a rate of 33 per cent.

Calculate the capital gearing of Smith plc based on (a) market values, and (b) book values, and discuss why a market-based estimate of capital gearing is generally considered to be superior.

3 Carbon and Short plc both operate in the same industry with the same business risk. Their earnings, capital structure, share prices and other data are as follows:

	Carbon plc	*Short plc*
	£000	*£000*
Annual dividends	500	1000
Annual interest	—	200
Annual cash flow	500	1200
Equity market value	3125	6000
Debt market value	—	2000
Total market value	3125	8000
Cost of equity capital	16%	16.6%
Cost of debt capital		10%
WACC	16%	15%
No. of shares in issue	3.25m	5m
Market price per share	96p	120p

(a) If Kitson, an investor, holds £1000 worth of shares in Short plc and can borrow at the same rate as Short, show how he can increase his wealth through arbitrage. Ignore taxes and transaction costs.

(b) If the rate of corporation tax is 40 per cent, calculate an equilibrium price for the shares of the two companies in a modified Miller and Modigliani world (i.e. one which allows for taxation).

4 Paisley Brothers plc, a company producing loud paisley shirts, has a net operating income of £2000 and is faced with the following three options of how to structure its debt and equity:

(a) to take no debt and pay shareholders a return of nine per cent;

(b) borrow £5000 at three per cent and pay shareholders an increased return of 10 per cent;

(c) borrow £9000 at six per cent and pay a 13 per cent return to shareholders.

Assuming no taxation and a 100 per cent payout ratio, calculate the WACC for each of the options and determine which method is optimal.

5 The calculation of WACC is straightforward in theory, but in practice it not an easy task. Outline any possible difficulties that might be experienced when trying to calculate WACC.

QUESTIONS FOR DISCUSSION

1 The following information has been extracted from the accounts of Merlin plc:

Balance sheet as at 30 June 19X8

	Notes	*£000*	*£000*	*£000*
Fixed assets:				
Freehold property				712
Plant and equipment				160
				872
Current assets:				
Stocks			240	
Debtors			300	
Cash			33	
			573	
Current liabilities:				
Trade creditors		120		
Bank overdraft		200		
			320	
Net current assets				253
Total assets less current liabilities				1125
Long-term liabilities:				
12% debentures	(a)		500	
9% convertible loan stock	(b)		250	
				750
				375
Capital and reserves:				
Ordinary shares, £1 each	(c)			225
Reserves				150
				375

Notes

(a) The 12 per cent debentures are redeemable in five years' time at par. Annual interest has just been paid. The current ex-interest market price of the debenture is £114.

(b) The nine per cent loan stock is convertible in three years' time into 40 ordinary shares of Merlin plc per £100 block, or in four years' time into 35 ordinary shares per £100 block. The current ex-interest market price of the convertible loan stock is £119.

(c) The current ex-dividend market price of the ordinary shares of Merlin plc is £3.14. Both dividends and share price are expected to increase by seven per cent per year for the foreseeable future.

(d) Corporation tax is at a rate of 33 per cent.
   (i) Calculate the redemption yield of the straight debentures.
   (ii) If ordinary loan stock of a similar risk class is expected to be trading at £125 in three years' time, and at £128 in four years' time, calculate the return required by investors holding the convertible loan stock.
   (iii) If a dividend of 35p per ordinary share has just been paid, calculate the return required by ordinary shareholders.
   (iv) Calculate the weighted average after-tax cost of capital of Merlin plc.

2 Critically discuss whether you consider that companies, by integrating a sensible level of gearing into their capital structure, can minimise their weighted average cost of capital.

3 You are given the following information about Jordan plc:

Balance sheet at January 1997

	£000	£000
Ordinary shares (50p)		200
Reserves		150
7% preference shares (£1)		300
9% debentures (redeemable January 2005)		650
9% bank loans		560
		1860
Fixed assets		1511
Current assets	672	
Current liabilities	323	349
		1860

You are also given the following information:

Yield on government Treasury bills	7%
Company equity beta	1.21
Market risk premium	9.1%
Current ex-div ordinary share price	£2.35
Current ex-div preference share price	66p
Current ex-interest debenture market value	£105
Corporation tax rate	35%

Calculate the company's WACC using market weightings.

REFERENCES

Altman, E. (1984) 'A further empirical investigation of the bankruptcy cost question', *Journal of Finance*, Vol. 39, pp. 1067–89.
Baskin, J.B. (1989) 'An empirical investigation of the pecking order hypthosesis', *Financial Management*, Vol. 18, pp. 26–35.
Baxter, N. (1967) 'Leverage, risk of ruin and the cost of capital', *Journal of Finance*, Vol. 26, pp. 395–403.
Donaldson, G. (1961) *Corporate Debt Capacity*, Harvard University Press.
Hawanini, G. and Vora, A. (1982) 'Yield approximations: an historical perspective', *Journal of Finance*, March, pp. 145–56.
Miller, M. (1977) 'Debt and taxes', *Journal of Finance*, Vol. 32, pp. 261–75.
Miller, M. and Modigliani, F. (1958) 'The cost of capital, corporation finance and the theory of investment', *American Economic Review*, Vol. 48, pp. 261–96.
Miller, M. and Modigliani, F. (1963) 'Taxes and the cost of capital: a correction', *American Economic Review*, Vol. 53, pp. 433–43.
Myers, S. (1984) 'The capital structure puzzle', *Journal of Finance*, Vol. 39, pp. 575–92.
Warner, J. (1977) 'Bankruptcy costs: some evidence', *Journal of Finance*, Vol. 26, pp. 337–48.

RECOMMENDED READING

Alexander, I. (1995) *Cost of Capital*, Oxera Press. This text is solely dedicated to the subject of cost of capital and its calculation and is extremely enlightening.

Stern, J. and Chew, D. (eds) (1986) *The Revolution in Corporate Finance*, Basil Blackwell; and Ward, K. (ed.) (1994) *Strategic Issues in Finance*, Butterworth-Heinemann. Both these texts collect together a number of very readable and interesting articles on the capital structure debate, including in Ward reprints of Miller and Modigliani's two seminal papers.

Important and informative papers and articles recommended for further reading on the subject of cost of capital and capital structure include the following:

Neish, S. (1994) 'Building the best balance sheet', *Corporate Finance*, March, pp. 26–31.
Rajan, R. and Zingales, L. (1997) 'Debt, folklore and financial structure', in *Mastering Finance*, Part 2, *Financial Times*, May.
Wilson, S.A. (1991) 'Industrial and commercial companies' gearing', *Bank of England Quarterly Bulletin*, May, pp. 228–33.

CHAPTER 9

PORTFOLIO THEORY AND THE CAPITAL ASSET PRICING MODEL

INTRODUCTION

An important relationship which underpins the majority of modern corporate finance theory is that of the trade-off between risk and return. This trade-off is important both from a company perspective, where companies face the risk of variability in cash flows from projects varying, and from an investor's point of view, where shareholders' returns vary due to fluctuations in share prices and dividends.

The aim of both companies and shareholders will be to minimise the risk they face given the return that they expect to receive. In order for them to do this though, they will need to have a firm understanding of why the risk they face exists in the first place. They may then be able to quantify the risk and hence manage or control it. Traditionally risk has been measured by the standard deviation of returns, the calculation of which will be considered in Section 9.1. Subsequent sections will examine how, by the careful combination of different investments, investors can 'trade-off' the amount of risk they face given the level of their expected return. This forms the basis of the portfolio theory which was developed by Markowitz (1952). The relationship between risk and return is then taken a step further by considering the capital asset pricing model developed by Sharpe (1964), which provides us with a framework by which to value individual securities according to their level of risk.

LEARNING OBJECTIVES

After studying this chapter, you should have achieved the following learning objectives:

- an ability to calculate the standard deviation of an investment's returns and to calculate the risk and return of a two-share portfolio;
- a firm understanding of both systematic and unsystematic risk and the concept of risk diversification using portfolio investment;
- the ability to explain the foundations of Markowitz's portfolio theory and discuss the problems associated with its practical application;
- an understanding of the capital asset pricing model and the assumptions upon which it is based;
- the ability to calculate the required rate of return of a security using the capital asset pricing model;
- the ability to explain how the capital asset pricing model can be used to calculate risk-adjusted discount rates for use in investment appraisal;
- an appreciation of the empirical research that has been undertaken to establish the applicability and reliability of the capital asset pricing model in practice.

9.1 THE MEASUREMENT OF RISK

Risk plays a very important role in the decision-making process for both investors and companies, so it is important that the level of risk associated with investment can be quantified. Risk is measured by the standard deviation (σ) of returns of a security, calculated using either the historical returns over time or the expected returns in the future.

9.1.1 Calculating risk and return using probabilities

In Exhibit 9.1 we can see the possible returns and associated probabilities of two securities A and B, where:

P_A = probability of return on A
R_A = the corresponding return on A
P_B = probability of return on B
R_B = the corresponding return on B.

EXHIBIT 9.1

A plc		*B plc*	
P_A	R_A (%)	P_B	R_B (%)
0.05	10	0.05	18
0.20	20	0.25	12
0.50	20	0.40	28
0.20	25	0.25	28
0.05	25	0.05	38
1.00		1.00	

The possible returns and associated probabilities of securities A and B

The expected returns and standard deviations of the two securities are given by the following formulae:

$$\text{Expected return of a security } (\bar{R}) = \sum_{i=1}^{n} P_i \times R_i$$

$$\text{Standard deviation } (\sigma) = \sqrt{\sum_{i=1}^{n} P_i \times (R_i - \bar{R})^2}$$

where: $P_1 \ldots P_n$ = the probabilities of the n different outcomes
$R_1 \ldots R_n$ = the corresponding returns associated with the n different outcomes.

By using the above formulae and the information provided we can calculate both the expected returns and the standard deviations for the two securities.

Expected return of security A:
$(0.05 \times 10) + (0.20 \times 20) + (0.50 \times 20) + (0.20 \times 25) + (0.05 \times 25) = 20.75$ per cent

Expected return of security B:
$(0.05 \times 18) + (0.25 \times 12) + (0.40 \times 28) + (0.25 \times 28) + (0.05 \times 38) = 24$ per cent

Standard deviation of security A:
$((0.05 \times (10 - 20.75)^2) + (0.20 \times (20 - 20.75)^2) + (0.50 \times (20 - 20.75)^2) + (0.20 \times (25 - 20.75)^2) + (0.05 \times (25 - 20.75)^2))^{1/2} = 3.27$ per cent

Standard deviation of security B:
$((0.05 \times (18 - 24)^2) + (0.25 \times (12 - 24)^2) + (0.40 \times (28 - 24)^2) + (0.25 \times (28 - 24)^2) + (0.05 \times (38 - 24)^2))^{1/2} = 7.62$ per cent

Here we can see that while security B has a higher expected level of return compared to A, it also has a correspondingly higher level of risk.

9.1.2 Calculating risk and return using historical data

The mean and standard deviation of the annual returns of a security, calculated over a number of years, can be found using the following equations.

$$\text{Mean return } (\bar{R}) = \frac{\sum_{i=1}^{n} R_i}{n}$$

$$\text{Standard deviation } (\sigma) = \sqrt{\frac{\sum_{i=1}^{n} (R_i - \bar{R})^2}{n}}$$

Exhibit 9.2 is a table of data detailing the historic returns of two securities, S and T, over the past five years.

EXHIBIT 9.2

Year (t)	*S return (%)*	*T return (%)*
– 4	6.6	24.5
– 3	5.6	– 5.9
– 2	– 9.0	19.9
– 1	12.6	– 7.8
0	14.0	14.8

The historic returns of two securities, S and T

Using the historical returns data and the formulae above:

Mean return of security S:

$(6.6 + 5.6 + (-9.0) + 12.6 + 14.0)/5 = 5.96$ per cent

Mean return of security T:

$(24.5 + (-5.9) + 19.9 + (-7.8) + 14.8)/5 = 9.10$ per cent

Standard deviation of security S:

$(((6.6 - 5.96)^2 + (5.6 - 5.96)^2 + (-9.0 - 5.96)^2$
$+ (12.6 - 5.96)^2 + (14.0 - 5.96)^2)/5)^{1/2} = 8.16$ per cent

Standard deviation of security T:

$$(((24.5 - 9.10)^2 + (-5.9 - 9.10)^2 + (19.9 - 9.10)^2 + (-7.8 - 9.10)^2 + (14.8 - 9.10)^2)/5)^{1/2}$$
$$= 13.39 \text{ per cent}$$

We can see that while security T has a higher historic level of return when compared to S, it also has a higher standard deviation. In Exhibit 9.3 we can see a graphical representation of the distribution of returns of the two securities. T has a higher mean or expected return, but has a flatter normal distribution curve when compared to S, due to its higher standard deviation.

EXHIBIT 9.3

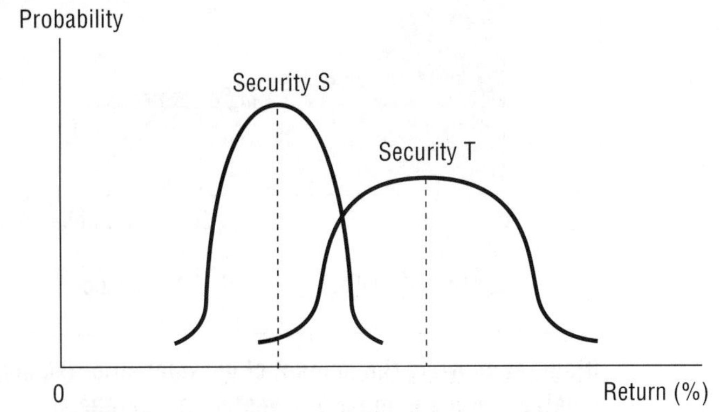

Graph showing the distribution of returns of securities S and T

9.2 THE CONCEPT OF DIVERSIFICATION

Earlier we mentioned that in order for investors to control and manage risk it is important for them to understand why risk exists in the first place. Therefore, it is useful to consider that the overall level of risk that investors and companies face can be separated into systematic and unsystematic risk. Systematic risk (also known as non-diversifiable, non-specific, unavoidable or market risk) represents how an investment's returns are affected by systematic factors, i.e. business cycles, the application of tariffs, the possibilities of war, etc. Systematic risk accounts for roughly 30 per cent of an individual share's total risk.

Unsystematic risk (or diversifiable, specific, avoidable or non-market risk) is the risk specific to a particular security, i.e. the risk of the individual company performing badly or going into liquidation. While this type of risk accounts for approximately 70 per cent of an individual share's total risk, investors can progressively reduce unsystematic risk by spreading their investments over a larger number of different securities. It is this possibility of investors reducing unsystematic risk through holding diversified portfolios of shares that forms the basis of Markowitz's portfolio theory. A graphical illustration of the relationship between systematic and unsystematic risk relative to the number of different investments held by an investor is shown in Exhibit 9.4. If an investor spreads their investment over approximately 12 shares of companies in different industries, about 90 per cent of all unsystematic risk will be eradicated. This increases to 95 per cent if the number of investments is increased to approximately 30 investments.

EXHIBIT 9.4

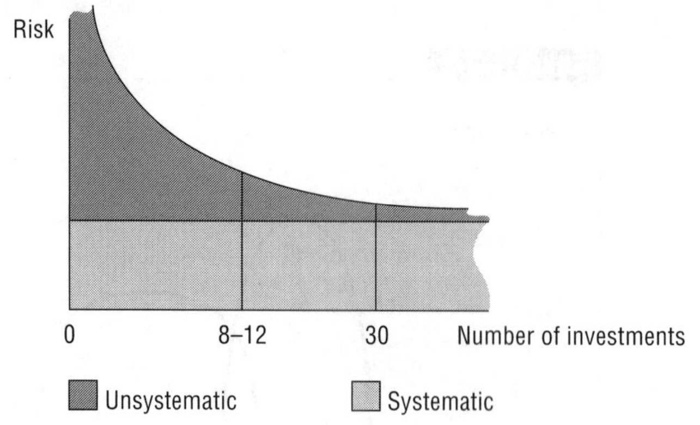

Diagram showing the amount of unsystematic risk diversification obtained as the number of investments increases

9.2.1 Diversifying unsystematic risk using a two-share portfolio

The simplest form of diversification to consider is that using a two-share portfolio. The extent to which investors will be able to reduce unsystematic risk using a two-share portfolio depends upon the correlation that exists between the two investments' returns. This correlation can be quantified by calculating the correlation coefficient (ρ) of the returns of the two securities, which can take any value in the range –1 to 1. What does the value of the correlation coefficient imply?

If $\rho_{x,y} = 1$ No unsystematic risk can be diversified away.
If $\rho_{x,y} = -1$ All unsystematic risk will be diversified away.
If $\rho_{x,y} = 0$ No correlation between the two securities' returns.

Therefore, when picking a two-share portfolio it is most beneficial to choose two shares whose correlation coefficient is as close to –1 as possible. However, as long as the correlation coefficient is not exactly +1 some unsystematic risk will be diversified away. In practice it may be difficult to find two securities whose correlation coefficient is exactly –1, but the most commonly quoted example is that of an umbrella manufacturer and an ice cream company. Work this one out for yourselves!!

The correlation coefficient ($\rho_{x,y}$) can be calculated by the formula below:

$$\rho_{x,y} = \frac{Cov_{x,y}}{\sigma_x \sigma_y}$$

where $Cov_{x,y}$ = covariance of returns of securities x and y.

Therefore, if using expected return data, ρ_{xy} is given by:

$$\frac{\sum_{i=1}^{n} P_i (R_{ix} - \bar{R}_x) \times (R_{iy} - \bar{R}_y)}{\sigma_x \times \sigma_y}$$

and if using historical data $\rho_{x,y}$ is given by:

$$\frac{\sum_{i=1}^{n} (R_{ix} - \bar{R}_x) \times (R_{iy} - \bar{R}_y)}{n\sigma_x \sigma_y}$$

The formulae to calculate the return and risk of a two-share portfolio are given below. The return of a two-share portfolio formula is a weighted average of the two shares' expected returns, while the standard deviation formula is more complex due to the diversification of unsystematic risk that occurs.

Return of a two-share portfolio (R_p):

$$R_p = (W_x \bar{R}_x) + (W_y \bar{R}_y)$$

Standard deviation of a two-share portfolio (σ_p):

$$\sigma_p = \sqrt{(W_x)^2 (\sigma_x)^2 + (W_y)^2 (\sigma_y)^2 + 2W_x W_y \sigma_x \sigma_y \rho_{xy}}$$

where:
- W_x = percentage of funds invested in investment x
- W_y = percentage of funds invested in investment y
- $\bar{R}_x$ = mean return of investment x (per cent)
- $\bar{R}_y$ = mean return of investment y (per cent)
- σ_x = standard deviation of investment x's returns
- σ_y = standard deviation of investment y's returns
- $\rho_{x,y}$ = correlation coefficient between x and y's returns.

Using annual returns of the two securities S and T from our earlier example we can calculate the return and risk of a series of portfolios consisting of differing amounts of S and T. First, though, we need to calculate the correlation coefficient between the returns of the two securities:

$\rho_{S,T}$ = ((6.6 – 5.96) × (24.5 – 9.10) + (5.6 – 5.96) × (–5.9 – 9.10) + (–9.0 – 5.96) × (19.9 – 9.10) + (12.6 – 5.96) × (–7.8 – 9.10) + (14.0 – 5.96) × (14.8 – 9.10))/(5 × 8.16 × 13.39) = –0.389

We can now calculate the risk and return of two-share portfolios made up of securities S and T. For example, the risk and return of a portfolio consisting of 80 per cent of S and 20 per cent of T are as follows:

Return of portfolio = $(0.8 \times 5.96) + (0.2 \times 9.1) = 6.59$ per cent
Risk of portfolio = $((0.8^2 \times 8.16^2) + (0.2^2 \times 13.39^2) + (2 \times 0.8 \times 0.2 \times 8.16 \times 13.39 \times -0.389))^{1/2} = 6.02$

The results of these calculations are given numerically in Exhibit 9.5, where:

A = 80 per cent S + 20 per cent T
B = 60 per cent S + 40 per cent T
C = 40 per cent S + 60 per cent T
D = 20 per cent S + 80 per cent T.

EXHIBIT 9.5

	All S	*A*	*B*	*C*	*D*	*All T*
Mean	5.96	6.59	7.21	7.84	8.47	9.10
Variance	66.59	36.18	32.26	54.80	103.81	179.29
Standard deviation	8.16	6.02	5.68	7.40	10.18	13.39

Diversification of risk in a portfolio containing securities S and T

The results of the above calculations are also illustrated graphically in Exhibit 9.6.

EXHIBIT 9.6

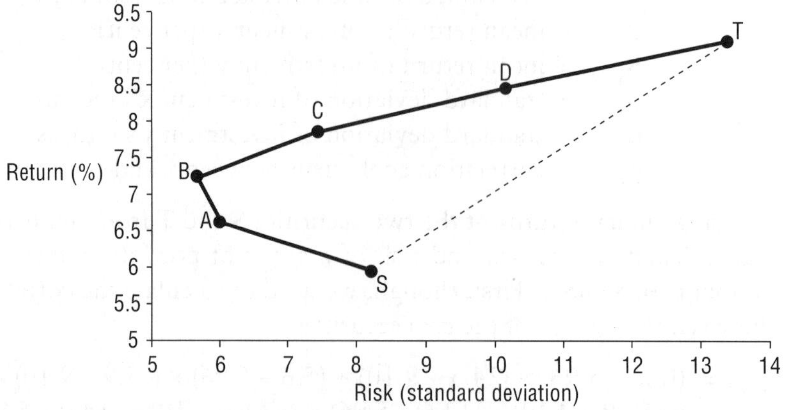

A graphical representation of the risk and return of portfolios consisting of different combinations of securities S and T

From Exhibit 9.6 it can be seen that an investor can locate themselves anywhere along the arc SABCDT according to how they divide their portfolio between the shares S and T. The points along the arc are superior to those on the straight line between security S and security T due to the diversification of unsystematic risk that occurs when more than one security is held.

9.2.2 Diversifying unsystematic risk using a three-share portfolio

With the introduction of an additional share into the portfolio there is even further scope for the diversification of unsystematic risk. The introduction of a higher risk and return share R into the earlier example is represented graphically in Exhibit 9.7, where:

ST represents portfolios of securities S and T;
SR (dotted line) represents portfolios of securities S and R;
TR represents portfolios of securities T and R;
SR (bold line) represents portfolios of securities T, S and R.

EXHIBIT 9.7

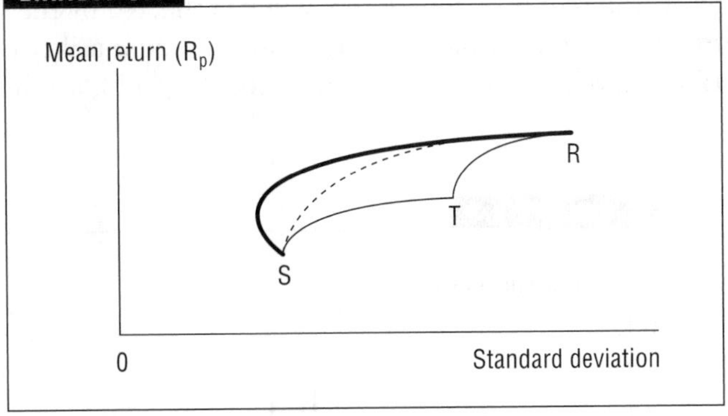

A graphical representation of the risk and return of portfolios consisting of combinations of securities S, T and R

Here we can see that the optimal set of portfolios is achieved when all three shares are invested in (i.e. the bold line SR). This optimal frontier is superior to investing in just S and T due to a greater ability to diversify away unsystematic risk when investing in all three shares. As more shares are added to the investment portfolio, progressively more and more unsystematic risk will be diversified away. This principle forms the basis of Markowitz's portfolio theory, where the investor's choice of investments is not just limited to three shares but includes all available risky securities. Before we go on to consider Markowitz's theory, however, let us first consider investor attitudes to risk and return.

9.3 INVESTOR ATTITUDES TO RISK

How much risk will an investor accept in the first place? The answer to this question depends upon how much utility an individual investor or company receives from taking risk. The three possible attitudes that investors and companies can have towards risk can be summarised as follows:

- *risk loving*, where the investor has a preference for high return in exchange for taking a high level of risk;
- *risk neutral*, where the investor is indifferent to the level of risk they face;
- *risk averse*, where the investor has a preference for low-risk, low-return investments.

While attitudes towards risk may differ, one thing that must be consistent is that investors act rationally and do not expose themselves to higher levels of risk without the possibility of higher returns. A common misconception that is often levelled at risk-loving investors is that they are acting irrationally. This is not the case, however, as investors with a preference for taking risks will only be prepared to incur a higher level of risk if it is accompanied by a correspondingly higher level of possible return.

The attitudes of investors to risk will be reflected by the shape of their utility (or indifference) curves, which join up points of equal utility or satisfaction. Two sets of utility curves for two different investors, U and I, are shown in Exhibit 9.8.

EXHIBIT 9.8

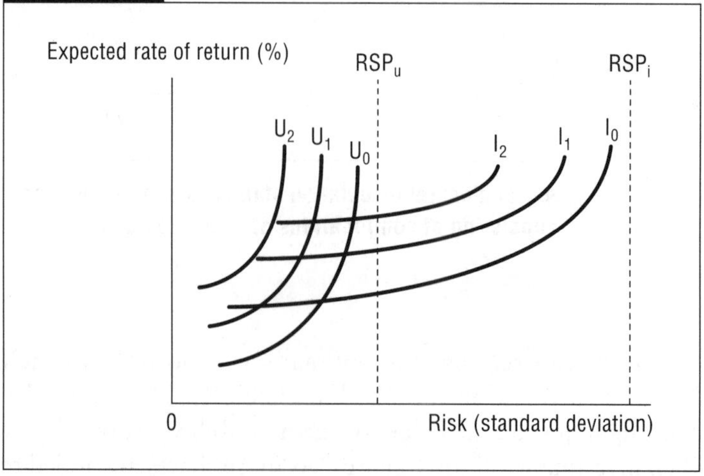

Utility curves for risk-loving (I) and risk-averse (U) investors

Both sets of curves slope upwards from left to right due to the fact that as risk increases an investor will require higher return to keep their utility constant. The utility curves slope upwards at an increasing rate due to an increasing marginal rate of substitution, i.e. in order for an investor to take on progressively more units of risk, progressively higher rates of return are required to compensate them and keep their utility constant. Investors will try to increase their level of utility by seeking the highest return for a given level of risk, or by seeking the lowest risk for a given level of return. The higher the utility or indifference curve, the more satisfied will be the investor.

While there are similarities between the utility curves of investor U and investor I, a major difference between them is the rate at which they slope upwards. Investor U's curves quickly steepen at low levels of risk, indicating that this investor is risk averse; the opposite is true for risk-loving investor I, whose curves are much flatter. The risk saturation point, i.e. the level of risk that an investor will not go beyond, is much lower for investor U (indicated by the vertical line RSP_u) when compared to that of investor I (RSP_i).

Having earlier considered the portfolio choices available to investors in Section 9.2, we are now in a position to combine these choices with the utility curves of investors, thereby allowing investors to select portfolios which satisfy their preference for risk and return.

9.4 MARKOWITZ'S PORTFOLIO THEORY

The cornerstone of Markowitz's seminal theory, for which he was awarded a Nobel Prize in Economics in 1990, is the ability of investors to diversify away unsystematic risk by holding portfolios consisting of a number of different shares. Markowitz's starting point is to construct what is known as the *envelope* curve which represents a set of portfolio choices available to investors when investing in different combinations of risky securities. The envelope curve is represented by the shaded area AMEGH in Exhibit 9.9. Investors can construct a portfolio with risk and return characteristics anywhere in this shaded area by holding different combinations of risky securities in differing proportions.

While investors are able to locate themselves anywhere within the envelope curve, rational investors will only invest in those portfolios on the *efficient frontier* represented by the arc BME. It is called the efficient frontier because all portfolios on this arc are superior to (i.e. more efficient than) all other portfolios within the envelope curve, giving either the maximum return for a given level of risk, or the minimum risk for a given level of return. For example, if we compare portfolios A and N on the boundary of the envelope curve, which both have the same level of risk, we can see that portfolio N offers a higher return without incurring any additional risk. Portfolio N is said to dominate portfolio A. In fact, all the portfolios on the arc between A and B are dominated by portfolios on the arc BME, and so cannot be regarded as efficient.

For an investor with utility curves represented by I_1, I_2 and I_3 in Exhibit 9.9, an optimal portfolio of risky investments will occur at the point N where the utility curve is tangential to the efficiency frontier. Investor choice, however, is not just restricted to risky securities. By assuming that investors can lend and borrow at a

EXHIBIT 9.9

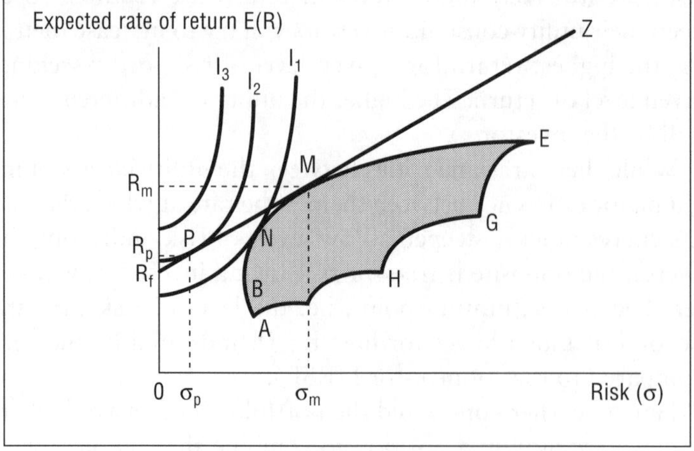

A graphical representation of Markowitz's portfolio theory

risk-free rate of return, we can construct what is known as the capital market line, represented here by the line R_fMZ. The starting point is to locate the rate of return on what is known as the risk-free asset, R_f, and plot it on the vertical axis. This risk-free rate is approximated by the yield on government treasury bills, which can be assumed to be virtually risk-free. If a line pivoting about R_f is then rotated clockwise until it reaches a point of tangency with the efficient frontier, we can locate the *market portfolio* M. This portfolio represents the optimal combination of risky securities given the existence of risk-free investments. Investors can now move along the capital market line by splitting their investment between risk-free assets and the market portfolio. Risk-averse investors will locate themselves at R_f by investing all their money in risk-free assets, while an investor putting all their funds into risky securities will locate themselves at M. Where investors locate themselves along the capital market line will depend on their risk preferences and hence the point of tangency of their utility curves with the capital market line. The investor we considered earlier in Exhibit 9.9 will locate at point P by putting the majority of his funds into risk-free assets and the remainder into the market portfolio.

Risk-loving investors will locate themselves to the right of M on the capital market line. They do this by putting all their money into the market portfolio and, in addition, borrowing at the risk-free rate and investing their borrowings in the market portfolio.

It is particularly important to understand the significance of the risk-free asset in Markowitz's portfolio theory. For a portfolio containing a large number of securities, the calculation of the portfolio risk (in order to facilitate an optimal investment decision for a given investor) involves incorporating correlation coefficients for every possible pair of securities. The number of expressions grows exponentially with the number of securities. However, the introduction of the risk-free asset simplifies enormously the calculation of portfolio risk since no security's returns are correlated with the return on the risk-free asset. All investors will choose to hold a combination of the market portfolio and the risk-free asset, i.e. a portfolio located on the capital market line, since any other portfolio will be dominated by a portfolio on the capital market line.

9.4.1 Problems with the practical application of portfolio theory

There are problems associated with trying to apply portfolio theory in practice, some of which are summarised below.

- It is unrealistic to assume that investors can borrow at the risk-free rate. Individuals and companies are not risk-free and will therefore not be able to borrow at the risk-free rate; they will be charged a premium to reflect their higher level of risk.
- There are problems associated with identifying the market portfolio, as this will require knowledge of the risk and return of all risky investments and their corresponding correlation coefficients.
- Having identified the make-up of the market portfolio it will then be expensive, from a transaction cost point of view, to construct. These costs will be prohibitive in the case of smaller investors.
- The market portfolio will change over time. This will be due both to shifts in the risk-free rate of return and in the envelope curve and hence the efficient frontier.

One way for smaller investors to get round the problems mentioned above is by buying a stake in a large diversified portfolio, for example by buying into unit trusts or investment trusts and what are called *index tracker funds*.

9.5 AN INTRODUCTION TO THE CAPITAL ASSET PRICING MODEL

In the previous section we discussed how risk can be split into systematic risk and unsystematic risk. We then went on to consider Markowitz's portfolio theory, which provided us with a framework of portfolio selection whereby investors can combine a diversified portfolio of risky securities with risk-free assets in order to maximise their utility. The capital asset pricing model (CAPM), which also considers the relationship between risk and return, is the method of share valuation developed by Sharpe (1964), who in his seminal paper attempted to 'construct a market equilibrium theory of asset prices under conditions of risk'. Sharpe, like Markowitz, was in 1990 awarded the Nobel Prize for Economics for his efforts.

The CAPM is in fact an extension of Markowitz's portfolio theory. While the 'normative' portfolio theory considers the total risk and return of portfolios and advises investors on which portfolios to invest in, the 'positive' CAPM uses the systematic risk of individual securities to determine their 'fair' price. In order to ignore the influence of unsystematic risk on the valuation of a security, it is required that investors have diversified away unsystematic risk by holding diversified portfolios.

As with most academic models, the CAPM is based on a simplified world using the following assumptions:

- investors are rational and therefore maximise their utility and do not take risk for risk's sake;
- all information is freely available to investors and having interpreted it investors arrive at similar expectations;
- investors are able to borrow and lend at the risk-free rate;
- investors hold diversified portfolios, eliminating all unsystematic risk;
- capital markets are perfectly competitive. The conditions required for this are: a large number of buyers and sellers; no one participant can influence the market; no taxes and transaction costs exist; no entry or exit barriers to the market; securities are divisible;
- shareholding occurs over a single standardised holding period.

While clearly these assumptions are at odds with the real world, we should refrain from dismissing the CAPM as unrealistic and impractical since, as Sharpe (1964) observed, 'the proper test of a theory is not the realism of its assumptions but the acceptability of its implications'. The issue of the CAPM's applicability and usefulness will be considered later in the chapter.

9.6 USING THE CAPM TO VALUE SHARES

Central to the CAPM is the existence of a linear relationship between risk and return. This linear relationship is defined by what is known as the security market line (SML), where the systematic risk of a security is compared with the risk and return of the market and the risk-free rate of return in order to calculate a required return for the security and hence a fair price. A graphical representation of the SML is given in Exhibit 9.10. From this the equation of the SML can be defined as:

$$R_j = R_f + \beta_j (R_m - R_f)$$

where: R_j = the rate of return of security j predicted by the model
R_f = the risk-free rate of return
β_j = the beta coefficient of security j
R_m = the return of the market.

In order for the CAPM to be applied to the valuation of capital assets, an understanding of the components that make up the SML and how they can be calculated or approximated is required. First, we will consider the beta coefficient, which is used to quantify a security's level of systematic risk.

EXHIBIT 9.10

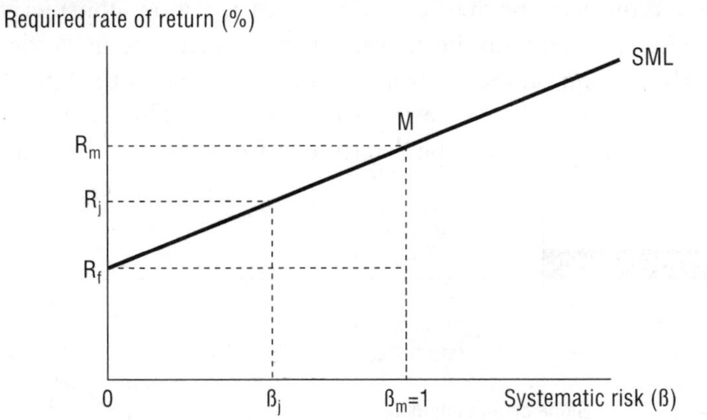

The security market line indicating the relationship between systematic risk (measured by beta) and the required rate of return on capital assets

9.6.1 The meaning and calculation of beta

The beta of a security can be defined as an index of responsiveness of the changes in returns of the security relative to a change in the stock exchange or 'market'. It measures the sensitivity of the returns on a company's ordinary share to changes in systematic factors. For example, for a security with a beta of 0.8 (i.e. less systematic risk than the market), if the market return increases by 10 per cent, the security's return will increase by eight per cent. If the market return decreases by 10 per cent, the return of the security decreases by eight per cent. This security represents what is known as a *defensive* security and is most attractive to investors when the stock exchange is falling. Alternatively, for a security with a beta of 1.5 (i.e. more systematic risk than the market), if the return of the market increases by 10 per cent, the security's return will increase by 15 per cent. If the market return decreases by 10 per cent, the return of the security decreases by 15 per cent. This is what is termed an *aggressive* security and is most attractive to investors when the market is rising. By definition, the beta of the market is 1 and this acts as a benchmark against which the systematic risk of securities can be measured.

The relationship between the beta of a security and the risk and return of the security and the market is given by the following equation:

$$\beta_j = \frac{\sigma_j \times \sigma_m \times \rho_{j,m}}{(\sigma_m)^2} = \frac{\sigma_j \times \rho_{j,m}}{\sigma_m}$$

where: σ_j = standard deviation of security j's returns
σ_m = standard deviation of returns of the market
$\rho_{j,m}$ = correlation coefficient between the security's returns and the market returns.

The calculation of a share's beta coefficient involves collecting data on the periodic returns of the market and the security under consideration. This data should then be plotted with the returns of the security on the vertical axis and the returns of the market on the horizontal axis. The slope of the line of best fit, or characteristic line, will then give the value of beta. This is illustrated in Exhibit 9.11. Alternatively, beta can be determined from the data by using regression analysis.

EXHIBIT 9.11

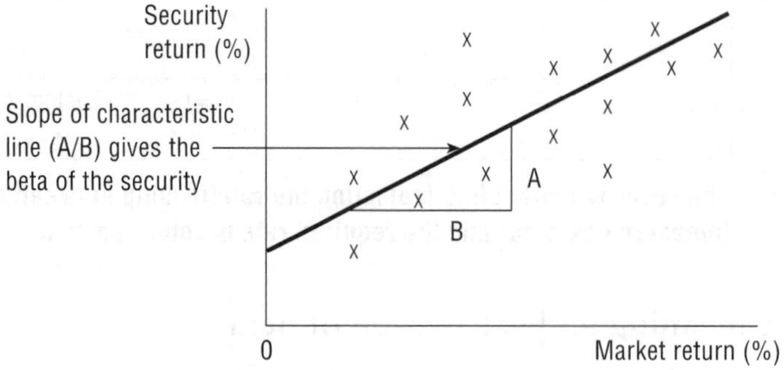

Finding the beta of a security by plotting the security's returns against those of the market

If regression analysis is used, the coefficient of variation (R^2) gives us an indication of the extent to which the regression equation, and hence the determined value of beta, explains the distribution of correlated returns. Put another way, the closer R^2 is to 100 per cent, the more of the total variability of a security's returns are explained by systematic factors as opposed to unsystematic factors.

A much easier way to find a security's beta is to leave it up to the experts! The Risk Measurement Service of the London Business School publishes quarterly beta books of companies' beta coefficients. They calculate the betas of all major companies by regressing securities' monthly returns against the monthly returns of the FT actuaries all-share index over the previous five years. An extract from one of the pages of the LBS's beta books is shown in Exhibit 9.12.

Not only do the beta books give company betas, they also provide other important information. The Variability column indicates the total variability of a share's returns measured by standard deviation. The Specific risk column gives the variability of a share's returns which is explained by specific factors measured by standard deviation. The Standard error column indicates the reliability of the beta coefficient calculated – the closer this is to zero the better. Finally, the R-squared column indicates, in percentage form, the amount of a share's total variability of returns that is explained by systematic factors. The relationship that exists between the total variability, the systematic variability and the specific variability of a share's returns is indicated on page 248.

EXHIBIT 9.12

Company	*Beta*	*Variability*	*Specific risk*	*Std error*	*R sq.*
Allied Domecq	1.05	20	15	0.14	44
Asda Group	1.07	36	33	0.25	15
BICC	1.18	29	24	0.20	28
Blue Circle Industries	1.11	29	25	0.21	25
BOC Group	0.69	16	13	0.13	30
Boots Co	1.00	19	14	0.14	44
British Airways	1.26	26	21	0.18	38
British Gas	0.80	19	16	0.15	29
British Petroleum	1.04	22	18	0.16	37
British Telecom	0.73	17	14	0.13	31
BTR	1.16	23	18	0.16	40
Cadbury-Schweppes	0.82	17	13	0.13	39
Courtaulds	1.07	24	20	0.18	32
EMI Group	1.09	21	16	0.15	43
General Electric	0.66	17	15	0.14	25
GKN	0.92	23	20	0.18	25
Glaxo Wellcome	0.63	22	20	0.18	14
Grand Metropolitan	1.14	20	14	0.14	51
Guinness	0.96	21	18	0.16	33
Hanson	0.87	19	15	0.14	35
ICI	0.66	18	16	0.15	21
Lucas Varity	1.40	31	25	0.21	34
Marks & Spencer	0.95	18	13	0.13	46
Nat West Bank	1.20	22	15	0.15	49
Peninsular and Orient	1.29	30	25	0.21	30
Reuters Holdings	1.04	22	17	0.16	37
Royal & Sun Alliance	1.28	25	20	0.18	41
SmithKline Beecham	0.63	22	20	0.18	14
Tate and Lyle	0.83	19	16	0.15	31
Vodafone Group	1.30	27	21	0.19	38

Extract from the beta books produced by the London Business School showing the beta, variability, specific risk, standard error of beta and R-squared of the constituents of the FT-30 Share Index

Source: London Business School, Risk Measurement Service, January–March 1997

Total variability of returns = systematic variability + specific variability

$$\sigma_j^2 = \beta_j^2 \times \sigma_m^2 + \sigma_{j.sp}^2$$

Algebraically 'R-squared' is represented by:

$$\frac{\beta_j^2 \times \sigma_m^2}{\sigma_j^2}$$

A frequency distribution of company betas is shown in Exhibit 9.13. It can be seen that the majority of company betas lie in the range between 0.7 and 1.4, with a beta of 1.1 being the most common. While it is mathematically possible for beta to be negative it is very rare in practice as few companies experience increasing returns in times of economic downturn. The most important determinant of a company's beta is the industry in which it operates. Companies with betas greater than one tend to be those in industries such as consumer durables, leisure and luxury goods. Companies with betas less than one usually come from industries such as food retailers, utilities and other necessity goods producers. A useful exercise is to look through the section of industrial betas that the London Business School includes in its beta books.

EXHIBIT 9.13

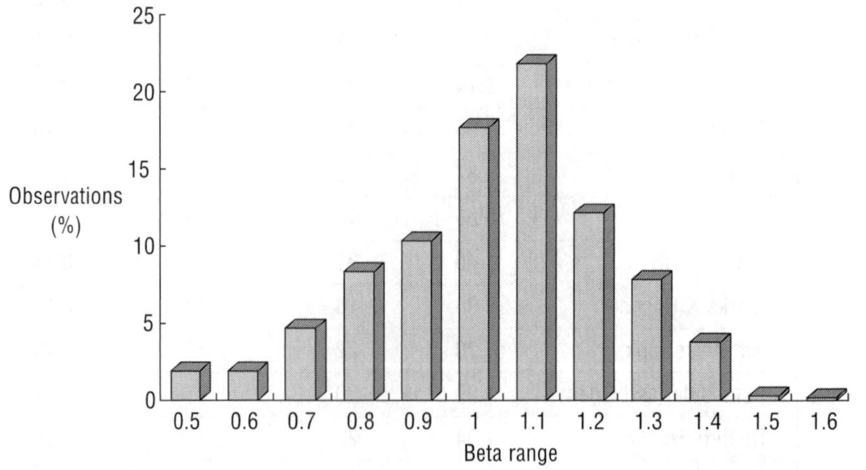

Bar chart showing the frequency distribution of equity betas of FT non-financials index companies

An important use of security betas is that they can be used to find the beta of a portfolio of shares. This allows the calculation of the required rate of return from the portfolio as a whole. An example is given in Exhibit 9.14.

EXHIBIT 9.14

Security	*Beta*	*Weighting (%)*	*Weighted beta*
BTR	0.90	20	0.180
Tesco	1.25	10	0.125
Rowntree	1.10	15	0.165
RTZ	1.15	20	0.230
BP	0.70	35	0.245
Portfolio beta		100	0.945

An example of how the beta of a portfolio can be calculated by weighting the betas of its constituent securities according to their relative market value

The beta of a portfolio is obtained by weighting the individual security betas by their relative market value (i.e. the number of shares multiplied by their price and divided by the total market value of the portfolio). In the example in Exhibit 9.14, the portfolio beta is 0.945, indicating that the portfolio has slightly less systematic risk than the market portfolio. One factor that must be noted with this example, though, is that a portfolio of only five shares will not diversify away all unsystematic risk, and therefore the risk of this portfolio will not just consist of systematic risk.

Having now built up a firm understanding of what beta represents and how it can be determined, we can now go on to consider the other variables required to use the CAPM.

9.6.2 Determining the risk-free rate and the return of the market

The risk-free rate, R_f, represents the rate of return earned by investing in risk-free assets. In reality, while no investments are risk-free, securities issued by the governments of politically and economically stable countries are generally considered to be free from the risk of default. Therefore, the risk-free rate can be approximated by taking the current rate of return or yield on short-dated government loan stock. In the UK this equates to the current yield on short-dated Treasury bills, which can be easily found in the *Financial Times*.

The return of the market, R_m, is a little more difficult to calculate. It is usually approximated by using stock exchange indices such as the FTSE 100 or FT actuaries all-share index, as a representation of the market. To find the return of the market, the capital gains of the chosen index over a period, say one year, should be added to the dividend yield of the shares in the index over the same period. This is given by the following formula, which allows us to approximate the return of the market over the period:

$$R_m = \frac{P_1 - P_0}{P_0} + Div$$

where: P_0 = the stock exchange index at the beginning of the period
P_1 = the stock exchange index at the end of the period
Div = average dividend yield of the stock exchange index over the period.

Due to the occurrence of short-term fluctuations in stock exchange indices it is advisable to make a number of calculations and then take a time-smoothed average in order to estimate the return of the market. For instance, if using monthly data, calculate the monthly return of the index over say a three-year period. Alternatively, if using annual data, calculate a moving average by shifting the year period back a month at a time to cover a number of years.

A number of empirical studies attempting to quantify the return of the market or rather the *market risk premium* ($R_m - R_f$), which represents the excess of market returns over and above those associated with investing in risk-free assets, have already been carried out. Dimson and Brealey (1978), using historical market returns for the UK over the period 1918–77, found an average market risk premium of nine per cent. A more recent estimation by Allan *et al.* (1986) over the longer time period 1919–84 found an average market risk premium of 9.1 per cent. A similar study carried out by Ibbotson Associates (1990) using US data over the period 1926–89 found an average risk premium of 8.6 per cent. While these calculations give similar results, it must be recognised that the premium calculated will vary according to the base period selected. This was demonstrated by Ibbotson and Sinquefield (1979), who calculated risk premiums over 18-, eight- and five-year time periods with very differing results.

While the use of a market risk premium of between eight and nine per cent has traditionally been put forward by academics, others have argued, for a variety of reasons, that this represents an overstatement. Jenkinson (1994) showed that if the market risk premium is calculated using a geometric average, rather than the more frequently used arithmetic average, the resulting premium is significantly reduced. Other arguments explaining why the use of historical data to predict the expected future market risk premium leads to its overestimation are the subject of discussion in Vignette 9.1.

9.6.3 A numerical example of the CAPM's use

Now that we have a firm understanding of the components of the CAPM, we can now work through an example to illustrate its use. Consider the following data:

Beta of company j (β_j) = 1.23
Yield of short-dated Treasury bills (R_f) = 6.5 per cent
Market risk premium ($R_m - R_f$) = 9.1 per cent

Using $R_j = R_f + \beta_j (R_m - R_f)$

VIGNETTE 9.1

Equity risk

FT

What extra return do investors require for assuming the risk of holding shares rather than gilts? The standard academic answer, based on calculating the actual premium shareholders have received since the first world war, is seven to eight per cent a year.

But this is almost certainly an overestimate. First, the premium previous generations of shareholders were expecting over gilts was probably lower than what they received – not least because the returns on gilts were eroded by unexpectedly high inflation. Second, today's investors are probably looking for a lower premium than their predecessors because they are better able to diversify their risks. Not only have pooled investments like unit trusts and pension funds largely displaced direct private investment which was a prominent feature of the inter-war stock market, but there has been a growing trend to diversification through investment in foreign shares. One could even argue that economic risk has fallen as macroeconomic management has become more responsible.

Why does this matter? Largely because companies typically take academic estimates of the risk premium to calculate their cost of capital, which they then use to judge which investments to approve. An excessive risk premium means overestimating the cost of capital and rejecting good investments. Paradoxically, the search for inappropriately high returns on investment may be holding back shareholder returns.

Source: Lex Column, *Financial Times*, 23 November 1996

we have R_j = 6.5 per cent + (1.23 × 9.1 per cent) = 17.7 per cent

From the data provided, the CAPM predicts that the required rate of return of shareholders and hence the company's cost of equity is 17.7 per cent.

9.6.4 Summary of the implications of the CAPM

The implications of the CAPM when applying it to pricing shares can be summarised as follows:

- investors calculating the required rate of return of a security will only consider systematic risk to be of relevance, as unsystematic risk can be eradicated by holding diversified portfolios of shares;
- shares that exhibit high levels of systematic risk are expected to yield a higher rate of return;
- on average there should be a linear relationship between systematic risk and return, and securities that are correctly priced should plot on the security market line (SML).

A graphical representation of the final implication is shown in Exhibit 9.15. Security B is correctly priced and plots on the SML. Security A is considered to be underpriced, giving higher returns compared to those required by investors given its level of systematic risk. Therefore, investors will buy the share, causing its price

EXHIBIT 9.15

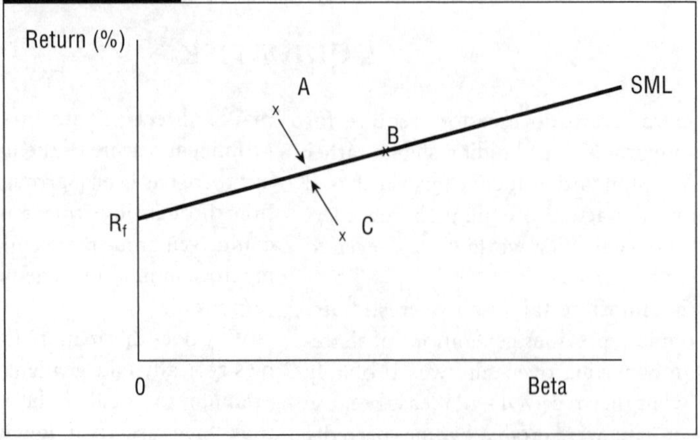

The security market line (SML) showing an underpriced share (A), an overpriced share (C) and a correctly valued share (B)

to rise and its return to decrease, and the share to move on to the SML. Security C is overpriced and hence the opposite situation will occur. If securities take a long time moving on to the SML, the linear relationship between risk and systematic return will be weakened. Therefore, we see the importance of the assumption made by the CAPM that capital markets are perfect, as under these conditions a share's price will tend to move accurately and quickly to reflect information about the share.

9.7 THE CAPM AND INVESTMENT APPRAISAL

So far, we have only discussed the use of the CAPM from the perspective of share valuation, where the model can be used by shareholders to calculate the required rate of return of a company's equity shares. This equates to the company's cost of equity finance and can therefore be used in the calculation of a company's weighted average cost of capital. The WACC calculated with the assistance of a CAPM-derived cost of equity finance can be used as the required rate of return for a company's investment projects. However, the CAPM can be used to find a required rate of return which directly reflects the risk of a project and hence replaces the use of WACC in this respect.

The utilisation of the CAPM in the investment appraisal process is especially useful when a company is appraising a project which possesses significantly different risk characteristics to that of the average level of risk of the company as a whole. The advantage here is that the CAPM can take into account the risk of projects and therefore lead to better investment decisions. This is something for which the WACC approach (which was considered in Chapter 8) makes no allowance.

9.7.1 Equity betas and asset betas

When applying the CAPM to investment appraisal, it is appropriate to introduce the concept of asset and equity betas. The betas we have referred to so far in this chapter have been what are known as equity betas or 'geared' betas. An equity beta represents the total systematic risk of a company. This systematic risk can be broken down into two components:

1 business risk representing the sensitivity of a company's operating cash flows to changes in the economic climate. This is dependent on the industry within which the company is operating;
2 financial risk, representing the sensitivity of a company's cash flows to changes in the interest payments it has to make on its debt finance. The level of financial risk faced by a company increases with its level of gearing.

Both types of risk are reflected in a company's equity beta. A company's asset beta or 'ungeared' beta, however, reflects only a company's business risk. A company's asset beta, in turn, reflects the asset betas of a company's individual projects. For example, a company with only two projects, both equal in value, one with an asset beta of 1.2 and the other with an asset beta of 0.8, will have an overall company asset beta of 1.

The algebraic relationship between a company's equity and asset betas is given by the following equation:

$$\beta_e = \beta_a \times \frac{(E + D(1 - C_T))}{E}$$

where: β_e = equity or geared beta
β_a = asset or ungeared beta
D = value of debt
E = value of equity
C_T = corporate tax rate.

This formula is derived from the expression of a company's asset beta as the weighted average of its equity and debt betas, weighted to reflect the market values of its debt and equity finance. This is represented by the following equation:

$$\beta_a = \left[\beta_e \times \frac{E}{D(1 - C_T) + E} \right] + \left[\beta_d \times \frac{D(1 - C_T)}{D(1 - C_T) + E} \right]$$

If we assume that companies do not default on their interest payments we can take the beta of debt to be zero. The last term of the equation therefore disappears and, by rearranging the remaining expression, we arrive at the earlier equation. We can see from this equation that a company's equity beta will always be greater than its asset beta. This is, of course, unless a company is all-equity financed, in which case its equity and asset betas will be identical.

9.7.2 Using the CAPM to calculate a project's hurdle rate

The process of using the CAPM in investment appraisal is very similar to its use in the share valuation process. In common with share valuation it is assumed that only the systematic risk of a project is relevant. The unsystematic risk is considered irrelevant on the grounds that shareholders of the company will be holding diversified portfolios. In order to use the CAPM in the investment appraisal process, we again require estimates of the risk-free rate, the market risk premium and, in addition, the beta of the project. It is the last of these three pieces of data which often proves the most difficult to find. We will now address this problem by considering the steps involved in using the CAPM to derive a hurdle rate for appraising a project.

1 Identify quoted companies engaged mainly or entirely in the same type of operation as the project under appraisal. These companies should have similar systematic risk characteristics to the project and so their betas can be used as suitable surrogates or proxies.
2 Once the surrogate companies and their equity betas have been identified, these betas must be adjusted to allow for gearing effects (i.e. financial risk). This is because the surrogate companies' financing will be different from the financing of the company appraising the project and is therefore irrelevant. The formula to 'ungear' a company's equity beta was given earlier.
3 The next step is either to take an average of the ungeared proxy betas, or to select the proxy beta considered most appropriate, and then to regear to reflect the financial risk of the company undertaking the project, using the formula utilised in step 2.
4 The regeared beta will now reflect the business risk of the project under consideration, plus the appraising company's financial risk. This beta can now be inserted into the CAPM in order to yield a required rate of return which accurately reflects the systematic risk of the project.

The required rate of return calculated by this method represents the appropriate hurdle rate for appraising the new project if it is being wholly financed by retained earnings or by newly raised equity finance. If the project is being financed by a mixture of debt and equity finance, however, the required rate of return of equity may need to be used in conjunction with a weighted average cost of capital formula.

9.7.3 The benefits of using CAPM instead of WACC

As mentioned earlier, the use of the CAPM in project appraisal should lead to better investment decisions. This is illustrated in Exhibit 9.16.

Consider two projects, A and B, where X marks the plot of their expected level of return and level of systematic risk as measured by beta. Project A would be rejected using WACC due to its expected return being less than the company's WACC. However, using CAPM, which takes into account the low-risk nature of the project, it would be accepted due to A plotting above the SML. The converse

EXHIBIT 9.16

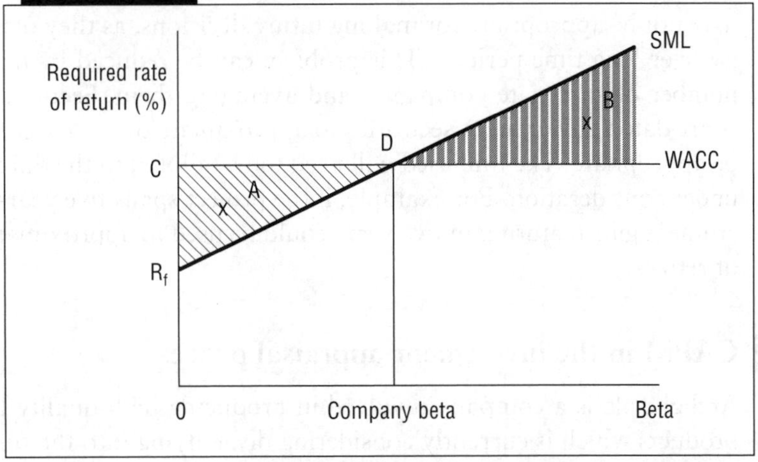

Diagram showing how the use of the CAPM in preference to WACC in the investment appraisal process will lead to better investment decisions

is true of Project B. This would be accepted using WACC, but rejected using the CAPM. Therefore, by using the CAPM and taking into account the systematic risk of projects, better investment decisions will be made in two areas of the diagram:

- the area shaded with diagonal lines which represents low-risk, low-return projects, previously rejected using WACC, which will now be accepted;
- the area shaded with vertical lines which represents high-risk, high-return projects, previously accepted using WACC, which will now be rejected.

9.7.4 Problems using the CAPM as an investment appraisal tool

While leading to better investment decisions, there are many practical problems associated with using the CAPM as an investment appraisal tool, as follows:

- the CAPM's general assumptions are not applicable to the real world and hence may undermine the applicability of the model;
- companies may have difficulty identifying suitable surrogate companies which possess similar levels of systematic risk to the project under consideration. Companies are often involved in a diversified range of activities rather than in the activity specific to the project being appraised;
- difficulties may be experienced when attempting to identify relevant capital structure data with which to ungear surrogate companies' equity betas;
- the CAPM assumes that transactions take place over a single period of time, which is usually taken to be no more than a year.

Clearly, the last point represents a difficulty, as investments span several time periods. Two problems arise here. First, equity betas calculated using historic data may not be appropriate for making future decisions, as they often exhibit instability over long time periods. This problem can be reduced by taking the betas of a number of surrogate companies and averaging them. Second, using the yield of short-dated government securities to approximate the risk-free rate will no longer be appropriate. The rate used will need to be tailored to the duration of the project under consideration. For example, if the project spans five years, the yield on government gilts maturing in five years could be used to approximate the risk-free rate of return.

Example CAPM in the investment appraisal process

Arclight plc is a company involved in producing high-quality household lighting products which is currently considering diversifying into the furniture business. It is trying to decide upon an appropriate discount rate in order to appraise the new venture, which has an expected return of 17 per cent. Arclight plc will use the CAPM to establish this discount rate and has the following information about suitable surrogate companies.

Furnisure plc
This company has an equity beta of 1.23 and is wholly involved in furniture making. It is financed by 35 per cent debt and 65 per cent equity.

Home Furnish plc
This company has an equity beta of 1.27 and is also wholly involved in furniture making. It is financed by 40 per cent debt and 60 per cent equity.

Lux Interior plc
This company has an equity beta of 1.45 and is financed by 30 per cent debt and 70 per cent equity. It is split into two divisions of equal size: one produces furniture and the other produces luxury wallpaper. The wallpaper division is seen as 50 per cent more risky than the furniture division.

Other information:

- Arclight plc has traditionally adopted a financing mix of 33 per cent debt and 67 per cent equity – although the project, if accepted, will be financed entirely by equity finance;
- the current yield on Treasury bills stands at seven per cent while the return on the stock exchange is 14 per cent;
- the corporation tax rate is 31 per cent for all companies;
- corporate debt can be assumed to be risk-free.

Using the above information, calculate an appropriate discount rate for appraising the project and decide whether it should be accepted.

1 Extract the appropriate asset betas by ungearing the surrogate companies' equity betas using the equation:

$$\beta_a = \beta_e \times \left[\frac{E}{E + D(1 - C_T)} \right]$$

Furnisure plc:

$$\beta_a = 1.23 \times 65/(65 + 35 \times (1 - 0.31)) = 0.90$$

Home Furnish plc:

$$\beta_a = 1.27 \times 60/(60 + 40 \times (1 - 0.31)) = 0.87$$

Lux Interior plc:

$$\beta_a = 1.45 \times 70/(70 + 30 \times (1 - 0.31)) = 1.12$$

We have to make a further calculation here as Lux Interior's asset beta partly reflects the business risk of its wallpaper division, which is of no relevance to the project under consideration. We can find the asset beta of its furniture division (β_{af}) as follows:

$$1.12 = (0.5 \times 1.5 \times \beta_{af}) + (0.5 \times \beta_{af})$$

Hence $\beta_{af} = 1.12/1.25 = 0.90$

2 Take an average of the three asset betas:

$$\text{Surrogate asset beta} = (0.90 + 0.87 + 0.90)/3 = 0.89$$

3 Regear the surrogate asset beta to reflect Arclight's financial risk:

$$\text{Surrogate equity beta} = 0.89 \times (67 + 33 \times (1 - 0.31))/67 = 1.19$$

4 Insert the surrogate equity beta into the CAPM to calculate the hurdle rate:

$$R_j = 0.07 + 1.19 \times (0.14 - 0.07) = 0.1533, \text{ i.e. } 15.33 \text{ per cent}$$

Therefore, as the expected rate of return of the project (17 per cent) is greater than the hurdle rate (15.33 per cent), Arclight plc should accept the project.

9.8 EMPIRICAL TESTS OF THE CAPM

Earlier in the chapter we acknowledged that the assumptions of the CAPM are unrealistic from the perspective of the real world. If we refer back to Section 9.5, for example, we can see that a key assumption of the CAPM is that capital markets are perfect. While capital markets are not perfect, however, as transaction costs and taxes clearly do exist in practice, markets have been found through various empirical tests to exhibit high levels of efficiency. The point we are trying to make here is that although the assumptions do not totally mirror reality, reality may not be so far away from the assumptions as to invalidate the model. The model, therefore, should not be prejudged on its assumptions but assessed on the results of its application.

There have been a large number of tests on the validity of the CAPM's applications and uses. Research carried out has concentrated on two main areas – the first concerning the stability of beta coefficients over time and the second considering the strength and nature of the linear relationship that exists between risk and return.

9.8.1 Tests of the stability of beta

While the CAPM is a forward-looking model, due to the availability of only past data, betas are calculated using historical returns of shares in relation to the historical returns of the market. Therefore the usefulness of historical betas in both the processes of pricing of shares and the appraisal of projects will depend heavily upon the stability of beta coefficients over time. This was the subject of the investigation by Sharpe and Cooper (1972), who examined the stability of US equity betas over the time period 1931–67. They started by splitting up their sample of shares into ten different risk classes, each class containing an equal number of shares, allocated according to their beta at the start of the test period. As a rule of thumb, stability was defined as any share that either remained in its existing class or moved by only one class over a five-year time period. Their results suggested that shares with high and low betas demonstrated higher levels of stability when compared with shares with mid-range betas. Additionally they found that approximately 50 per cent of shares' betas could be considered stable (according to their earlier definition) over a five-year time period.

While empirical evidence on the stability of individual betas is inconclusive, there is general agreement that the betas of portfolios of shares exhibit much higher levels of stability over time. The most common reasons put forward to explain this are that any errors associated with the estimation of an individual share's beta or any actual changes in the systematic risk characteristics of individual shares will tend to average out when shares are combined in a portfolio.

9.8.2 Tests of the security market line

Many empirical tests have used regression analysis to derive a '*fitted*' security market line which is then compared to the '*theoretical*' SML. Deriving the fitted line involves a two-stage process. The first stage is to select a wide-ranging sample of shares and, by using market returns and security returns over a specified time period (say monthly data over a five-year period), calculate the average return of the securities and their beta coefficients using a series of regressions. The second stage is to then regress the individual shares' beta coefficients against their average returns in order to derive a fitted SML. The theoretical SML is located by estimating the risk-free rate of return (R_f) to give the intercept on the vertical axis and then calculating the return of the market (R_m) and plotting it against a beta of one. Some of the best known tests include those carried out by Jacob (1971), Black *et al.* (1972) and Fama and Macbeth (1973). The conclusions of their tests can be summarised as follows:

- the intercept of the fitted line was above the one derived using the theoretical model, indicating that some other factor in addition to systematic risk was determining securities' rates of return;
- the slope of the fitted line was flatter than that suggested by the theoretical SML;
- the fitted line indicated the existence of a strong linear relationship between systematic risk and return, albeit different from the one suggested by the theoretical SML.

These points are illustrated in Exhibit 9.17.

EXHIBIT 9.17

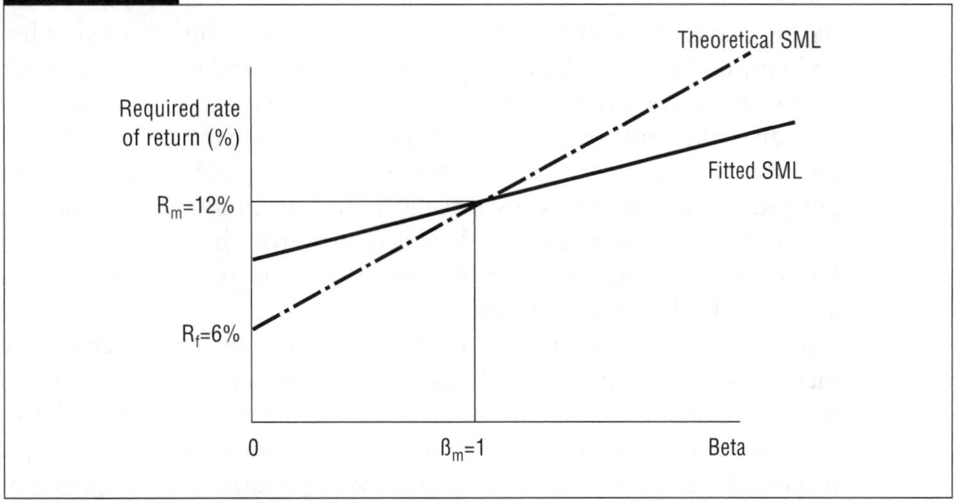

Diagram showing that the fitted SML, while providing strong evidence of a linear relationship between risk and return, suggests a less steep linear relationship when compared to the theoretically derived SML

The broad conclusions drawn from these tests is that the CAPM does not fully explain observed data, although systematic risk does go a long way to explaining the expected returns of individual securities.

While the tests do not support the validity of the CAPM, Roll (1977) argued that the CAPM is difficult, if not almost impossible, to test. The reason is that the stock exchange indices that are used to approximate the market return are poor surrogates. Not only do stock exchange indices fail to include all tradable shares, they also omit untradable shares and other financial and non-financial assets (such as bonds, property, land, antiques, etc.). Roll therefore concluded that, without a market portfolio which accurately reflects all risky assets, it is impossible to properly test the validity of the CAPM.

So is the CAPM worthless and are students of corporate finance wasting their time by learning about the model? The answer to this question has to be an unconditional 'no'. First, we should only discard a theory or model if there is a better one with which to replace it. A potential 'heir to the throne' of the CAPM, the arbitrage pricing model (APM), is currently only in its early stages of development and has some considerable way to go before it displaces the CAPM. Second, while the CAPM is limited from the perspective of its practical application by companies, it does provide us with a framework with which to quantify and translate risk into an easily understandable required rate of return. Remember that, in Chapter 8, the CAPM was considered to be a more superior way to calculate a company's cost of equity finance than the Gordon growth model.

9.9 CONCLUSION

In this chapter we considered the important relationship that exists between risk and return. We started by looking at how the risk and return of individual investments can be measured and then went on to demonstrate that investors, by holding well-diversified portfolios, can eradicate the unsystematic risk they face. This forms the basis of Markovitz's portfolio theory, which combines investing in the optimal portfolio of risky shares (known as the market portfolio) with investing in risk-free assets. The combinations of risk and return given by this linear relationship is known as the capital market line. Investors can locate themselves on the line according to their risk preferences.

Sharpe's capital asset pricing model is a development of Markovitz's portfolio theory. The model identifies a linear relationship between the return of individual securities and their systematic risk as measured by their beta factor. This relationship then allows investors to calculate the required return for a security given its systematic risk and hence determine whether the security is fairly priced or not. The capital asset pricing model can, in addition to being used to price securities, be used to determine risk-adjusted discount rates for appraising new investment projects. While the assumptions upon which the model is based are unrealistic, empirical tests of the model do provide evidence of the existence of a linear relationship between risk and return, albeit one which is slightly different from that suggested by theory.

KEY POINTS

1 The relationship between risk and return plays an important role within corporate finance. Risk is measured by the standard deviation of an investment's returns and can be calculated using either historical returns or expected future returns.

2 The risk of an investment can be split into systematic and unsystematic risk. Unsystematic risk can be diversified away by investors spreading their funds over a number of different shares.

3 The simplest form of diversification is to invest in a two-share portfolio. The key determinant of the amount of risk that can be diversified away is the level of correlation that exists between the two shares' returns.

4 The more shares investors include in their portfolio, the more unsystematic risk they will eradicate.

5 Markowitz's portfolio theory provides a framework within which investors combine the most efficient portfolio of risky investments with risk-free securities in order to construct a portfolio which satisfies their risk and return requirements and hence maximises their utility.

6 There are a number of difficulties associated with putting portfolio theory into practice for smaller investors, for whom the transaction costs can be prohibitive. However, smaller investors can overcome this problem by buying into diversified portfolios, i.e. investment trusts and unit trusts.

7 The CAPM, which builds on portfolio theory, defines a linear relationship between the systematic risk of a security and its required rate of return. This linear relationship is represented by the security market line (SML).

8 Systematic risk is measured by beta, which indicates the sensitivity of a security's returns to systematic factors, relative to the market return and the risk-free rate of return.

9 If securities are correctly priced, they should plot on the security market line.

10 The CAPM can be used in the investment appraisal process. If an appropriate project beta can be estimated, then a discount rate for appraising a project can be tailored to reflect its risk.

11 While empirical tests do not reinforce the validity of the CAPM, the model does provide us with a useful aid to understanding the relationship between systematic risk and the required rate of return of securities.

QUESTIONS

Answers to these questions can be found on pages 424–6.

1 Explain why certain levels of risk cannot be avoided even in a highly diversified portfolio.

2 Discuss whether diversification at company level has any value to a company's ordinary shareholders.

3 Distinguish between an efficient portfolio and an optimal portfolio.

4 List the limitations of portfolio theory as an aid to investment decisions.

5 Which of the following companies is likely to have the highest equity beta?
 (a) a highly geared supermarket company;
 (b) a low geared electricity generating company;
 (c) a highly geared building materials company;
 (d) a low geared retail bank;
 (e) an all-equity financed industrial conglomerate.

6 For which of the following reasons might a company that is perceived as risky have a lower beta factor than an equivalent company that is perceived as less risky?
 (a) the risky company has a lower financial gearing level;
 (b) inaccuracies in the estimation of beta from linear regression analysis;
 (c) the risky company has lower systematic risk but higher unsystematic risk;
 (d) the risky company is larger in size;
 (e) because of differing asset betas.

7 A firm has an equity beta of 1.30 and is currently financed by 25 per cent debt and 75 per cent equity. What will be the company's new equity beta if the company changes its financing policy to 33 per cent debt and 67 per cent equity? Assume corporation tax to stand at 35 per cent.

8 How do we approximate the risk-free rate in practice? In reality will the capital market line be a straight line?

9 The market is currently yielding a return of 16 per cent while Treasury bills are yielding 10 per cent. Shares of Lime Spider plc have a covariance of 7.5 with the market while the market has a variance of 4.5. What is the required rate of return for Lime Spider plc's shares?

10 Explain why an asset beta of a company will always be lower than its equity beta, unless of course the company is all-equity financed.

QUESTIONS FOR REVIEW

Answers to these questions can be found on pages 426–8.

1 Discuss how portfolio theory can help individual investors maximise their utility.

2 You are considering investing in one or both of two securities, X and Y, and are given the following information:

Security	*Possible return (%)*	*Probability*
X	30	0.3
	25	0.4
	20	0.3
Y	50	0.2
	30	0.6
	10	0.2

(a) Calculate the expected return for each security separately and for a portfolio comprising 60 per cent X and 40 per cent Y.

(b) Calculate the expected risk of each security separately and of the portfolio as defined above if the correlation coefficient of the two returns is +0.15.

3 Icicle Works plc is a frozen food packaging company and is looking to diversify its activities into the electronics business. The project it is considering has a return of 18 per cent and Icicle Works plc is trying to decide whether the project should be accepted or not. To help it decide it is going to use the CAPM. The company has to find a proxy beta for the project and has the following information on three companies in the electronics business:

(a) *Supertronic plc*

Equity beta of 1.33. Financed by 50 per cent debt and 50 per cent equity.

(b) *Electroland plc*

Electroland plc has an equity beta of 1.30, but it has just taken on a totally unrelated project, accounting for 20 per cent of the company's value, that has an asset beta of 1.4. The company is financed by 40 per cent debt and 60 per cent equity.

(c) *Transelectro plc*

Equity beta of 1.05. Financed by 35 per cent debt and 65 per cent equity.

Assume that all the debt is risk-free and that corporation tax is at a rate of 35 per cent. Icicle Works plc is financed by 30 per cent debt and 70 per cent equity. The return of risk-free securities stands at 10 per cent and the return on the market portfolio is 14 per cent. Should the company accept the project?

4 Simpson plc over the past few years has been investing surplus funds in a small portfolio of equity shares. Details of the portfolio are as follows:

Company	*No. shares*	*Beta*	*Share price (£)*	*Dividend yield (%)*	*Expected return (%)*
Kitson	70 000	1.27	3.75	5.6	17
Pembridge	150 000	1.53	4.25	3.5	21
Taylor	100 000	1.01	2.50	4.2	19
Short	80 000	0.95	4.50	6.2	14.5
Johnson	130 000	0.82	3.50	4.8	20

The current market return is 17 per cent and the rate earned on Treasury bills is 10 per cent.

(a) Is Simpson's portfolio more or less risky than that of the market portfolio? Support your answer with appropriate calculations.

(b) Give Simpson plc advice on how it should change the composition of its portfolio, giving a rationale for the changes that you recommend.

5 Discuss the problems that may be encountered in applying the capital asset pricing model (CAPM) in investment appraisal.

QUESTIONS FOR DISCUSSION

1 Loring plc has paid the following dividends in recent years:

Year	*1991*	*1992*	*1993*	*1994*	*1995*
Dividend per share	64p	nil	7p	69p	75p

The dividend for 1995 has just been paid. The risk-free rate of return is six per cent and the market rate of return is 15 per cent.

(a) If Loring plc has an equity beta of 1.203, what will be the market price of one of its shares?

(b) Discuss the meaning of the term 'equity beta' and explain how the equity beta of a public limited company may be determined.

(c) Critically discuss the limitations of the CAPM as a method of determining the required return on an investment.

2 You have the following information about the returns for the securities of Super Lux plc and the returns for the market:

Time	*Return of Super Lux (%)*	*Return of the market (%)*
t_1	18	10
t_2	21	11
t_3	20	8
t_4	25	12
t_5	26	14

Given that the rate of return on Treasury bills is eight per cent and that the correlation coefficient between the security and the market is +0.83, calculate the required rate of return on Super Lux's shares using the CAPM.

3 The securities of companies Z and Y have the following expected returns and standard deviations:

Company	Z	Y
Expected return (%)	15	35
Standard deviation (%)	20	40

If the correlation coefficient between the two securities is +0.25, calculate the expected return and standard deviation for the following portfolios:

(a) 100 per cent Z;

(b) 75 per cent Z and 25 per cent Y;

(c) 50 per cent Z and 50 per cent Y;

(d) 25 per cent Z and 75 per cent Y;

(e) 100 per cent Y.

4 Critically discuss whether the CAPM makes portfolio theory redundant.

REFERENCES

Allen, D., Day, R., Hirst, I. and Kwiatowski, J. (1986) 'Equity, gilts, treasury bills and inflation', *Investment Analyst*, Vol. 83, pp. 11–18.

Black, F., Jensen, M. and Scholes, M. (1972) 'The capital asset pricing model: some empirical tests', in Jensen, Frederick A. (ed.) *Studies in the Theory of Capital Markets*, New York, Praeger, Inc.

Dimson, E. and Brealey, R. (1978) 'The risk premium on UK equities', *Investment Analyst*, Vol. 52, pp. 14–18.

Fama, E. and Macbeth, J. (1973) 'Risk, return and equilibrium: empirical tests', *Journal of Political Economy*, May/June, pp. 607–36.

Ibbotson Associates (1990) 'Stocks, bonds, bills and inflation', *Ibbotson Associates 1990 Yearbook*.

Ibbotson, R. and Sinquefield, R. (1979) *Stocks, bonds and inflation*, Financial Analysts Research Foundation.

Jacob, N. (1971) 'The measurement of systematic risk for securities and portfolios: some empirical results', *Journal of Financial and Quantitative Analysis*, Vol. 6, pp. 815–33.

Jenkinson, T. (1994) 'The equity risk premium and the cost of capital debate in the UK regulated utilities', University of Oxford, mimeo.

Markowitz, H. (1952) 'Portfolio selection', *Journal of Finance*, Vol. 7, pp. 13–37.

Roll, R. (1977) 'A critique of the asset pricing theory's tests: part 1; on past and potential testability of the theory', *Journal of Financial Economics*, Vol. 4, pp. 129–76.

Sharpe, W. (1964) 'Capital asset prices: a theory of market equilibrium under conditions of risk', *Journal of Finance*, Vol. 19, pp. 768–83.

Sharpe, W. and Cooper, G. (1972) 'Risk-return classes of New York Stock Exchange common stocks 1931–67', *Financial Analysts Journal*, Vol. 28, pp. 46–54.

RECOMMENDED READING

For an in-depth account of risk and return, portfolio theory, the CAPM and its application in the investment appraisal process *see*:

Samuels, J., Wilkes, F. and Brayshaw, R. (1995) *Management of Company Finance* (6th edn) Chapman and Hall, Chapters 8–10.

The following book includes a number of very readable and interesting articles, including both Markowitz's and Sharpe's seminal articles and an excellent overview article of the CAPM by Mullins:

Ward, K. (ed.) (1994) *Strategic Issues in Finance*, Butterworth-Heinemann.

Important and informative papers and articles recommended for further reading include the following:

Appleyard, A. and Strong, N. (1989) 'Beta geared and ungeared: the case of active debt management', *Accounting and Business Research*, Vol. 19, No. 74, pp. 170–4.

Dimson, E. (1995) 'The capital asset pricing model', in *Mastering Management*, Part 4, *Financial Times*, Nov.

Dimson, E. (1997) 'Capital budgeting: a beta way to do it', in *Mastering Finance*, Part 1, *Financial Times*, May.

Fielding, J. (1989) 'Is beta better?' *Management Accounting*, Nov, pp. 38–40.

Gregory, A. (1990) 'The usefulness of beta in the investment-appraisal process', *Management Accounting*, Jan, pp. 42–3.

CHAPTER 10

WORKING CAPITAL MANAGEMENT

INTRODUCTION

Long-term investment and financing decisions give rise to future cash flows which, when discounted by an appropriate cost of capital, determine the market value of a company. Such long-term decisions will not result in the expected benefits for a company if attention is not also paid to short-term decisions regarding current assets and liabilities. Current assets and liabilities, that is assets and liabilities with maturities of less than one year, need to be carefully managed. Net working capital is the term given to the difference between current assets and current liabilities, which may include inventories of raw materials, work-in-progress and finished goods, debtors, short-term investments, cash, trade creditors and short-term debts.

The level of current assets is a key factor in a company's liquidity position. A company must be able to generate or have in reserve enough cash to meet its short-term needs if it is to continue in business. Therefore, working capital and its management is a key factor in the company's long-term success, since without the 'oil' of working capital the 'engine' of fixed assets will be unable to function. The greater the extent to which current assets exceed current liabilities, the more solvent a company is likely to be, depending of course on the nature of its current assets.

LEARNING OBJECTIVES

After studying this chapter, you should have achieved the following learning objectives:

- an appreciation of the importance of working capital management in ensuring the profitability and liquidity of companies;
- the ability to describe the cash conversion cycle and to explain its significance to working capital management;
- an understanding of the need for working capital policies concerning the level and financing of current assets, and of the significance of aggressive, moderate and conservative approaches to working capital management;
- the ability to describe and discuss a range of methods for managing stock, cash, debtors and creditors;
- the ability to evaluate at an introductory level the costs and benefits of proposed changes in working capital policies;
- an understanding of how factoring and invoice discounting can assist in the management of working capital.

10.1 THE OBJECTIVES OF WORKING CAPITAL MANAGEMENT

To be effective, working capital management requires a clear specification of the objectives to be achieved. As discussed by Pass and Pike (1984), the two main objectives of working capital management are to increase the profitability of a company and to ensure that it has sufficient liquidity to meet short-term obligations as they fall due and so continue as a going concern. Profitability in this sense can be related to the goal of shareholder wealth maximisation, so that investment in current assets should only be made if an acceptable return is obtained. While liquidity is needed for a company to continue as a going concern, a company may choose to hold more cash than is needed for operational or transaction purposes, for example for precautionary or speculative motives. The twin goals of profitability and liquidity will often conflict, because as assets become more liquid they will give rise to lower returns. Cash kept in a safe will not generate any return at all, for example, while a six-month deposit may earn a reasonable amount of interest in exchange for loss of access for the period.

10.2 WORKING CAPITAL POLICIES

Because the operational management of working capital is so important, a company will need to formulate or to have already in place clear policies concerning the various components of working capital. Central to such working capital policies are decisions taken by management regarding the level of investment in working capital for a given level of business activity, and decisions regarding the extent to which working capital is financed from short-term funds such as bank overdrafts.

A company should have working capital policies covering the management of stock, debtors, cash and short-term investments in order to minimise the possibility of decisions being made which are not in the best interests of the company. Examples of such sub-optimal decisions are the granting of credit to customers who are unlikely to pay and the ordering of unnecessary stocks of raw materials. Sensible working capital policies will reflect corporate decisions on the total investment needed in current assets, i.e. the overall level of investment; decisions on the level of investment needed in each type of current asset, i.e. the mix of current assets; and decisions on the way in which current assets are to be financed.

Working capital policies will need to take into account the nature of the company's business, since different businesses will have different working capital requirements. A manufacturing company may need to invest heavily in spare parts and components and may be owed considerable amounts of money by its customers. A food retailer may have large stocks of goods for resale but may have no debtors to speak of. The manufacturing company clearly has a need for a carefully thought out policy on the management of debtors, while the food retailer may not grant credit at all.

Working capital policies will also need to reflect the credit policies of a company's competitors, since it would be foolish to lose business because of an unfavourable comparison of trade terms. Any forecast fluctuations in the supply or demand for goods and services, for example if part of a company's business is seasonal in nature, must also be considered, as must be the impact of a company's manufacturing period on its current assets.

10.2.1 The level of working capital

An *aggressive* policy with regard to the level of investment in working capital means that a company chooses to operate with lower levels of stock, debtors and cash, for a given level of activity or sales. An aggressive policy will increase profitability, since less cash will be tied up in current assets, but it will also increase risk, since the possibility of cash shortages or running out of stock (stockouts) is increased.

A *conservative* or more flexible working capital policy for a given level of turnover would be associated with maintaining a larger cash balance, perhaps even investing in short-term securities, offering more generous credit terms to customers and holding higher levels of stock. Such a policy will give rise to a lower risk of financial or stock problems, but at the expense of reducing profitability.

A *moderate* policy would tread a middle path between the aggressive and conservative approaches. All three approaches are shown in Exhibit 10.1.

It should be noted that the working capital policies of a company can only be characterised as aggressive, moderate or conservative by comparing them with the working capital policies of similar companies. There are no absolute benchmarks of what may regarded as aggressive or otherwise, but these characterisations are

EXHIBIT 10.1

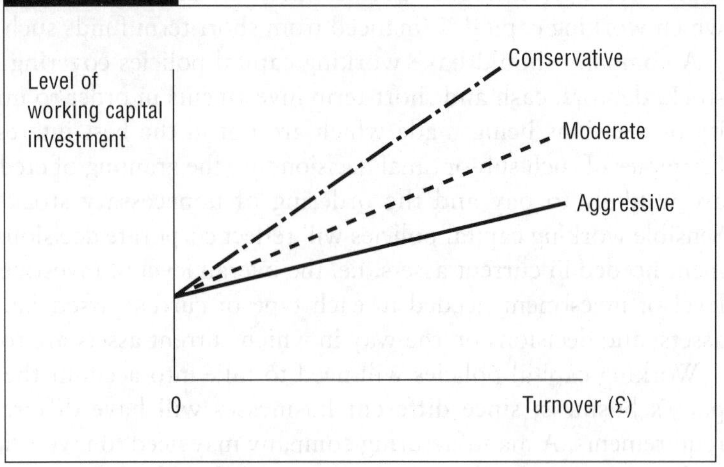

Diagram illustrating different policies regarding the level of investment in working capital

useful for analysing the ways in which individual companies approach the operational problem of working capital management.

10.2.2 Financing working capital

The trade-off between risk and return which occurs in the policy decisions regarding the level of investment in current assets is also significant in the policy decision on the relative proportions of finance of different maturities in the balance sheet, i.e. on the choice between short- and long-term funds to finance working capital. In order to assist us in the analysis of policy decisions regarding the financing of working capital, a company's assets can be divided into three different types, as discussed by Cheatham (1989): fixed assets, permanent current assets, and fluctuating current assets. Fixed assets are long-term assets from which a company expects to derive benefit over several periods, for example factory buildings and production machinery. Permanent current assets represent the core level of investment needed to sustain normal levels of trading activity, such as investment in buffer stocks and investment in the average level of a company's debtors. Fluctuating current assets represent the variations in the level of current assets arising from normal business activity.

Short-term sources of finance are usually cheaper and more flexible than long-term sources of finance. Short-term interest rates are usually lower than long-term interest rates; for example, an overdraft is more flexible than a long-term loan on which a company is committed to pay fixed amounts of interest every year. However, short-term sources of finance are riskier than long-term sources from the borrower's point of view, in that they may not be renewed (an overdraft is, after all, technically repayable on demand), or may be renewed on less favourable terms. Another source of risk for the borrower is that interest rates are more volatile in the

EXHIBIT 10.2

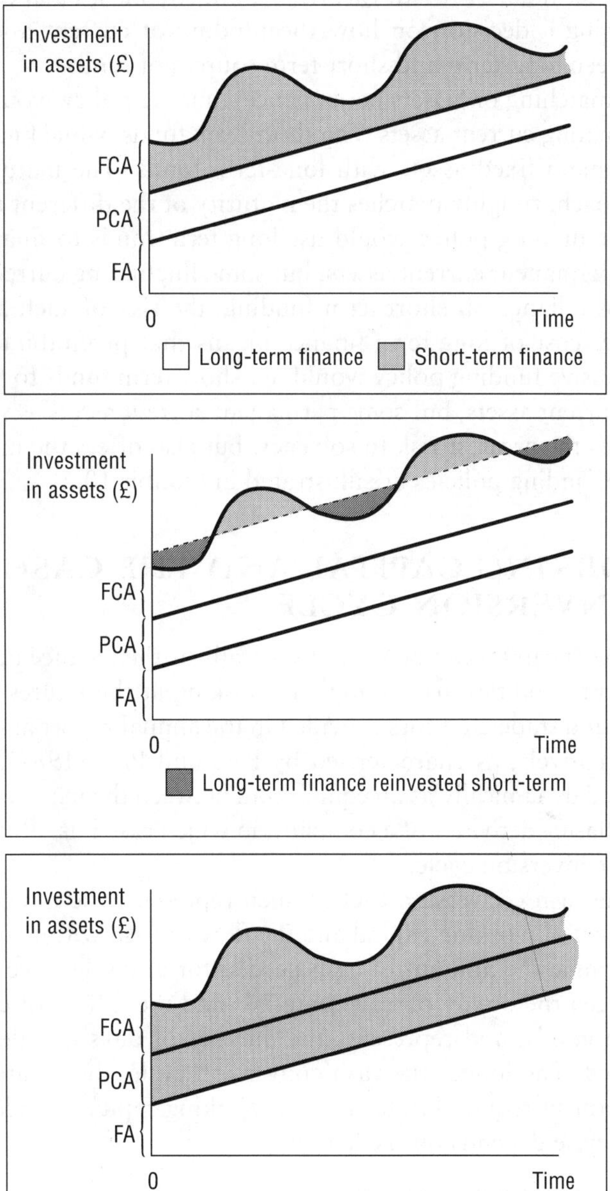

Key: Fluctuating current assets = FCA
Permanent current assets = PCA
Fixed assets = FA

Three diagrams illustrating the matching, conservative and aggressive approaches to the relative proportions of long- and short-term debt used to finance working capital

short term than in the long term and this risk will be compounded if floating rate short-term debt is used. Clearly, a company must balance profitability and risk in reaching a decision on how the funding of current and fixed assets is divided between long-term and short-term sources of funds.

A matching or 'assets permanence' funding policy would be one which financed fluctuating current assets with short-term funds, while financing permanent current assets and fixed assets with long-term funds. The maturity of the funds, in this approach, roughly matches the maturity of the different types of assets. A conservative funding policy would use long-term funds to finance not only fixed assets and permanent current assets, but some fluctuating current assets as well. As there is less reliance on short-term funding, the risk of such a policy is lower, but the higher cost of long-term finance means that profitability is reduced as well. An aggressive funding policy would use short-term funds to finance not only fluctuating current assets, but some permanent current assets as well. An aggressive policy carries the greatest risk to solvency, but also offers the highest profitability. These three funding policies are illustrated in Exhibit 10.2.

10.3 WORKING CAPITAL AND THE CASH CONVERSION CYCLE

Working capital can be viewed statically as the balance between current assets and current liabilities, for example by looking at the figures for stock, trade debtors, cash and trade creditors provided in the annual report and accounts of a company. Alternatively, as characterised by Pass and Pike (1984), working capital can be viewed dynamically as an equilibrium between the income-generating and resource-purchasing activities of a company, in which case it is intimately connected with the cash conversion cycle.

The cash conversion cycle, which represents the interaction between the components of working capital and the flow of cash within a company, can be used to determine the amount of cash needed for any sales level. It is the period of time between the outlay on raw materials and the inflow of cash from the sale of finished goods, and represents the number of days of sales for which financing is needed. The longer the cash conversion cycle, the greater will be the amount of investment required to be made in working capital. The length of the cash conversion cycle depends on the length of:

- the stock conversion period;
- the debtor collection period;
- the creditor deferral period.

The stock conversion period is the average time taken to use up raw materials, added to the average time taken to convert raw materials into finished goods, added to the average time taken to sell finished goods to customers. The debtor collection period is the average time taken by credit customers to settle their accounts. The creditor deferral period is the average time taken by a company to settle accounts with its suppliers. If we approximate these three periods by using the financial ratios of stock turnover, debtors' ratio and creditors' ratio, the length of the cash conversion cycle (CCC) is given by:

CCC = (stock turnover) plus (debtors' ratio) minus (creditors' ratio)

The cash conversion cycle is shown in Exhibit 10.3.

EXHIBIT 10.3

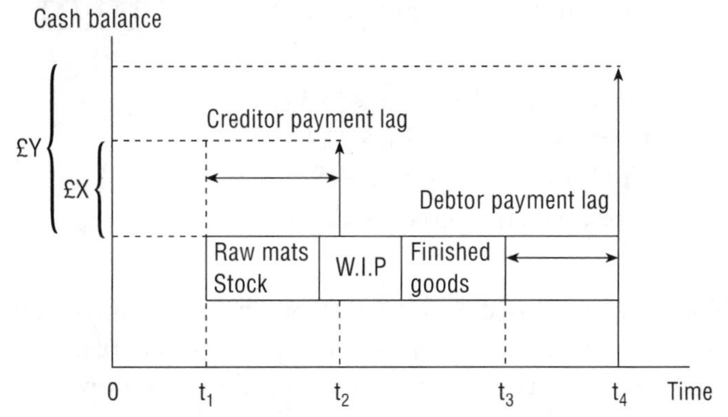

The cash conversion cycle of a firm, showing the relationship between the inventory conversion period ($t_1 - t_3$), the debtor deferral period ($t_3 - t_4$) and the creditor deferral period ($t_1 - t_2$)

Example Calculation of required working capital

The amount of working capital required by a company can be estimated if we can produce information on the value of relevant working capital inputs and outputs, such as raw material costs and credit purchases, together with information on the length of the components of the cash conversion cycle. Let us suppose that Carmed plc expects sales in the next year to be £18m and has budgeted production costs as follows:

	£m
Raw materials	4
Direct labour	5
Production overheads	3
Total production costs	12

Raw materials are in stock for an average of three weeks and finished goods are in stock for an average of four weeks. All raw materials are added at the start of the production cycle, which takes five weeks and incurs labour and production overheads at a constant rate. Credit taken from suppliers of raw materials is approximately four weeks, while customers are allowed 12 weeks to pay. If production takes place evenly throughout the year, what is Carmed plc's total working capital requirement?

Working capital requirement:

		£	£
Raw materials:	4m × (3/52) =		230 769
Work-in-progress:			
raw materials:	4m × (5/52) =	384 615	
labour:	5m × (5/52) × 0.5 =	240 385	
overheads:	3m × (5/52) × 0.5 =	144 231	
			769 231
Finished goods:	12m × (4/52) =		923 077
Debtors:	18m × (12/52) =		4 153 846
Creditors:	4m × (4/52) =		(307 692)
Working capital required:			5 769 231

Note that, in this calculation, it has been assumed that all raw materials are added at the start of the production process, whereas labour and overheads are consumed evenly as production proceeds. If work-in-progress is half-finished, then labour and overheads have to be multiplied by 0.5 as only half the amounts of labour and overheads present in finished goods have been added.

On the information given, Carmed plc has to finance £5.77m of working capital. The relative proportions of long- and short-term funds used in this financing will depend upon Carmed plc's working capital policies.

10.3.1 The cash conversion cycle and working capital needs

Forecasts of working capital requirements can be based on forecasts of sales if a relationship between net working capital and sales is assumed to exist. Such a relationship could be made explicit by the formulation of a policy on the level of investment in working capital, as described in Section 10.2.1. However, even with such a policy in existence, the relationship between sales and working capital is unlikely to remain static as levels of business and economic activity change. Since budgeted production is based on forecast sales, care must be taken in periods of reduced economic activity that over-investment in stocks of raw materials, work-in-progress and finished goods does not occur. Although the overall amount of working capital needed can be estimated from forecast sales and the cash conversion cycle, there is likely to be a difference between forecast activity and actual activity. There can be no substitute, then, for regularly reviewing working capital needs in the light of changing levels of activity.

The cash conversion cycle also shows where management should focus attention if it wishes to reduce the amount of cash tied up in current assets. As pointed out by Cheatham (1989), apart from reducing sales and reducing the cost per unit sold, there are a number of possibilities for reducing the cash invested in current assets by shortening the length of the cash conversion cycle. The cash conversion cycle can be shortened by reducing the stock conversion period, by reducing the debtor collection period, or by increasing the creditor deferral period.

The stock conversion period can be reduced by shortening the length of the production cycle, for example by more effective production planning or by outsourcing part of the production process. The amount of stock within the production process can be reduced by using just-in-time (JIT) production methods (*see* Section 10.5.3) or by employing production methods which are responsive to changing sales levels.

The debtor conversion period can be shortened by offering incentives for early payment, by reducing the period of credit offered to customers and by more stringent assessment of the creditworthiness of customers in order to screen out slow payers.

10.4 OVERTRADING

Overtrading, or undercapitalisation, occurs if a company is trying to support too large a volume of trade from too small a working capital base, and emphasises the need to make adequate provision for investment in working capital. It is essentially the result of the supply of funds failing to satisfy the demand for funds within a company. Even if a company is operating at a profit, overtrading can result in a liquidity crisis, with the company being unable to meet its debts as they fall due, because cash has been absorbed by growth in fixed assets, stock and debtors. Overtrading, then, can lead to serious and sometimes fatal problems for a company.

Overtrading can be caused by a rapid increase in turnover, perhaps as a result of a successful marketing campaign, if the necessary associated investment in fixed and current assets has not been made. Overtrading can also arise in the early years of trading if a business starts off with insufficient capital. This may be due to a mistaken belief that sufficient capital could be generated from trading profits and ploughed back into the business, when in fact the early years of trading are often difficult ones. Overtrading may also be due to erosion of a company's capital base, perhaps due to the non-replacement of long-term loans following their repayment.

There are several appropriate strategies to deal with overtrading, as follows.

- *The introduction of new capital.* This is likely to be an injection of equity finance rather than debt since, with liquidity under pressure due to overtrading, management will be keen to avoid further straining cash flow by increasing interest payments.
- *Improved working capital management.* Overtrading could also be attacked through better control and management of working capital, for example by chasing overdue accounts. Since overtrading is more likely if an aggressive funding policy is being followed, adoption of a matching or more relaxed approach to funding could pay dividends.
- *Reducing business activity.* If necessary, a company could choose to rein back the

level of its business activity in order to consolidate its trading position and to allow time for its capital base to build up through retained earnings, though this is considered somewhat drastic.

Indications that a company may be overtrading could include:

- rapid growth in sales over a relatively short time period;
- rapid growth in the amount of current assets, and perhaps fixed assets;
- deteriorating stock turnover and debtors' ratio;
- increasing use of trade credit to finance growth in current assets;
- declining liquidity, indicated perhaps by a falling quick ratio;
- declining profitability, perhaps due to using discounts to increase sales;
- a lack of cash and liquid investments.

10.5 THE MANAGEMENT OF STOCK

Significant amounts of working capital can be invested in stocks of raw materials, work-in-progress and finished goods. Stocks of raw materials and work-in-progress can act as a buffer between different stages of the production process and so ensure its smooth operation. Stocks of finished goods allow the sales department of a company to satisfy customer demand without unreasonable delay and potential loss of sales. These benefits of holding stock must be weighed against any costs incurred, however, if optimal levels of stock for a company are to be determined. Costs which may be incurred include:

- holding costs, such as insurance, rent and utility charges;
- replacement costs, including the cost of obsolescent stock;
- the cost of the stock itself;
- the opportunity cost of cash tied up in stock.

10.5.1 The economic order quantity

This classical stock management model establishes an optimum level of stock by balancing the costs of holding stock against the costs of ordering fresh supplies. It then uses this optimal level of stock as the basis of a minimum cost procurement policy. The economic order model assumes that, for the period under consideration, costs and activity are constant and known with certainty. Because these steady-state assumptions are made, it is also called a *deterministic* model. It makes no allowance for the existence of buffer stocks.

If a constant rate of stock consumption is assumed, holding costs will increase as average stock levels and order quantity increase, while ordering costs will decrease as order quantity increases and the number of orders falls. The economic order quantity occurs when the total cost, which is the sum of the holding cost and the ordering cost, is at a minimum. The cost equation is:

$$\text{Total cost} = \text{Holding cost} + \text{Ordering cost}$$

Algebraically, then:

$$TC = \frac{(Q \times H)}{2} + \frac{(S \times F)}{Q}$$

where: H = holding cost per unit per year
S = annual demand in units per year
F = ordering cost per order
Q = order quantity in units.

This relationship is illustrated in Exhibit 10.4.

EXHIBIT 10.4

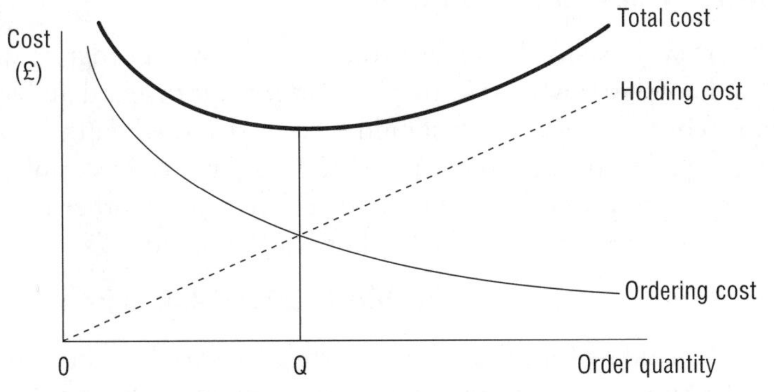

The costs of holding stock and the economic order quantity model

The minimum total cost occurs when holding cost and ordering cost are equal, as can be shown by differentiating the total cost equation with respect to Q and setting to zero. Putting holding cost equal to ordering cost and rearranging gives:

$$Q = \sqrt{\frac{2 \times F \times S}{H}}$$

Q is now the economic order quantity, i.e. the order quantity which minimises the sum of holding costs and ordering costs. This expression is known as the economic order quantity (EOQ) model.

More sophisticated stock management models have been developed which relax some of the classical model's assumptions, while some modern approaches, such as just-in-time methods and material resource planning (MRP), question whether there is a need to hold any stock at all.

Example Use of the EOQ model

Oleum plc sells a soap called Fragro, which it buys in boxes of 1000 bars with ordering costs of £5 per order. Retail sales are 200 000 bars per year and holding costs are 50p per year per 1000 bars. What is the economic order quantity and average stock level for Fragro?

$$F = \text{£}5 \text{ per order}$$
$$S = 200\,000 \text{ bars per year}$$
$$H = \text{£}0.50 \text{ per } 1000 \text{ bars}$$

so
$$Q = (2 \times 5 \times 200\,000/(0.5/1000))^{1/2}$$
$$= 63\,245 \text{ bars or approximately } 63 \text{ boxes}$$

The average stock level = Q/2 = 63 000/2 = 31 500 bars.

10.5.2 Buffer stocks and lead times

Orders will usually be subject to a delay between ordering and physical delivery, and this delay is what is known as *lead time*. If demand and lead time are assumed to be constant, new stock should be re-ordered when the stock in hand falls to a level equal to the demand during the lead time. For example, if demand is 10 400 units per year and the lead time for delivery of an order is two weeks, new stock should be ordered when the level of stock in hand falls to:

$$10\,400 \times (2/52) = 400 \text{ units}$$

If demand or lead times are uncertain or variable, the company may choose to hold a buffer stock in order to reduce or eliminate the possibility of stock outs. The company could seek to optimise the level of buffer stocks by balancing their holding costs against the potential costs of stock outs. However, the EOQ model could still be used to determine an optimum order size.

In Exhibit 10.5, we can see the pattern of stock levels where a company chooses to operate with buffer stock OB. From a knowledge of the average annual demand, regular orders of size BQ are placed. Because lead time is known and is equal to ab, new orders are placed when stock levels fall to OR. The company can meet unexpected demand during the lead time from the buffer stocks held. The average stock level will be:

$$(\text{buffer stock}) + (\text{half of regular order quantity}) = OB + (BQ/2)$$

This can be used to determine the expected holding cost for the year.

10.5.3 Just-in-time stock policies

Many companies in recent years have reduced stock costs by minimising stock levels. The main purpose of a just-in-time (JIT) purchasing policy is to minimise or eliminate the time which elapses between the delivery and use of stock. Such

EXHIBIT 10.5

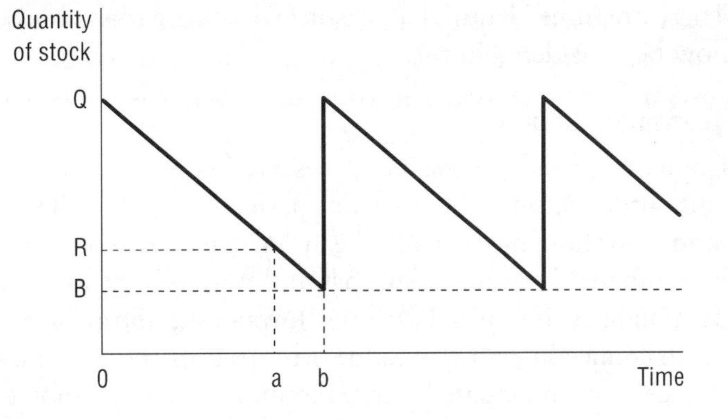

Average stock levels, re-order level and buffer stock

policies have been applied in a wide range of commercial operations in recent years and call for a close relationship between the supplier and the purchaser of raw materials and bought components. The purchaser requires guarantees on both quality and reliability of delivery from the supplier in order to avoid disruptions to production. In return for these commitments, the supplier can benefit from long-term purchase agreements, since a company adopting JIT purchasing methods will concentrate on dealing with those suppliers who are able to offer goods of the required quality at the required time. The purchaser will benefit from a reduction in the costs of holding, ordering and handling stock since materials will move directly from the reception point to the production line.

The main purpose of a JIT manufacturing policy is to minimise stock acting as a buffer between different stages of production. Apart from developing closer relationships with suppliers, this could also be achieved by changing factory layout, in order to reduce shopfloor queues of work-in-progress, and by cutting set-up times in order to reduce the size of production batches. Good production planning is essential if a JIT manufacturing policy is to be successful.

10.6 THE MANAGEMENT OF CASH

Cash management, which is part of the wider task of treasury management, is concerned with optimising the amount of cash available to the company, by maximising the interest earned by spare funds not required immediately and by reducing any losses caused by delays in the transmission of funds. Holding cash to meet short-term needs carries the opportunity cost of the return which could have been earned if the cash had been invested or put to productive use. However, choosing to reduce this opportunity cost by operating with very small cash balances will increase the risk of being unable to meet debts as they fall due.

10.6.1 The need for cash

There are three identifiable reasons why companies choose to hold cash. These will now be considered in turn.

Transactions motive

Companies need to have a cash reserve in order to balance short-term cash inflows and outflows, since these are not perfectly matched. This is called the transactions motive for holding cash and the approximate size of such a reserve for a period can be estimated by forecasting cash inflows and outflows and by the preparation of cash budgets. If unusual cash outflows of significant size are anticipated, for example in connection with investment projects or refurbishment, then cash may be held to meet such anticipated future requirements in addition to the cash reserve needed to meet day-to-day operational needs.

Precautionary motive

Forecasts of future cash flows are subject to uncertainty and it is possible that the company may experience unexpected demands for cash. This gives rise to the precautionary motive for holding cash. Reserves held for precautionary reasons could be in the form of easily realised short-term investments, which are discussed below.

Speculative motive

Companies may also build up cash reserves in order to take advantage of attractive investment opportunities that may arise, for example in the corporate take-over market. Such reserves are held for speculative reasons. If a company has significant cash reserves for which it cannot see an advantageous use, it may choose to return them to shareholders, for example by means of a share repurchase scheme or a special cash dividend (*see* Section 7.6).

10.6.2 Optimum cash levels

Given the variety of needs that a company may have for cash and the different reasons that it may have for holding cash, the optimum cash level will vary between companies and over time. For a given company, the optimum amount of cash to hold will depend upon the following factors:

- forecasts of the future cash inflows and outflows of the company;
- the efficiency with which the cash flows of the company are managed;
- the availability to the company of liquid assets;
- the company's borrowing capability;
- the company's tolerance of risk.

10.6.3 Cash flow problems

A company may experience cash flow problems for a number of reasons. It may, for example, be making losses: while this need not be a problem in the short term, making losses on a regular basis for several periods will lead to serious cash flow problems and perhaps even to liquidation or take-over. Inflation may also be a source of cash flow problems, since historic profit may prove to be insufficient to fund the replacement of necessary assets. As we have seen in our discussion of overtrading, growth requires investment in fixed assets and working capital; if the funds needed for this investment are not obtained from an appropriate source, cash flows can be severely strained. Careful cash management is needed when dealing with a seasonal business since cyclical sales patterns can lead to cash flow imbalances. Finally, cash flow problems may arise due to sizeable one-off items of expenditure, such as repayment of debt capital or investment in fixed assets. Companies may choose to anticipate the need to repay significant amounts of debt capital by setting up a 'sinking fund', in which regular contributions of cash and accumulated interest combine to produce the required lump sum.

When faced with cash flow shortages, a company may consider one or more of a number of possible remedies. It may, for example, identify and choose to postpone non-essential capital expenditure. It may be able to accelerate the rate at which cash is flowing into the business, for example by offering discounts for early payment by debtors, by chasing overdue accounts or by having a sale to clear unwanted stock. If a company has investments, perhaps purchased with surplus cash from an earlier period, it may choose to sell them in order to generate income. Finally, a company may be able to identify ways to reduce or postpone cash outflows. It may, for example, be able to take longer credit from its suppliers or reschedule its loan repayments. As a last resort, it may decide to reduce or pass a dividend payment, although this is usually taken to be a sign of financial weakness by the capital markets.

10.6.4 Cash budgets

Cash budgets are central to the management of cash. They show expected cash inflows and outflows over a period or periods and highlight anticipated cash surpluses and deficits. Their preparation assists management in the planning of borrowing and investment and facilitates the control of expenditure. Computer spreadsheets allow management to undertake 'what if' analysis to anticipate possible difficulties that may arise, as well as the examination of possible future scenarios. To be useful, cash budgets should be regularly updated as a result of comparing estimated figures with actual results, perhaps by using a rolling cash budget system. Significant variances from planned figures must always be investigated.

10.6.5 Management of cash flows

Cash flows should, of course, be efficiently managed. This means that, ideally, debts should be collected in line with agreed credit terms and cash should be banked as quickly as possible. Prompt banking will either reduce the interest charged on amounts outstanding on agreed overdraft accounts, or will increase the interest earned on cash deposited. Available credit offered by suppliers should be used to the full and payments made as late as possible, as long as the benefit of this course of action is greater than the net benefit to be derived from accepting any discounts offered for early payment.

Float is the term given to the amount of money tied up in the period between the initiation of payment and the point at which money appears in a company's bank account. Float can vary between four and nine days and consists of:

- transmission delay, which is time taken for a payment to pass from payer to payee;
- lodgement delay, which is the delay in banking payments received;
- clearance delay, which is the time taken by a bank to clear a presented instruction to pay.

Float can be reduced by minimising lodgement delay and by simplifying and speeding up the handling of cash. Good cash management will take steps to keep float to a minimum.

10.6.6 The investment of surplus cash

Companies, as discussed above, have a number of reasons why they may want to hold funds in liquid or near-liquid form. Cash which is surplus to immediate needs should earn a return by being invested on a short-term basis without risk of capital loss. There must be no risk of capital loss with the investment of short-term cash surpluses, since these funds are required to support a company's ongoing working capital needs. For this reason, it is important for large companies to set limits on the amount that they will deposit with individual banks, as discussed by Leadill (1992). As recent examples such as the collapses of the Bank of Credit and Commerce International (BCCI) and Barings have shown, banks can and do fail, and so credit risk should be taken into account by placing funds with a number of acceptably rated institutions. The factors which should be considered when choosing an appropriate investment for short-term cash surpluses are:

- the size of the surplus, as some investments have minimum amounts;
- the ease with which an investment can be realised;
- the maturity of the investment;
- the risk and the yield of the investment;
- any penalties which may be incurred for early liquidation.

Short-term instruments that can be useful in the management of corporate liquidity include money market deposits, sterling certificates of deposit, Treasury bills, sterling commercial paper and gilt-edged government securities. These will now be discussed in turn.

Money market deposits

Cash can be put on deposit to earn interest, with the interest rate depending on the size of the deposit, its maturity and the notice required for withdrawals. The interest rate will vary between banks because they compete for funds and so, to maximise returns, more than one quotation should be obtained before a deposit is made.

In the UK, large companies can lend directly to banks on the interbank market, at rates close to the London Interbank Offered Rate (LIBOR). Smaller companies can lend onto the market through their banks.

Sterling certificates of deposit

Sterling certificates of deposit are negotiable bearer securities which are issued by banks and building societies. They are for amounts which range from £500 000 to £1m and have maturities which range from 28 days to five years. The holder of a certificate of deposit at maturity is entitled to receive both principal and interest.

Because certificates of deposit can be sold before maturity and so are more liquid than money market deposits, they carry a lower rate of interest. They may be useful if a company's cash flows are not predictable enough for a money market deposit to be made. It is also possible that the anonymity of bearer securities may be attractive to some investors.

Treasury bills

Treasury bills of two-, three- and six-month maturity are issued on a discounted basis by the UK government. They are bought and sold on the part of the London money market called the discount market. The yield on Treasury bills is lower than on other money market instruments because of the lower default risk associated with government borrowing. In fact, the Treasury bill rate is often used as a surrogate for the 'risk-free rate'.

Sterling commercial paper

Sterling commercial paper refers to short-term promissory notes with a fixed maturity of between seven days and three months. They are bearer securities which are issued at a discount by companies, banks and building societies and are unsecured. The minimum amount of sterling commercial paper that can be issued is £100 000 and issuing companies, or their guarantors, must be listed on the Stock Exchange. However, the default risk of sterling commercial paper is higher than the risk associated with government securities such as Treasury bills.

Gilt-edged government securities

Gilt-edged government securities (gilts) are the long-term equivalent of Treasury bills, with maturities usually greater than five years. Newly-issued gilts are not suitable for the investment of short-term cash surpluses, since their long maturities will make their market prices very sensitive to interest rate changes and the risk of capital loss in the short term could be high. Gilts which are close to maturity may be regarded as liquid assets, similar to Treasury bills, and may be used for short-term investment.

10.7 THE MANAGEMENT OF DEBTORS

A company's credit management policy should be formulated so as to maximise its expected profits. It will need to take into account the company's current and desired cash position, as well as the company's ability to satisfy expected demand. In order to put the credit management policy into effect successfully, management and staff may need training or new staff may need to be recruited.

A key variable affecting the level of debtors will be the terms of sale which are prevalent in the company's area of business and the ability of the company to match and service comparable terms of sale. There is also a relationship between the level of debtors and the company's pricing policy: for example, it may choose to keep selling price relatively high while offering attractive terms for early payment. The effectiveness of debtor follow-up procedures used by the company will also influence the overall level of debtors and the likelihood of bad debts arising.

The debtor management policy decided upon by senior management should also take into account the administrative costs of debt collection, the ways in which the policy could be effectively implemented and the costs and effects of easing credit. It should balance the benefits to be gained from offering credit to customers against the costs of doing so. Longer credit terms may increase turnover, but they will also increase the risk of bad debts. The cost of increased bad debts and the cost of any additional working capital required should be less than the increased profits generated by the higher turnover. In order to operate its debtor policy, the company needs to set up a credit analysis system, a credit control system and a debtor collection system.

10.7.1 Credit analysis system

Information about a business is needed if a sensible decision about whether to trade with it or not is to be made. The risk of bad debts can be minimised if the creditworthiness of new customers is carefully assessed before credit is granted and if the creditworthiness of existing customers is reviewed on a regular basis. Relevant information can be obtained from a variety of sources. New customers can be asked to provide bank references to offer an indication of their financial standing, and trade references can be obtained to give an insight into the satisfactory conduct of business affairs. Published information, such as the audited annual report and accounts of a prospective customer, may also provide a useful indication of creditworthiness. The company's own experience of similar companies will also be a useful aid to forming an opinion as to the wisdom of offering credit, as will the experience of other companies within a group.

For a fee, a report may be obtained from a credit reference agency, such as Dunn & Bradstreet or Infocheck. A credit agency report includes a company profile, recent accounts, financial ratios and industry comparisons, analysis of trading history, payment trends, types of borrowing, previous financial problems and a credit limit. Bearing in mind the cost of assessing creditworthiness, the magnitude of likely regular sales could be used as a guide to the depth of the credit analysis.

10.7.2 Credit control system

Once an assessment of creditworthiness has been made and a credit limit agreed, the company should take steps to ensure that the credit limit and the terms of trade are adhered to. Customer accounts should be kept within the agreed credit limit and credit limits granted should be reviewed periodically to ensure that they remain appropriate. In order to facilitate prompt payment, invoices and statements should be despatched promptly and carefully checked to ensure their accuracy. Under no circumstances should goods be obtainable by customers who have exceeded agreed credit limits.

10.7.3 Debtor collection system

Since the purpose of offering credit is to maximise profitability, the costs of debt collection should not be allowed to exceed the amounts recovered. On a regular basis, the company should prepare an aged debtor analysis and take steps to chase late payers. It will be useful to establish clear procedures for the pursuit of late payments, setting out the circumstances under which reminders are to be sent out by credit control staff and the stage at which recourse should be made to legal proceedings. The company could consider charging interest on overdue accounts as an encouragement to timely payment, depending upon the legality of such an action and the likely reaction of customers.

10.7.4 Insurance against bad debts

Although expensive, the risk of bad debts can be covered by insurance. Whole turnover insurance will cover any debt below an agreed amount against the risk of non-payment. Specific account insurance will allow the company to insure key accounts against default and may be useful for major customers. Williams (1994) reports that credit insurance is used much more widely in continental Europe than in the UK.

10.7.5 Discounts for early payment

Cash discounts may encourage early payment, but the cost of discounts offered must be compared with any financing savings resulting from lower debtor balances, any financing or administrative savings arising from shorter average collection periods and any benefits from a reduction in bad debts.

Example Evaluation of a change in debtor policy

Mine plc has annual credit sales of £15m and allows its customers 90 days credit. The financial manager is considering the introduction of a three per cent discount for payment within 15 days, and the reduction of the credit period to 60 days. It is estimated that 60 per cent of Mine plc's customers will take advantage of the discount, while the volume of sales will not be affected. The cost of each item sold by Mine plc is £12, and the selling price is £14 per unit. The company finances working capital from an overdraft at a cost of 15 per cent. Is the proposed change in policy worth implementing?

	£000	£000
Current level of debtors: 15 000 × (90/365) =		3699
Proposed level of debtors:		
15 000 × (60/365) × 40 per cent =	986	
15 000 × (15/365) × 60 per cent =	370	
		1356
Reduction in debtors		2343

	£
Saving in finance costs: 2343 × 0.15 =	351 450
Cost of discount: 15 000 × 3 per cent × 60 per cent =	270 000
Net benefit of proposed policy change	81 450

The policy change is financially attractive. However, the difficulty of forecasting accurately the effects of changes in creditor management policy should be borne in mind when reaching a decision as to whether or not to recommend its introduction.

10.7.6 Factoring

Factoring companies offer a range of services in the area of sales administration and the collection of amounts due from debtors. A factor can take over the administration of sales invoicing and accounting for a client company, together with the collection of amounts due from debtors and the chasing up of any slow payers. A factor can offer an advance of cash against the security of accounts receivable, allowing a company ready access to cash as soon as credit sales are made. For an additional fee, a factor can take on any bad debts that may arise through non-payment of amounts due. Since here the factor does not have recourse to the company in the event of non-payment, this is termed non-recourse factoring.

While a factor will advance up to 80 per cent of the face value of debtors, interest will be charged on the sum advanced. In exchange for accelerated cash receipts, then, the company will have to pay an interest charge, which can be compared with the cost of short-term borrowings. This charge is in addition to the service fee levied by the factor, which is usually between 0.5 per cent and 2.5 per cent of gross annual turnover. However, there will be a reduction in the company's administration costs to be considered, as well as the value of the factor's expertise in credit analysis and control.

The advantages that factoring may offer to a company include the following:

- the prompt payment of suppliers, leading perhaps to obtaining the benefit of early payment discounts;
- a reduction in the amount of working capital tied up in debtors;
- the financing of growth through sales;
- savings on sales administration costs;
- benefits accruing to a company from the factor's experience in credit analysis and control.

10.7.7 Invoice discounting

Invoice discounting involves the sale of selected invoices to a third party while retaining full control over the sales ledger, and is a service often provided by factoring companies. The principal charge for invoice discounting is a discount charge linked to bank base rates, although a fee of between 0.2 per cent and 0.5 per cent of turnover is often levied. The value of invoice discounting to a company lies in the resulting improvement in cash flow.

An evaluation of the costs and benefits of factoring can be carried out in a similar way to the method used for evaluating discounts for early payment that has already been demonstrated.

Example Cost–benefit analysis of factoring

Trebod plc has annual credit sales of £4.5m. Credit terms are 30 days, but because its management of debtors has been poor, the average collection period has been 50 days, with 0.4 per cent of sales resulting in bad debts. A factor has offered to take over the task of debt administration and credit checking, at an annual fee of 2.2 per cent of credit sales. Trebod plc estimates that it would save £35 000 per year in administration costs. Due to the efficiency of the factor, the average collection period would fall to 30 days and bad debts would be eliminated. The factor would advance 80 per cent of invoiced debts at an interest rate of 14 per cent. Trebod plc currently finances debtors from an overdraft costing 13 per cent per year.

Assuming that credit sales occur smoothly throughout the year, determine whether the factor's services should be accepted.

	£
Current level of debtors is £4.5m × (50/365) =	616 438
Under the factor, debtors would fall to £4.5m × (30/365) =	369 863

The costs of the current policy are as follows:

	£
Cost of financing current debtors: 616 438 × 13 per cent =	80 137
Cost of bad debts: 4.5m × 0.4 per cent =	18 000
Costs of current policy:	98 137

The costs under the factor are as follows:

	£
Cost of financing new debtors through factor:	
(£369 863 × 0.8 × 0.14) + (£369 863 × 0.2 × 0.13) =	51 041
Factor's annual fee: £4.5m × 0.022 =	99 000
Saved administration costs:	(35 000)
Net cost under factor:	115 041

The cost–benefit analysis shows that the factor's services are more expensive than the current arrangements by £16 904 per year. On financial grounds, the services of the factor should not be accepted.

10.8 CONCLUSION

Effective working capital management lies at the heart of a successful company, playing a crucial role in the increase of shareholder wealth and the realisation of benefits from capital investment. In fact, poor management of working capital is one of the more common reasons for corporate failure. It is essential that company managers have an understanding of this key area in corporate finance.

KEY POINTS

1 The main objectives of working capital management are profitability and liquidity.

2 Companies may adopt aggressive, moderate or conservative working capital policies regarding the level and financing of working capital.

3 The cash conversion cycle can be used to determine the working capital requirement of a company as well as helping management to look for ways of decreasing the cash investment in current assets.

4 Overtrading can lead to business failure and must be corrected if found. Corrective measures could include introducing new capital, improving working capital management and reducing business activity.

5 Because there can be significant amounts of cash tied up in stocks of raw materials, work-in-progress and finished goods, steps must be taken both to reduce the amount of stock held and to reduce the time it is held for.

6 The EOQ model can be used to determine an optimum order size and directs

attention to the costs of holding and ordering stock, but there is a growing trend to minimise the holding of stock within companies.

7 Cash may be held for transactions, precautionary and speculative reasons, but companies should optimise holdings of cash according to their individual needs.

8 Cash flow problems can be minimised through the forecasting of cash needs, for example by using cash flow forecasts and cash budgets.

9 Surplus cash should be invested to earn a return in appropriate short-term instruments.

10 The effective management of debtors requires assessment of the creditworthiness of customers, effective control of credit granted and efficient collection of money due. Effective management of debtors can be assisted by factoring and invoice discounting.

QUESTIONS

Answers to these questions can be found on pages 429–31.

1 Explain the different strategies a firm may follow in order to finance its cumulative capital requirements.

2 Describe the cash conversion cycle and explain its significance in determining the working capital needed by a company.

3 Describe the strategies that could be followed by a company seeking to deal with the problem of overtrading.

4 Explain the difference between factoring and invoice discounting.

5 Discuss the possible reasons why a company might experience cash flow problems and suggest ways in which such problems might be alleviated.

6 Explain why a company may choose to have reserves of cash.

7 Discuss ways in which a company might invest its short-term cash surpluses, explaining briefly the factors which it should consider in making its selection.

8 How might the creditworthiness of a new customer be checked?

9 Is it worth offering discounts to debtors to encourage prompt payment?

10 Suggest ways in which companies can exercise control over their levels of working capital.

QUESTIONS FOR REVIEW

Answers to these questions can be found on pages 431–2.

1 Sec plc uses a large quantity of salt in its production process. Annual consumption is 60 000 tonnes over a 50-week working year. It costs £100 to initiate and process an order and delivery follows two weeks later. Storage costs for the salt are estimated at 10p per tonne per annum. The current practice is to order twice a year when the stock falls to 10 000 tonnes. Recommend an appropriate ordering policy for Sec plc, and contrast it with the cost of the current policy.

2 MW Ltd has budgeted its sales to be £700 000 per annum. Its costs as a percentage of sales are as follows:

	%
Raw materials	20
Direct labour	35
Overheads	15

Raw materials are carried in stock for two weeks and finished goods are held in stock before sale for three weeks. Production takes four weeks. MW Ltd takes four weeks' credit from suppliers and gives eight weeks credit to its customers. If both overheads and production are incurred evenly throughout the year, what is MW Ltd's total working capital requirement?

3 MC plc has current sales of £1.5m per year. Cost of sales is 75 per cent of sales and bad debts are one per cent of sales. Cost of sales comprises 80 per cent variable costs and 20 per cent fixed costs, while the company's required rate of return is 12 per cent. MC plc currently allows customers 30 days credit, but is considering increasing this to 60 days credit in order to increase sales.

It has been estimated that this change in policy will increase sales by 15 per cent, while bad debts will increase from one per cent to four per cent. It is not expected that the policy change will result in an increase in fixed costs and creditors and stock will be unchanged.

Should MC plc introduce the proposed policy?

4 A company is considering offering a discount for payment within 10 days to its customers, who currently pay after 45 days. Only 40 per cent of credit customers would take the discount, although administrative cost savings of £4450 per year would be gained. If sales, which are unaffected by the discount, are £1 600 000 per year and the cost of short-term finance is 11 per cent, what is the maximum discount that could be offered?

QUESTIONS FOR DISCUSSION

1 The finance director of Stenigot Ltd is reviewing the working capital management of the company. He is particularly concerned about the lax management of the company's debtors. The trade terms of Stenigot Ltd require settlement within 30 days, but its

customers are taking an average of 60 days to pay their bills. In addition, out of total credit sales of £20m per year, the company suffers bad debts of £200 000 per year. Stenigot Ltd finances working capital needs by an overdraft at a rate of 10 per cent per year. The finance director is reviewing two options which have been suggested to him.

Option 1: Offering a discount of one per cent for payment within 30 days. It is expected that 35 per cent of customers will take advantage of the discount, while the average time taken by the remaining debtors to settle their accounts will remain unchanged. It is also expected that bad debts will fall by £60 000 per year and that administration costs will fall by £20 000 per year.

Option 2: The debt administration and credit control of Stenigot Ltd could be taken over by Great Coates plc, a factoring company. The annual fee charged by Great Coates plc would be 1.75 per cent of sales. This would be offset by administration cost savings for Stenigot Ltd of £160 000 per year and by an 80 per cent reduction in bad debts. Great Coates plc would be able to reduce the credit period taken by Stenigot Ltd to 30 days and would advance 80 per cent of invoiced debts at an interest rate of 15 per cent.

(a) Calculate the benefit, if any, to Stenigot Ltd of the two suggested options and, in the light of your findings, recommend an appropriate course of action to the finance director.

(b) Critically discuss whether it is possible for a company to optimise its working capital position. Your answer should include a discussion of the following matters:

(i) the risk of insolvency;

(ii) the return on assets;

(iii) the level, mix and financing of current assets.

2 Saltfleet plc, a wholesale merchant supplying the construction industry, has produced moderate profits for a number of years. It operates through a number of stores and depots throughout the UK and has a reputation in the sector as a steady if unspectacular performer. It has one subsidiary, Irby Ltd, which manufactures scaffolding and temporary security fences. The finance director of Saltfleet plc, who is based at the company headquarters in Sheffield, has been reviewing the way in which the company manages its working capital and has been discussing with you, a recently appointed graduate trainee in his department, a number of proposals which he hopes will lead to greater efficiency and effectiveness in this important area.

The proposals that the finance director has been discussing with you are:

(a) the appointment of a credit controller to oversee the credit management of the branches and depots;

(b) the appointment of a factoring company, Pyewipe plc, to take over the sales administration and debtor management of Irby Ltd;

(c) the investment of short-term cash surpluses on the London Stock Exchange. The finance director is especially interested in investing in the shares of a small company recently tipped in an investment magazine.

(i) Critically discuss the importance of credit management to a company like Saltfleet plc, explaining the areas to be addressed by a credit management policy.

(ii) Distinguish between factoring and invoice discounting, and explain the benefits which Irby Ltd may receive from a factor such as Pyewipe plc.

(iii) Discuss whether Saltfleet plc should invest short-term cash surpluses on the London Stock Exchange.

3 The following information has been extracted from the financial statements of Rowett plc by its finance manager:

Profit and loss account extracts

	£000	£000
Turnover		12 000
Cost of sales		
Raw materials	5800	
Labour	3060	
		8 860
Gross profit		3 140
Administration/distribution		1 680
Operating profit		1 460

Balance sheet extracts

	£000	£000
Current assets		
Stocks of raw materials	1634	
Stocks of finished goods	2018	
Debtors	1538	
Cash and bank	500	
		5690
Current liabilities		
Trade creditors	1092	
Overdraft	300	
Accrued expenses	76	
		1468
		4222

Powell plc, a factoring company, has offered to take over the debt administration and credit control of Rowett plc on a non-recourse basis for an annual fee of 1.8 per cent of sales. This would save Rowett plc £160 000 per year in administration costs and reduce bad debts from 0.5 per cent of sales to nil. Powell plc would be able to reduce the credit period allowed to Rowett's customers to 40 days, and will advance 75 per cent of invoiced debts at an interest rate of 15 per cent.

Rowett plc finances working capital from an overdraft at 12 per cent.

(a) Calculate the length of the cash conversion cycle of Rowett plc and discuss its significance to the company.

(b) Discuss ways in which Rowett plc could improve the management of its debtors.

(c) Using the information given, assess whether Rowett plc should accept the factoring service offered by Powell plc. What use should the company make of any finance provided by the factor?

4 The finance director of Menendez Ltd is trying to improve the company's slack working capital management. Although the trade terms of Menendez Ltd stipulate settlement by the end of the month following delivery, its customers in fact take an average of 45 days to pay their bills. In addition, out of total credit sales of £15m per year, the company suffers bad debts of £235 000 per year.

It has been suggested that the average settlement period could be reduced if a cash discount were given for early payment, and the finance director is considering offering a reduction of 1.5 per cent of the face value of the invoice for payment within 30 days. Informal discussions with customers have indicated to him that 40 per cent of customers would take advantage of the discount, but that the average time taken by the remaining customers would not be affected. It is also expected that, if the new credit terms are introduced, bad debts will fall by £60 000 per year and a small saving in credit administration costs of £15 000 per year will be made.

(a) If total sales are unchanged and if working capital is financed by an overdraft at nine per cent per year, are the new credit terms of any benefit to Menendez Ltd?

(b) Discuss whether Menendez Ltd should finance its working capital needs from an overdraft.

(c) It has been suggested by the managing director of Menendez Ltd that the way to optimise the company's overall level of working capital is by minimising its cash conversion cycle. Critically discuss whether the finance director should follow the suggestion of the managing director.

(d) Briefly discuss ways in which Menendez Ltd could use its debtors as a source of finance.

REFERENCES

Cheatham, C. (1989) 'Economising on cash investment in current assets', *Managerial Finance*, Vol. 15, No. 6, pp. 20–5.

Leadill, S. (1992) 'Liquidity and how to manage it', *Accountancy*, Nov, pp. 17–18.

Pass, C. and Pike, R. (1984) 'An overview of working capital management and corporate financing', *Managerial Finance*, Vol. 10, No. 3/4, pp. 1–11.

Williams, P. (1994) 'Who will you put your money on?', *Accountancy*, Oct, pp. 36–40.

FURTHER READING

An interesting discussion of stock management methods can be found in:

Samuels, J., Wilkes, F. and Brayshaw, R. (1995) *Management of Company Finance* (6th edn), Chapman and Hall.

An excellent discussion of cash management can be found in:

Weston, J. F. and Copeland, T. E. (1992) *Managerial Finance*, Cassell.

CHAPTER 11

MERGERS AND TAKE-OVERS

INTRODUCTION

Mergers and take-overs play a vital role in corporate finance. For many companies they represent an important source of external growth where no organic growth opportunities are available, while to other companies they represent a constant threat to their continuing existence.

The decision to take over another company may, on the face of it, appear to be just another investment decision. In actuality though, taking over another company is a far more complex process than simply buying a machine or building a factory. First, valuing a target company and estimating the potential benefits of taking it over is a far more difficult proposition than valuing a simple investment project. Second, the take-over process is often complicated by bids being contested by the victim company and hence it may be drawn out into a long and unpleasant fight to the death. This often results in the predator company paying considerably in excess of what it had previously budgeted. Third, due to the size of many take-over deals, there are often serious financial implications for the predator company after it has paid for its acquisition. We must also take into account the amount of valuable senior management time that is taken up with the take-over process.

The subject area of mergers and take-overs is a very large one indeed and a large number of books have been written on it. In this chapter, therefore, we are not going to be able to give the subject detailed treatment, but it is important to obtain more than just a general understanding of this key area of corporate finance.

LEARNING OBJECTIVES

By the end of this chapter, you should have achieved the following learning objectives.

- a familiarity with the different classifications and types of mergers and take-overs;
- a firm understanding of the justifications and motives behind merger and take-over activity;
- the ability to value target companies using a range of valuation techniques and then to decide upon the most appropriate valuation;
- an awareness of the different types of finance that can be utilised to fund mergers and take-overs;
- an understanding of the strategies and tactics that are employed in the take-over process from both a predator and a victim company perspective;
- an appreciation of the effects of merger and take-over activity on the various interest groups involved.

11.1 TERMINOLOGY ASSOCIATED WITH MERGERS AND TAKE-OVERS

Although the terms merger and take-over tend to be used synoymously, in practice there is a distinction between the two, albeit sometimes a fairly narrow one. A merger can be defined as a friendly reorganisation of assets into a new organisation, i.e. A and B merge to become C, a new business entity, which has the agreement of both sets of shareholders. Generally speaking, mergers tend to involve companies of similar size, reducing the likelihood of one of the parties dominating the other. A take-over is the acquisition of one company's ordinary share capital by another company, financed by a cash payment, an issue of securities, or a combination of both. Here, the company initiating the take-over is usually larger than the target company. In practice the vast majority of 'corporate restructurings' tend to be take-overs rather than mergers as, even if two companies declare that they are merging, more often than not one of the two companies is in fact the dominant player.

Take-overs can be classified into three broad types. A brief explanation of these types will now be given.

- *Horizontal take-over*. This involves two companies operating in the same industry, at a similar level of production, combining their operations.
- *Vertical take-over*. This involves two companies who are active at different stages of production within the same industry, and can involve a move forward in the production process to secure an outlet for a company's products, or a move backward in the production process to secure supply of raw materials.

- *Conglomerate take-over*. This involves the acquisition of a company involved in a totally different line of business to that of the acquirer.

Examples of these different classifications are shown in Exhibit 11.1. Take-overs can also have an international dimension, when they are referred to as *cross-border* acquisitions. An example of an international horizontal merger is Hong Kong and Shanghai Bank's take-over of Midland Bank plc.

EXHIBIT 11.1

Date	*Bidder*	*Target*	*Deal value (£m)*	*Classification of take-over*
1984	BAT	Eagle Star	968	Conglomerate
1985	Burton	Debenhams	571	Horizontal
1986	Hanson	Imperial Group	2564	Conglomerate
1986	Guinness	Distillers	2531	Horizontal
1988	BP	Britoil	2323	Vertical backwards
1988	Nestlé	Rowntree	2666	Horizontal
1995	De La Rue	Portals	682	Vertical backwards
1995	Glaxo	Wellcome	9150	Horizontal
1995	Hanson	Eastern Electric	2400	Conglomerate
1996	Granada	Forte	3600	Horizontal

Major UK take-overs including total value of bid and classification

11.2 JUSTIFICATIONS FOR ACQUISITIONS

A whole variety of justifications are used by company management to support take-over and merger activity. Ultimately, however, a take-over should only go through if the wealth of the shareholders of the acquiring company is enhanced. Merger activity can only be justified if the wealth of both groups of shareholders involved increases. Possible motives or justifications for take-over activity can be grouped into three broad areas. These motives will be examined in the following pages and assessed from the point of view of the enhancement of shareholder wealth.

11.2.1 Economic factors

The economic motive for take-overs is the belief by company management that shareholder wealth will be enriched by the transaction, as the two companies are worth more in combination with each other than as separate business entities. Algebraically, this can be shown as:

$$PV_{X+Y} > (PV_X + PV_Y)$$

where PV represents present value and X and Y are the two companies involved. Economic gains can be generated from a number of sources and for a number of reasons, including the following.

Synergy

Synergy occurs where the assets and/or activities of two companies complement each other, so that the sum of their separate outputs before merger is less than their combined output once merged, i.e. 1 + 2 = 4. For example, a company may have to buy in, at substantial expense, a particular service which it cannot provide for itself. By taking over a company which can supply such a service it may then be able to reduce its costs. The problem with the synergy rationale is that, before assets have been combined, it is difficult to quantify and measure; and after assets have been combined, it is difficult to realise, due to the fact that a high level of post-merger asset integration is required before such benefits begin to materialise.

Economies of scale

These are similar to synergy benefits but occur due to a larger scale of operations after the take-over. They are most likely to arise with horizontal mergers but may also be present in vertical mergers as well. Many different types of economies of scale exist, including those associated with production, marketing, distribution, management and finance. An example of a production economy is represented by the case where two companies producing the same good and using the same kind of machine can, upon merging, produce their combined output by using a single, larger, more sophisticated machine which is cheaper and easier to run than two smaller machines. A distribution economy would be represented by two companies that previously distributed their product by each employing the use of a transit van distributing their combined output using a large articulated lorry. Other examples of economies of scale include the scaling-down of duplicated resources and the ability to enjoy bulk-buying discounts when purchasing larger quantities of raw materials and components.

Elimination of inefficient management

A company may be being poorly run by its current management, perhaps because they are satisfying their own requirements rather than those of their shareholders. The company's share price will therefore decline, attracting prospective buyers of the company who are of the opinion that they can manage the company's assets more efficiently and who may decide to launch a take-over bid. If the take-over bid is successful, the inefficient management will be replaced by more effective personnel who will be expected to deliver the level of performance envisaged at the inception of the bid. The elimination of inefficient management as a result of a take-over deal may represent a more attractive alternative to their elimination by being voted out of office by shareholders (which may be difficult to achieve for practical reasons) or as a result of the company going into liquidation.

Entry to new markets

Companies may want to develop into new areas, both geographically and from a business or product perspective, in order to meet their strategic objectives. Organic or internal growth may be deemed to be too slow or too costly and hence take-over may be chosen as a more efficient route to expansion. This is especially true of the retail trade, where starting operations from scratch is both time-consuming and costly. The costs involved will result from the purchasing and refurbishment of premises, the hiring and training of personnel and the building up of market share. An example of the use of a take-over to break into a new market is Iceland plc's acquisition of Bejam in 1987, by means of which Iceland established for itself a retail foothold in the north of England. The alternative course of action, of competing with Bejam and other retailers in the area from a zero base, would have been prohibitively expensive.

To provide critical mass

Smaller companies may experience a lack of credibility due to their size. In addition, due to the increasing importance of research and development and brand investment, merging companies can pool resources to establish the critical mass required to provide sufficient cash flows to finance such requirements.

As a means of providing growth

Once a company has reached the mature stage of its growth cycle it may find it hard to grow organically. In this situation, take-over provides a quick solution for a company which is following a growth strategy. An example of this would be BAT's take-over of Allied Dunbar and Eagle Star. An alternative to acquisition for a mature company which has a substantial amount of surplus cash is for it to return the funds to its shareholders through a share repurchase or special dividend.

Market power and share

Horizontal mergers and take-overs will increase market share and hence enhance a company's ability to earn monopoly profits, while vertical integration will increase power in raw material or distribution markets. The only problem here, which is particularly applicable to horizontal mergers, is the legislative obstacle of possible referral to the Monopolies and Mergers Commission and the harm that such a referral can do, both financially and in terms of damage to a company's reputation (*see* Sections 11.2.4 and 11.6.2).

Risk reduction

A company may acquire another company in a different line of business (a conglomerate take-over) in order to reduce the volatility of its cash flows. Its management may seek to justify this acquisition to shareholders by stating that they are reducing the risk that investors face.

All of the arguments we have considered above represent perfectly good justifications for merger and take-over activity from the point of view of the enhancement of shareholder wealth, with the exception of one. Only the risk-reduction argument cannot be justified from a shareholder wealth viewpoint, as shareholders are theoretically assumed to have already eliminated unsystematic risk by holding a diversified portfolio of shares. Therefore, by diversifying its operations, a company will have little impact on the level of unsystematic risk faced by its shareholders. The potential downside to conglomerate diversification is represented by the company losing economies of scale and the ability to manage its operations efficiently, becoming effectively a jack of all trades but a master of none.

There is no doubt about the general validity of the economic justifications we have considered with respect to their ability to enhance shareholder wealth. The potential for economic gains in specific cases is not guaranteed and if such potential does exist, it is not certain that economic gains can be realised by companies after post-take-over integration. This issue will be considered in further detail in Section 11.7.

11.2.2 Financial motives

Acquisitions can also be justified on the grounds of the financial benefits they bring to shareholders in the companies involved. These are now considered in turn.

Target undervaluation

Some acquisitions are justified on the grounds that the target company is considered to be a bargain, in the sense that its shares are underpriced. The implication of this argument is that the capital markets are not totally efficient, since allowing companies to be undervalued for long periods of time is not consistent with pricing efficiency. Whether a take-over can be justified on these grounds, therefore, depends on the view taken towards stock market efficiency. While the evidence considered in Chapter 2 gave strong support for the efficiency of the capital markets, companies are in practice difficult to value with any degree of certainty, which leaves scope for the occurrence of undervaluation.

Tax considerations

It may be beneficial for a company that is in a tax-exhausted position to take over another company that is not tax-exhausted, so it can bring forward the realisation of any tax-allowable benefits. This may apply to companies that do not have sufficient profits against which to set off their capital allowances and interest payments, or to companies that have unrelieved advanced corporation tax (ACT) due to paying high dividends relative to their profit level in previous years. The latter case is particularly true of UK multinational companies who earn a large proportion of their profits overseas while paying high dividends in the UK, due to their inability to offset ACT against foreign profits.

Increasing earnings per share

If a bidding company has a higher price/earnings ratio compared to its target company, the bidder can increase its overall earnings proportionally more than it has to increase its share capital if the take-over is financed by a share-for-share issue. The result is that its post-acquisition earnings per share (EPS) is higher than its pre-acquisition earnings per share: its EPS has been boosted through acquisition. This boosting can be beneficial to the company, as EPS is deemed to be a key ratio by market analysts and its increase can, potentially, lead to a share price rise. The process whereby companies seek to increase their EPS through take-over activity is sometimes known as 'boot-strapping'. A numerical example of how boot-strapping can increase a bidding company's EPS is shown below. This motive cannot be used to justify take-overs from a shareholder wealth perspective, however, as changes in the level of a company's EPS are not a satisfactory indicator as to whether a merger is wealth-creating or not. There are many drawbacks associated with the focus on the EPS ratio as a guide to company performance, including the fact that it ignores cash flow and risk and that it uses historic numbers based on accounting profit, which is subject to both arbitrary accounting policies and to possible manipulation by company management. In fact, 'boot-strapping' can be considered merely as another exercise in creative accounting.

Example Boot-strapping

Big plc is to take over Little plc and, as a means of payment, is offering its shares in return for Little's shares.

	Big plc	*Little plc*
Number of shares	200m	25m
Earnings	£20m	£5m
EPS	10p	20p
P/E ratio	25	5
Share price	£2.50p	£1
Market value	£500m	£25m

If we assume that Big has to pay £25m to take over Little, Big must issue 10 million new shares. Details of the combined companies are as follows:

Number of shares	210m
Earnings	£25m
EPS	11.9p

Here we can see that Big has managed to manufacture an increase in its EPS. Big plc hopes that the market will then apply its original P/E ratio of 25 to its higher post-take-over EPS. If this is the case, then Big's shares and hence its market value will increase:

EPS	11.9p
P/E ratio	25

Share price	£2.97p
Market value	£623.7m

Whether in practice the market applies a P/E ratio of 25 will depend on its expectations of the performance of Little once it has been taken over by Big. If there is an expectation that Big will pull Little's performance up to its own level, then the market may well apply the P/E ratio of 25 to Big's EPS. A more likely scenario, though, is for the market to apply some other P/E ratio to the earnings of the combined companies, perhaps a weighted average of the two companies' P/E ratios.

11.2.3 Managerial motives

Take-overs can also arise due to the agency problem that exists between shareholders and management, whereby managers are more concerned with enhancing their own utility rather than that of the shareholders. From this perspective, the motives behind some take-overs may be to increase managers' emoluments and power, or to make their jobs more secure. The belief is that the larger an organisation is, the less likely it is to be taken over by another company and hence the less likely it is that its current management team will be out of a job. From a shareholder wealth perspective, take-overs made on these grounds cannot be justified, as managers are likely to increase their own wealth at the expense of the company's shareholders.

11.2.4 The case against acquisition

So far we have only put forward the arguments that can be used for justifying mergers and take-overs. To arrive at a more balanced picture, we need to take into consideration the arguments that can be put forward *against* growth by acquisition and merger.

Possible referral to the Monopolies and Mergers Commission (MMC)

A referral to the MMC can be very damaging to both the image of a predator company and to its pocket. If a formal investigation results from such a referral, it may delay the proposed take-over for a considerable amount of time. Depending on the result of the investigation, the take-over may not even be allowed to proceed.

The bid is contested

If a bid is contested, the predator company may well end up paying a large premium on top of the original market price in order to acquire its target. Indeed, with take-over premiums averaging around the 50 per cent mark, acquisition is viewed by many as a relatively expensive way of expanding.

Are mergers and take-overs beneficial?

Research on post-merger performance, which is considered later, suggests that the expected benefits arising from synergy and economies of scale very rarely materialise and that, in general, the only beneficiaries from take-over activity are the target company's shareholders.

The cost of financing a take-over

If a take-over bid is financed by a share-for-share offer, the predator company will have to find money to pay dividends on the new shares that have been issued. There may also be changes in its ownership structure. Conversely, if a take-over bid is financed by debt, it may increase the predator company's gearing to levels where it may have difficulties meeting interest payments in the future. Consideration must also be given to the arrangement and issue fees that will be incurred by issuing securities to finance the take-over.

Other difficulties

There are a plethora of other difficulties that companies engaging in take-over activity may encounter. Cultural problems are likely to exist, especially when acquiring companies in different industries, or in different countries if the take-over is a cross-border one. Cross-border take-overs are also subject to exchange rate risk, from both a transaction and a translation perspective. These risks are looked at in greater detail in Chapter 12. Take-over transactions can involve complicated taxation and legal issues and, partly in consequence, may incur large advisory fees. Finally, in some cases, the quality of the assets purchased may turn out to be lower than initially expected. An example of this occurred following the purchase of the US Crocker Bank by Midland Bank plc in the early 1980s, when a large amount of the advances previously made by the Crocker Bank turned out to be bad debts rather than assets.

11.3 TRENDS IN TAKE-OVER ACTIVITY

One thing that becomes apparent if we study Exhibit 11.2 (which gives information on the number of take-overs, the total outlay involved and the methods of financing) is that merger and take-over activity tends to occur in 'waves'. Such waves occurred in 1972–3, the late 1970s, the end of the 1980s and the mid-1990s, with the last wave being by far the largest in terms of total outlay. These waves have been different in nature. The late 1980s saw high levels of take-over activity by conglomerate companies, who purchased what they considered to be underpriced targets in a diverse range of industries, in many cases subjecting them to restructuring and break-up. In contrast, the most recent wave of the mid-1990s has involved horizontal acquisitions concentrated in a number of specific industries such as electrical distribution, pharmaceuticals and financial services. Here, acquiring companies have sought to create economies of scale and synergy in areas such as research and development and marketing by acquiring businesses with similar operations.

While the characteristics of merger waves may differ, a question that is frequently asked is, 'why do mergers and take-overs tend to occur in waves?' A large

EXHIBIT 11.2

Year	*Number acquired*	*Outlay (£m)*	*Cash (%)*	*Shares (%)*	*Debt and preference shares (%)*
1970	793	1 122	22	53	25
1971	884	911	31	48	21
1972	1210	2 532	19	58	23
1973	1205	1 304	53	36	11
1974	504	508	68	22	9
1975	315	291	59	32	9
1976	353	448	72	27	2
1977	481	824	62	37	1
1978	567	1 140	57	41	2
1979	534	1 656	56	31	13
1980	469	1 475	52	45	3
1981	452	1 144	68	30	3
1982	463	2 206	58	32	10
1983	447	2 343	44	54	2
1984	568	5 474	54	34	13
1985	474	7 090	40	52	7
1986	842	15 370	26	57	17
1987	1528	16 539	35	60	5
1988	1499	22 839	70	22	8
1989	1337	27 250	82	13	5
1990	776	8 235	77	18	5
1991	506	10 343	70	29	1
1992	432	5 941	63	36	1
1993	542	6 846	80	17	3
1994	674	8 268	64	34	2
1995	503	32 536	78	20	2
1996	547	27 863	67	32	1

The scale and method of financing of take-over activity in the UK between 1970 and 1996

Source: CSO Business Monitor and Financial Statistics

number of reasons have been advanced in an attempt to answer this question, but no consensus has yet been reached. The combination of a booming stock exchange (enabling companies to use shares to finance acquisitions) and an increase in companies' real liquidity and profitability levels is often cited as a factor encouraging take-over activity. This argument is contradicted, though, when we consider that one of the biggest booms in take-over activity followed the 1987 Stock Exchange crash. There can be no doubt, however, that certain factors have helped to accommodate the financing side of take-overs. Deregulation in the capital markets, for example, making external sources of finance such as debt more available, in combination with low levels of corporate gearing in the early 1980s, certainly increased the capacity of companies to acquire debt for the purpose of financing take-overs and to accommodate borrowings on their balance sheets.

11.4 VALUATION OF THE TARGET COMPANY

An important consideration in any take-over is the ability of the predator company to place a value on the company it is trying to acquire. Once it has established a value for its target, a predator company can then compare this value with the expected cost of the acquisition itself. Unfortunately, placing a value on a company is a very complicated process, if only due to the many different methods of valuation that can be used. In this sense, business valuation is considered by many to be more of an 'art' than a science.

There are two broad approaches that can be used when valuing companies. A company's value can be calculated according to the value of the assets of the company itself or, alternatively, by reference to the future earnings or cash flows that are expected to be obtained through the ownership and utilisation of its assets. The latter approach is sometimes referred to as a *going concern valuation*. Due to the existence of many different techniques within these two broad approaches, it is possible to come up with a number of different valuations of a single company. Indeed, two predator companies can come up with different valuations of the same target company due to the differing plans that each has for the target. Each method of valuation has its associated advantages and disadvantages and will be more or less appropriate according to the intentions of the acquirer towards its victim; for example, does the purchaser want to break up its acquisition or does it want to integrate its assets into its own operations?

The different methods of company valuation are now considered in turn and are illustrated with the help of a numerical example.

Example Take-over (Simpson and Stant)

Simpson plc has distributable earnings of £72.7m, a weighted average cost of capital of 14 per cent and a P/E ratio of 18.7. It is in the process of taking over Stant plc whose financial details are as follows:

Stant plc – Key financial data

Profit before interest and tax (PBIT)	£66m
Interest paid	£7.2m
Corporation tax	£17.64m
Distributable earnings	£41.16m
Current dividend	15p
Last 4 years' dividends:	10p, 12p, 12p, 14p
Earnings per share (EPS)	16.7p
P/E ratio	12.87
Market price of ordinary shares	£2.15
Equity beta	1.17

Stant plc – Balance sheet

	£m	*£m*
Fixed asset		265
Current assets	60	
Current liabilities	43	
		17
		282
10 per cent debentures (redemption 2015)		72
		210
Financed by:		
ordinary shares (50p)		123
reserves		87
		210

Simpson plc is optimistic that it will be able to maintain an annual increase in distributable earnings of five per cent per annum due to anticipated synergy as a result of the take-over. The company will also be able to sell duplicated assets which will realise £60m in one year's time. The risk-free rate of return is nine per cent and the return on the market as a whole is 15 per cent.

11.4.1 Stock market valuation

This method of valuation is straightforward in that it is calculated by taking the number of ordinary shares of a company and multiplying it by their current market price. Whether this represents a fair price will depend, naturally, on the efficiency of the stock market. It must also be recognised that a company's quoted share price does not reflect the value of all of a company's shares, since only a small proportion of shares are traded at any one time. The quoted share price, then, only reflects marginal trading. In addition, this method of valuation is unlikely to be available if the target company has issued ordinary shares but they are not frequently traded, or if the target company has not been floated on a recognised stock exchange at all.

For Stant, number of ordinary shares = 123m × 2 = 246m
Stock market valuation = 246m × £2.15 = £529m

For take-over purposes, the stock market valuation of a target company's shares is useful as an initial starting point or floor as to what the purchase price will be, since it represents the minimum that shareholders of the target are likely to accept. A substantial purchase premium will need to be added to this floor value as an incentive to persuade the shareholders to give up their shares. Furthermore, the market value does not reflect the full value of the target company to the predator company, as it fails to incorporate the post-acquisition intentions of the predator company.

11.4.2 Asset valuation

There are several different ways in which a company's assets can be valued.

Book value

The most straightforward asset valuation is the balance sheet or book value of a company's assets. Book or asset valuation can be defined as:

Net asset value (NAV) = fixed assets + net current assets – long-term debt

In our example, using Stant's balance sheet values:

NAV = 265m + 17m – 72m = £210m

While this valuation method has the advantage that it uses historical costs that are both factual and available, it also has a number of disadvantages. For example, balance sheet historical cost values do not reflect current asset valuations, debtor and stock figures may be unreliable, and intangible assets such as goodwill, human capital and brands are ignored. Therefore, net asset value, even at its most reliable, only offers a lower limit of a company's value.

Realisable or break-up value

It is possible that, instead of using book values, assets can be valued according to their net realisable value. This valuation is based on the amount that could be realised if the target company's assets were sold on the open market. It can be formally defined as 'the residual value left after the realisation of assets, the deduction of liquidation costs and the paying off of liabilities'. In theory, the market value of a company should be higher or at least no less than its break-up value. If its market value is lower than its break-up value, the implication is that the company is undervalued, perhaps due to inefficiencies in the stock market, and a predator company can make a risk-free windfall gain by acquiring the company and stripping it of its assets.

The calculation of the net realisable value of a company's assets is not easy. The book values of the assets are unlikely to be indicative of their market value, as they are based on historic cost. In the case of property, balance sheet figures often underestimate its true value. With respect to stock, despite the requirement of accounting standards that it be recorded at the lower of cost and net realisable value, book values may overestimate realisable value if items need to be sold quickly, or if they have become obsolete. Another factor to consider is that the assets of certain companies are unique and may not be able to be easily sold on an appropriate 'second-hand' market. The break-up values of such assets can only ever be estimates. A further problem is that provisions for unforeseen liabilities may need to be made.

In the case of most take-overs, the break-up value is not the most appropriate method of valuation anyway, as very few take-overs involve a total break-up of the victim company. This method may be partially applicable if part of the victim is to be sold off and part is to be integrated into the predator company's operations.

Replacement value

This method seeks to determine the cost of acquiring the separate assets of a target company on an open market basis. It has an advantage over a book valuation in that replacement cost estimates of asset values are more relevant than historic cost estimates. Unfortunately, though, it does not take account of goodwill. It also requires the identification of the company's separate assets and the determination of the replacement cost for these individual assets. Given that the majority of corporate assets are part-used, it will prove difficult finding second-hand assets of equivalent condition.

Due to a lack of information, we have not calculated the realisable and replacement values of Stant's assets. This is likely to be the case for most predator companies who, while being able to obtain the book value of a company's assets through its annual published accounts, will have great difficulty in determining their replacement cost and realisable value without obtaining access to the necessary inside information.

11.4.3 Going concern valuation

The valuation of a target company as a going concern is appropriate if the intention of the predator company is for it to continue in business for the foreseeable future with no significant changes in operations, as opposed to it being broken up or asset-stripped following the acquisition. There are many ways to calculate the value of a company as a going concern. These are now considered and illustrated quantitatively using the example of Stant plc.

Capitalised earnings valuation

Under this method, a valuation is calculated by capitalising a company's annual maintainable expected earnings by an appropriate required earnings yield or return on investment. Annual maintainable expected earnings can be estimated by taking an average of historical earnings, weighted or otherwise, and allowing for any expected future increase in earnings due to synergy or economies of scale. The discount rate used to capitalise this earnings stream should reflect factors such as the size of the company and the industry in which it is operating. The valuation using this method is as follows:

$$\text{Capitalised earnings value} = \frac{\text{Annual maintainable expected earnings}}{\text{Required earnings yield}}$$

In our example, the approximated capitalisation rate is as follows:

Required earnings yield = EPS/share price = (16.7/215) × 100 = 7.8%
This is also the reciprocal of the P/E ratio: (1/12.87) × 100 = 7.8%

We only have the current distributable earnings, but if we assume that they are equivalent to the annual maintainable expected earnings and capitalise them, we have:

Capitalised earnings value = £41.16m/0.078 = £528m

Because of the way we have determined the required earnings yield, this is the same as the stock market valuation obtained earlier. An advantage of using this method is that, in terms of expected earnings, it is a forward-looking measure and so encourages forecasts of future performance to be made. The disadvantages associated with its use include the uncertainty that surrounds the accuracy of the earnings figure, which may be subject to differing accounting policies and to different treatments of exceptional and extraordinary items.

Price/earnings ratio valuation

This valuation method involves multiplying the target company's distributable earnings by an appropriate P/E ratio where:

$$\text{P/E ratio} = \frac{\text{Market value of company}}{\text{Distributable earnings}}$$

A major determining factor of the valuation arrived at by this method is the P/E ratio selected. Possible P/E ratios will include the predator's P/E ratio, the victim company's P/E ratio and a weighted combination of the two. If the target company's P/E ratio is used, we obtain the following result for Stant:

Company value = 12.87 × £41.16m = £528m

This yields a figure similar to the capitalised earnings valuation since, as mentioned earlier, the P/E ratio of a company is the reciprocal of its earnings yield. Alternatively, if the predator company is sure that it will be able to bring the level of performance of its victim up to its own performance, it is more appropriate to use its own P/E ratio. In our example, if Simpson is convinced that it can improve Stant's financial performance, then:

Company value = 18.70 × £41.16m = £770m

If the future performance of neither predator nor victim is expected to change, it is logically more appropriate to apply a weighted average of the two companies'

P/E ratios. If we weight the P/E ratios of Stant and Simpson by their current distributable earnings, we obtain:

$$(12.87 \times (41.16/113.86)) + (18.70 \times (72.7/113.86)) = 16.59$$
$$\text{Company value} = 16.59 \times £41.16\text{m} = £682\text{m}$$

While this method is relatively straightforward in terms of calculation, it can be seen from the examples given that the valuation arrived at fluctuates widely according to which P/E ratio is applied. Therefore, in addition to the problems associated with using distributable earnings, such as the fact that different companies use different bases to calculate them, there are the further difficulties associated with estimating an appropriate post-merger P/E ratio to apply.

Gordon growth model

The value of a company can be estimated by using the Gordon growth model (*see* Section 7.3.4) to calculate the present value of future dividends accruing to its shares. Here:

$$P_0 = \frac{D_0(1 + g)}{(r - g)}$$

where: D_0 = current total dividend payment
g = expected annual growth rate of dividends
r = required rate of return of the company's shareholders.

In order to apply this model to Stant plc, we need to calculate a value for the annual growth, g. We can do this by using the values of its historical dividends, as follows:

$$10 \times (1 + g)^4 = 15$$

Hence:

$$g = \sqrt[4]{\frac{15}{10}} - 1 = 10.7\%$$

We can find the total amount of dividends paid recently (D_0) by multiplying the dividend per share by the number of Stant's shares:

$$£0.15 \times 246\text{m shares} = £36.9\text{m}$$

The only information we require now is r, the required return of Stant's shareholders. It is appropriate to use the required rate of return of shareholders of the target company, rather than those of the predator company, since it is the former shareholders who are being asked to sell their shares and this valuation method gives an indication of what they are giving up. We can calculate the required return of Stant's shareholders by using the CAPM and the data supplied earlier:

$$r = 9\% + 1.17 \times (15\% - 9\%) = 16\%$$

If we put our calculated data into the Gordon model we obtain:

$$\text{Company value} = \frac{£36.9\text{m} \times (1 + 0.107)}{(0.16 - 0.107)} = £771\text{m}$$

The limitations of this model were discussed in Section 7.3.4. The major drawback noted there was the sensitivity of the model to the value of g.

Discounted cash flow valuation

The maximum amount that Simpson should be prepared to pay for Stant is the difference between the present values of its pre- and post-acquisition cash flows:

$$PV_{X+Y} - PV_Y$$

Determining these present values requires the estimation of relevant cash flows and the selection or calculation of an appropriate discount rate. Discounted cash flow valuations are theoretically and academically preferred, but there are a number of problems which must be dealt with before any useful information is obtained from this approach to determining the value of a target company.

- One problem that must be solved is the difficulty of quantifying and incorporating into future cash flow predictions any expected synergy benefits or economies of scale and deciding upon the rate at which these cash flows are expected to grow in the future.
- We must decide on an appropriate time period over which to estimate future cash flows and determine a terminal value for the company at the end of this period. Corporate forecasting is usually geared to a five-year time horizon and so, as a rough guideline, a five-year time span and multiples thereof may be most appropriate.
- Which discount rate should be used? The most appropriate discount rate is likely to be the predator company's cost of capital, but the difficulties associated with its calculation must be overcome. There are certain situations, however, where the predator company's WACC is not appropriate, for example when the victim company possesses significantly different risk characteristics to those of the predator company. In such circumstances, the CAPM can be used to determine a discount rate which takes into account the systematic risk of the victim company.

Referring back to the example of Stant plc, we have insufficient information to determine the difference between the pre- and post-acquisition cash flows of the company. However, if we use distributable earnings as an approximate substitute, we have:

Current distributable earnings	£72.7m
Stant's distributable earnings	£41.16m
Total post-acquisition earnings	£113.8m

Simpson expects to be able to increase earnings by five per cent per year. Simpson also expects to be able to sell surplus assets for £60m in one year.

In the absence of a better alternative, we can discount by Simpson's WACC:

Present value of post-acquisition earnings	
= ((113.8 × 1.05)/(0.14 − 0.05)) + (60/1.14) =	£1380m
Present value of pre-acquisition earnings = (72.7/0.14) =	£519m
Maximum price that Simpson should be prepared to pay:	£861m

This valuation is based on the assumption that growth in distributable earnings will occur only if the acquisition goes ahead and has used the Gordon model.

11.4.4 Summary

We stated earlier that company valuation was considered to be more of an art than a science and that a wide range of valuation techniques can be applied to a target company under consideration. These different techniques have been illustrated by the calculation of a range of values for Stant plc in our example. Estimates have ranged from £210m up to £861m. The accuracy of the different valuations will depend on the reliability of the data used. Which valuation method is most appropriate will depend upon the information available to the predator company and its intentions for the target company.

Summary of the valuations of Stant plc that have been obtained:

	£m
Stock market valuation	529
Net asset value (using book values)	210
Capitalised earnings valuation	528
P/E ratio valuation	528 or 682 or 769
Gordon growth model valuation	771
DCF valuation	861

11.5 THE FINANCING OF ACQUISITIONS

Due to the sheer size of many take-overs, the financial implications of these transactions for the companies involved are significant. There are many ways in which a take-over can be financed, with differing methods of financing having significantly different financial implications. When deciding upon its method of financing, it is important for the predator company to recognise that the needs of both sets of shareholders involved must be satisfied.

If we refer back to Exhibit 11.2, we can observe the ways in which take-over activity has been financed in the past. A large percentage of the take-overs between 1985 and 1987 were financed through share-for-share offers, primarily due to the boom in company share prices during this period. Since 1987, however, there has been an increase in cash financing in the aftermath of the stock market crash of October 1987.

11.5.1 Cash offers

Here the target company's shares are purchased using cash. A cash offer is attractive to the target company's shareholders because the compensation they receive for giving up their shares is certain – which is not the case with a share-for-share offer since the value of the predator company's shares is not certain and is likely to change during the take-over. Target company shareholders can then adjust their portfolios (without incurring selling costs) once they have received their cash remuneration. These advantages must be balanced against the disadvantage that if the shares are sold at a higher price than their original purchase price, sellers may be liable to pay capital gains tax on the disposal. Clearly, this will be unattractive to shareholders with large portfolios, as they are more likely to have used up their capital gains allowance. From the point of large institutional investors, cash offers are more attractive since pension funds and unit trusts are exempt from paying capital gains tax. The differing tax positions of small and large private and institutional investors helps to explain why mixed cash and share-for-share issues have grown in popularity. These are considered later in Section 11.5.5.

There are also significant advantages of cash offers to the bidding company and its shareholders. First, it allows them to see exactly how much is being offered for the victim company. Second, cash offers will not affect the number of equity shares the predator company has in issue, and so will not alter the predator company's ownership structure or lead to dilution of its earnings per share.

A major issue concerning cash issues is where the cash is raised from. In a large number of cases, due to the size of take-overs, the predator company rarely has to hand sufficient cash generated from retained earnings and will therefore have to find cash from external sources. A source that has been frequently used in the past is debt finance, raised either through borrowing from banks (often in the form of *mezzanine* finance) or by the issue of debt securities. Where large amounts of cash are borrowed in order to make the cash payment, the take-over is referred to as a *leveraged* take-over. A problem for companies with high levels of gearing is that they may experience difficulty in finding a sufficient number of banks or other financial intermediaries that are prepared to supply them with the large amounts of debt finance they require.

Because high gearing is undesirable, many companies that increase their gearing to very high levels in order to finance a take-over will subsequently sell off parts of the acquired business in order to bring their gearing down to a more acceptable level.

In 1988 in the UK there was a large increase in the number of cash offer take-overs financed by debt (*see* Exhibit 11.2). The fact that, as a result, many companies experienced high levels of gearing was not seen as problematic because interest rates were at a relatively low level. As the 1980s drew to a close, however, interest rates increased rapidly and the gearing levels of these 'highly leveraged' companies became a cause for concern. As a result, a number of companies that had borrowed heavily to finance take-over activity had to seek re-financing, through rights issues for example, in order to 'repair' their balance sheets.

There were also a large number of leveraged take-overs in the US during the 1980s. A common occurrence was for small companies to borrow massive amounts of money from banks or to issue unsecured high-risk, high-return *junk bonds* in order to take over companies much larger than themselves. An example of this is the $25bn take-over of RJR Nabisco in 1988 by the small private company Kohlberg, Kraves and Roberts (KKR). KKR financed the transaction through borrowing and issuing junk bonds, and subsequently sold off part of RJR Nabisco to reduce its gearing level.

11.5.2 Share-for-share offers

Here, the victim company's shareholders are offered a fixed number of shares in the predator company in exchange for the shares they hold in their own company. For the victim company's shareholders, one advantage of a share-for-share offer is that they still have an equity interest in the company that they originally invested in, even though it is now part of a larger concern. In addition, they do not incur the brokerage costs associated with reinvesting any cash received, nor do they incur any capital gains tax liability arising from the disposal of their shares.

A disadvantage to both the acquiring company and its shareholders is that equity payments tend to work out as more expensive than cash offers. Because the value of the shares being offered will vary over time, the share-for-share offer made will have to err on the side of generosity in order to prevent it becoming unattractive should the predator company's share price fall. There are also possible disadvantages arising from the predator company increasing the number of its shares in circulation. The actual effect on the company's share price is unknown, although a fall in price is likely, which will be unpopular with its shareholders. It is also likely that a dilution of control may occur due to the issue of the new shares. On a more subtle level, the decrease in gearing that will result from issuing more shares may move the predator company away from its optimal capital structure and therefore increase its cost of capital.

Share-for-share offers can be used by predator companies with high P/E ratios to engineer an increase in their EPS if their victim has a lower P/E ratio. This was dismissed in Section 11.2.2 as an acceptable justification for taking over a company as, while the predator company's EPS may increase, it does not involve any intrinsic increase in the wealth of its shareholders.

11.5.3 Vendor placings and vendor rights

These methods of financing are variations on the theme of a cash offer and exploit a loophole in the Accounting Standards definition of a merger, allowing companies to apply merger rather than take-over accounting rules to the post-merger company. If a company offers cash to target company shareholders, the transaction is classified as a take-over and merger accounting cannot be used. Merger accounting is allowed, however, when the two parties of shareholders involved continue, or have the option to continue, their shareholding as before but on a combined basis.

With a vendor placing, the acquiring company offers shares to the target company shareholders, giving them the option to continue their shareholding. However, the acquiring company simultaneously arranges for the new shares to be placed with institutional investors, and for the cash to be paid to the target company's shareholders. A vendor rights issue works in a similar manner, differing only with respect to the final destination of the offered shares. Instead of being placed with institutional investors, the shares are offered to the acquiring company's shareholders. If they are accepted, the cash is then paid to the victim company's shareholders. Any rights shares not taken up are placed with institutions.

11.5.4 Security packages

The use of securities other than the ordinary shares of the predator as a means of payment to target company shareholders is now rare. It can be seen from Exhibit 11.2 that the use of security packages, which can include bonds, convertibles and preference shares, has played only a minor role in the financing of take-overs since the mid to late 1980s, although it represented a popular financing choice for companies up until the late 1960s. The popularity of the use of debt security packages was finally killed off by the high levels of inflation (and the correspondingly higher levels of interest) caused by the oil crises of the 1970s. The problems of using these securities as a method of payment are now considered.

Straight debentures and loan stock

A major problem with using ordinary debt securities as a means of payment is their acceptability from the point of view of the target company's shareholders. Investors who have previously bought shares to satisfy their preferences for high risk and high return may be unhappy to exchange their shares in the victim company for low risk and low return debt securities. On the plus side, issuing debt may not lead to any dilution of the predator company's EPS, and interest payments are also tax efficient. While the use of bonds will lead to an increase in the predator company's gearing, over the life of such bonds it can build up cash reserves with which to pay off the stock on maturity.

Convertible bonds

Some of the problems associated with the use of straight bonds may be partially resolved by offering convertible bonds to the victim company's shareholders. Convertibles are attractive to them because they offer their holders a means of benefiting from future corporate growth on conversion. Considerable advantages exist from the predator company's point of view. When using convertibles rather than ordinary shares as a method of payment, dilution of EPS will not occur immediately but will be delayed until the securities are converted. Also, due to their relative attractiveness when compared with straight or *vanilla* debt, convertibles tend to pay a lower coupon rate which can greatly ease the cash flow situation of the predator company. Even though banks may not be prepared to lend money to a predator company because of the high post-acquisition gearing level that would arise, target shareholders may be prepared to accept convertibles as payment in the expectation that, at some date in the future, the company's gearing level will be reduced as the conversion into ordinary equity occurs.

Preference shares

The use of preference shares as a means of payment is even less common than the use of bonds. For the predator company, preference shares are less attractive than ordinary equity because preference dividends are less flexible than ordinary share dividends. Preference dividends are also distributions of after-tax profit and are not an allowable deduction against taxable profit. For the victim company's shareholders, preference shares offer neither the ownership aspects of equity shares nor the security of a cash offer.

11.5.5 Mixed bids

Mixed bids, where a share-for-share offer is supported by a cash alternative, have become an increasingly popular method of payment in the UK. There are two major reasons for their increase in popularity. The first is that mixed bids are perceived as being more acceptable to the target company's shareholders as they can select the method of payment that best suits their liquidity preference and tax position. Second, Rule 9 of the City Code on Take-overs and Mergers (1988), requires companies acquiring 30 per cent or more of a target company's shares to make a cash offer (or cash alternative if a share-for-share payment is being used) at the highest price paid by the predator for the victim company's shares over the previous 12-month period.

11.6 STRATEGIC AND TACTICAL ISSUES

11.6.1 An introduction

When a company is engaging in acquisitional behaviour it is vital that it gives due consideration to the strategy and tactics it is going to employ. Before it becomes involved in take-over activity, it must satisfy itself that acquisition represents a more efficient alternative than organic growth or the independent purchase of required assets. Once a company has satisfied itself on these points, the strategic process that it should follow towards acquiring a target company can be summarised as follows.

1 Identify suitable target companies.
2 Obtain as much information about the target companies as possible.
3 Using the information obtained, value each of the possible target companies and decide upon the maximum purchase price that might be countenanced for each alternative.
4 Decide which of the potential target companies is most appropriate.

5 Decide upon the best way to finance the acquisition, taking into account which methods of payment are acceptable to both sets of shareholders.

Once a predator company has gone through this strategic process it must then decide upon the take-over tactics it will employ. Failure to employ the right tactics can result in a predator paying over the odds or, in the worst-case scenario, failing to acquire its target altogether. In addition, companies must be aware of the rules and regulations governing mergers and take-overs.

Before we look in more detail at the regulatory environment governing merger and take-over activity, it is important to establish the significance, both legal and otherwise, of the various levels of shareholding. A summary of levels of shareholding and their associated implications is given in Exhibit 11.3.

EXHIBIT 11.3

Voting rights held (%)	*Implications and legal obligations of shareholding level*
90 and over	Once 90% of shares are held the company has a right to purchase compulsorily the remaining shares.
75 and over	The acquiring company can change the articles of association of the company taken over and put it into liquidation.
50 and over	The company can influence dividend policy and appoint management.
30 and over	Implies effective control with respect to public companies and hence requires the launch of a formal take-over bid.
25 and over	Minority influence to dividend policy and management and an ability to block changes to the company's articles.
20 and over	According to the 1981 Companies Act implies related company status.
10 and over	Can prevent a complete take-over.
5 and over	Taking a holding over 5% in a company requires formal notification.

Table showing the implications associated with different proportions of shareholding

The most significant level of shareholding from an acquisition perspective is that associated with holding 50 per cent of a company's voting rights. Once a predator company has more than 50 per cent of its victims shares, it has the power to dismiss and appoint directors and effectively has control of the victim company's decision-making process.

11.6.2 Merger regulation and control

There are, broadly speaking, two types of regulation that govern merger and take-over activity, which we can characterise as legal controls and self-regulatory controls.

Legal controls

Take-over activity is subject to a number a statutory controls, the most important of which is the Fair Trading Act of 1973. Under this Act, the Director General of Fair Trading is required to review all mergers and take-overs that involve the formation of a company that accounts for greater than a 25 per cent share of a particular market, or that involve the purchase of assets that amount to over £30m. The Director General collects information on mergers and take-overs that meet these criteria and, after reviewing the evidence, approaches the Secretary of State if he considers a merger or take-over should be investigated by the Monopolies and Mergers Commission (MMC). Investigations by the MMC usually take up to six months, during which time the Commission considers if the merger or take-over is in the public interest or not. If it decides that it is not, it can prohibit the transaction. The criteria that are considered in deciding whether a merger should be referred are meant to indicate whether a merger will maintain or promote the public interests as regards:

- effective competition within the industry;
- the interests of consumers, purchasers and users of the goods and services of that industry with respect to quality, price and variety;
- the reduction of costs and the introduction of new products and techniques.

In practice, only a small number of mergers reviewed by the Director General are actually referred, and an even smaller proportion are found by the MMC to be against the public interest. Companies can usually receive an informal indication as to whether their take-over activities are likely to be subject to referral. On finding out that they are likely to be referred, the majority of companies subsequently drop their proposed transactions due to the delay and potentially adverse publicity associated with an investigation by the MMC.

Self-regulatory controls

The London Stock Exchange has its own rule book which member companies must adhere to. The Stock Exchange itself answers to the Securities and Investment Board (SIB), a self-regulatory organisation (SRO) set up by the Financial Services Act 1986. One of the Stock Exchange requirements is that its member companies keep their shareholders adequately informed. In addition, the Council of the Securities Industry issues a City Code that must also be obeyed. This is based on a number of general principles, some of which are rooted in the concept of equity between shareholders. While these principles are not enforceable by law, non-compliance can result in the facilities of the capital market being withdrawn.

11.6.3 The bidding process

When a company launches a bid, it is often carried out in consultation with financial advisers such as merchant banks and, as mentioned earlier, it is important for the company to consider carefully the tactics it employs. Having decided upon a maximum price that it is prepared to pay, the acquiring company will aim to pay as far below this price as possible. The market price of the shares of the target company will act as a lower limit, on top of which the acquiring company can expect to pay a premium. Jensen (1993) found that, historically, the premiums paid in successful take-overs have not tended to be less than 30 per cent, while averaging out at approximately 50 per cent. Major determinants of the acquisition price finally paid include whether or not a take-over is contested and whether the predator company employs the most appropriate tactics during the take-over process.

As mentioned in the previous section, the City Code must be adhered to during the bidding process. This is to protect the interests of the various groups of shareholders involved. The code includes the following procedures:

- The acquiring company must notify its potential victim five days after it has built up a five per cent holding of its shares. This reduces the possibility of what are known as *dawn raids*, where predator companies sneak up on their victims before they have had time to organise their defences. Predators can get round this by using *concert parties*, where friendly companies form a coalition in which no one company holds more than the notifiable five per cent level of shareholding.
- Once 30 per cent of the victim company's shares are held, the predator has to make a cash offer to all remaining shareholders at a price no less than the highest price paid in the preceding 12-month period.
- When the acquiring company makes the offer, it must first inform the board of the target company of the nature and terms of its offer. This information must then be passed on by the victim company's board to the shareholders. The acquiring company then has to post the terms of its offer to the victim company's shareholders 28 days after its announcement.
- Once the offer has been received, the victim company's board will express their views as to the acceptability of the offer. The acquiring company may also be required by the Stock Exchange rule book to get approval from its own shareholders with respect to the proposed bid. Offers once posted are open for 21 days. If any amendments to the initial offer are made then a further 14 days is allowed.
- An offer becomes unconditional when the acquiring company has obtained more than 50 per cent of the victim company's shares. Once the offer has become unconditional, existing shareholders have 14 days either to sell their shares or to become minority shareholders in the new company.
- Partial bids, where the acquiring company bids for a specific percentage of the victim company's share capital, are allowed only in certain circumstances and require prior approval from the Take-over Panel. Permission is usually only

given for partial bids of less than 30 per cent of the target company's overall equity.

11.6.4 Bid defences

When a company receives a bid for its shares the management must decide whether they will contest the bid or not. If they decide to contest the bid, they should make this decision on the grounds that the offer is not in the best interests of their shareholders and not just because they don't want to lose their jobs. They must communicate their decision to contest the bid to their shareholders. It may be difficult for them to convince shareholders to reject the bid if it appears to be in the financial interests of shareholders to accept it. They may, then, seek to convince shareholders that the acquiring company's share price is artificially inflated and will drop after the proposed take-over, or perhaps argue that their own shares are currently undervalued by the market. Bid defences can be conveniently grouped into two types according to whether they were employed before or after a bid was received.

Pre-bid defences

Pre-bid defences are put into place prior to a formal take-over bid being made, with the purpose of making a company both difficult and expensive to take over, so as to dissuade bids being made in the first place. This defence is helped if the management of a company can, by monitoring the make-up of its share ownership, detect the possibility of a take-over bid long before it is formally launched. There are a number of ways for management to achieve these objectives which are consistent with the objective of maximising the wealth of the shareholders to whom they are responsible. These include the following defences.

1 *Improving operational efficiency*. Rationalising production, cutting overheads and improving labour productivity can raise a company's EPS and share price, making a potential take-over both more expensive and less likely.
2 *Examining asset portfolios and making necessary divestments*. Managers can sell off non-core, low-growth business and concentrate on the markets in which they have relative strengths. Again, this should lead to higher profits and a higher EPS and share price.
3 *Restructuring of equity*. A number of tactics are available within this area. For example, companies can repurchase their own shares to make it more difficult for predators to build up a controlling position, or they can increase their gearing level in order to make themselves less attractive to bidding companies. More intriguingly, companies can plant 'poison pills' within their capital structure, for example options giving rights to shareholders to buy future loan stock or preference shares. If a bidding company tries to take over the company before the rights have to be exercised, it is obliged to buy up the securities, hence increasing the cost of the acquisition.

4 *Management retrenchment devices*. The best known of these are 'golden parachutes', which give extremely generous termination packages for senior management and thereby increase the cost of the take-over, as substantial amounts of money have to be paid to get rid of incumbent managers.

5 *Ensuring good investor relations*. Maintaining good relations with both investors and analysts can make a take-over both more difficult and more expensive. The company should keep investors well informed about company strategy, policies and performance and also try to satisfy investors' risk/return preferences.

6 *Strategic defence via cross-holdings*. This device is used to ensure that a significant proportion of equity is in 'friendly hands' through companies arranging to take a mutual shareholding in each other in order to block potential take-over bids.

Post-bid defences

Post-bid defences are used by target companies to repel a bid once one has been made. Post-bid defences that are often used include the following.

1 *Rejection of the initial offer*. When a take-over bid is made, the bid is attacked to signal to the predator that the target company will contest the take-over. In some cases, this may be sufficient to scare the predator off.

2 *A pre-emptive circulation of shareholders*. Target companies can appeal to their own shareholders, explaining why the bid is not in their favour from both a logical and a price perspective.

3 *Formulation of a defence document*. The board of the target company can prepare a formal document for circulation amongst their own shareholders which praises their company's performance and criticises the bidding company and its offer.

4 *Profit announcements and forecasts*. The defending company can produce a report that indicates its forecast profits for the future will be much better than those expected by the market. If these revised forecasts are accepted by the market, this acceptance will force up the market price and make the proposed take-over more expensive. A major problem here is that, if the company does not meet these increased forecasts in the future, its share price is likely to fall, putting it at risk from another take-over bid and making it less likely that such a defence will be successful when used again.

5 *Dividend increase announcements*. A company can announce an increase in current dividend and an intention to pay increased dividends in the future. This expected increase in shareholder returns may dissuade them from selling their shares. Equally, they may query why increased returns were not paid prior to the arrival of a take-over bid.

6 *Revaluation of assets*. Before or after a bid is made a company can revalue certain assets on its balance sheet, such as land and buildings, or capitalise intangible assets in its balance sheet, such as brands and goodwill, in order to

make the company look stronger or more valuable. While this may lead to the predator company having to make an increased offer, it could be argued that, if capital markets are efficient, no new information is being offered to the market and the existing share price is a fair one.

7 *Searching for a white knight.* The target company can seek a more suitable company to take it over, although this tactic tends to be used only as a last resort. The City Code on mergers and take-overs allows this tactic, but if the target company passes any information to the 'white knight' it must also be passed to the initial predator company. A variation of this technique is to issue new shares to a 'white knight' in order to dilute the predator company's holdings. The defending company must get its shareholders' approval before it defends the take-over bid in this way, however.
8 *Pac-man defence.* This defence involves the target company making a counter-bid for the shares of the predator company. This option is difficult to organise and expensive to carry out, but it has been used on occasion in the US.
9 *Acquisitions and divestments.* The target company can either buy new assets or companies that are incompatible with its predator's business, or sell the 'crown jewels' or assets that the predator company is particularly interested in. This tactic is more common in the US than in the UK, since in the UK the City Code restricts the selling off of assets once a take-over bid has been made.

11.7 EMPIRICAL RESEARCH ON ACQUISITIONS

There have been a large number of empirical investigations looking into the performance of mergers and take-overs which have considered the impact of acquisition activity on the wealth of the various interest groups involved. It is difficult to establish whether mergers or take-over have been successful, however, as evaluation of success or failure in many cases involves a series of subjective judgements. In theory, benefits such as economies of scale and synergy are available to companies involved in take-overs and mergers. Whether companies manage to crystallise these potential gains in practice is another matter and will depend very heavily upon post-merger planning and management.

There is also a large body of information and research concerning how companies can increase the chances of successful take-overs and mergers, as well as studies of post-merger integration and the success of mergers that have taken place. De Noble *et al.* (1988) published a paper in which they laid out a number of lessons for merger success. These included involving line management in take-over activity, searching out any hidden costs that take-overs incur, management being aware of the existence of culture differences and appreciating the vital link between corporate structure and strategy.

The best way to build up a picture of whether merger activity is beneficial as a whole is to identify the groups affected by mergers and take-overs and then to consider the evidence regarding the impact of merger and take-over activity upon them. These interest groups are now considered in turn.

11.7.1 The economy

The most important question to ask here is whether or not take-overs produce a social gain for the economy as a whole. The answer to this question, in theory, is 'yes', as the potential for mergers and take-overs to create an economy-wide gain does exist if, as a consequence of acquisitional activity, assets are transferred from the control of inefficient management to the control of efficient management. Unfortunately though, the motives behind acquisitions often owe more to managerial self-interest than to the increased efficiency of the use of assets.

The weight of empirical evidence suggests that merger and take-over activity has, at best, a neutral effect and that there are no extreme efficiency gains. Cowling *et al.* (1980) used cost–benefit analysis to examine nine mergers that occurred between 1965 and 1970 in the UK, in order to determine whether increased efficiency through economies of scale outweighed the welfare loss from increased industrial concentration. They concluded that no real general efficiency gains were made and that in the UK, where most take-overs were of a horizontal nature, any such gains were neutralised by increased monopoly power. There were benefits in one or two instances where superior management gained control. Subsequent research has echoed the findings of Cowling *et al.* that the effect of mergers and take-overs on the economy is on the whole neutral. Although the economic wealth to be shared out between parties may not increase, scope still exists for certain parties to benefit at the expense of others.

11.7.2 The shareholders of the companies involved

Instead of considering the impact of merger and take-over activity at an economy-wide level, their impact can be assessed at a company level by examining the effect that acquisitional behaviour has on the wealth of predator and victim company shareholders. Two broad approaches can be used here.

The first is to use accounting and financial data to assess the performance of companies pre- and post-merger. The results of such surveys, including those carried out by Singh (1971) in the UK between 1955 and 1960 and Kelly (1967) in the US between 1946 and 1960, concluded that mergers have proved unprofitable from the acquiring company's viewpoint. It must be noted, however, that the results of such investigations rely very heavily on the quality and reliability of the accounting data used.

The second, and more commonly used method to quantify the benefits of mergers to the two shareholder groups, is to examine pre- and post-bid announcement share prices. Research in this area uses the capital asset pricing model (CAPM) to calculate expected returns for both predator and victim companies' shares before and after the announcement of a take-over bid. These are then compared with actual returns to allow the identification of any abnormal returns that are generated during the take-over period. The results of empirical studies employing this methodology have concluded that target company shareholders tend to enjoy significant positive abnormal returns while predator companies experience statistically insignificant negative or positive abnormal returns. Following on from this, many surveys conclude that, in the majority of cases, the gain made by the target company's shareholders outweighed the loss made by the bidding company. A study by Jensen and Ruback (1983) in the US showed average abnormal returns to bidding company shareholders of four per cent for successful bids, compared with a one per cent loss for failed bids. This contrasted heavily with shareholders of the target company, who on average experienced benefits of 30 per cent for successful bids and losses of three per cent for failed bids. In the UK, studies by Franks *et al.* (1988) and Firth (1980) found that predator companies experienced little or no abnormal gain during the take-over period.

A possible explanation of the benefits that accrue to target company shareholders is that they represent a bid premium which must be paid in order for target company shareholders to be persuaded to part with their shares. The observed lack of benefits to predator company shareholders at the time of take-overs may be explained by the efficiency of capital markets, i.e. the market predicts take-overs long before they actually occur and consequently impounds the benefits of the take-over into the predator company's share price a number of months before its announcement. This explanation was supported by Franks *et al.* (1977) who found evidence that the market began to anticipate mergers and take-overs at least three months before they were announced.

Finally, a number of surveys have considered the abnormal returns of predator and victim companies over the periods well before take-overs were made. The results suggest that predator companies, on average, earned positive abnormal returns over these periods while their victim companies experienced negative abnormal returns. This may give support to the idea that merger and take-over activity facilitates the transfer of assets and resources from less efficient to more efficient management.

Concluding this section, empirical surveys appear to be in agreement that substantial benefits accrue to victim company shareholders. There is less agreement over the benefits to predator company shareholders – some surveys finding no gains, others finding small statistically insignificant gains and losses. Many surveys have concluded that merger and take-over activity is not wealth *creating*, but instead involves the *transfer* of wealth from predator company shareholders to shareholders in the target company.

11.7.3 Management and employees of predator and victim companies

It is generally agreed that the predator company's management benefit from a successful take-over. This is due to the increased power and status of running a larger company, which is often reflected by an increase in management's financial rewards. In addition, the directors' jobs become more secure, as it is more difficult for other companies to take over the enlarged company. In contrast, the management of the victim company lose out, as in the majority of cases they are dismissed, either because they are deemed to be inefficient or because they are surplus to requirements. The same situation applies to the employees of the victim company.

Redundancies tend to follow the vast majority of take-overs. An obvious area in which to exploit economies of scale is to economise on the use of human capital by laying off workers in duplicated functions and by closing down unwanted parts of the acquired business in a streamlining process.

11.7.4 Financial institutions

Financial institutions, predominantly merchant banks, are involved in fee-making advisory roles in the merger and take-over process as advisors to both acquiring and target companies. They help in many aspects, from advising over bid values and organising defence tactics to the arrangement of financing for mergers and acquisitions. In the take-over boom year of 1995 it has been estimated that merchant banks in the City of London made advisory fees totalling in the region of £950m, clearly demonstrating that they are one of the parties to benefit most from merger and take-over activity.

11.7.5 Summary

The clear winners from take-over activity appear to be the shareholders of victim companies who receive substantial premiums over and above pre-merger share prices. Other parties that benefit from merger activity are investment banks, lawyers and accountants, who earn substantial fee income from offering advice, and the managers of the predator companies, who experience increased job security and remuneration. Evidence suggests that little or no benefit is felt by the shareholders of predator companies, especially when take-overs are contested and the predator company ends up paying over the odds for its target. There appears to be no clear evidence of any economic benefits of merger and take-over activity; however, if individual mergers involve the transfer of assets from inefficient to more efficient use, society will ultimately gain. The clear losers are the management and employees of victim companies who stand a high chance of losing their jobs once their company has been taken over.

11.8 CONCLUSION

In this chapter we have given a thorough consideration to take-overs and mergers, an area that continues to maintain a high profile in modern corporate finance and that has implications for companies' dividend, financing and investment policies. Many justifications have been offered for take-over and merger activity, not all of which have been accepted as valid by academics. The existence of many methods of company valuation illustrates the fact that determining a fair price for a target company is a very imprecise science. The financing implications of take-overs are also far from straightforward and can have serious implications for a company's balance sheet; the two methods most commonly used are share-for-share offers and cash payments.

Take-overs can take months to complete, especially if the target company considers the bid to be hostile and tries to repel it. This is not only because of the payment of substantial bid premiums, but also because of the failure of predator companies to obtain the expected post-acquisition benefits. These benefits fail to materialise due to the difficulties faced by the predator company in achieving a successful integration of the assets of the two companies. Predator company shareholders rarely benefit from the take-over process. Parties that do tend to gain from the acquisition process are the predator company management and the shareholders in the target company.

KEY POINTS

1 Mergers and take-overs have significant effects on companies' assets and financial structures.

2 Acquisitions tend to be far more common than mergers due to the relative sizes of the companies involved.

3 Mergers and take-overs can be classified as being either vertical, horizontal or conglomerate.

4 The motives put forward by companies to justify merger and take-over activity can be economic, financial and managerial in nature.

5 Economies of scale and synergy are the economic benefits most frequently cited to justify mergers and take-overs, especially those which are horizontal in nature.

6 When a company is considering entering into a merger or take-over it is important for it to consider the associated costs and disadvantages as well as the benefits.

7 Merger and take-over activity tends to come in waves, usually coinciding with booms in the economy and times of high corporate liquidity.

8 An accurate valuation of the target company is crucial to the success of take-over activity.

9 The two broad approaches that can be used to value a company are based either on the value of the assets of the company itself or on the future cash flows associated with the ownership of the assets.

10 The most common ways for companies to finance take-overs are by using share-for-share offers, cash offers, or mixed offers which give the choice of either shares or cash.

11 It is important that companies consider the implications of their chosen method of financing on their shareholders' wealth, their level of gearing, their liquidity and their ownership structure.

12 Companies must have an understanding and an awareness of the regulatory framework that governs merger and take-over activity.

13 The strategic and tactical aspects of mergers and take-overs play an important part in determining whether such activity is successful or not.

14 Victim companies have a number of ways by which they can defend themselves against an unwanted take-over bid. A better strategy, though, is to use pre-bid defences to dissuade potential predators from making a bid in the first place.

15 Empirical evidence suggests that merger and take-over activity has a fairly neutral effect on the economy as a whole, while benefiting the target company's shareholders and the management of the predator company.

QUESTIONS

Answers to these questions can be found on pages 432–4.

1 Explain briefly why take-overs are much more common than mergers.

2 Briefly outline the economic reasons for take-over activity.

3 Briefly outline the financial reasons for take-over activity.

4 Why might growth by acquisition not be in the best interests of a company?

5 Explain why mergers and take-overs come in waves.

6 Discuss the use of the P/E ratio and Gordon growth methods of determining the value of a target company.

7 Explain why the DCF valuation method is preferred by academics.

8 Briefly discuss the advantages and disadvantages of financing a take-over by an issue of convertible debentures.

9 Briefly describe four defences that could be used by a company after its board has received a take-over bid from a predator.

10 Describe briefly some of the important contributing factors which explain why shareholders of predator companies rarely benefit from take-overs.

QUESTIONS FOR REVIEW

Answers to these questions can be found on pages 435–6.

1 Explain the major justifications that are likely to be put forward to explain the following types of take-over:

(a) horizontal take-overs;

(b) vertical backwards and forwards take-overs;

(c) conglomerate mergers.

2 Restwell plc, a hotel and leisure company, is currently considering taking over a smaller private limited company, Staygood Ltd. The board of Restwell is in the process of making a bid for Staygood but first needs to place a value on the company. Restwell has gathered the following data:

Restwell	
Weighted average cost of capital	12%
P/E ratio	12
Shareholders' required rate of return	15%
Staygood	
Current dividend payment	27p
Past five years' dividend payments	15p, 17p, 18p, 21p, 23p
Current EPS	37p
Number of ordinary shares in issue	5m

It is estimated that the shareholders in Staygood require a rate of return 20 per cent higher than the shareholders of Restwell due to the higher level of risk associated with Staygood. Restwell estimates that cash flows at the end of the first year will be £2.5m and these will grow at an annual rate of five per cent. Restwell also expects to raise £5m in two years' time by selling off hotels of Staygood that are surplus to its needs.

Given the above information, estimate values for Staygood using the following valuation methods:

(a) price/earnings ratio valuation;

(b) Gordon growth model;

(c) discounted cash flow valuation.

3 Carsley plc and Powell plc are planning to merge to form Stimac plc. It has been agreed that Powell's shareholders will accept three shares in Carsley for every share in Powell they hold. Other details are as follows:

	Carsley plc	*Powell plc*
Number of shares	40m	10m
Annual earnings	£10m	£5.8m
P/E ratio	8	10

Post-merger annual earnings of the enlarged company are expected to be eight per cent higher than the sum of the earnings of each of the companies before the merger, due to economies of scale and other benefits. The market is expected to apply a P/E ratio of 9 to Stimac plc.

Determine the extent to which the shareholders of Powell will benefit from the proposed merger.

4 What are the major considerations that the predator company has to take into account when deciding on how to finance a proposed take-over?

QUESTIONS FOR DISCUSSION

1 The board of Hanging Valley plc wishes to take over Rattling Creek Ltd. Shown below are summarised financial data for the two companies:

	Hanging Valley	*Rattling Creek*
Profit before interest and tax	£420 000	£200 000
Ordinary share dividends	6.9p	14.0p
Corporation tax rate	35%	35%

Balance sheet extracts:

	Hanging Valley	*Rattling Creek*
Net fixed assets	1 750 000	800 000
Current assets	800 000	500 000
Current liabilities	(450 000)	(200 000)
Total assets less current liabilities	2 100 000	1 100 000
		(200 000)
	2 100 000	900 000
Financed by:		
ordinary shares, £1	1 500 000	500 000
reserves	600 000	400 000
	2 100 000	900 000

Hanging Valley's earnings and dividends have been increasing at approximately 15 per cent per year in recent times, while over the same period the earnings and dividends of Rattling Creek have remained static. The current market price of Hanging Valley's ordinary shares is £1.60. The board of Hanging Valley considers that the shareholders of Rattling Creek will accept a share-for-share offer, in the proportion of four shares in Hanging Valley plc for every five shares in Rattling Creek Ltd.

(a) Using three different valuation methods, determine the effect on the wealth of Hanging Valley plc's shareholders if Rattling Creek Ltd's shareholders accept the proposed share exchange.

(b) Critically discuss the *economic* reasons why one company may seek to take over another.

2 Two companies called Blur plc and Oasis plc are considering a merger. Financial data for the two companies is given below:

	Blur	*Oasis*
Number of shares issued	3m	6m
Distributable earnings	£1.8m	£0.5m
P/E ratio	12.0	10.3

The two companies have estimated that due to economies of scale the newly merged company would generate cost savings of £200 000 per year.

(a) It is initially suggested that 100 per cent of Oasis's shares should be exchanged for shares in Blur at a rate of one share for Blur for every three shares in Oasis. What would be the expected dilution of EPS of the merger from the point of view of Blur's shareholders?

(b) An alternative to this is for Blur's shares to be valued at £7.20 and for the total share capital of Oasis to be valued at £10 500 000 for merger purposes. A certain percentage of Oasis's shares would be exchanged for shares in Blur, while the remaining shares of Oasis would be exchanged for 6.5 per cent loan stock (issued at £100 par value) in the new company. Given that the corporation tax rate is 35 per cent, how much 6.5 per cent loan stock would be issued as part of the purchase consideration, in order for there to be no dilution of EPS from Blur's existing shareholders' point of view?

3 The managing directors of Wrack plc are currently considering what value to place on Trollope plc, a company which they are planning to take over in the near future. Wrack plc's share price is currently £3.21 and the company's earnings per share stands at 29p. Wrack's weighted average cost of capital is 15 per cent.

The board estimates that annual after-tax synergy benefits resulting from the take-over will be £10m, that Trollope's distributable earnings will grow at an annual rate of three per cent and that duplication will allow the sale of £25m of assets, net of corporation tax (currently standing at 35 per cent), in a year's time. Information referring to Trollope plc, including the current balance sheet and profit and loss account, is as follows:

Balance sheet of Trollope plc

	£m	£m
Fixed assets		296
Current assets	70	
Current liabilities	52	
		18
		314
Financed by:		
ordinary shares (£1)		156
reserves		75
Net equity interest		231
10 per cent debentures		83
		314

Profit and loss account (extracts)

	£m
Profit before interest and tax	76.0
Interest payments	8.3
	67.7
Corporation tax payments	23.7
Distributable earnings	44.0

Other information:

current ex-div share price	£2.25
latest dividend	12p
past four years' dividend payments	9p, 9p, 10p, 11p
Trollope's equity beta	0.875
Treasury bill yield	7%
return of the market	15%

(a) Given the above information, calculate the value of Trollope plc using the following valuation methods:

   (i) price/earnings ratio;

   (ii) dividend valuation method;

   (iii) discounted cash flow method.

(b) Discuss the problems associated with using the above valuation techniques. Which of the values would you recommend the board of Wrack to use?

(c) Critically discuss which factors will influence a company to finance a take-over by either a share-for-share offer or a cash offer financed by an issue of debentures.

REFERENCES

Cowling, K., Stoneman, P., Cubbin, J. *et al.* (1980) *Mergers and Economic Performance*, Cambridge University Press.

De Noble, A., Gustafson, L. and Hergert, M. (1988) 'Planning for post-merger integration – eight lessons for merger success', *Long Range Planning*, Vol. 2, No. 4, pp. 82–5.

Firth, M. (1980) 'Take-overs, shareholders' returns and the theory of the firm', *Quarterly Journal of Economics*, Mar, pp. 235–60.

Franks, J., Broyles, J. and Hecht, M. (1977) 'An industry study of the profitability of mergers in the United Kingdom', *Journal of Finance*, Dec, pp. 1513–25.

Franks, J., Harris, R. and Mayer, C. (1988) 'Means of payment in take-overs: results for the UK and US', in Avernick, M. (ed.) *Corporate Take-overs: Causes and Consequences*, University of Chicago Press.

Jensen, M. (1993) 'The take-over controversy: analysis and evidence', in Chew, D. (ed.) *The New Corporate Finance – where theory meets practice*, McGraw-Hill.

Jensen, M. and Ruback, R. (1983) 'The market for corporate control: the scientific evidence', *Journal of Financial Economics*, Vol. 11, pp. 5–50.

Kelly, E. (1967) *The Profitability of Growth through Mergers*, Pennsylvania State University, University Park.

Panel on Take-overs and Mergers (1988) *Code on Takeovers and Mergers*, Jan.

Singh, A. (1971) *Takeovers: Their Relevance to the Stock Market and the Theory of the Firm*, Cambridge University Press.

RECOMMENDED READING

For a book totally dedicated to the topic of mergers and take-overs *see*:

Cooke, T. (1988) *International Mergers and Acquisitions*, Basil Blackwell.

The following books include a number of very readable and interesting articles on the subject of mergers and take-overs:

Chew, D. (ed.) (1993) *The New Corporate Finance – where theory meets practice*, McGraw-Hill.
Stern, J. and Chew, D. (eds) (1986) *The Revolution in Corporate Finance*, Basil Blackwell.

Important and informative papers and articles recommended for further reading include the following:

Benzie, R. (1989) 'Take-over activity in the 1980s', *Bank of England Quarterly Bulletin*, Vol. 29, pp. 78–85.

Borstadt, L., Zwirlein, T. and Brickley, J. (1991) 'Defending against hostile take-overs: impact on shareholder wealth', *Managerial Finance*, Vol. 17, No. 1, pp. 25–33.

Ravenscraft, D. (1991) 'Gains and losses from mergers: the evidence', *Managerial Finance*, Vol. 17, No. 1, pp. 8–13.

Severiens, T. (1991) 'Creating value through mergers and acquisitions: some motivations', *Managerial Finance*, Vol. 17, No. 1, pp. 3–7.

Sudarsanam, P. (1991) 'Defensive strategies of target firms in UK contested take-overs', *Managerial Finance*, Vol. 17, No. 6, pp. 47–56.

CHAPTER 12

RISK MANAGEMENT

INTRODUCTION

The importance of interest rate and exchange rate management has increased dramatically over the last 20 years. The continuing expansion in international trade and the increased volatility of exchange rates since the collapse of the Bretton Woods fixed exchange rate system in 1972 has increased the importance for companies of managing their exchange rate risk, while the volatility of interest rates and the size and complexity of company borrowing have generated the need for hedging interest rate risk.

In this chapter we consider the different types of exchange rate and interest rate risk that companies can be exposed to and then go on to consider the techniques available to them to control and manage such exposures. A large part of this chapter is devoted to a consideration of the increasingly complex derivatives that are available for the external hedging of interest and exchange rate exposures. Derivatives have become a highly topical area for discussion, perhaps for the wrong reasons, following the recent collapse of Barings bank due to the misuse of derivatives by one of its employees.

LEARNING OBJECTIVES

By the end of this chapter, you should have achieved the following learning objectives:

- an understanding of the theoretical and practical issues underlying interest rate and exchange rate risk;
- an understanding of the internal and external methods that can be used to manage interest rate and exchange rate risk;
- the ability to select and evaluate appropriate risk management techniques in accordance with the nature of the exposure being faced;
- an appreciation of both the benefits and the costs associated with the utilisation of risk management techniques.

12.1 INTEREST AND EXCHANGE RATE RISK

12.1.1 An introduction

Recent years have witnessed an increasing awareness by the corporate sector of the potential benefits to be gained by managing or *hedging* their interest and exchange rate exposures. The importance to companies of hedging depends largely upon the potential losses that can result from unfavourable movements in interest and exchange rates. With respect to interest rate exposures, the magnitude of such losses is dependent upon the volatility of interest rates, the level of companies' financial and income gearing and the proportion of corporate debt linked to floating interest rates. The increased need in recent years for companies to manage their interest rate exposures is illustrated in Exhibit 12.1, which shows the high volatility of short-term interest rates, and in Exhibit 12.2, which emphasises the rising trend of corporate income gearing ratios over the period 1985–93.

The incidence of exchange rate risk has increased greatly since the early 1970s, when the collapse of the Bretton Woods exchange rate regime led to the major currencies of the world floating against each other. When this factor is considered in tandem with the growth in world trade over the last 20 years, so that now virtually all companies are involved in transactions denominated in a foreign currency, it is not really surprising that the management of foreign exchange exposure has also become of increasing importance to companies. Adverse movements in exchange rates that are not hedged can lead to companies having profits on foreign deals eliminated and, even worse, can drive a company into bankruptcy. Demirag and Goddard (1994) additionally cite the increased visibility of foreign exchange gains and losses as a reason for the increasing importance of exposure management.

So what do we mean exactly when we talk about interest and exchange rate management? Perhaps one of the easiest ways to explain interest and exchange rate management is as a form of insurance, whereby companies insure themselves

EXHIBIT 12.1

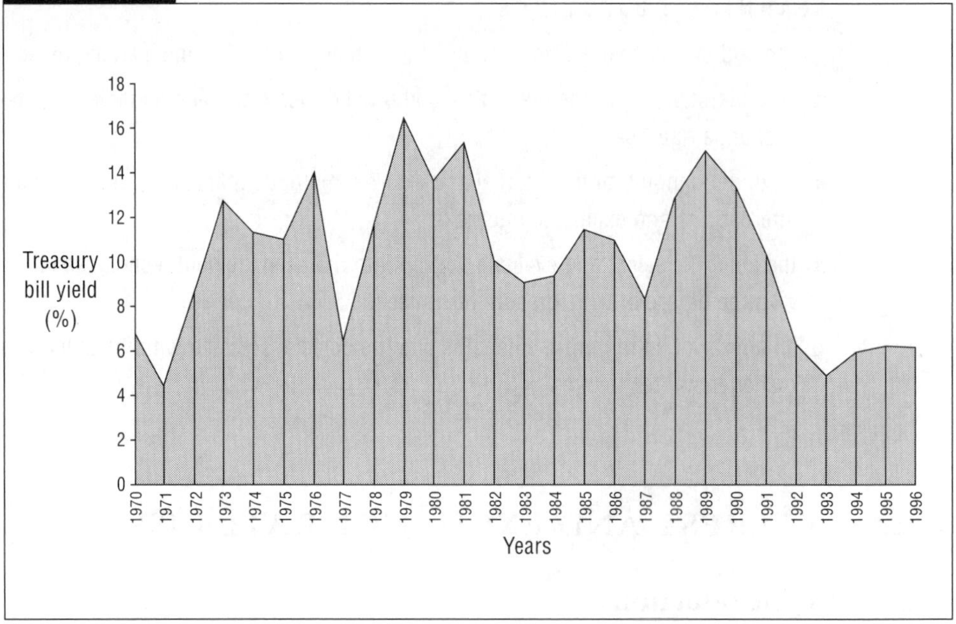

Annual average yield on three-month Treasury bills over the period 1970–96
Source: Office for National Statistics

EXHIBIT 12.2

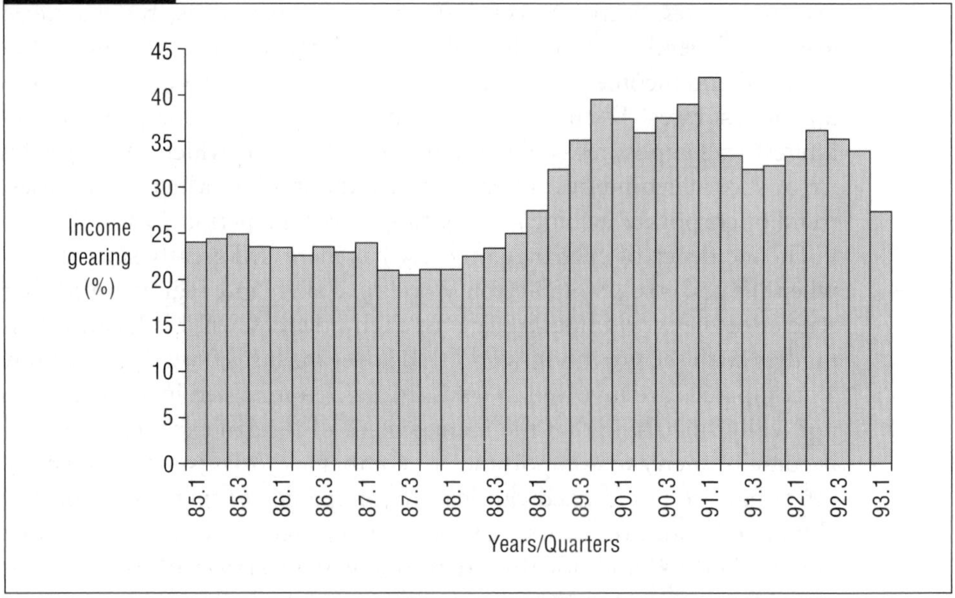

UK industrial and commercial companies' incoming gearing ratios (1985–93)
Source: Datastream

against adverse movements in exchange and interest rates in the same way as we insure ourselves against personal injury or against a loss of personal possessions.

12.1.2 Interest rate risk

The most common form of interest rate risk faced by a company is that associated with having a high proportion of floating interest rate debt. One consequence of volatility in interest rates for such a company is that forecasting and planning its future cash flows will not be easy. More seriously, the company will be afraid of interest rates increasing sharply in the future, since significantly increased interest payments will increase financial risk, and may, in extreme cases, lead to the risk of bankruptcy (financial risk and bankruptcy risk were discussed in Sections 8.5.1 and 8.5.2 of Chapter 8).

However, a company with a high proportion of fixed interest rate debt will also face interest rate risk. Here the concern is that interest rates may fall sharply in the future. The commitment to fixed interest payments will lead to loss of competitive advantage compared to rival companies whose borrowings are primarily at floating rates, even if financial planning is made easier due to the fixed rate debt. Rival companies, apart from having reduced debt servicing costs, will experience a fall in their cost of capital, increasing the profitability of their existing projects and widening the portfolio of attractive projects they can choose from in the future.

Interest rate risk is not faced solely by companies with debt liabilities, but also by those holding debt investments. For example, a cash-rich company that has invested surplus cash on the money markets at a floating interest rate will face the risk of interest rates falling, while one that has purchased fixed rate gilts will face the risk of interest rates rising.

In reality, the incidence of interest rate risk may not be quite as obvious as in the examples we have just considered. *Basis risk* and *gap exposure* represent more subtle types of interest rate exposure that companies may encounter.

Basis risk

A company may have assets and liabilities of similar sizes, both with floating interest rates, and at first sight may not appear to have any interest rate risk exposure. If the two floating rates are not determined using the same basis, however (e.g. one is linked to LIBOR but the other is not), it is unlikely that they will move perfectly in concert with each other; that is, as one rate increases by one per cent, the other also increases by one per cent.

Gap exposure

Even more subtle still is the situation where a company has assets and liabilities which are matched in terms of size and where the floating interest rates on each are determined on the same basis, for example by reference to LIBOR. It is still possible for interest rate risk to exist, as the rates on loans may be revised on a three-monthly basis while the rates on assets may be revised on a six-monthly basis.

12.1.3 Spot and forward rates

Before we go on to consider different types of exchange rate risk we must consider the meaning of the term 'exchange rate'. In practice many exchange rates exist, not only the buy and sell rates between different currencies, but also between the same currencies over different time horizons. The different rates can be illustrated with an example which considers the exchange rate between sterling and the dollar.

$ spot rate	1.5617 – 1.5773
One-month $ forward rate	1.5945 – 1.6136
Three-month $ forward rate	1.6280 – 1.6523

The *spot rate* refers to the rate of exchange if buying or selling the currency immediately. The higher of the two spot rates (1.5773) is the buy rate (i.e. the number of dollars you have to give up to receive one pound), while the lower spot rate (1.5617) is the sell rate (i.e. the number of dollars you receive for giving up one pound). The difference between the two spot rates is called the *spread*.

The rates below the spot rate are called *forward rates* and these allow the fixing of buy and sell rates for settlement and delivery at a specific date in the future. The forward rates are in fact a consensus estimate of the future spot rate, and their accuracy will depend upon how efficient the foreign exchange market is at forecasting future spot rates and the factors that influence them.

Forward rates can be at either a *premium* or a *discount* to the current spot rate. In our example, the one- and three-month rates are at a discount to the spot rate, indicating that the foreign exchange market is expecting an appreciation in the value of the pound against the dollar (i.e. the market expects that you will receive more dollars for your pound in the future).

12.1.4 What is meant by exchange rate risk?

Exchange rate risk is commonly divided into transaction risk, translation risk and economic risk. The meaning of these terms will now be discussed.

Transaction risk

Transaction risk occurs because, as a consequence of either importing or exporting raw materials, goods and services, companies expect either to pay or to receive amounts of foreign currency in the future. The amount of domestic currency either paid or received in these foreign currency transactions may change due to movements in the exchange rate.

For example, suppose that a UK company sells a car to a German customer for DM 30 000 and gives three months credit, with payment to be received in DM. At the current spot rate of DM 2.95 to the pound, the company expects to receive 30 000/2.95 = £10 170. If the German customer pays at the end of the three-month credit period and in the interim the exchange rate has moved to DM 3.05 to the pound, the UK company will only receive £9836 when it exchanges its deutschmarks into sterling. This is 3.3 per cent less than expected.

Companies expecting to *receive* foreign currency in the future, then, will be concerned about the possibility of the domestic currency *appreciating* against the foreign currency, while companies expecting to *pay* foreign currency in the future are concerned about the possibility of the domestic currency *depreciating* against the foreign currency.

Translation risk

Translation risk is mainly of relevance to companies with overseas operations and subsidiaries. As part of the process of producing consolidated accounts, the balance sheet values of the assets and liabilities of overseas subsidiaries, denominated in a foreign currency, will need to be translated into the domestic currency. The foreign currency denominated profit and loss account will also need to be translated and consolidated. Translation risk refers to the possibility that, as a result of the translation of overseas assets, liabilities and profits into the domestic currency, the holding company may experience a loss or a gain due to changes in the exchange rate. While these losses or gains only appear on paper and do not represent actual cash flows, they may affect the perceptions and opinions of investors and financial institutions regarding a company's well-being. However, as Buckley (1996) points out, translation risk is simply a function of the accounting treatment of foreign assets and liabilities on consolidation, and does not give any indication of the real effect of currency fluctuations on the value of a company.

Translation risk can be illustrated by considering a UK company that purchases a Spanish hotel and finances the purchase with sterling borrowing. The hotel is initially valued at 40m pesetas, which at the then current exchange rate of 200 pesetas to the pound gives a sterling value of £200 000. A year later, the hotel is still valued at 40m pesetas but the exchange rate now stands at 230 pesetas to the pound. The sterling value of the liability used to finance the hotel will be the same, but the value of the hotel, translated into sterling for consolidation purposes, has fallen to £173 913.

Economic risk

Economic risk is a more general type of exchange rate risk than transaction and translation risk. While companies can avoid transaction and translation risk by not being involved in foreign currency transactions and by not engaging in overseas operations, economic risk is almost impossible to avoid. It refers to the risk of long-term movements in exchange rates and national economies undermining the international competitiveness of a company.

For example, a company based solely in the UK buys all its raw material and sells all its finished goods in the domestic market. While not facing any transaction or translation risk, if the company faces domestic competition from a US company and if the pound appreciates against the dollar, hence reducing the sterling cost of the US company's dollar-denominated imports, the UK company will lose its competitive edge.

Now that we have examined the different types of interest rate and exchange rate risk that companies can be exposed to, we can move on to consider the methods companies can use to manage them.

12.2 INTERNAL RISK MANAGEMENT

12.2.1 An introduction

Internal risk management refers to the hedging of either interest or exchange rate risk by the way in which a company structures its assets and liabilities. Internal risk management is cheaper than external hedging, as the use of external methods incurs a range of costs and arrangement fees, as we will see later. Unfortunately, companies can rarely hedge all their exposures in this way, as there are a number of factors which will limit the amount of risk that can be hedged internally.

12.2.2 Internal management of interest rate risk

There are two general methods of internal hedging that can be used to manage interest rate exposure within a company's balance sheet.

Smoothing

Smoothing is where a company tries to maintain a balance between its fixed rate and floating rate borrowing. If interest rates *rise*, the advantage of the relatively cheaper fixed rate loan will be cancelled out by the relatively more expensive floating rate loan. If interest rates *fall*, the advantage of the relatively cheaper floating rate loan will be cancelled out by the relatively more expensive fixed rate loan. One drawback of this method is that it ignores the comparative advantage a company may have, depending on its commercial environment, in using fixed rate debt relative to floating rate debt or vice-versa. On top of this, the company may incur two lots of transaction and arrangement costs.

Matching

Matching involves the internal matching of liabilities and assets which both have a common interest rate. Consider a decentralised group which has two subsidiaries. One subsidiary may be investing in the money markets at LIBOR, while the other subsidiary is borrowing through the same money market at LIBOR. If LIBOR rises, one subsidiary's borrowing cost increases while the other subsidiary's returns increase: the assets and liabilities are matched. One problem with this method is that it may be difficult for commercial and industrial companies to match the characteristics of their liabilities and assets, as many companies, while having to pay interest on their liabilities, do not receive their income in the form of interest payments. Matching is most likely to be used, then, by financial institutions such as banks, who derive a large amount of their income from interest received on advances.

12.2.3 Internal management of exchange rate risk

There are a number of techniques that can be used for hedging internally the exchange rate risks faced by companies. It is easier to hedge transaction and translation risk internally than to hedge economic risk, due to the difficulties associated with quantifying economic risk and the long time periods over which exposure to economic risk occurs.

Matching

This technique can be used to reduce the amount of translation or transaction risk that a company faces. For example, in order to mitigate translation risk, a company acquiring a foreign asset should borrow funds denominated in the currency of the country in which it is purchasing the asset, matching if possible the term of the loan to the expected economic life of the asset. Then, as the exchange rate varies, the translated values of the asset and liability will increase and decrease in concert. To mitigate transaction risk, a company selling its goods in the US with prices denominated in dollars could import raw materials through a supplier that invoices in dollars.

Netting

This is utilised primarily by multinational companies with overseas subsidiaries or large organisations where financial transactions are made on a decentralised basis. Here, companies net out all their different foreign currency transactions at group office level and then hedge any net exposure.

Consider a UK company with a French subsidiary. The UK company may have to pay $5m to a supplier in three months' time, while the French subsidiary may be expecting to receive payment of $7m in three months' time for goods supplied. If this information is centralised at the group office, the net exposure of $2m to be received in three months' time can be identified and then be hedged externally. This will be cheaper than the UK company and its French subsidiary hedging their respective exposures of $5m and $7m independently.

Leading and lagging

Leading and *lagging* of payments can be used by companies that face transaction risk due to the need to settle foreign currency denominated overseas debtors. This technique involves settling foreign currency accounts either at the beginning (leading) or after the end (lagging) of the allowed credit period. The choice of whether to lead or lag the settlement will depend upon the company's expectations of future exchange rate movements.

Invoicing in the domestic currency

A company exporting goods could invoice for them in its domestic currency, rather than in the currency of the company to which it is exporting. The transaction risk is then transferred to the foreign company buying the goods. The drawback of this method is that it may deter potential customers, as they may transfer their orders to companies that invoice in their own currency.

12.3 EXTERNAL RISK MANAGEMENT

Having considered internal hedging methods and having recognised that companies are limited in the amount of risk they can hedge using them, we now turn our attention to the many types of external hedging that are available to companies. Over the last 20 years the choice of external hedging instruments has increased dramatically. Two of the longest standing external methods of hedging interest and exchange rate risk are the use of forward contracts and borrowing and lending in the money markets. Nowadays, companies can choose from a number of *derivative* instruments, including futures contracts, swaps and options. Derivatives can also be divided according to whether they are standardised *traded* derivatives or bank-created *over-the-counter* derivatives. We shall begin by considering forward contracts and the use of the money markets.

12.3.1 Hedging using forward contracts

There are two types of forward contract. *Forward rate agreements* (FRAs) enable companies to fix, in advance, either a future borrowing rate or a future depositing rate, based on a nominal principal amount, for a given time period. *Forward exchange contracts* (FECs) enable companies to fix, in advance, future exchange rates on an agreed quantity of foreign currency, for delivery or purchase on an agreed date. Forward contracts are generally set up via banking institutions and are non-negotiable, legally binding contracts.

An advantage of forward contracts is that they can be tailormade with respect to maturity and size in order to meet the requirements of the company. In this sense, they are different from their traded equivalent, financial futures. Due to their lack of standardisation, FECs cannot be traded. While there will be an initial arrangement fee, FECs do not require the payment of margin as with financial futures, nor do they require the payment of a premium, as with traded options. Cash flows occur only on the execution date of the agreement. While a company knows that protection from any adverse interest rate or exchange rate movements is assured, the binding nature of a forward contract means that the company must forego any potential benefit from favourable movements in rates.

Example Forward rate agreement

A company is wanting to borrow £5.6m in three months' time for a period of six months. Interest rates are currently standing at 12 per cent and the company, being afraid that in three months' time the interest rate may have increased, decides to hedge using a FRA. The bank guarantees the company a rate of 12.5 per cent on a notional £5.6m for six months starting in three months' time. If interest rates have increased after three months to say 14 per cent, the company will have to pay 14 per cent interest on the £5.6m loan that it wants to take out: 1.5 per cent more than the rate agreed in the FRA. The bank will make a compensatory payment of £42 000 (1.5 per cent × £5.6m × 6/12) to the company, covering the higher cost of its borrowing. On the other hand, if after three months interest rates have dropped to 11 per cent, the company will have to make a £42 000 payment to the bank.

12.3.2 Hedging using the money markets and eurocurrency markets

Companies can also hedge interest and exchange rate risk by using the money markets and the eurocurrency markets. These types of transaction are sometimes referred to as *cash market* hedges. Take for example a company that wants to borrow £1m in three months' time for six months, but is afraid that interest rates will rise. The company can use the money markets to borrow the money now and then re-deposit it on the money markets for the first three months. If interest rates rise during the first three months, the company will benefit by receiving a higher rate of interest on its money market deposit.

Using the eurocurrency markets to hedge exchange rate risk is more complicated and is best illustrated with a numerical example. Suppose that a company expects to receive $180 000 in three months' time and wants to lock into the current exchange rate of $1.65/£1 because it is afraid that the pound will appreciate against the dollar. If the company borrows dollars now and converts them to sterling at the current spot rate, then when the dollar loan matures it can be paid off by using the expected dollar receipt. If the *annual* dollar borrowing rate is seven per cent and Z is the amount of dollars that must be borrowed now, then:

$$Z \times (1 + 7\%/4) = \$180\ 000$$

and so:

$$Z = \$180\ 000/1.0175 = \$176\ 904$$

This dollar loan can be converted into sterling at the current spot rate of $1.65/£1 to give £107 215 as the cash available to the company now.

12.4 FUTURES CONTRACTS

A futures contract can be defined as an agreement to buy or sell a standard quantity of a specific financial instrument or foreign currency at a future date at a price agreed between two parties. Financial futures resemble traded options in that both are contracts of a standardised nature, but financial futures are a binding contract locking both buyer and seller into a particular rate: there is no option on the part of the buyer not to proceed. When a company takes out a futures contract it has to place *initial margin*, which represents approximately three per cent of the contract value, with the clearing house of the futures exchange. On £500 000 short sterling contracts, this would be a margin of £1200 per contract. As the interest or exchange rate specified in the futures contract changes on a daily basis, money is either credited or debited from the company's margin account, depending on whether the rate change represents a favourable or adverse movement. If the initial margin drops below a certain safety level, *variation margin* will be called for to keep it topped up.

Financial futures were first traded in the US on the Chicago Mercantile Exchange (CME) in 1972. In the UK, the London International Financial Futures Exchange (LIFFE) was set up in 1982 to trade futures contracts. LIFFE has subsequently merged with the London Traded Options Market (LTOM) to form a single unified UK market for trading derivative securities.

The mechanics of hedging interest and exchange rate exposure using financial futures is best demonstrated by the use of examples.

12.4.1 Using futures contracts to hedge interest rate risk

When hedging interest rate risk, companies must *buy* futures contracts if they want to guard against a *fall* in interest rates and *sell* futures contracts to guard against a *rise* in interest rates. The contracts run in three-month cycles and have a nominal value of £500 000. The two most useful contracts for hedging sterling interest rate risk are the three-month LIBOR sterling and long gilt contracts. Futures contracts are priced in nominal terms by subtracting the value of the specified interest rate from 100. Profits or losses made on a futures contract are determined by reference to changes in this nominal price. Contract price changes are given in *ticks*, a tick being equal to a movement of one basis point or 0.01 per cent of the contract price. In value terms on a £500 000 short sterling contract, a movement of one tick is worth £12.50 (i.e. £500 000 × 0.0001 × 0.25).

Example: Using interest rate futures

A company wants to borrow £500 000 in three months' time for a period of three months, but is expecting interest rates to rise above the current level of 10 per cent. In order to hedge its position, therefore, it *sells* one £500 000 interest rate contract at 90 (i.e. 100 – 10).

Suppose that, after three months, the interest rate has gone up by three per cent and the contract price has moved by the same amount. The seller of the contract now *buys* a contract at 87 (i.e. 100 – 13), thereby 'closing out' his position. The contract price movement in terms of ticks is 3/0.01 = 300 ticks.

$$\text{Profit made by selling and buying futures} = 300 \times £12.50 = £3750$$

The company can use this profit to compensate it for the higher cost of borrowing £500 000 in three months' time. Here, this is three per cent for three months, giving (500 000 × 0.03)/4 = 15 000/4 = £3750. Because the contract price movement matched the change in the interest rate, the company has exactly offset its higher borrowing cost and hence hedged its interest rate risk.

12.4.2 Using futures contracts to hedge exchange rate risk

These contracts are no longer available on LIFFE, as the exchange discontinued its currency futures contracts in 1990 due to a lack of demand. They are available, however, on the Chicago Mercantile Exchange (CME) and on its Far East partner, the Singapore Mercantile Exchange (SIMEX).

Example Using US currency futures

It is 1 January and a UK company is expecting to receive \$300 000 in three months' time on 1 April. Being concerned about the pound strengthening against the dollar, it decides to use futures to hedge its transaction risk.

Current spot rate:	\$1.54 – \$1.55
Sterling futures price (1 April):	\$1.535
Standard size of futures contracts:	£62 500

The first thing to establish is whether the company should buy or sell futures contracts. Given that holding a futures contract (often referred to as *taking a long position*) allows future delivery of a foreign currency and that in this case *sterling* is the foreign currency, the company should *buy* US sterling futures. This allows the company to take delivery of sterling in return for the dollars it expects to receive. The futures price quoted is the amount of US dollars needed to buy one unit of the foreign currency. Translating the dollar receipt into sterling at the exchange rate implicit in the currency future, we have:

\$300 000/1.535 = £195 440
Number of contracts required = 195 440/62 500 = 3.13

The company therefore purchases three contracts, allowing it to take delivery of £187 500 in return for a payment of \$287 813. Given that the company is to receive \$300 000, it will have to sell the \$12 187 surplus in the foreign exchange market in three months' time. In this example, we can see that the company has locked into a particular exchange rate (\$1.535/£1) and knows how much sterling it will receive when converting its future dollar receipts, except for the \$12 187 surplus.

12.4.3 Advantages and disadvantages of using futures to hedge risk

An informed decision on hedging with financial futures will consider the advantages and disadvantages of choosing this risk management method. One advantage of futures is that, unlike options, there is no up-front premium to be paid. Another advantage of futures is that, unlike their over-the-counter counterparts, they are tradable and can be bought and sold on a secondary market. Finally, because contracts are *marked to the market*, favourable movements in interest and exchange rates are immediately credited to a company's margin account.

Arguably the biggest drawback associated with futures is that, unlike options, they do not allow a company to take advantage of favourable movements in interest and exchange rates. A further problem is that, because the contracts are standardised, it is difficult to find a perfect hedge with respect to the principal to be hedged and its maturity. This is illustrated in our earlier example, where four currency futures would over-hedge the exposure and three currency futures contracts would under-hedge it. As regards cost, while there are no premiums to be paid with futures contracts, there is still the opportunity cost of the margin requirement. Extra margin may also be required as interest or exchange rates move adversely. Finally, basis risk may exist if changes in exchange and interest rates are not perfectly negatively correlated with changes in the prices of futures contracts. For example, a one per cent increase in interest rates may not lead to a one per cent drop in the price of the futures contract. Basis risk, therefore, affects the hedge efficiency of futures contracts.

12.5 OPTIONS

Currency and interest rate options give their holders the right, but not the obligation, to borrow or lend at a specific interest rate or to buy or sell foreign currency at a specific exchange rate. This gives the users of options the flexibility to take advantage of favourable interest and exchange rate movements. A price has to be paid for this flexibility, however, in the form of an option premium. There are two distinct categories of options available to companies to hedge their exposures, namely over-the-counter options and traded options, which will now be considered.

12.5.1 Over-the-counter options

Over-the-counter (OTC) options can be purchased from financial institutions such as banks and can be tailormade to meet company requirements. OTC options, which can be subdivided into caps, floors and collars, specify a principal amount, a time period over which the option runs and a particular currency or interest rate.

With an interest rate cap, if the specified interest rate goes above a predetermined level the financial institution is required to pay the excess, thereby guaranteeing or capping the maximum rate of interest the company will pay. Alternatively, a UK company wanting to convert an amount of dollars into sterling at some future date can purchase an exchange rate cap. The company will be guaranteed a certain rate of exchange – say $1.5 to the pound. If the exchange rate in the foreign exchange markets increases to $1.67 to the pound, the company can use the cap to exchange at the more favourable rate of $1.5 to the pound with the bank from which it purchased the cap.

With an interest rate floor, if a specified interest rate falls below a certain rate, the financial institution will pay the company the difference. Interest rate floors allow companies receiving floating rate interest income to guarantee a minimum level of receipts. Correspondingly, an exchange rate floor will guarantee a UK company wanting to buy foreign currency in the future a minimum rate of exchange should the pound depreciate against the currency in question.

A collar, which is the combination of a floor and a cap, keeps an agreed interest rate or exchange rate between an upper and lower limit. The use of a collar works out cheaper for companies when compared to using caps or floors on their own. If a company with floating rate income takes out a collar to keep the interest rate between six per cent and eight per cent, it is effectively purchasing a floor of six per cent from the bank and at the same time selling the bank a cap of eight per cent. It should be easy to appreciate why a collar will work out cheaper than a floor, as any beneficial interest rate changes over and above eight per cent are paid to the bank. Conversely, a collar for a company wanting to keep its borrowing rate between an upper and lower limit involves the combination of purchasing a cap and selling a floor.

12.5.2 Traded options

Traded options are similar to OTC options except that they are standardised with respect to the principal amount and the maturity date specified by the contract. The standardised nature of these contracts allows them to be bought and sold on a secondary market. The world's largest options market is the Chicago Board Options Exchange (CBOE) which trades share, interest and currency options. In the UK, equity and interest rate options trade on LIFFE.

Traded options mature in three-month cycles (March, June, September and December) and the standardised size of a three-month sterling option, for instance, is £500 000. Traded options are of two kinds: *put* options carry the right to *sell* currency or to *lend* at a fixed rate; while *call* options carry the right to *buy* currency or to *borrow* at a fixed rate. Puts and calls can be further divided into American options, which are exercisable up to and on their expiry date, and European options, which are exercisable only on the expiry date.

12.5.3 Using traded options to hedge interest rate risk

The interest options traded on LIFFE use futures contracts as the underlying asset rather than the cash market, because futures positions can be closed out by buying or selling contracts whereas cash market transactions require delivery. The diagrams in Exhibit 12.3 show the profit or loss associated with buying or selling put and call interest rate options, where K represents the *strike price* at which futures can be bought or sold and P represents the premium paid, if the option is bought, or the premium received, if the option is sold.

It can be clearly seen from these diagrams that when selling or *writing* call and put options, the downside risk (i.e. the risk of loss) is unlimited. For these reasons, only the buying of puts and calls is recommended for hedging commercial transactions, since this limits the downside risk for a company to the loss of the premium paid for the option.

EXHIBIT 12.3

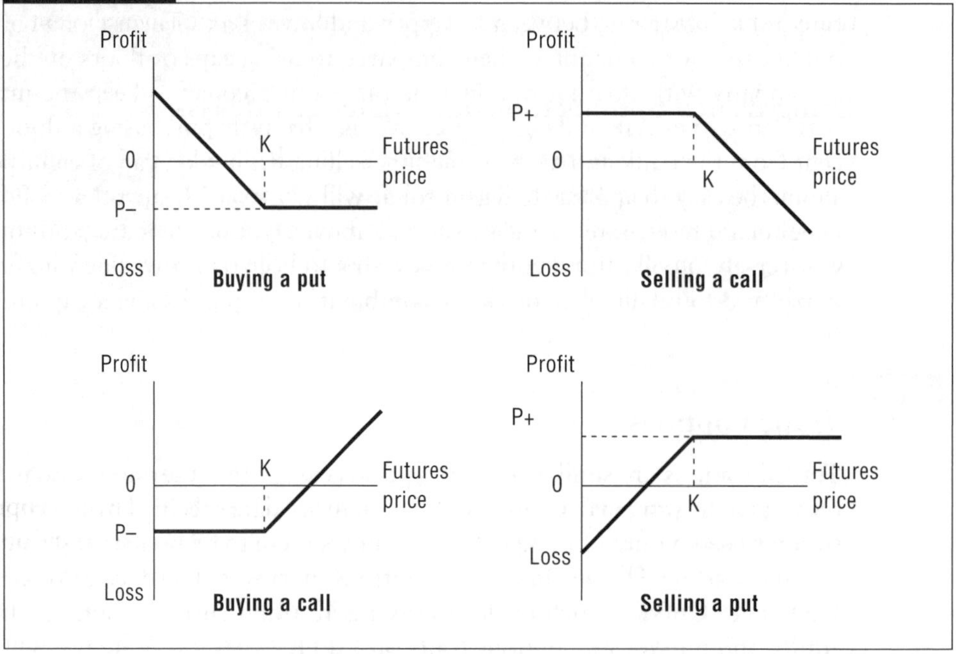

Diagrams showing the pay-offs associated with the purchasing and selling of put and call options on futures contracts

Example Using interest rate options

It is 15 December and a company wants to borrow £2m, for a period of three months, in three months' time. On this date, the three-month LIBOR rate stands at six per cent and the company wants to guard against any increase in interest rates. To give the company the option to borrow at an effective rate of six per cent, it will purchase four 15 April LIBOR sterling put option contracts of £500 000 each which have a strike price of 94. The price the company has been quoted for these option contracts is 0.17 per contract. This signifies a cost of 17 ticks per option contract. Given that ticks have a predetermined value of £12.50, this represents a cost per contract of £212.50 (17 × £12.50). The cost of four option contracts to the company is therefore £850.

If interest rates have increased to eight per cent on 15 April, the company will exercise its option contracts, allowing it to sell futures contracts at 94. The futures price, assuming no basis risk (*see* Section 12.4.3), will have dropped to 92 (i.e. 100 – 8), so the company can make a two per cent gain on its futures transactions by purchasing futures at 92 and selling futures at 94. This represents a gain of 200 ticks at £12.50 each per contract, giving a total gain on the options of 200 × £12.50 × 4 = £10 000. This exactly balances the two per cent increase in its cost of borrowing, which is 2 per cent × £2m × 1/4 = £10 000. By paying an option premium of £850, then, the company has guaranteed a maximum borrowing rate of six per cent. If interest rates had dropped to five per cent on 15 April, the company would let its option contracts expire and would borrow at the lower market rate of five per cent.

12.5.4 Using traded options to hedge exchange rate risk

Currency options were first traded on the Philadelphia Stock Exchange in 1982. They were introduced on the London Traded Options Market in 1985, but were discontinued in 1990 due to their lack of popularity. Currently, the most important currency options are those of the Chicago Mercantile Exchange (CME), closely followed by the Philadelphia Stock Exchange.

Example Using exchange rate options

It is 1 January and a UK company is expecting to receive \$1m in three months' time in payment for exports. The company wants to guard against the pound appreciating against the dollar, which currently stands at \$1.5/£1. As currency options are not available on LIFFE, the company will have to use US currency options. It decides to use the CME's sterling currency options, which have futures contracts as the underlying asset and come in contract sizes of £62 500. Remember that, from the US perspective, sterling is the foreign currency, so the company will have to purchase call options. By buying sterling currency call options, the company can obtain the right but not the obligation to sell dollars and buy sterling at a rate of \$1.5 to the pound. To find the appropriate number of contracts required, the dollar amount to be received must be translated into pounds at the option striking price, giving £666 667 (i.e. \$1m/\$1.5). This is then divided by the standard contract size to give the number of contracts required as 10.7 (i.e. £666 667/£62 500). In this situation it is impossible to get a perfect hedge due to the standard size of the contracts. The company will therefore have to either under-hedge by buying ten contracts or over-hedge by buying 11 contracts. Any shortfalls or excess amounts of dollars can be corrected by using currency market transactions when the options are exercised. In this example we have assumed that the company decides to purchase 11 contracts.

If March sterling currency call options with a \$1.5 strike price are currently trading at a premium of six cents (per pound of contract) then the total cost of 11 contracts is given by:

$$62\ 500 \times 11 \times 0.06 = \$41\ 250$$

By purchasing March sterling currency call options with a \$1.5 strike price the company will, in the worst-case scenario, exchange its dollars at a rate of \$1.56 to the pound (i.e. \$1.5 plus the six cents premium). If in three months' time the spot rate is below \$1.50/£1, the company will allow the option to expire and exchange its dollars in the spot market.

Conversely, if the company had imported goods and therefore needed to buy dollars in three months' time, it would have purchased US sterling currency put options, giving it the option to sell sterling and receive dollars at a predetermined rate.

As with OTC options, traded options can be combined to create collars and so decrease the costs of hedging with options. The different combinations of put and call options required in order to create interest rate and currency collars are shown in Exhibit 12.4.

EXHIBIT 12.4

Using LIFFE interest rate options on interest futures	
Borrower's collar: to keep interest rate between an upper and lower limit	Buy a put option and sell a call option
Lender's collar: to keep interest rate between an upper and lower limit	Buy a call option and sell a put option
Using US sterling currency options	
Exporter's collar: to keep exchange rate between an upper and lower limit	Buy a sterling call option and sell a sterling put option
Importer's collar: to keep exchange rate between an upper and lower limit	Buy a sterling put option and sell a sterling call option

Table showing the combinations of put and call options that are required to create interest and currency collars

12.5.5 Factors affecting the price of traded options

The determination of option premiums is a very complex process due to the large number of factors that influence the price of traded options. These factors are as follows.

Strike price

The higher the strike price specified in an interest rate option contract, the lower the price of a call option and the higher the price of the corresponding put option. A put option to lend at 10 per cent, for example, will cost more than a put option to lend at eight per cent. Similarly, a put option to sell the dollar at a rate of $1.5 to £1 will cost less than a put option to sell the dollar at a rate of $1.3 to £1.

Changes in interest and exchange rates

Rising interest rates will increase the value of interest rate call options but decrease the value of interest rate put options. For example, a call option to borrow at 12 per cent will become more valuable if interest rates rise from, say, 11 per cent to 13 per cent. Similarly, a US sterling put option to sell sterling at $1.5/£1 will increase in value if the pound depreciates against the dollar.

Volatility of interest rate and exchange rates

Both call and put options will have a higher value if interest rates and exchange rates are more volatile, as potentially larger losses can now be mitigated by using options as a hedge.

Time to expiry of the option

The longer the time an option has to go before its expiry date, the more valuable it will be, as it can be used by a company to hedge against unfavourable movements in exchange or interest rates for a longer period of time. The value of an option can in fact be split into two parts:

Time value + Intrinsic value = Total value

The *intrinsic value* of an option represents the value of an option if it is exercised immediately. If the current exchange rate between the dollar and the pound is \$1.5/£1, then a dollar currency put option with a strike price of \$1.3/£1 will have some intrinsic value, while a similar option with a strike price of \$1.7/£1 will not. The first option is 'in the money' while the second option is 'out of the money'.

If an option is out of the money and thus has no intrinsic value, it may still possess *time value*. Take the put option with a strike price of \$1.7/£1. This option has no intrinsic value but, if it has three months before expiry, there is time for the exchange rate to rise from its current rate of \$1.5/£1 to above the option's \$1.7/£1 strike price. Time value, therefore, is proportionate to the time left before the option expires and is at a maximum when a contract starts and at a minimum (i.e. zero) when the contract expires.

12.5.6 Advantages and disadvantages of hedging with options

There are a number of distinct advantages and disadvantages associated with hedging exposures using options. While not representing the cheapest method of hedging, due to the premiums that are payable on them, options have the major advantage of offering the holder the opportunity to benefit from favourable movements in exchange and interest rates.

There are two situations where the cost of using options to hedge exposures can be justified. The first is where a company is expecting to make a transaction, but is not certain that it will occur. For example, it may be expecting to borrow money in the future or may be tendering for an overseas contract. If the transaction does not occur, the company can either let the option expire or, due to the tradability of options, sell it on to another party if it has any value. The second situation is where a company expects interest or exchange rates to move in a certain direction but, in addition, believes there is an outside chance that rates might move in the opposite direction. By using options, the company is in a position to take advantage of any favourable movements in rates.

In addition to the disadvantage of their expense, the use of options can make it difficult to create a hedge which matches perfectly both the duration and size of a company's exposure. Just as in the case of futures, this problem is due to the standardisation of traded option contracts. The use of OTC options may represent a more appropriate choice than traded options for the hedging of significant non-standard exposures.

12.6 SWAPS

12.6.1 An introduction to swaps

The currency swaps market was developed in the early 1980s to facilitate multinational companies' access to international capital markets. In these markets, companies raise funds in 'vehicle' currencies (in which they can borrow relatively cheaply but which is not the currency in which the debt is required) and swap into the preferred currency at a lower rate than if the funds were borrowed directly. The development of interest rate swaps followed closely on the heels of currency swaps and the market in interest rate swaps is now larger in terms of both size and importance.

Swaps are used extensively by companies and banks to capitalise on their comparative advantages in the different debt markets and to hedge their interest and exchange rate exposures. The counterparties (companies) of a swap deal are normally brought together by a dealer (usually a bank) acting as an intermediary. Where a swap partner cannot be found immediately, banks can 'warehouse' swaps, by acting as a temporary swap partner until an appropriate counterparty is found. Banks benefit, through acting as swap brokers, from the arrangement fees they receive from the counterparties.

A major advantage of swaps over other derivatives such as traded options, FRAs and financial futures is that they can be used to lock into interest and exchange rates for much longer periods of time and do not require frequent monitoring and reviewing.

12.6.2 Interest rate swaps

Winstone (1995) offers a definition of an interest rate swap as an exchange between two parties of interest obligations or receipts in the same currency on an agreed amount of notional principal for an agreed period of time. Interest rate swaps can be used to hedge against adverse interest rate movements or to achieve a chosen blend of fixed and floating rate debt. Companies may become involved in swap agreements because their borrowing or lending requirements do not coincide with their comparative advantages with respect to fixed and floating rate borrowing or lending. The most common type of interest rate swap is a 'plain vanilla' swap, where fixed interest payments based on a notional principal are swapped with floating interest payments based on the same notional principal. The swap documentation will include the following details of the agreement:

- the start and end dates of the swap;

- the notional principal on which the swap is based (amount and currency);
- which party is paying floating interest and receiving fixed interest in return, and vice-versa;
- the level of the fixed rate and the basis of the floating rate (e.g. one-, three- or six-month LIBOR) upon which the agreement is based.

Example Plain vanilla interest rate swap

Consider two companies, A and B. The interest rates at which they can borrow are shown in the first part of Exhibit 12.5.

EXHIBIT 12.5

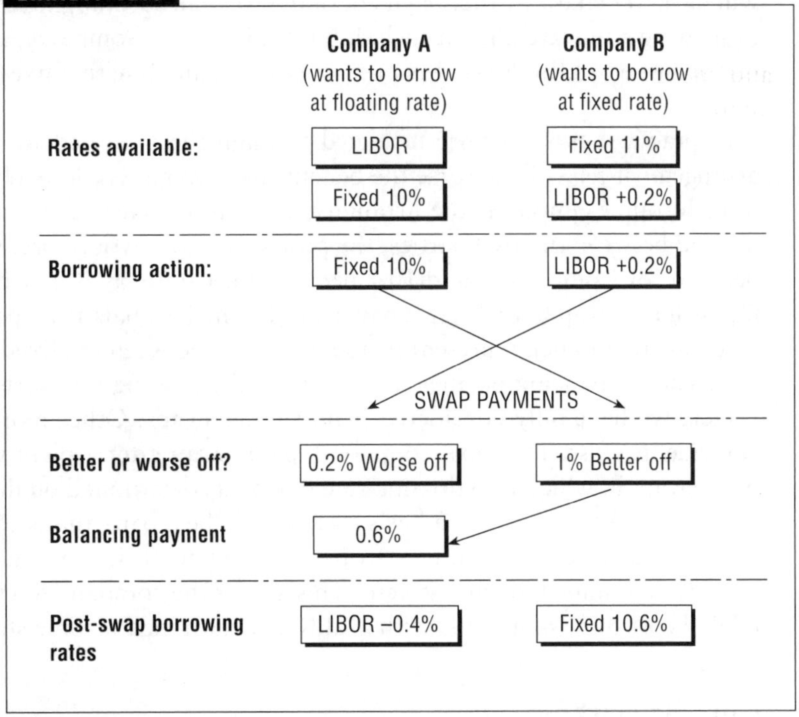

An example of a plain vanilla interest rate swap between two companies, A and B

Company A, due to a better credit rating, can borrow at a lower fixed and floating rate than Company B. We refer to Company A as having an absolute advantage over Company B. However, Company B has a comparative advantage over Company A with floating rate borrowing, as its floating rate is proportionately less expensive when compared to Company A's rates than its fixed rate. If, for example, LIBOR stands at eight per cent, then Company B's floating rate is 2.5 per cent more expensive than Company A's floating rate (i.e. 0.2 per cent/8 per cent).

This compares with Company B's fixed rate being 10 per cent more expensive (i.e. 1 per cent/10 per cent) when compared to Company A's.

The prerequisite for a swap agreement to proceed is for both companies to be able to benefit from it. For this to be the case, the companies must want to raise funds by borrowing in the rate in which they do not possess a comparative advantage. In our example, this means that Company A must want to borrow at a floating rate and Company B must want to borrow at a fixed rate. If Company A raises a fixed rate loan at 10 per cent and Company B raises a floating rate loan at LIBOR + 0.2 per cent, and they swap interest payments, then Company B is one per cent better off while Company A is 0.2 per cent worse off. If Company B makes a payment of 0.2 per cent to Company A, then Company A is neither better nor worse off, while Company B is still 0.8 per cent better off. If the benefits of the swap agreement are to be split evenly between the two parties, then Company B will have to make a further payment of 0.4 per cent to Company A. The post-swap borrowing rates are shown in Exhibit 12.5, where Company A ends up with a floating rate of LIBOR – 0.4 per cent and Company B with a fixed rate of 10.6 per cent.

In practice, as swaps are arranged through the intermediation of a bank, its arrangement fee will decrease the benefit that companies derive from the transaction. In our example, if the arranging bank took a fee of 0.2 per cent, equally divided between the two parties, the post-swap rates would become LIBOR – 0.3 per cent for Company A and 10.7 per cent for Company B. Furthermore, companies will not swap both interest payments, but make a balancing payment from one company to another, representing the difference between the fixed and the floating rate. These balancing payments will vary as the floating rate varies.

Here we have only considered plain vanilla swaps. Other more complex swap agreements exist. The most common type of swap after a plain vanilla swap is a *basis* swap, in which two floating rate payments determined on different bases are exchanged. An example of a basis swap would be a bank that swaps its base-rate-determined interest income (from the advances it has made) for say a LIBOR-determined income stream. This allows the company to match its LIBOR-related cost of raising funds with a LIBOR-determined income stream.

12.6.3 Currency swaps

A currency swap is a formal agreement between two parties to exchange principal and interest payments in different currencies over a stated time period. Currency swaps enable companies to gain the use of funds in a foreign currency but to avoid any exchange rate risk (transaction risk) on the principal or servicing payments. Alternatively, they can be used to obtain a particular currency at a more favourable rate than if a company borrowed the currency itself.

Currency swaps commence with the exchange of the agreed principal amounts at a par exchange rate (usually the prevailing spot rate), followed by the exchange of interest payments over the life of the swap. When the swap matures, the principal amounts are re-exchanged at the par exchange rate agreed earlier. An alternative to the initial exchange of the principal is for both counterparties to make the appropriate spot market transactions, followed by exchange of interest payments over the duration of the swap and re-exchange of principals on maturity.

The information included in currency swap contracts is similar to the information included in an interest rate swap agreement. In addition, though, it will specify which currency is to be paid, which currency is to be received and the exchange rate to be used as the par rate.

Implicit within currency swaps is an interest rate swap. The simplest form of currency swap is a *fixed to fixed* agreement, where the interest payments to be exchanged on the two currencies are both fixed. If the swap involves exchanging fixed and floating interest rates it is then called a *fixed to floating* or *currency coupon* swap.

An example of how currency swaps can be used to hedge exchange rate risk is explained in the following example and illustrated in Exhibit 12.6.

EXHIBIT 12.6

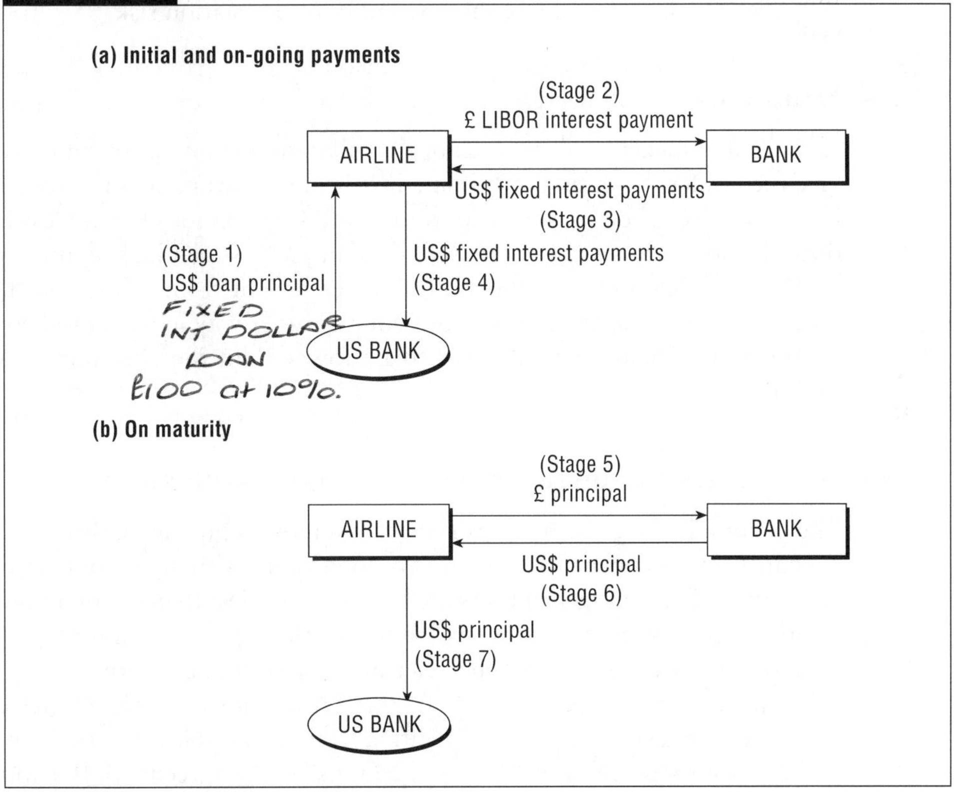

An example of a currency swap indicating (a) the initial and on-going payments and (b) the payments made on the swap's maturity. The chronological order of payments is indicated by the numbered stages in brackets

Example Fixed to floating currency swap

A UK airline is to purchase a new aeroplane. This has to be paid for in US dollars, so the airline will finance its purchase with a fixed interest dollar loan (Stage 1) from a US bank. Due to the company's income being received predominantly in pounds, it has approached another bank in order to establish a currency swap deal. Within this swap agreement will be a par exchange rate which is used to convert dollar cash flows into pounds. It will be used to convert the dollar loan into a sterling principal on which to determine the sterling LIBOR payments the airline will make to the bank (Stage 2), in return for the bank paying to the airline the dollar interest payments on the airline's dollar loan (Stage 3). These dollar interest payments will then be paid on to the US bank by the airline (Stage 4). Upon the swap agreement's maturity the airline will pay the sterling principal to the bank (Stage 5) and in return will receive a dollar payment (Stage 6) with which to pay off its maturing dollar loan (Stage 7). Looking at the swap as a whole, we can see that the airline has paid off a sterling loan principal and sterling LIBOR-determined interest payments, hence avoiding the possibility of translation risk.

12.6.4 Swaptions

As the name suggests, swaptions are a combination of an option and a swap. They give the holder the option to become involved in a swap, i.e. they are a derivative of a derivative. They are similar to traded and OTC options but are less flexible, as once the option to swap is exercised, the company is then locked into a particular exchange or interest rate and can no longer benefit from subsequent favourable movements in rates. Swaptions represent a cheaper way in which to hedge risk, as the premiums paid on them tend to be lower than the premiums charged for options.

12.6.5 Advantages and disadvantages of hedging with swaps

The major advantage with swaps is that they allow companies to hedge interest and exchange rate exposures for relatively long periods of time compared to other derivatives. The arrangement fees are usually much less than the premiums paid on options, while swaps are more flexible from a principal and duration point of view than standardised derivatives such as traded options and futures.

Swap agreements are not without their risks, however. Once entered into, a swap prevents a company from benefiting from favourable movements in exchange and interest rates, unless of course it defaults on the agreement. If a counterparty to a swap agreement defaults on paying the other company's interest payments, the latter party is still legally required to make the servicing payments as it originally took out the loan. This risk of interest default is referred to as *counterparty risk*. It is therefore advisable that companies entering into swap agreements do so only with counterparties of an acceptable credit standing.

12.7 ISSUES IN RISK MANAGEMENT

12.7.1 The need for a risk management strategy

Hedging exchange rate and interest rate risk is both a complicated and a dynamic process. Hedging strategy, therefore, and the techniques and instruments employed to execute a hedging strategy, will vary from company to company, depending upon the markets that companies operate in, their attitudes towards risk, and their awareness and understanding of the techniques available. When formulating hedging strategies, it is important for companies to be clear about their objectives, to identify and quantify their likely exposures, and to select appropriate hedging techniques. Interestingly, Rawls and Smithson (1993) report that, even though many companies regard risk management as important, few have produced formal statements of risk management policy.

The objectives of hedging policy

Companies must clearly define the objectives of their hedging policy. Is the objective one of securing a certain interest income or interest cost? Is the objective to minimise foreign currency expense, or to maximise or fix the sterling value of foreign currency income? An important determining factor here is whether a company's treasury department is designated as a cost centre or a profit centre. Within a cost centre, hedging will be seen solely as a means of reducing risk and providing a service to the rest of the company. If the treasury department is classified as a profit centre, however, there is in-built pressure to use derivatives in a more speculative manner, the consequences of which can be disastrous, as witnessed by the number of recent high profile losses arising from the misuse of derivatives.

On a rational note, Cornell and Shapiro (1988) argue that, since currency risk affects all aspects of a company's operations, exposure management should not be left solely in the hands of financial managers, but rather should be integrated into the general management of the company as a whole. On this analysis, exchange rate expectations should inform production, marketing and other operational decisions, so that hedging is an anticipatory strategy.

Identifying and quantifying the exposure

Companies must identify and quantify their exchange and interest rate risk exposures and implement an appropriate hedging strategy. They will have to decide whether they wish to hedge exposures selectively or to hedge on a continuous basis. This choice will depend on a company's attitude to risk. Another important factor is the expectations that companies have concerning future exchange and interest rate changes. For example, a company may only choose to hedge its interest rate exposure selectively if it expects interest rates to change significantly.

Selection of hedging method

The final component of a company's hedging strategy is the selection of appropriate methods of hedging, given the nature of an exposure. A sensible strategy is to try to hedge as much of the interest and exchange rate risk as possible by using internal hedging techniques. Any remaining exposure can then be hedged using the most appropriate external techniques. A number of factors restrict a company's ability to hedge internally, however (*see* Section 12.2), increasing the need to use external methods. While there is a wide range of external instruments to choose from, the choice of derivative will depend heavily upon the relative importance to a given company of the particular costs and benefits of the derivatives available. Some of the considerations to be taken into account are as follows:

- for exposures of non-standard size and duration, tailormade derivatives (swaps, FRAs, OTC options) represent more appropriate hedging tools than traded options and futures;
- options, while costing more, are appropriate when a company is not completely certain of making a transaction or where it is not completely certain about the direction in which interest or exchange rates will move;
- bank-created products may be more appropriate for smaller companies, as their treasury functions are likely to lack the required experience and knowledge needed to use more complex traded derivatives.

12.7.2 The pros and cons of exposure management

Considerable debate has continued for some years, on both an academic and a practical level, as to the desirability of hedging by companies. Common sense tells us that a company should hedge an exposure if, and only if, the costs of executing the hedge are outweighed by the benefits. The actions of financial managers would seem to support the importance and benefits of hedging, given the enormous growth in the use of exchange and interest rate management instruments in recent years. It has been known for some time that large UK companies, including Cadbury-Schweppes and Tate and Lyle, have found benefits in adopting such instruments. The potential benefits which may arise from hedging exposures include the following.

Maintaining competitiveness

Adverse changes in interest and exchange rates may reduce the competitive position of a company compared to other companies with lower levels of gearing or smaller exchange rate exposures, or compared to companies who have taken the precaution of hedging against rate changes.

Reduction of bankruptcy risk

Adverse movements in interest and exchange rates may jeopardise the continued operation of a company. A classic example is that of a highly geared company with a large proportion of floating rate debt being forced into bankruptcy due to an increase in interest rates.

Restructuring of capital obligations

Interest rate hedging instruments can be used to restructure a company's capital profile by altering the nature of its interest obligations, thereby avoiding the repayment of existing debt or the issuing of new securities. In consequence, considerable savings can be made in respect of call fees and issue costs. At the same time, a wider range of financial sources becomes available to the company.

Reduction in the volatility of corporate cash flows

Reducing the volatility of net cash flows may increase the market rating of the company and will facilitate the process of forward planning.

Enhancement of companies' debt capacity

If interest rate hedging techniques are being used to manage interest rate exposure, companies may be able to increase gearing levels or enhance their debt capacities.

The benefits of hedging must be balanced against a number of problems which, ultimately, may dissuade some companies from engaging in it.

The complicated nature of hedging instruments

A combination of unfamiliarity with the range of hedging methods available and a belief by potential users that such methods are complex may result in treasurers choosing not to hedge exchange and interest rate exposures.

The costs associated with derivatives

Companies may be dissuaded from using derivatives by the various fees, premiums, margin requirements and transaction costs associated with them.

The risks associated with using external hedging instruments

The perceived risk associated with using hedging instruments can sometimes dissuade potential users. This has recently been exacerbated by a number of high profile derivative disasters. In 1994 Proctor and Gamble lost $102m on two interest rate swap agreements with US bank Bankers Trust. Instead of providing protection from steeply increasing interest rates, the transactions turned out to be highly speculative bets. Proctor and Gamble has subsequently taken legal action against Bankers Trust on the grounds that it was misled by the bank.

In February 1995, in a now legendary disaster, Barings bank went into receivership after making losses in excess of £860m on Nikkei index futures deals on SIMEX in Singapore and on the Osaka derivatives exchange in Japan. The losses were accumulated by their former 'star' trader Nick Leeson, who was responsible for both trading and back office records of his deals.

The legality of swap agreements with certain counterparties was undermined by a 1991 Law Lords judgment against Fulham and Hammersmith Council and its operations in the swap market, which were deemed to be *ultra vires* (not within its powers).

The complicated tax and financial reporting treatments of derivatives

The accounting and tax treatment of derivatives has tended to lag behind the pace of their development due to the dynamic nature of their markets. The major problem regarding the accounting treatment of derivatives is knowing exactly what information to disclose and how to disclose it. At present, in the absence of a definitive accounting standard, companies tend to report only superficial information and general strategies, rather than disclosing detailed information. As far as the tax treatment of derivatives is concerned, it may be necessary for companies to seek specialist advice before engaging in the derivatives market. This represents a further cost and may contribute to the reluctance of many companies to use derivatives.

Diversification by shareholders may be superior to hedging

An alternative to hedging by individual companies is for shareholders to diversify away interest and exchange rate risk themselves by holding a diversified portfolio of shares, hence saving the costs associated with hedging at a corporate level. If shareholders hold diversified portfolios, there is a school of thought that argues that hedging of exposures by individual companies is motivated purely by management's desire to safeguard their jobs, rather than a desire to enhance shareholder wealth.

Despite the drawbacks we have just considered, there can be little doubt that, if used properly, derivatives can and do bring real benefits to the user company. In the cases cited where companies have made huge losses through the trading of derivatives, the problems were not so much with the derivatives themselves but rather with the way that they were used (or misused). Some of these financial disasters have involved unauthorised trading (e.g. the Barings fiasco), raising the possibility that a significant number of companies may not have in place appropriate controls or monitoring procedures to regulate their derivative dealings. The lesson for such companies is that they cannot ignore the need for well-defined risk management policies, which must include specific reference to:

- the types of derivative instrument that are permitted;
- limits on the volume and principal amount of derivative transactions allowed;
- requirements to calculate, say on a monthly basis, the market value of the company's derivative positions;
- systems and procedures to prevent unauthorised dealings.

It is also sensible for companies to outlaw the use of derivatives for speculative purposes. Once such policies are implemented, a company's derivatives transactions should be both more visible and more easily understood.

Spare a parting thought for corporate treasurers who, when it comes to risk management, are effectively in a 'no win' situation. Deciding not to hedge a particular exposure and doing nothing can be construed as speculation if an unfavourable movement in rates occurs. However, should the treasurer hedge the exposure, locking into a particular rate, and the market subsequently move in what would have been a favourable pre-hedge direction, it is considered bad judgement on his part!

12.8 CONCLUSION

The area of risk management has grown rapidly in importance over the past 20 years and treasurers now find themselves spending an increasing amount of their time engaged in hedging company exposures to risk. This elevation of importance has been mainly due to the increased volatility of interest and exchange rates and to the rapid growth in the risk management tools and techniques available.

Risk can be managed by the use of both internal and external techniques. Internal techniques allow companies to hedge risk within their own balance sheet by the way in which they structure their assets and liabilities. Alternatively, companies can employ one or more of the many external techniques now available such as swaps, options, futures and forwards. While these derivative instruments give more scope and flexibility to companies to manage their risk, their associated costs and their complicated nature must be taken into account.

There have been a number of huge losses reported by companies in recent years due to the misuse of derivatives. This should not detract, however, from the very real benefits that can be derived from hedging, whether by internal or external methods, provided that these techniques are used in an appropriate manner.

KEY POINTS

1 Interest and exchange rate management has played an increasingly important role within corporate finance due to recent instability of interest and exchange rates.

2 Interest rate risk is faced by companies regardless of whether they lend or borrow at fixed or floating rates of interest.

3 Exchange rate risk can be classified into transaction, translation or economic risk. The first two types of risk are only faced by companies with some form of overseas operations, but all companies face economic risk.

4 Interest and exchange rate risk can be hedged internally by the way in which companies structure their assets and liabilities, but the degree to which companies can hedge their exposures internally is often limited.

5 The large number of external derivatives now available to companies can be sub-divided into traded derivatives and over-the-counter (OTC) derivatives.

6 Before the advent of derivatives, external hedging took the form of forward contracts arranged with banks and the use of money market hedges. These techniques remain a popular form of hedging risk.

7 Financial futures are standardised agreements to buy or sell an underlying financial asset. They are exchange-traded and allow companies to lock into particular interest or exchange rates for set periods.

8 Options give the holder, on payment of a premium, the right but not the obligation to pay or receive interest, or sell or buy currency, at a predetermined rate. Traded options are standardised with respect to maturity and principal, while OTC options can be tailormade.

9 Interest rate swaps are agreements to exchange interest payments based on a specified principal. They allow companies to hedge interest rate risk over long periods of time and to raise funds at more favourable rates than if they raised funds directly. Currency swaps are similar to interest rate swaps, but also involve exchanges of principal. They allow companies to hedge translation and transaction risk and to raise currency more cheaply than if they were to borrow it directly.

10 For companies to hedge effectively, it is important they have a well thought out strategy. This involves specifying hedging objectives, identifying and quantifying exposures and selecting appropriate hedging tools.

11 Advantages of using derivatives include the greater level of certainty companies face with respect to interest rates and currency transactions, while disadvantages include the expense and complicated nature of such instruments.

12 Recent derivatives disasters have stemmed more from derivatives misuse than from fundamental problems with the instruments themselves. If companies have well-defined guidelines to control the use of derivatives and the required expertise and knowledge to monitor them, then they should benefit from their use.

QUESTIONS

Answers to these questions can be found on pages 436–8.

1 In the following cases, state which type of exchange rate risk the company is facing and whether this risk is upside or downside in nature:

(a) A power generating company imports coal from Germany, purchasing the coal in deutschmarks. The company is expecting the pound to weaken against the deutschmark over the next few months.

(b) A UK toy-producing company supplies only to the domestic market. Its only major competitor in the domestic market is a US toy company. The pound is expected to weaken against the dollar over the next year.

(c) A UK company has purchased a factory in France but has financed its purchase with sterling borrowing. Over the next year the pound is expected to appreciate against the French franc.

2 Recommend internal hedging methods that a company can utilise in order to reduce the exposure caused by translation risk and transaction risk.

3 A company is expecting to have to pay $345 000 in three months' time. It is afraid

that over this period the pound will depreciate against the dollar. Given that the current exchange rate is \$1.78/£1 and that the current dollar deposit rate is 8.5 per cent, how can the company use the money markets to hedge the transaction risk it is facing?

4 What are the major differences between OTC options and traded options?

5 A company is going to borrow £6m in three months' time for a period of six months. The company is afraid that interest rates will rise between now and the time that the loan is taken out. Therefore the company is going to try to hedge the exposure using futures contracts. Given that the contract size of interest futures is £500 000, which of the following transactions will enable the company to hedge its exposure successfully?

(a) selling 12 futures contracts;
(b) buying 12 futures contracts;
(c) selling 24 futures contracts;
(d) buying 24 futures contracts;
(e) selling 6 futures contracts.

6 Which factors influence a company's decision to hedge interest rate risk?

7 Which factors determine whether a company, having decided to hedge its interest rate exposure, uses internal hedging methods or external instruments? If it decides to hedge interest rate risk externally, what factors will determine which instruments will be used?

8 Which of the following will *not* help a company to hedge successfully against an *increase* in interest rates?

(a) the selling of interest rate futures contracts;
(b) swapping floating rate interest for fixed interest rate payments;
(c) the purchase of a bank-created floor;
(d) splitting borrowing between fixed and floating rate interest loans;
(e) the purchase of a put option on futures contracts.

9 What are the drawbacks of hedging exchange rate risk by using a swap agreement?

10 Given the following list of dollar currency options (all with three months to run) and the fact that the current spot rate is \$1.55/£1, which of the following options do you expect to have the highest market value?

(a) put option, strike price \$1.76;
(b) call option, strike price \$1.43;
(c) put option, strike price \$1.55;
(d) call option, strike price \$1.52;
(e) put option, strike price \$1.42.

QUESTIONS FOR REVIEW

Answers to these questions can be found on pages 438–40.

1 Discuss the factors that may persuade a company to hedge an interest rate exposure by using OTC options rather than financial futures contracts.

2 Carrycan plc will have to make a payment of $364 897 in six months' time. It is currently 1 January. The company is considering the various choices it has in order to hedge its transaction exposure.

Exchange rates:	
$ spot rate	1.5617–1.5773
Six-month $ forward rate	1.5455–1.5609

Money market rates:

	Borrow (%)	*Deposit* (%)
US dollars	6	4.5
Sterling	7	5.5

Foreign currency option prices (cents per £ for contract size £12 500):

Exercise price	*Call option (June)*	*Put option (June)*
$1.70	3.7	9.6

By making the appropriate calculations decided which of the following hedging alternatives is the most attractive to Carrycan plc:

(a) forward market (i.e. a forward exchange contract);

(b) money market;

(c) currency options.

3 Discuss the factors which influence the price of traded options.

4 Two companies A and B are considering entering into a swap agreement with each other. Their corresponding borrowing rates are as follows:

	Floating rate	*Fixed rate*
Company A	LIBOR	12%
Company B	LIBOR + 0.3%	13.5%

Company A requires a floating rate loan of £5m while Company B requires a fixed rate loan of £5m.

(a) Which company has a comparative advantage in floating rate loans and which company has a comparative advantage in fixed rate loans?

(b) At what rate will Company A be able to obtain floating rate finance and Company B be able to obtain fixed rate finance, if the two companies engage in a swap agreement and the benefits of the swap are split equally between the two parties? Ignore any bank charges.

5 Slammer plc has an excellent rating on the corporate bond market and is able to borrow at a fixed rate of 11.5 per cent, while Can plc, which is regarded as riskier, can borrow at a fixed rate of 12 per cent. For floating rate finance, whether obtained through a floating rate bond issue or a long-term bank loan, Slammer plc can borrow at LIBOR + 0.2 per cent while Can plc can borrow at LIBOR + 0.4 per cent. If Slammer plc wants a floating interest rate loan and Can plc wants to lock into current interest rate levels through a fixed interest rate loan, show how an interest rate swap agreement can benefit both companies. If the benefits from the swap are divided equally between the two companies, calculate their post-swap borrowing rates.

QUESTIONS FOR DISCUSSION

1 Goran plc is a UK company with export and import trade with the USA. The following transactions, in the currency specified, are due within the next six months:

Purchases of goods, cash payment due in three months:	£116 000
Sale of finished goods, cash receipt due in three months:	\$197 000
Purchase of goods, cash payment due in six months:	\$447 000

Data relating to exchange rates, interest rates and option prices is as follows:

Exchange rates (London market)

	\$/£
Spot	1.7106–1.7140
Three months forward	0.82–0.77 cents premium
Six months forward	1.39–1.34 cents premium

Interest rates	*Borrow (%)*	*Deposit (%)*
Sterling	12.5	9.5
Dollars	9.0	6.0

(a) Discuss four techniques that a company like Goran might use to hedge against the foreign exchange risk involved in foreign trade.

(b) Calculate the net sterling receipts/payments that Goran might expect for both its three-month and six-month transactions if the company hedges foreign exchange risk using (i) the forward foreign exchange market and (ii) the money market.

2 Give an in-depth explanation of how interest rate risk can be hedged using options *or* swaps. What are the particular advantages and disadvantages of the hedging method you have chosen?

3 Explain how a company can use financial futures to hedge its interest rate risks and identify any advantages and disadvantages that arise from their use.

REFERENCES

Buckley, A. (1996) *Multinational Finance*, Prentice-Hall.

Cornell, B. and Shapiro, A. (1988) 'Managing foreign exchange risks', in Chew, D. (ed.) *New Developments in International Finance*, Basil Blackwell.

Demirag, I. and Goddard, S. (1994) *Financial Management for International Business*, McGraw-Hill.

Rawls, S. and Smithson, C. (1993) 'Strategic risk management', in Chew, D. (ed.) *The New Corporate Finance – where theory meets practice*, McGraw-Hill.

Winstone, D. (1995) *Financial Derivatives: Hedging with futures, forwards, options and swaps*, Chapman and Hall.

RECOMMENDED READING

For a book totally dedicated to giving a clear and easily understandable account of derivatives and their use, *see*:

Winstone, D. (1995) *Financial Derivatives*, Chapman and Hall.

The following two books have sections on risk management which include a number of very readable and interesting articles on the subject of hedging and derivatives:

Chew, D. (ed.) (1993) *The New Corporate Finance – where theory meets practice*, McGraw-Hill.

Stern, J. and Chew, D. (eds.) (1986) *The Revolution in Corporate Finance*, Basil Blackwell.

Important and informative books, papers and articles recommended for further reading include the following:

Black, F. and Scholes, M. (1973) 'The pricing of options and corporate liabilities', *Journal of Political Economy*, Vol. 18, pp. 637–59.

'Corporate risk management survey' (1996) *The Economist*, 10 Feb.

Dodd, H. (1994) 'Corporate hedging revisited', *The Treasurer*, July/Aug, pp. 23–6.

Hull, J. (1995) *Options, Futures and Other Derivative Securities*, Prentice-Hall.

Ross, D. (1990) 'Interest rate management: risk and how to measure it', *Accountancy*, Aug, Oct, Nov and Dec issues.

'Survey of derivatives' (1995) *Financial Times*, 16 Nov.

'The over-the-counter derivatives market in the UK' (1996) *Bank of England Quarterly Bulletin*, Feb, pp. 30–6.

'The pricing of over-the-counter options' (1995) *Bank of England Quarterly Bulletin*, Nov, pp. 375–81.

Walsh, D. (1995) 'Risk management using derivative securities', *Managerial Finance*, Vol. 21, No. 1, pp. 43–65.

CHAPTER 13

INTERNATIONAL INVESTMENT DECISIONS

INTRODUCTION

Many companies now undertake operations at the international level, either through exporting goods and services or through setting up operations in foreign countries. Whatever the reasons for choosing to undertake international operations, the choice has significant implications for corporate financing and investment decisions. The currency risk arising from trading with foreign countries may need to be hedged, while a decision to invest directly in a foreign country will naturally raise the question of whether finance should be sought in the local currency or in the currency of the parent company. Evaluation of international investment proposals is more complex than the evaluation of domestic investment, but the primary financial test in both cases is the extent to which a proposed investment will lead to an increase in the wealth of shareholders. With international investment proposals, there will arise the need to make forecasts of exchange rates, to take account of the effect on project cash flows of different taxation systems, and to assess the risk associated with adverse actions by foreign governments. Rather than investing directly in a foreign subsidiary, a company may choose to undertake international operations through licensing or franchising, which have lower attendant risks, or through setting up a foreign branch through which to conduct local operations. This is especially true in the early stages of becoming an international company.

LEARNING OBJECTIVES

After studying this chapter, you should have achieved the following learning objectives:

- an appreciation of the different reasons, strategic or otherwise, for a company to undertake foreign investment;
- the ability to describe the various methods by which a company may seek to internationalise its trading activities, including exporting, licensing, participating in a joint venture and creating a subsidiary, and the reasons why direct investment may be preferred;
- an understanding of the various risks associated with foreign direct investment and how they can be mitigated;
- an understanding of the differences between domestic and international investment appraisal and the ability to evaluate international investment decisions from the perspective of both parent company and host country;
- an appreciation of the difficulties involved in determining an appropriate cost of capital for use in foreign direct investment.

13.1 THE REASONS FOR FOREIGN INVESTMENT

It is rare for foreign investment to be undertaken for a single, overriding motive. It is more likely to occur as a result of the interaction of a number of different motives, not all of which may be explicit. There has been a great deal of research into the reasons why companies invest directly abroad and into how it is possible for international companies to be able to compete successfully with local companies. We shall look at the strategic and economic reasons for foreign investment, but the distinction has been drawn solely for the purposes of discussion; the interaction between corporate strategy and economics is a complex one.

13.1.1 Strategic reasons for foreign investment

Brooke (1996) gives a detailed analysis of the strategic reasons for foreign investment through a classification of *defensive* and *aggressive* motives for foreign investment in checklist form. A company could establish a foreign manufacturing subsidiary, suggests Brooke, as a strategy to defend existing business due to:

- government action on tariff barriers, import controls or legislation;
- demands for local manufacture;
- transport costs and delays;
- problems with agents and licensees;
- technical difficulties abroad, e.g. problems with after-sales service;

- the need to protect patents and intellectual property;
- the need to ensure supplies of raw materials and components;
- the need to internationalise to match competitors, suppliers or customers;
- the need to protect parent company shareholders against recession.

Aggressive reasons for establishing a foreign manufacturing subsidiary suggested by Brooke include:

- the search for more profitable uses for under-employed resources;
- the search for lower factor costs;
- the development of global plans and strategies;
- the desire for access to foreign knowledge;
- the need to expand beyond the domestic arena.

Aharoni (1966) studied 38 US companies which had considered foreign investment in Israel and identified the following external reasons for foreign investment:

- invitation from an outside source, such as a foreign government offering incentives for inward investment;
- fear of losing a market;
- the 'band wagon' effect, i.e. the need to match competitors who have already been successful in foreign markets;
- strong competition from abroad in the home market.

13.1.2 Economic reasons for foreign investment

In a perfect market, foreign subsidiaries would be unable to compete with local companies because of the additional costs imposed by the distance from their parent companies. In order for a foreign subsidiary to compete successfully, the additional costs of operating at a distance from its parent must therefore be overcome. This means that *market imperfections* must offer compensating advantages which are not available to local companies and which are of sufficient size to make investment in the local market attractive to international companies. According to Buckley (1996), market imperfections may occur in product differentiation, marketing skills, proprietary technology, managerial skills, better access to capital, economies of scale, government imposed market distortions (e.g. incentives for inward investment) and financial markets. After considering diversification to reduce earnings volatility and economies of scale as examples of compensating advantages, we shall look at reasons why companies may choose to locate subsidiaries in particular areas.

Economies of scale

The improvement of profit margins and earnings by achieving lower average costs per unit through increasing the scale of operations, discussed in Section 11.2 as one of the justifications for acquisitions and mergers, is also an economic reason for undertaking foreign investment. Such scale economies can arise in any area of business activity, for example in purchasing, production, marketing, distribution, research or finance. Barclay (1995) notes that economies of scale are expected to be one of the main effects of the economic integration accompanying the development of regional blocs such as the European Union (EU) and the North American Free Trade Agreement (NAFTA). These scale economies arise because of access to larger, tariff-free markets and are most marked where a regional bloc integrates a number of smaller domestic markets. Economies of scale are also facilitated by the removal of non-tariff barriers to trade, thereby making markets less fragmented. Such non-tariff barriers may be physical, i.e. border controls and transit documents; technical, i.e. different connectors for electrical appliances in different countries; and fiscal, i.e. differences in indirect taxes such as VAT (value-added tax) between countries.

Diversification to reduce earnings volatility

Companies may undertake foreign investment in order to guard against overexposure to any one economy. Since different economies are unlikely to move exactly in parallel, a company may be able to reduce the variability of its cash flows by investing in projects in different countries. Here, the intention of international diversification is to reduce risk. Theoretically, the company's shareholders will not benefit if a company reduces the variability of its cash flows, since this represents unsystematic risk which shareholders themselves can eliminate through portfolio diversification. From a practical point of view, however, a company with volatile earnings may have higher interest costs, a lower credit rating, liquidity problems and a higher cost of capital due to being perceived as riskier than similar companies. This could result in lower earnings being available for shareholders. Here, the intention of international diversification is to increase shareholder returns. Reviewing the evidence, Siegel *et al.* (1995) found that diversification did not appear to increase shareholder returns and that the risk advantage of multinational companies appeared to be decreasing over time.

Locational factors

Even if a company has compensating advantages encouraging foreign investment, it will still need to select the location which offers the best overall return. Locational factors which need to be considered include production costs, marketing considerations and government policy.

In order to maximise the benefits of foreign investment, companies can set up production facilities in locations where land and labour costs are lower, or where the proximity to growing markets offers a reduction in distribution costs. These opportunities are likely to be features of 'emerging markets'. Dawes and Ivanov (1995) suggest the example of exploiting cheap labour by producing goods in Vietnam, coupled with selling not only in Vietnam but also to its Pacific Rim neighbours, such as China and Japan. Madura (1995) cites lower costs of production as a reason why Honeywell has established subsidiaries in Mexico, Malaysia,

Hong Kong and Taiwan, and notes that the establishment of subsidiaries in Mexico by US-based multinational companies has contributed significantly to the growth of Mexico's economy.

An example of the ways in which economic integration and locational factors can encourage foreign investment is given in Vignette 13.1 on page 370.

13.2 DIFFERENT FORMS OF INTERNATIONAL TRADE

It is unusual for a company to make setting up a foreign subsidiary its first step in internationalising its business operations. There are a number of other methods of conducting operations which may be preferred when a company is taking its first steps on the international stage, and which may be preferred to foreign investment, even by established international companies. These methods are illustrated in Exhibit 13.1 and include direct exporting, licensing, setting up an overseas branch and participating in a joint venture. If we accept that companies adopt a risk-minimising process of gradual expansion into the international arena, these different methods of conducting international operations could be seen as intermediate stages of increasing risk along the path to setting up a foreign subsidiary. It has been found that, while most companies do begin the process of internationalisation through exporting, they do not necessarily undertake all of the intermediate stages mentioned. As Buckley (1996) points out, this incremental model of the internationalisation process only moves in one direction, and therefore cannot explain divestment or reorientation as strategic choices. This may be because the model is too simplistic in its representation of a complex process.

EXHIBIT 13.1

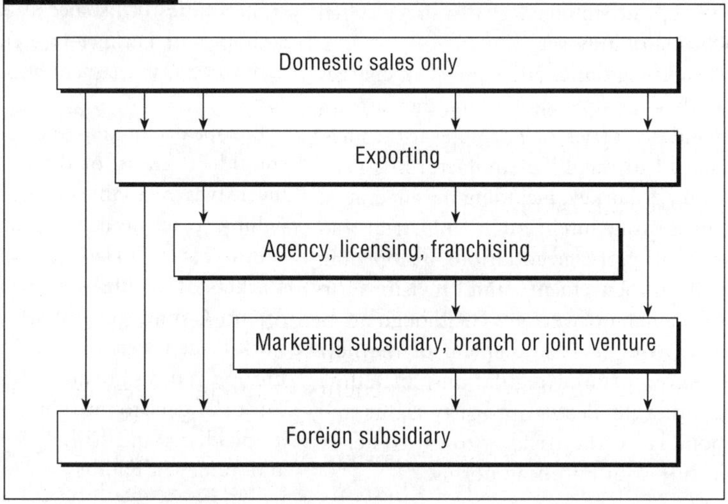

Diagram illustrating different ways in which a company may conduct international operations, culminating in the establishment of a foreign subsidiary

VIGNETTE 13.1

New access to top trading partner

FT

While reports of political turmoil and macroeconomic woes in Turkey are unsettling investors, many European exporters are painting a rosier picture, capitalising on the EU's newfound access to the rapidly developing Turkish market of 63m consumers. Once heavily protected, Turkey last year opened its doors to the European Union in a landmark customs union deal, bolstering what was already a strong trade partnership – Turkey was one of Europe's top 10 trading partners in 1995. The customs union, which entered into force in January 1996, has enhanced opportunities for EU manufacturers looking to sell to Turkey or to manufacture in Turkey for export to promising developing markets in the Middle East, Central Asia and Europe.

With the duty-free access to the Turkish market ushered in by the customs union, EU imports to Turkey jumped 19 per cent in 1996, a year that registered a 7.9 per cent growth rate, making Turkey the seventh largest importer of EU goods. Raw materials and investment goods topped the import list, reflecting the way in which rising industrial production is fuelling economic expansion. Consumer goods, in demand by a young and increasingly urban population, also registered high on the list of imports.

As well as lifting duties and equivalent charges on EU goods, excluding agriculture, the customs union includes a series of harmonisation measures designed to put EU manufacturers on an equal footing in Turkey, including the enactment of laws protecting intellectual, industrial and commercial property, negotiations on opening government procurement and revisions in Turkey's discriminatory tax laws. Although problems remain with the enforcement of the new customs union-inspired regulations, including laws regulating intellectual property rights and child labour laws, the trend is towards steady harmonisation with European norms.

'We would like to see more retail and food industry coming into Turkey,' says Mr Mike Stevenson, commercial secretary at the British Embassy, citing the impressive results of the country's first Marks and Spencer outlet in Istanbul, as well as the excellent performance of joint ventures involving European hypermarket chains, including Germany's Metro and the Swiss Migros.

Turkey's emergence as a key business partner for the emerging economies of the Central Asian Turkic republics of the former Soviet Union is also creating excellent opportunities for European countries. 'The emergence of Central Asia as a focus for trade and investment has given Turkey a new role,' says IBS Research and Consultancy in its *Doing Business in Turkey Guide*. Turkey's geographic position assures it a key role in bringing the substantial oil and gas reserves of the Caspian and Central Asian basins to international markets. Added to that, says IBS, are the solid commercial strengths Turkey has built up in the area. Turkish companies, helped by cultural and language links, now lead the foreign business community in many Black Sea and Caspian Sea communities. This success has led to increasing examples of Turkish–foreign co-operation in the contracting, investment goods and telecoms sectors.

Europeans looking to enter the Turkish market should be aware of the numerous government incentives available, especially for companies willing to set up in the country's less developed south-eastern provinces, away from the chief markets of Istanbul and Izmir, according to Mr Ayhan Copur, general secretary of the private Turk-trade Foreign Trade Association of Turkey. European firms are also advised to find a reliable Turkish agent to introduce and develop sales for its products and to be prepared to invest time and money in building business relationships.

Source: Kelly Couturier, FT Exporter, *Financial Times*, July 1997 (adapted)

13.2.1 Exporting

Export sales have a lower risk than foreign investment, as they offer quick returns and do not require a commitment to substantial capital expenditure. However, selling and distribution costs will be higher with exporting compared with local production and there is also the risk that tariffs may be imposed on imports as a result of government policy. Establishing strong business links with foreign customers will be more difficult without a local manufacturing or sales presence, and it will take longer to build up a detailed picture of foreign markets.

Many of the difficulties associated with exporting can be overcome by setting up a branch in the foreign country, perhaps staffed by local employees, as this offers a low-cost way for a company to establish a local presence.

13.2.2 Licensing

This involves a contractual agreement with a local company to manufacture the company's products in return for a royalty or similar payment and is therefore an example of the trade in knowledge. It offers a way of expanding foreign sales without the need for substantial capital expenditure and may facilitate penetration of markets where export sales are either not possible or restricted by barriers to trade. It also offers a route by which funds can be remitted back to the parent company even if repatriation of funds is difficult. However, the returns obtained through licensing may be small compared with those generated by a foreign subsidiary.

One of the main dangers mentioned in connection with licensing is the possibility of encouraging the setting up of a competitor as a result of the transfer of knowledge and expertise. If the licensee terminates the agreement and sets up in competition to the principal company, it may be difficult to restrain him. Difficulties could then arise from competition between the products manufactured by the licensee and the firm's existing products.

13.2.3 Joint ventures

A joint venture represents an alternative ownership strategy to that of owning all or most of the equity in a foreign subsidiary and involves distribution of the subsidiary's shares amongst the independent participants in the project. Each participant will be involved in the management of the project and in return will have particular resources to offer. These resources may be finance, expertise, local knowledge and contacts, a distribution network, and so on. By pooling financial resources, the participants may be able to undertake a project too big or too risky for an individual company to consider, for example the development and construction of the European Airbus. Some countries (e.g. India) insist on a joint venture and require a proportion of a subsidiary's equity to be in local hands.

There are particular advantages to using a joint venture if one of the partners is based in the foreign country with which it is hoped to trade. Such a partner may have local business knowledge, access to local finance, established distribution channels and access to local raw materials. It is also possible that, if the local partner has political contacts, these could be used to reduce the risk of adverse government action.

Brooke (1996) states that the disadvantages of joint ventures are as follows:

- lack of adequate control;
- the partner may not have the requisite skills and the parent company may find itself doing more work than expected;
- rigidity, in that the joint venture is difficult to control or amend;
- division of interest, in that policies that are advantageous to a company as a whole may not be advantageous to an individual subsidiary. Transfer pricing, dividend policy, sourcing of materials and marketing plans are examples of policy areas that may present problems.

13.2.4 Foreign subsidiary

A subsidiary may be established by acquisition of an existing company or by setting up a new one. Acquiring an existing company may offer considerable cost advantages if the acquisition has a good reputation, a good distribution network and an established client base, although naturally these advantages will have a price. However, these advantages may be reduced by post-acquisition integration problems, arising from cultural or operational differences. Whichever method is used, a subsidiary represents a significant commitment of parent company resources.

A subsidiary may be preferred to a branch because it can be financed wholly or in part by local currency debt, allowing both transaction and translation risk to be hedged by matching (*see* Section 12.2.3). A subsidiary is also likely to offer tax advantages over a branch. Since a branch is not a separate legal entity from the parent, its profits are taxed at the domestic rate as they are earned. The profits of a foreign subsidiary are subject to the local tax system, which may be more favourable than the domestic system. Domestic tax liability will not arise until profits are remitted back to the home country.

Selling and distribution costs for goods produced by a foreign subsidiary will be lower than for exported goods; profit margins will also be improved by the avoidance of import tariffs and other fiscal penalties attached to imported goods. Business links with foreign customers will be easier to establish and customer loyalty can be fostered by the provision of after-sales care.

An example of how a multinational company can adopt different forms of international operations to suit local conditions is given in Vignette 13.2.

VIGNETTE 13.2

Positive experience in difficult markets

FT

The experience of pharmaceuticals giant SmithKline Beecham in North Africa is that investment-related export sales may allow a company to consolidate its position even in the most difficult markets. Maghreb countries have been a focus for many years and the company has a joint venture in Algeria, a subsidiary in Morocco, a licensing agreement in Tunisia and operations in Libya.

Investor-friendly Tunisia is 'something of a model in terms of its one-stop investment office that works quite efficiently', says Mr Paul Barrett, director and vice-president for Africa. 'There are plenty of regulatory obstacles,' he says. 'But this tends to be the case with all developing markets.'

Operating is possible even in the most difficult conditions, however, if a company approaches the challenges in an appropriate manner. In Algeria, where tens of thousands have been killed in more than five years of civil conflict, 'the problems attached to security are entirely manageable', says Mr Barrett.

Indeed, SmithKline Beecham's joint venture in Algeria is progressing 'very positively', according to Mr Barrett. 'We have just taken a decision to invest in the second phase of our local manufacturing project, a basic medicines factory at Boudouaou,' he says.

The project was held up by the security situation, but Mr Barrett says SmithKline's Algerian partner built its own factory and demonstrated it was possible to obtain high standards using local staff with only minimal European supervision, 'So we are going ahead with an antibiotic plant on the existing site.'

The Algerian market has shrunk by about half in the last year due to cutbacks on authorised imports by the authorities, which are trying to encourage local manufacturers. Import permits are going to exporters with a firm intent to set up locally or which have an involvement with local manufacturing companies.

Past investments have brought SmithKline's pharmaceutical operations in the region to a stage where they 'are now mature', Mr Barrett says. But this does not mean a lack of new opportunities. Consumer products, particularly healthcare, offer potential. The North African market also needs quality, but affordable, generic materials.

SmithKline has a local manufacturing presence in Morocco and Tunisia, where competition is fierce. Local manufacturers have been operating in the Moroccan market for years, whereas pharmaceuticals investments by Rhone-Poulenc, Roussel Uclaf and others in Tunisia are recent, intensifying competition. 'There are now seven synthetic penicillin plants in Tunisia,' Mr Barrett says.

Morocco is an important market. Here, SmithKline's local subsidiary has an antibiotics facility in production. Pointing to the potential offered by establishing a regional manufacturing base, exports from this plant are expected to start next year.

The company is also a major supplier for Libya, despite the political problems. Libya remains a state-controlled market, where watching closely for public tenders is essential.

Source: Jon Marks, FT Exporter, *Financial Times*, July 1997

13.3 THE EVALUATION OF FOREIGN INVESTMENT DECISIONS

A distinction can be made between foreign direct investment and foreign portfolio investment. Foreign portfolio investment occurs when a company participates in international investment but has no control of the business, for example by purchasing a minority of shares in a foreign company. As a result of such purchases, the investing company will receive returns in the form of dividends and capital gains, and may enhance business relationships. We are not concerned here with this kind of foreign investment.

Foreign direct investment may be defined as a long-term investment in an economy other than that of the investing company, where the investing company has control over the business. The main example of such an investment is the setting up or purchase of a foreign subsidiary.

13.3.1 The distinctive features of foreign direct investment

Foreign direct investment decisions are not conceptually different from the domestic investment decisions considered in Chapters 3 and 4 and so can be evaluated using broadly the same investment appraisal techniques discussed there, including net present value and internal rate of return. However, international investment decisions do have some distinctive features which make their evaluation more difficult:

- project cash flows may need to be evaluated in a foreign currency;
- exchange rate movements create currency risk, which may need hedging;
- foreign taxation systems may differ from the domestic taxation system;
- project cash flows and parent cash flows will be different;
- remittance of project cash flows may be restricted;
- the investment decision may be evaluated from different viewpoints;
- the investment may be subject to political risk.

13.3.2 Methods of evaluating foreign direct investment

The financial evaluation of foreign direct investment proposals can help to eliminate poor projects, check whether marketing assumptions are valid, and give an indication as to the amount and type of finance needed. Following on from Chapter 3, the academically preferred method of evaluating foreign direct investment proposals is the net present value method, since shareholder wealth will be increased by the selection of projects with a positive net present value. This also suggests that, since it is the shareholders of the parent company whose wealth is of paramount importance, it is the net present value of the after-tax cash flows accumulating to the parent company which should be used to judge the worthiness or otherwise of a foreign direct investment proposal. We should recognise, however, that evaluation at the level of the host country is also possible.

A number of empirical studies of international investment appraisal have been summarised by Demirag and Goddard (1994), Buckley (1996) and Kim and Ulferts (1996). The empirical evidence suggests that, rather than using the academically preferred net present value method, companies evaluating foreign direct investment decisions use a whole range of different methods. We can summarise the main findings as follows:

- the majority of multinational companies use discounted cash flow (DCF) methods of investment appraisal as the primary method for evaluating foreign investment projects, with internal rate of return being preferred to net present value;
- there does not appear to have been an increasing use of DCF methods of investment appraisal in recent years;
- only a minority of companies used sophisticated risk adjustment methods such as risk-adjusted discount rate and the certainty equivalent approach;
- a large proportion of companies do not use after-tax cash flows to the parent company as the main measure of income in the evaluation;
- an increasing number of companies appear to base the required rate of return for foreign investment decisions on the cost of debt;
- smaller firms tended to use less sophisticated investment appraisal methods such as accounting rate of return and payback;
- UK companies tended to use less sophisticated investment appraisal methods than US companies.

This divergence between the methods used by companies and the methods recommended by theory echoes the findings of the empirical surveys of investment appraisal methods discussed in Chapter 4.

13.3.3 Evaluation of foreign direct investment at local level

The foreign direct investment project can be evaluated in local terms and in local currencies, for example by comparing it with similar undertakings in the chosen country. This evaluation ignores the extent to which cash flows can be remitted back to the parent company and also ignores the overall value of the project to the parent company's shareholders. Whether foreign direct investment is to be evaluated at local level or parent company level, the project cash flows in the local currency will need to be determined. Such project cash flows can be categorised as follows.

Initial investment

This will be the outlay on fixed assets such as land, buildings, plant and machinery. This may be derived from an issue of equity or debt, and the debt finance may be raised locally or be provided by the parent company. The initial outlay may also include a transfer of real assets such as plant and equipment, in which case the transferred assets should be valued at the opportunity cost to the parent company.

Investment in working capital

This may be part of the initial investment or may occur during the start-up period as the project establishes itself in operational terms. Investment in working capital may be achieved in part by transfer of stocks of components or part-finished goods from the parent company.

Local after-tax cash flows

These will be after any local operating costs for materials and labour and after local taxation. Interest payments may need to be considered if the investment is partly financed by locally raised debt, such as loans from banks or other financial institutions. A particular difficulty will be the treatment of goods provided by the parent company, when the price charged to the subsidiary (the transfer price) must be seen by local taxation authorities to be a fair one. In cash flow terms, such goods will be a cost at local level but a source of revenue to the parent company, and will have tax implications at both levels.

The terminal value of the project

It will be necessary to determine a terminal value for the project, either because the evaluation is being truncated for ease of analysis or because it is expected that at some future date the parent company's interest in the project will cease, for example through sale of the subsidiary.

Even though evaluating the investment project solely in terms of the cash flows accruing in the foreign country may indicate that it is apparently worth undertaking, making a decision to proceed with the investment on these grounds may be incorrect. The net present value of the project to the parent company depends to a large extent on the future cash flows which can be transferred or remitted. If the transfer of funds is restricted, this value may be reduced. The effect of the project on existing cash flows, for example existing export sales, must also be considered.

13.3.4 Evaluation of foreign direct investment at parent company level

At parent company level, project cash flows will be the actual receipts and payments in the parent company's own currency. These project cash flows are as follows.

Initial investment

This will consist of cash that has been invested by the parent company and may be in the form of debt or equity. It will also include transferred plant and equipment at opportunity cost.

Returns on investment

The parent company will receive dividends from the project and, if debt finance has been provided, interest payments and repayments of principal.

Receipts from inter-company trade

The parent company may receive a variety of cash payments in exchange for goods and services provided to the project. Goods and components sold to the company will generate income based on agreed transfer prices. Royalties may be received on patents. Management fees may be received in exchange for the services of experienced personnel.

Accrued contribution

If remittances have been subject to exchange controls, the parent company will at some point receive accrued contributions, perhaps at the termination of the project.

Taxation

Cash flows accruing to the parent company will be liable to taxation under the domestic tax system. Relief may be given for tax paid abroad.

Cash flows from the foreign direct investment will need to be converted in the home currency, which means that exchange rates will need to be forecast over the life of the project. A further problem is that an appropriate discount rate for the project will need to be determined: this is discussed in Section 13.4.

13.3.5 Taxation and foreign direct investment

The taxation systems of the host country and the home country are likely to be different. If profits were subjected to taxation in both countries, i.e. if 'double taxation' existed, there would be a strong disincentive to investment. 'Double taxation relief' is usually available, either by treaty between two countries or on a unilateral basis, whereby relief is given for withholding tax paid abroad on income received. The net effect of a double taxation treaty is that the parent company will pay the higher of local tax or domestic tax on dividends remitted by the foreign subsidiary. Withholding taxes paid abroad will only affect the amount of taxation received by each country, unless the withholding tax rate is greater than the domestic tax rate.

For computational purposes, the UK tax liability can be assessed from the taxable profits of the foreign subsidiary. This is easier than grossing up receipts from overseas investments and also avoids the possibility of wrongly assessing capital cash flows for UK corporation tax. The UK liability can then be reduced by withholding tax already paid to determine UK tax payable.

Example Foreign direct investment evaluation

Wobble plc is a UK company which is considering setting up a manufacturing subsidiary in the small republic of Bandanna, whose currency is the Bar (B). The initial investment of £1 000 000 in plant and machinery would be payable in sterling. Initial investment in working capital of B500 000 would be financed by a loan from a local bank, at an annual interest rate of 10 per cent. At the end of five years, the subsidiary would be sold as a going concern to a local conglomerate for B4 950 000 and part of the proceeds will be used to pay off the bank loan.

The subsidiary is expected to produce cash profits of B1 500 000 per year over the five-year period. Writing down allowances are available on the initial investment on a straight-line basis at a rate of 20 per cent per year. As a result of setting up the subsidiary, Wobble expects to lose export sales to Bandanna of £20 000 per year (after tax).

Profits in Bandanna will be taxed at a rate of 20 per cent after interest and writing down allowances. All after-tax cash profits are remitted to the UK at the end of each year. UK taxation of 31 per cent is charged on UK profits, but a double taxation agreement between Bandanna and the UK allows tax paid in Bandanna to be set off against any UK liability. Taxation is paid in the year in which it arises.

Other companies with similar business in Bandanna have a weighted average after-tax cost of capital of 10 per cent. Wobble requires its foreign investments to be discounted at 15 per cent. The current exchange rate is B4.50/£1, but as the Bar is expected to depreciate against sterling, the exchange rate will deteriorate by B0.50 per year.

Should Wobble undertake the investment in Bandanna?

Initial investment in Bandanna:	£1 000 000 × 4.50 = B4 500 000
Annual writing down allowance:	B4 500 000 × 0.2 = B900 000
Annual interest payment:	B500 000 × 0.1 = B50 000

As the subsidiary is sold as a going concern, working capital is not recovered.

The calculation of the cash flows of the Bandanna subsidiary is given in Exhibit 13.2. Notice that a separate tax calculation has not been carried out, but instead the writing down allowances have been deducted from operating cash flows and then added back after local tax has been calculated.

EXHIBIT 13.2

Year	*0* *(B000)*	*1* *(B000)*	*2* *(B000)*	*3* *(B000)*	*4* *(B000)*	*5* *(B000)*
Operating cash flows		1500	1500	1500	1500	1500
Writing down allowances		(900)	(900)	(900)	(900)	(900)
Interest		(50)	(50)	(50)	(50)	(50)
Profit before tax		550	550	550	550	550
Withholding tax		(110)	(110)	(110)	(110)	(110)
After-tax cash flows		440	440	440	440	440
Initial investment	(4500)					
Working capital	(500)					
Loan capital	500					(500)
Sale of subsidiary						4950
Add back WDAs		900	900	900	900	900
Project cash flows	(4500)	1340	1340	1340	1340	5790
10 per cent discount factors	1.000	0.909	0.826	0.751	0.683	0.621
Present values	(4500)	1218	1107	1006	915	3596

Calculation of the project cash flows and present values for Wobble plc's subsidiary in Bandanna

To determine the acceptability of the project at local level, the project cash flows can be discounted at the weighted average after-tax cost of capital of local companies carrying out similar business. Using the present values from Exhibit 13.2, we have:

$$NPV = (4\ 500\ 000) + 1\ 218\ 000 + 1\ 107\ 000 + 1\ 006\ 000 + 915\ 000 + 3\ 596\ 000 = B3\ 342\ 000$$

At the local level, the project appears to be acceptable.

As a first step to determining the acceptability of the project at the company level, the cash flows remitted to the UK are translated into sterling. The tax payable on the sterling cash flows can then be found by reference to the taxable profits of the Bandanna subsidiary, after taking account of local tax already paid, as follows:

Year 1 taxable profit (B)	= 550 000
Year 1 taxable profit (£)	= 550 000/5.00 = 110 000
UK tax liability	= 110 000 × 0.31 = £34 100
Local tax paid	= 110 000 × 0.20 = £22 000
UK tax payable	= 34 100 – 22 000 = £12 100

This calculation can be repeated for subsequent years, always bearing in mind that the exchange rate continues to change. After bringing in the value of the lost export sales, which are already after tax, the parent company cash flows and their present values can be determined, as shown in Exhibit 13.3.

EXHIBIT 13.3

Year	*0*	*1*	*2*	*3*	*4*	*5*
Remitted to UK (B000)	(4500)	1340	1340	1340	1340	5790
Exchange rate (B/£)	4.50	5.00	5.50	6.00	6.50	7.00
	£000	*£000*	*£000*	*£000*	*£000*	*£000*
Sterling equivalent	(1000)	268	244	223	206	827
UK tax		(12)	(11)	(10)	(9)	(9)
	(1000)	256	233	213	197	818
Exports lost, after tax		(20)	(20)	(20)	(20)	(20)
Parent cash flow	(1000)	236	213	193	177	798
15 per cent discount factors	1.000	0.870	0.756	0.658	0.572	0.497
Present values	(1000)	205	161	127	101	397

Calculation of the project cash flows and present values for Wobble plc's subsidiary at parent company level

We have:

NPV = (1 000 000) + 205 000 + 161 000 + 127 000 + 101 000 + 397 000
= minus £9000

At the parent company level, it appears that the project should be rejected. The reasons why there is a difference between the two evaluations is clear:

- operating cash flows in Bandanna are constant but exchange rates have deteriorated;
- UK taxation is greater than Bandanna taxation;
- parent company cash flows are discounted more heavily;
- Wobble plc has lost exports to Bandanna.

13.4 THE COST OF CAPITAL FOR FOREIGN DIRECT INVESTMENT

The arguments for and against using the weighted average cost of capital (WACC) or the capital asset pricing model (CAPM) as the source of a discount rate for use in investment appraisal have been discussed in Chapters 8 and 9. Similar arguments are relevant when considering the appropriate discount rate to be used in evaluating foreign direct investment. For example, Stanley (1990) notes that theorists have made the following suggestions concerning the cost of capital for foreign direct investment:

- a project-specific cost of capital should be employed since the discount rate should reflect the value to the firm of undertaking particular activities;
- the weighted average cost of capital should be used for projects of similar risk to existing activities, otherwise a project-specific cost of capital should be employed;
- the appropriate cost of capital is that of local firms in the same industry.

All three suggestions point towards the need for a cost of capital which takes account of the risk and characteristics of individual projects. Each suggestion also implies that a single cost of capital can adequately take account of the complex interaction between sources of finance, taxation, exchange rates, exchange controls and risk which is a feature of foreign direct investment.

In contrast, it has been suggested that the basic investment project, shorn of taxation and financing aspects, should be discounted at the parent company's ungeared cost of equity, and that taxation and financing implications should be treated as adjustments to this 'base-case NPV' by discounting their cash flows at an appropriate cost of debt. This is the *adjusted present value* (APV) method of investment appraisal, which has the advantage of being able to deal with project-specific financing in different capital markets. It suffers from the disadvantage that estimating the side-effects of adjustments to the base-case NPV and their associated discount rates is far from easy, calling for considerable expertise.

The CAPM was recommended in Chapter 9 as being the best way of finding the cost of equity for use in investment appraisal, but there are a number of difficulties that arise within the context of foreign direct investment.

- The risk-adjusted discount rate found by using the CAPM takes account of systematic or market risk, but which market portfolio should be used in determining the project beta?
- The CAPM is sensitive to financial market prices and these will change frequently. Over what time frame should the cost of equity be determined?
- What is the value of the market premium? Studies comparing the returns of capital markets of different countries, while offering some evidence of increasing integration, suggest that integration is by no means complete. Should a global risk premium be determined?

While the resolution of these problems is as yet incomplete, steps have been taken towards the development of an international capital asset pricing model (ICAPM), for example as discussed by Buckley (1996).

On the question of whether the cost of capital should in general be higher or lower for foreign direct investment than for domestic investment, it could be assumed from a common sense point of view that foreign direct investment, especially in countries regarded as politically unstable, ought to require a higher risk premium. On the other hand, Holland (1990) suggests that, if foreign investment provides otherwise unattainable diversification benefits to parent company shareholders, the discount rate used could be lower. It seems that the safe course is to assume that the cost of capital for each foreign direct investment may need to be determined individually by selecting from the range of techniques available, depending upon the sophistication of the analyst involved. It will be recalled from Section 13.3.2 that internal rate of return was found from empirical evidence to be the favoured technique for evaluating foreign direct investment. Given the difficulties in determining an appropriate cost of capital for such investment, this may not be so surprising.

13.4.1 The international financing decision

The main objective of the international financing decision is to minimise the company's after-tax cost of capital at an acceptable level of risk, since minimising the cost of capital will maximise the market value of the company. A multinational company with access to international capital markets has a greater opportunity to reduce its cost of capital than a domestic company. The financing decision, which has been considered in detail in Chapter 8, will need to consider:

- the relative proportions of equity and debt finance;
- the relative proportions of long-term and short-term finance;
- the availability of different sources of funds;
- the effect of different sources of finance on the risk of the company;

- the direct and indirect costs of different sources of finance;
- the effect of taxation on the relative costs of equity and debt.

13.4.2 Factors influencing the choice and mix of finance

The key factors influencing the choice and mix of finance for international operations include gearing, taxation, political risk and currency risk.

Gearing

Both the gearing of the company as a whole and the gearing of each subsidiary must be considered. If the holding company guarantees the debts of its subsidiaries, whether formally or informally, then as long as the group gearing is acceptable, the decision on the gearing of individual subsidiaries can be made independently. Advantage can then be taken of local interest rates and tax rules and subsidised finance as appropriate.

Taxation

Differences between the treatment in different tax systems of withholding taxes, gains, losses, interest and dividends can be exploited through the financing decision. In particular, since interest payments on debt are tax deductible while dividends are not, there is an incentive to use debt as the main source of finance for a foreign subsidiary. Some countries counter this tendency by imposing a maximum allowable level of gearing for tax purposes.

Political risk

One kind of political risk is the possibility of expropriation of assets by a foreign government. Expropriation of assets is less likely if foreign direct investment is financed as much as possible from local sources and if the financing arrangements involve international banks and government agencies. Buckley (1996) cites the example of investment along these lines by Kennecott in a Chilean copper mine project, on which the company was able to secure returns despite the subsequent coming to power of a regime committed to expropriating all foreign-held assets without compensation. Political risk is discussed in Section 13.5.

Currency risk

The financing mix chosen for foreign direct investment can be used by a company as part of its overall strategy of managing currency risk. The use of local debt finance, for example, will reduce translation exposure and allow the parent company to use the internal risk management technique of matching.

13.5 POLITICAL RISK

Goddard (1990) defines political risk as 'the possibility of a multinational company being significantly affected by political events in a host country or a change in the political relationships between a host country and one or more other countries'. Multinational companies making direct foreign investments must consider the possibility of political action. This may be favourable, such as the granting of investment incentives (e.g. to encourage inward investment to south-eastern Turkey, as in Vignette 13.1), or unfavourable, such as the expropriation of assets (e.g. during the Gulf War).

Political risk management involves two stages: first, the assessment of political risk and its potential consequences; and second, the development and implementation of policies to minimise political risk.

13.5.1 Assessment of political risk

Demirag and Goddard (1994) point out that, because there is no consensus definition of political risk or political risk events, the development of a reliable method for the measurement and analysis of political risk is not easy. Two approaches to the measurement of political risk are commonly cited, namely macro-assessment and micro-assessment. Macro-assessment seeks to assess political risk without considering factors which are business-specific, while micro-assessment looks at political risk from the perspective of the investing company.

Macro-assessment of political risk is at the country level and is intended to produce risk indices which give an indication of the level of political risk in each country. These indices focus on political stability and look at a range of political and social factors, including the relative power of political factions; the extent of division by language, race or religion; social conditions; internal conflict; bureaucratic infrastructure, and so on. Rankings of countries by political risk indices are produced regularly by financial magazines such as *Euromoney* and *Institutional Investor*, or are available by subscription.

Individual companies who are considering investing in a particular country can use a number of different methods to assess its political risk from both a micro- and a macro-assessment perspective, including the following.

- *Checklist approach*. This approach involves making a judgement on all the factors that contribute to political risk and then weighting them to produce a political risk index.
- *Delphi technique*. This involves the collection of a number of expert opinions, perhaps by use of a questionnaire, and then weighting or aggregating them.
- *Quantitative analysis*. Quantitative analysis techniques such as sensitivity analysis or discriminant analysis can be used to identify the key factors influencing the level of political risk of a country.
- *Inspection visits*. Also known as the grand tour, this involves company staff visiting the country under consideration on a fact-finding visit.

Goddard (1990) found that UK multinationals typically used a subjective rather than a systematic approach to the analysis of political risk, with little use being made of external advisors.

13.5.2 Policies to manage political risk

The simplest way to manage political risk is to choose not to invest in those countries which are perceived as having too high a level of political risk. However, this ignores the fact that the returns from such an investment might more than compensate for the risk incurred.

Insurance against political risk

It is possible to insure against political risk through private companies, such as Trade Indemnity and NCM, but most insurance of this kind is through government departments or agencies. The government agency responsible for political risk insurance in the UK is the Export Credits Guarantee Department (ECGD).

Negotiation of agreements

Political risk can be addressed by the negotiation of concession agreements with host governments, setting out the rules and restrictions under which the investing company can expect to conduct its business. The weakness of such agreements is that they may be renegotiated or repudiated by the same or subsequent governments, although this is much less likely to occur with developed nations.

Financing and operating policies

It is possible to reduce exposure to political risk by appropriate structuring of the company operations. Operating policies which have been suggested for consideration include locating different stages of construction in different countries; controlling the means by which finished goods are exported; concentrating key services such as research and development, marketing and treasury management outside of the host country; and avoiding becoming dependent upon the output of any particular manufacturing facility.

Exposure to political risk can also be reduced by choosing appropriate financing policies. As noted earlier, expropriation of assets is less likely if investment is financed locally as much as possible and if international banks and government agencies are involved in financing arrangements. Another financial strategy which could be employed is securing unconditional guarantees from the host government.

13.6 CONCLUSION

A company may undertake foreign direct investment for a number of strategic and economic reasons, but whether a proposed investment increases the wealth of the parent company's shareholders remains the primary financial test. The path to foreign direct investment is also not necessarily a straight one: a company may progress through a number of different methods of conducting international trade before it decides that creating or acquiring a foreign subsidiary is in the best interests of the company.

The evaluation of foreign direct investment is necessarily more difficult than the evaluation of domestic investment. Apart from the difficulty of determining relevant cash flows, exchange rates need to be forecast and an appropriate discount rate needs to be selected. The calculation of a discount rate for use in foreign direct investment is far from easy: here, we have concentrated on outlining the problems involved. The solution will depend upon the information that is available and the theoretical model that is preferred.

KEY POINTS

1 Companies can have defensive and aggressive motives for foreign investment.

2 If the additional costs of operating at a distance are to be overcome, market imperfections must offer compensating advantages to make foreign investment attractive.

3 Foreign investment may be undertaken to achieve economies of scale, which are encouraged by economic integration within regional blocs such as the EU and the NAFTA.

4 Foreign investment may be undertaken in order to reduce earnings volatility or overexposure to any one market, i.e. to reduce risk. Whether this reduction of risk has value for shareholders is debatable.

5 Locational factors to be considered in order to obtain the best overall return include production costs, marketing factors and government policy.

6 A company can conduct international operations through exporting, licensing, an overseas branch, a joint venture or a subsidiary. From one perspective, these represent stages in the internationalisation process.

7 Exporting is low risk, offers quick returns and does not need capital investment, but selling and distribution costs may be high and there is a risk that import tariffs may be imposed.

8 Licensing allows a local company to produce goods in return for royalties. While it may allow entry into difficult markets, returns may be lower than with direct investment. There is the danger of encouraging the setting up of a competitor.

9 A joint venture with a partner based in the target country may be useful, but joint ventures have problems with lack of control and divided interests.

10 A subsidiary can offer tax advantages, lower selling and distribution costs, higher profit margins and stronger business links.

11 NPV at parent company level should be used to judge a foreign direct investment, but evidence suggests IRR is preferred by multinationals. NPV at local level ignores the overall value to the company.

12 While the taxation systems of two countries may be different, double taxation relief is usually available.

13 The arguments for and against using WACC and CAPM in investment appraisal, discussed earlier in the book, also apply to the problem of finding the cost of capital for foreign investment. A cost of capital which reflects the risk of the individual project should be used.

14 It may be advantageous to use the APV method with foreign investment.

15 In using the CAPM with foreign investment, problems arise when considering which market portfolio to use in order to find beta; over which time period to conduct the analysis; and the value of the market premium.

16 The international financing decision seeks to minimise the after-tax cost of capital at an acceptable level of risk. The key factors in this decision are gearing, taxation, political risk and currency risk.

17 Political risk is concerned with the effect on a company's value of political events in the host country. It can be managed by assessing political risk and its consequences, and by developing policies to minimise it.

18 Individual companies can asses political risk by using the checklist approach, the Delphi technique, quantitative analysis and inspection visits. Many companies still use a subjective approach.

19 Political risk can be managed through insurance, negotiation of agreements, and financing and operating policies.

QUESTIONS

Answers to these questions can be found on pages 440–1.

1 For what strategic reasons may a company decide to build a manufacturing facility in another country?

2 Briefly describe the economic reasons why a company may choose to undertake foreign direct investment.

3 Explain the advantages and disadvantages of exporting, licensing and foreign direct investment as different ways of conducting international trade.

4 Describe the advantages and disadvantages of joint venture as a way of selling goods to another country.

5 List the ways in which foreign direct investment decisions are different from domestic investment decisions.

6 Discuss whether foreign direct investment should be evaluated at the local level or at the parent company level.

7 What difficulties may be faced by analysts seeking to use the capital asset pricing model to determine a discount rate for foreign direct investment?

8 Describe the main factors influencing the choice and mix of financing used in foreign direct investment.

9 Explain how political risk may be assessed by a company considering foreign direct investment.

10 Describe briefly the policies and strategies that a company could use to mitigate the problem of political risk.

QUESTIONS FOR REVIEW

Answers to these questions can be found on pages 441–4.

1 Scot plc is a successful manufacturing company based in the North of England. As a result of the changing relationship between the European Union and Eastern European countries, an opportunity has arisen to invest in Glumrovia. The directors of Scot plc have decided that, because of the risky nature of investments in this part of the world, they will require an after-tax return of at least 20 per cent on the project.

The government of Glumrovia is prepared to grant Scot plc a five-year licence to operate in the country. Market research suggests that cash flows from the project, in Glumrovian dollars (G$), will be as follows:

Year	*1*	*2*	*3*	*4*	*5*
G$000	250	450	550	650	800

However, much of the increase in the project cash flows is due to expected rates of inflation. The current G$/sterling exchange rate is G$3.00/£1, and the expected exchange rate in subsequent years is expected to be:

Year	*1*	*2*	*3*	*4*	*5*
G$/£	4.00	5.00	6.00	7.00	8.00

The project will cost G$600 000 to set up, but the present Glumrovian government will pay G$600 000 to Scot plc for the business at the end of the five-year period. It will also lend Scot plc the G$250 000 required for initial working capital at the advantageous rate of six per cent, to be repaid at the end of the five-year period.

Scot plc will pay Glumrovian tax on the after-interest profits at the rate of 20 per cent. Glumrovian tax is payable at the end of each year, at which time the balance of profits can be remitted to the UK. There is a tax arrangement between the two governments, so that any Glumrovian tax paid can be offset against UK tax liability. UK tax is payable at the rate of 30 per cent on gross remittances and you should assume that it is payable at the time that the cash is remitted to the UK.

As yet, there is no stock exchange in Glumrovia, as the current liberal government has been unable to complete the implementation of necessary economic reforms. A recent press report revealed that the people of Glumrovia are disappointed with the pace of liberal reform and that elections to be held next year might well see a significant renewal of communist influence.

(a) Prepare a report for the management of Scot plc that analyses the data available and makes argued recommendations as to whether or not the project should be taken on.

(b) Discuss the possible problems that might confront a company making the type of decision facing Scot plc.

2 Redek Mornag plc manufactures mobile telephones in a manufacturing facility in the UK which has some spare capacity. It currently exports 20 per cent of its annual production to Laresia, a developing nation which has recently elected a right-wing government after five years of military rule. It is expected that the market for mobile telephones will increase significantly in Laresia over the next few years, and Redek Mornag plc wants to increase its share of the market. Discuss the relative merits to Redek Mornag plc of the following ways of servicing the Laresian market:

(a) increasing exports to Laresia from the existing UK factory;

(b) licensing a Laresian manufacturer to produce mobile telephones there;

(c) constructing a factory in Laresia.

3 Critically discuss the ways in which international capital investment decisions can be distinguished from domestic capital investment decisions.

4 Brinpool plc, a UK manufacturer of machine parts, has been invited to build a factory in the small African state of Gehell by the government of that country. The local currency is the Ked (K) and data on current and expected exchange rates is as follows:

Year	*0*	*1*	*2*	*3*	*4*	*5*
K/£	3.50	4.00	4.40	4.70	4.90	5.00

Initial investment will be £1 500 000 for equipment, payable in sterling, and K1 000 000 for working capital. The Gehell government has offered a loan to cover working capital at 10 per cent per year, repayable in full after five years. The Gehell government has also expressed a wish to acquire the factory from Brinpool plc as a going concern after five years, and has offered K4 200 000 in compensation. Their loan would be recovered from the compensation payment.

Brinpool plc estimates that cash profits will be K3 000 000 per year, but also expects to lose current annual export sales to Gehell of £50 000 after tax. All after-tax cash profits are remitted to the UK at the end of each year.

Profits in Gehell are taxed at a rate of 15 per cent after interest and writing down allowances, which are available on the £1.5m initial investment on a straight-line basis at a rate of 20 per cent per year. UK taxation of 31 per cent is charged on UK profits and a double taxation agreement exists between Gehell and the UK. Taxation is paid in the year in which it arises.

Other companies with similar business in Gehell have a weighted average after-tax cost of capital of 12 per cent. Brinpool plc has estimated that, due to the political risk of Gehell, it should apply a cost of capital of 18 per cent.

Determine whether the proposed investment is financially acceptable to Brinpool plc.

5 Discuss the problem of political risk in the context of foreign direct investment, and the difficulties that companies may face as a result of it.

QUESTIONS FOR DISCUSSION

1 Lisant Mirrad International is evaluating a proposal to build a manufacturing facility in Weland. The initial investment of £1.6m is payable in sterling to UK contractors and Lisant Mirrad International expects before-tax operating cash flows of 1m Welandian dollars (W$) per year. It is expected that the sales from the new manufacturing facility will reduce existing exports by Lisant Mirrad International to Weland by about £17 000 per year in after-tax profit over the life of the project.

Under Welandian legislation, a withholding tax of 15 per cent is charged on profits which are remitted abroad. The directors of Lisant Mirrad International have proposed that all of each year's profits be remitted to the UK, where under UK legislation they will be treated as gross dividends (before withholding tax) and attract corporation tax at 33 per cent. Withholding tax paid in Weland is an allowable deduction against the UK tax liability.

In order to reduce the risk of the project, Lisant Mirrad International has agreed to sell the factory to the Welandian government after five years of operations for W$1.5m. The Welandian government has agreed that this sum may be remitted to the UK without further taxation.

Assume that cash transfers occur at the end of each year, and that tax liabilities are paid in the year that they arise. Lisant Mirrad International requires a return of at least 17 per cent on this kind of investment as regards cash flows received in the UK, while in order to compensate for the perceived risk of investing in Weland, it requires a return of 22 per cent at the level of the manufacturing facility.

The current exchange rate is W$1.5/£1 and expected exchange rates over the next five years are as follows:

Year	*1*	*2*	*3*	*4*	*5*
W$/£	1.620	1.750	1.890	2.041	2.204

Determine whether the project is acceptable on the following bases:

(a) from the point of view of the manufacturing facility;

(b) from the point of view of Lisant Mirrad International.

2 Critically discuss the following statement:

'Net present value is the best way to find out if a foreign investment project is a good one and all the big multinationals are using it now.'

REFERENCES

Aharoni, Y. (1966) *The Foreign Investment Decision Process*, Harvard Graduate School of Business Administration, Division of Research.

Barclay, J. (1995) 'Regional blocs', in Dawes, B. (ed.) *International Business: A European Perspective*, Stanley Thornes.

Brooke, M. (1996) *International Management*, Stanley Thornes.

Buckley, A. (1996) *Multinational Finance*, Prentice-Hall.

Dawes, B. and Ivanov, D. (1995) 'Emerging markets: characteristics and opportunities', in Dawes, B. (ed.) *International Business: A European Perspective*, Stanley Thornes.

Demirag, I. and Goddard, S. (1994) *Financial Management for International Business*, McGraw-Hill.

Goddard, S. (1990) 'Political risk in international capital budgeting', *Managerial Finance*, Vol. 16, No. 2, pp. 7–12.

Holland, J. (1990) 'Capital budgeting for international business: a framework for analysis', *Managerial Finance*, Vol. 16, No. 2, pp. 1–6.

Kim, S. and Ulferts, G. (1996) 'A summary of multinational capital budgeting studies', *Managerial Finance*, Vol. 22, No. 1, pp. 75–85.

Madura, J. (1995) *International Financial Management*, Minnesota, West Publishing Company.

Siegel, P., Omer, K., Rigsby, J. and Theerathorn, P. (1995) 'International diversification: a review and analysis of the evidence', *Managerial Finance*, Vol. 21, No. 9, pp. 50–77.

Stanley, T. (1990) 'Cost of capital in capital budgeting for foreign direct investment', *Managerial Finance*, Vol. 16, No. 2, pp. 13–16.

RECOMMENDED READING

A comprehensive discussion of the internationalisation process can be found in Buckley, A. (1996) *Multinational Finance*, Prentice-Hall.

A fascinating account of the various forms of international trade is given by Brooke, M. (1996) *International Management*, Stanley Thornes.

APPENDIX

ANSWERS TO END-OF-CHAPTER QUESTIONS

CHAPTER 1

Answers to Questions

1 The financial manager's job normally falls under the control of the financial director. He or she oversees the financial controller, who deals with the accounting side, and the corporate treasurer, who carries out the financial management tasks. These tasks will include the following:

- investment decisions, capital budgeting and investment appraisal;
- financing decisions, including raising debt and equity finance;
- working capital management, including cash management, credit control and inventory control;
- dividend policy formulation;
- interest rate and foreign currency management.

2 Examples could include the following:

- insufficient finance or expensively raised finance, leading to the rejection of investment projects;
- too high dividends, restricting the amount of retained earnings and therefore increasing the need for external finance;
- large number of attractive projects, leading to a higher level of retained earnings and therefore a lower dividend payment.

3
- *Profit maximisation*. Profit figures can be manipulated, have no time dimension if profits are maximised year after year and also don't take risk into account.
- *Sales maximisation*. Even further off the mark than the above. Market share may be an initial goal in order to obtain a market foothold. Sales maximisation, taken to the extreme, can lead, via overtrading, to bankruptcy.

- *Maximisation of benefit to employees and the local community.* Again, if taken to the extreme, could lead to bankruptcy. It is important to keep both employees and the local community happy, but this is not a main goal.
- *Maximise shareholder wealth.* The correct goal, since as owners their wealth should be maximised.

4 How does a financial manager maximise shareholder wealth? Shareholders derive wealth from share ownership through capital gains and dividend payments. The financial manager, then, should maximise the present value of these. If capital markets are efficient, the current market price of a share should be the net present value of all future benefits accruing to the share. Current market share price, then, can be used as a proxy for shareholder wealth. To maximise shareholder wealth, a financial manager should accept all projects with positive net present values, as this will maximise the market share price, therefore maximising shareholder wealth.

5 Examples of good financial management are given at the end of Section 1.3.

6 The correct answer is (d), because the use of restrictive covenants in bond deeds is of relevance to the providers of debt finance as a way of encouraging optimal behaviour by shareholders. It does not, then, lead to a reduction in the agency problems experienced by shareholders.

7 The agency problem arises because of a divorce of ownership and control. Within a public limited company (plc), there are a number of examples of the agency problem, the most important being that existing between shareholders (principal) and managers (agent). The problem exists because of divergent goals and an asymmetry of information. Managers act to maximise their own wealth rather than the shareholders' wealth.

8 There are various ways to reduce the agency problem:

- do nothing, if the costs of divergent behaviour are low;
- monitor agents, if contracting or divergent behaviour costs are high;
- use a reward/punishment contract, if monitoring costs and divergent behaviour costs are high.

As regards the shareholders/managers agency problem, monitoring costs and divergent behaviour costs are high, so shareholders use contracts to reward managers for good performance and could give managers shares in the company they manage, making them shareholders themselves.

9 Some possible managerial goals are given in Section 1.2.

10 The size of the agency problem reflects the relative power of shareholders with respect to managers. Since, in the UK, institutional investors now have significant holdings in UK public limited companies, they are able to bring significant pressure to bear on company management as a way of encouraging goal congruence. As in the US, shareholder groupings are growing as a way of enhancing and focusing this pressure. It can be argued, then, that for institutional investors in UK plcs, the agency problem is being progressively attenuated. For smaller investors, however, this may not be the case.

Answers to Questions for review

1 The definition of wealth is not straightforward, but one method is to consider the returns that investors expect in exchange for becoming shareholders. Such returns will be in the form of regular dividends and any gain made on disposal of the shares; that is, the returns will be either revenue or capital in nature. The maximisation of wealth then becomes the maximisation of such returns to the shareholder. If we introduce the element of time, the objective becomes the maximisation of the dividend flow to the shareholder over time, followed by receiving the gains of disposal.

Since investors have a required return, which is the opportunity cost of investing in a given company rather than investing elsewhere, future cash flows will need to be discounted. If disposal of the security is distant, we can ignore it, recognising that discounted distant returns are less valuable then those received in the near future. Maximisation of shareholder wealth then becomes maximisation of the present value of the stream of future dividends, and as Gordon and others have shown, the present value of future dividends can be equated to the current ex-dividend share price. Maximisation of the company's share price can therefore be used as a surrogate objective.

2 The maximisation of sales has a number of problems as a measure of maximisation of shareholder wealth:

- sales are measured in revenue rather than cash terms, so maximising sales may not result in cash inflows for a company;
- sales may be maximised by offering goods on extended credit terms or by making sales to disreputable companies who may default on payment;
- sales are theoretically maximised when marginal revenue is equal to marginal cost, but how do we know when this has occurred?
- sales or turnover is an historical measure and not necessarily a guide to expected future cash flows;
- sales may be maximised but on mispriced goods, leading to losses.

Sales maximisation is therefore a subjective measure. In contrast, a company's ordinary share price is an objective yardstick provided by the capital markets. It is independent of the company, forward-looking, and reflects an assessment of the company's prospects in both financial and strategic terms.

3 You should discuss the following points:

- divergence of ownership and control;
- divergence of goals between principal and agent;
- asymmetry of information, including access to dissimilar information sets and asymmetry of interpretation;
- managers' personal goals, which may not lead to maximisation of shareholder wealth;
- conflict between investors and managers in the areas of investment decisions and risk;
- ways in which principals can monitor the activities of agents;
- agency costs, including costs of monitoring, free rider problem and contract costs;
- optimal contracts and other ways of encouraging goal convergence.

CHAPTER 2

Answers to Questions

1 Retained earnings is the cash left after a company has met operating and recurrent investment needs. Retained profit is an accounting term signifying residual profit at the end of an accounting period. It is not cash.

2 This topic is discussed in Section 2.1.2. The main factors influencing the split between internal and external finance are as follows:

- the amount of finance needed;
- the profitability of current operations;
- the opportunity cost of retained earnings;
- the costs of external finance;
- the availability of finance;
- the dividend policy.

3 The relevance of the efficient market hypothesis for financial management is that, if the hypothesis holds true, the company's 'real' financial position will be reflected in the share price. If the company makes a 'good' financial decision, this will be reflected in an increase in the share price. Similarly, a 'bad' financial decision will cause the share price to fall. In order to maximise shareholder wealth, then, the financial manager need only concentrate on maximising the NPV of investment projects, and need give no consideration to matters such as the way in which the future position of the company will be reflected in the company's financial statements. The financial manager, then, may utilise rational decision rules and have confidence that the market will rapidly cause the effects of those decisions to be reflected in the company's share price.

4 The incorrect statement is (b), since if capital markets are strong form efficient, then nobody, not even people with insider information, will be able to make abnormal returns.

5 A perfect capital market has the following features:

- trading is costless, so there are no transaction costs or taxes. Trading is said to be 'frictionless';
- information is costless and freely available to all. This means that all investors make decisions based on the same information;
- there are many buyers and sellers, so prices are not distorted by the actions of individuals.

6 Allocational efficiency means that funds are allocated to their most productive use, to the benefit of the many. This allocation is done on the basis of assets being efficiently priced, so that prices correctly reflect all relevant information. For the market to respond quickly to new information, transactions must be frictionless, i.e. the market is operationally efficient.

7 It is hard to test for strong form efficiency directly, that is by studying the market's *use* of information, because it can always be objected that investors with access to inside information can make abnormal gains. Tests for strong form efficiency are therefore *indirect*, examining the performance of *users* of information who may have access to inside information or who have special training for share dealing, such as fund managers.

8 Ratios in isolation mean little. In order to assist in their interpretation, they can be compared with other benchmarks, including:

- target ratios set by managers;
- sector or industry norms;
- the ratios of similar companies;
- the ratios of the same company from previous years.

All such comparisons should be made with caution, due to the problems associated with undertaking ratio analysis, such as differing accounting policies and creative accounting.

9 The answer to this question is given in Section 2.3.2 and subsequently. You should be able to define *all* the ratios. If you cannot, you must study them until you can. Compare your calculations to the illustrative calculations given.

10 The problems that may be encountered in using ratio analysis to assess the health performance of companies include:

- all ratios are imperfect and imprecise and should be treated as guidelines;
- ratios are only as reliable as the accounting figures they are based on;
- no two companies are identical, so inter-company comparisons must be carried out with care;
- a ratio means little in isolation – it should be used to complement and support other information;
- ratio analysis tends to be performed on historical data, and so may not be an accurate guide to either current position or future activity.

Answers to Questions for review

1 The capital markets are markets for trade in long-term negotiable financial securities or instruments. There are essentially three kinds of securities traded on the capital markets: company securities, such as ordinary shares and debentures; public sector securities, such as Treasury bills and gilts; and Eurobonds.

The primary or new issues market enables firms to raise new finance by issuing new shares and debentures. The secondary market is where dealing takes place in previously issued securities. The secondary market plays a very important role in financial management, because this market:

(a) increases the liquidity of the shares and so increases their value;

(b) increases primary market efficiency by providing pricing information;

(c) provides a barometer of company performance and also of industrial and commercial performance as a whole (FTSE 100, FT All Share index etc.).

The Stock Exchange consists of the 'full' market, the Alternative Investment Market (AIM), and the gilts market.

The desirable characteristics of the primary capital market are as follows:

(a) all transaction costs in primary markets should be as low as possible;

(b) primary markets should have allocational efficiency, which means that they should direct funds to their most productive uses;

(c) activity in the primary market should have only a minimal effect on prices in the secondary market.

Secondary markets will encourage investment if they provide liquidity and flexibility, reduce price volatility, and are operationally and allocationally efficient:

(a) price volatility is reduced by having an active market with 'depth' and 'breadth';

(b) operational efficiency means that transaction costs should be low;

(c) allocational efficiency requires both operational and pricing efficiency.

Pricing efficiency will only occur if the prices of securities reflect available information, that is if markets are informationally efficient.

2 The solution to this question is given in Section 2.2.7.

3 Key ratios for Hoult plc are shown on page 397.

Hoult is experiencing deteriorating profitability, liquidity, debtors', current and quick ratios, and has an increased reliance on short-term funding. These are signs of overtrading (*see* Chapter 10). The main reason appears to be erosion of the company's capital base due to repayment of the debentures. If this had not been happening, even if fixed asset investment had been occurring, it is likely that the overdraft would have been much lower, a small cash surplus might have arisen, and lower interest payments would have led to increased profitability. Overall profitability would still have been low, but management action to improve profitability might have been possible if the focus of the company's activity had not been on redeeming the debentures. The dividend payment in 1995 is intriguing, since it cannot be justified in profitability terms. Is the company hoping to curry favour prior to a rights issue?

Overall profitability	*1995*	*1996*	*1997*
ROCE (%)	8.0	8.6	10.3
Net profit (%)	3.1	2.8	2.7
Asset turnover (n:1)	2.6	3.1	3.8
Gross profit (%)	30	28	27
Asset management			
Current ratio (n:1)	2.5	2.4	1.9
Quick ratio (n:1)	1.1	1.1	1.0
Stock turnover (days)	109	98	93
Debtors' ratio (days)	61	61	75
Creditors' ratio (days)	41	37	60
Sales/working capital (n:1)	4.5	4.7	5.5
Financial risk			
Total debt/capital employed (%)	51	46	47
LT debt/capital employed (%)	32	23	12
Total debt/equity (%)	74	59	54
Interest cover (n:1)	2.3	2.1	1.8
Investor ratios			
Dividend cover (n:1)	—	—	3.5
Increase in turnover (%)		+12.5	+13.0
Increase in overdraft (£000)		10	30

CHAPTER 3

Answers to Questions

1 The payback method cannot be recommended as the main method used by a company to assess potential investment projects because it has serious disadvantages. These include the following:

- payback ignores the time value of money;
- payback ignores the timing of cash flows within the payback period;
- payback ignores post-payback cash flows;

- the choice of payback period is arbitrary;
- payback does not measure profitability.

2 *Project A*

Average annual accounting profit = (13 000 – 10 000)/4 = £750

Average annual investment = 10 000/2 = £5000

Accounting rate of return = (750 × 100)/5000 = 15 per cent

Project B

Average annual accounting profit = (30 000 – 15 000)/5 = £3000

Average annual investment = 15 000/2 = £7500

Accounting rate of return = (3000 × 100)/7500 = 40 per cent

Project C

Average annual accounting profit = (24 000 – 20 000)/4 = £1000

Average annual investment = 20 000/2 = £10 000

Accounting rate of return = (1000 × 100)/10 000 = 10 per cent

Project	*ARR (%)*	*Ranking*
A	15	2
B	40	1
C	10	3

If the target rate of return is 12 per cent, projects A and B will be accepted.

3 The shortcomings of accounting rate of return as an investment appraisal method are that it ignores the time value of money; it does not take account of the timing of cash flows; it uses accounting profits rather than cash flows, and it does not take account of the size of the initial investment. However, accounting rate of return gives an answer as a percentage return, which is a familiar measure of return, and is a simple method to apply. It can be used to compare mutually exclusive projects, and can also indicate whether a project is a 'good' one compared to a target ARR. For these reasons, it is used quite widely in industry.

4 *Project A*

Year	*Cash flow (£)*	*12% discount factor*	*Present value (£)*
0	(10 000)	1.000	(10 000)
1	5 000	0.893	4 465
2	5 000	0.797	3 985
3	2 000	0.712	1 424
4	1 000	0.636	636
		Net present value	510

Project B

Year	*Cash flow (£)*	*12% discount factor*	*Present value (£)*
0	(15 000)	1.000	(15 000)
1	5 000	0.893	4 465
2	5 000	0.797	3 985
3	5 000	0.712	3 560
4	10 000	0.636	6 360
5	5 000	0.567	2 835
		Net present value	6 205

Project C

Year	*Cash flow (£)*	*12% discount factor*	*Present value (£)*
0	(20 000)	1.000	(20 000)
1	10 000	0.893	8 930
2	10 000	0.797	7 970
3	4 000	0.712	2 848
4	2 000	0.636	1 272
		Net present value	1 020

Summary

Project	*NPV (£)*	*Ranking*
A	510	3
B	6205	1
C	1020	2

Since all three projects have positive NPVs, they are all acceptable.

5 The advantages of the net present value method of investment appraisal are:
- takes account of the time value of money;
- takes account of the amount and timing of cash flows;
- uses cash flows rather than accounting profit;
- takes account of all relevant cash flows over the life of the project;
- can take account of both conventional and non-conventional cash flows;
- can take account of changes in discount rate during the life of the project;
- gives an absolute rather than a relative measure of the desirability of the project;
- can be used to compare all investment projects.

6 If an investment project has positive and negative cash flows in successive periods (non-conventional cash flows), it may have more than one internal rate of return. This may result in incorrect decisions being taken if the IRR decision rule is applied. The NPV method has no difficulty in accommodating non-conventional cash flows.

7 There is no conflict between the NPV and IRR methods when they are applied to a single investment project with conventional cash flows. In other situations, the two methods may give conflicting results. In all cases where this conflict occurs, the project with the highest NPV should be chosen. This can be proven by examining the incremental cash flows of the projects concerned. The reason for the conflict between the two methods can also be viewed graphically.

8 The answer to this question is contained in Section 3.4.

9 If a company is restricted in the capital available for investment, it will not be able to undertake all projects with a positive NPV and is in a capital rationing situation. Capital rationing may be either soft (due to internal factors) or hard (due to external factors). Soft capital rationing may arise if management adopts a policy of stable growth, or is reluctant to issue new equity, or wishes to avoid raising new debt capital. It may also arise if management wants to encourage competition for funds. Hard capital rationing may arise because the capital markets are depressed, or because investors consider the company to be too risky.

10 If projects are divisible and independent, they can be ranked by using the profitability index or cost–benefit ratio. If projects are not divisible, then combinations of projects must be examined to find the investment schedule giving the highest NPV.

Answers to Questions for review

1 *Payback*

A = 5 + (500/900) = 5.5 years

B = 5 + (500/1200) = 5.4 years

C = 2 + (1000/2000) = 2.5 years

Net present value

$NPV_A = (-5000) + (900 \times 6.145) = (5000) + 5530.5 = £530.5$

NPV_B is calculated as follows:

Year	*Cash flow (£)*	*10% discount factor*	*Present value (£)*
0	(5000)	1.000	(5000)
1	700	0.909	636
2	800	0.826	661
3	900	0.751	676
4	1000	0.683	683
5	1100	0.621	683
6	1200	0.564	677
7	1300	0.513	667
8	1400	0.467	654
9	1500	0.424	636
10	1600	0.386	618
			1591

$NPV_C = (-5000) + (2000 \times 2.487) + (1000 \times 0.683) = £657$

Internal rate of return

If $NPV_A = 0$, present value factor of IRR over 10 years = 5000/900 = 5.556

From tables, IRR $\approx$ 12 per cent.

IRR_B

Year	*Cash flow (£)*	*10% discount factor*	*Present value (£)*	*20% discount factor*	*Present value (£)*
0	(5000)	1.000	(5000)	1.000	(5000)
1	700	0.909	636	0.833	583
2	800	0.826	661	0.694	555
3	900	0.751	676	0.579	521
4	1000	0.683	683	0.482	482
5	1100	0.621	683	0.402	442
6	1200	0.564	677	0.335	402
7	1300	0.513	667	0.279	363
8	1400	0.467	654	0.233	326
9	1500	0.424	636	0.194	291
10	1600	0.386	618	0.162	259
			1591		(776)

Interpolating: $IRR_B = 10 + \dfrac{1591 \times 10}{(1591 + 776)} = 10 + 6.72 = 16.72$ per cent

IRR_C

Year	*Cash flow (£)*	*15% discount factor*	*Present value (£)*	*18% discount factor*	*Present value (£)*
0	(5000)	1.000	(5000)	1.000	(5000)
1	2000	0.870	1740	0.847	1694
2	2000	0.756	1512	0.718	1436
3	2000	0.658	1316	0.609	1218
4	1000	0.572	572	0.516	516
			140		(136)

Interpolating: $IRR_C = 15 + \dfrac{140 \times 3}{(140 + 136)} = 15 + 1.52 = 16.52$ per cent

Accounting rate of return

ARR_A:

Average capital employed = 5000/2 = £2500

Average accounting profit = (9000 – 5000)/10 = £400

ARR_A = (400 × 100)/2500 = 16 per cent

ARR_B:

Average accounting profit = (11 500 – 5000)/10 = £650

ARR_B = (650 × 100)/2500 = 26 per cent

ARR_C:

Average accounting profit = (7000 – 5000)/4 = £500

ARR_C = (500 × 100)/2500 = 20 per cent

Summary of results:

Project	*A*	*B*	*C*
Payback (years)	5.5	5.4	2.5
ARR (%)	16	26	20
IRR (%)	12.4	16.7	16.5
NPV (%)	530.5	1591	657

Comparison of rankings:

Method	*Payback*	*ARR*	*IRR*	*NPV*
1	C	B	B	B
2	B	C	C	C
3	A	A	A	A

2 Summary of answers:

	Project alpha	*Project beta*
ARR	33%	25%
NPV	£142 000	£210 000
IRR	25%	20%
Payback	2.8 years	3.2 years

Project beta appears to be preferable, as it has the highest NPV.

3 The first step is to work out the net cash flows:

Contribution = (3.00 – 1.75) × 50 000 = £62 500

Fixed costs = 40 000 – (100 000 – 5000)/5 = £21 000

Working capital = 15 000 + 20 000 – 10 000 = £25 000

Year	*Capital (£)*	*Contribution (£)*	*Fixed costs (£)*	*Adverts (£)*	*Working capital (£)*	*Net cash flow (£)*
0	(100 000)					(100 000)
1		62 500	(21 000)	(10 000)	(25 000)	6 500
2		62 500	(21 000)	(15 000)		26 500
3		62 500	(21 000)			41 500
4		62 500	(21 000)			41 500
5	5 000	62 500	(21 000)		25 000	71 500

The net cash flows can now be discounted to find the net present value.

Year	*Net cash flow (£)*	*10% discount factor*	*Present value (£)*
0	(100 000)	1.000	(100 000)
1	6 500	0.909	5 909
2	26 500	0.826	21 890
3	41 500	0.751	31 167
4	41 500	0.683	28 345
5	71 500	0.621	44 402
			31 713

The net present value of the project is £31 713.

4 Net present values of the different projects:

$NPV_A = -1000 + (3000 \times 0.467) = £401$

$NPV_B = -800 + (200 \times 0.909) + (300 \times 0.826) + \ldots = £451$

$NPV_C = -750 + (300 \times 3.791) = £387$

$NPV_D = -500 + (150 \times 4.868) = £230$

$NPV_E = -800 + (350 \times (4.868 - 0.909)) = £586$

Project	*A*	*B*	*C*	*D*	*E*
Profitability index	1.401	1.564	1.516	1.462	1.732

- *Non-capital rationing situation*: accept all projects.
- *Projects are divisible and only £2500 is available*:

Investment schedule: £800 in project E
£800 in project B
£750 in project C
£150 in project D

Total NPV = £1493

- *Projects are indivisible and only £2500 is available*:

Investment schedule: £800 in project E
£800 in project B
£750 in project C

Total NPV = £1424
Surplus funds = £150

CHAPTER 4

Answers to Questions

1 The cash flows which are relevant to an investment appraisal calculation are those which will arise or change as a result of undertaking the investment project. Direct costs incurred, such as purchased raw materials, are relevant, as are changes in existing cash flows (incremental cash flows) such as additional fixed costs. The opportunity cost of labour and raw materials which have alternative uses may be a relevant cost. Tax liabilities are also relevant.

2 The answer to this question can be found by referring to Section 4.2.1 and Exhibit 4.1.

3 The real cost of capital can be found by deflating the nominal (or money terms) cost of capital. Nominal project cash flows can be obtained by inflating estimated cash flows to take account of inflation which is specific to particular costs and revenues. Real project cash flows can be obtained by deflating nominal project cash flows to take account of general inflation. The NPV of the project can then be found either by discounting nominal cash flows by the nominal cost of capital (the nominal or money terms approach), or by discounting real cash flows by the real cost of capital (the real terms approach). The NPV will have the same value whichever method is used.

4 Evaluating investment projects is made more difficult by the existence of inflation. While it may be possible to forecast general inflation into the near future, it is much harder to forecast specific inflation rates for individual costs and revenues. If specific

inflation forecasts can be obtained and used, it is likely that the evaluation of an investment project will be more accurate than if account were only taken of general inflation. The incremental benefit of this increased accuracy would need to be weighed against the cost of obtaining and processing the necessary data, however. Failure to take account of inflation at all may lead to unrealistic estimates of the value of an investment project.

5 The answer to this question can be found by referring to the discussion at the start of Section 4.4, focusing in particular on the relationship between risk and the variability of returns.

6 Sensitivity analysis examines how responsive the project's NPV is to changes in the variables from which it has been calculated. There are two methods: in the first, variables are changed by a set amount and the NPV is recalculated; in the second, the amounts by which individual variables would have to change to make the project's NPV become zero are determined. In both methods, only one variable is changed at a time.

Both methods give an indication of the key variables within the project. These variables may merit further investigation and indicate where management should focus attention in order to ensure the success of the project. However, sensitivity analysis gives no indication of whether changes in key variables are likely to occur, or are even possible.

7 Several recent surveys have shown that payback is widely used in practice. Drury *et al.* (1992) showed that 63 per cent of firms surveyed used it often or always. However, their survey also indicated that only 14 per cent of firms used the payback method exclusively and did not combine it with a method that took account of the time value of money. The reasons why payback is commonly used as a way of dealing with risk in investment projects are as follows:

- it is a useful test for companies concerned about short-term liquidity;
- it focuses attention on the short term, which is more certain and hence less risky than the long term;
- it guards against unforeseen changes in economic circumstances.

8 The answer to this question can be found by referring to Section 4.4.4.

9 The answer to this question can be found by referring to Section 4.4.6.

10 The answer to this question can be found by referring to Sections 4.5.2 and 4.5.3.

Answers to Questions for review

1 (a) 100 per cent first-year capital allowances available.

Year	Capital (£)	Tax saving (£)	Net cash flow (£)	8% discount factor	Present value (£)
0	(100 000)		(100 000)	1.000	(100 000)
2		33 000	33 000	0.857	28 281
					(71 719)

The present value of the cost of borrowing is £71 719.

(b) Straight-line basis capital allowances over life of asset.

Year	Capital (£)	Tax saving (£)	Net cash flow (£)	8% discount factor	Present value (£)
0	(100 000)		(100 000)	1.000	(100 000)
2		8 250	8 250	0.857	7 070
3		8 250	8 250	0.794	6 550
4		8 250	8 250	0.735	6 064
5		8 250	8 250	0.681	5 618
					(74 698)

The present value of the cost of borrowing is £74 698.

(c) 25 per cent reducing balance capital allowances, zero scrap value.

Year	Capital (£)	Tax saving (£)	Net cash flow (£)	8% discount factor	Present value (£)
0	(100 000)		(100 000)	1.000	(100 000)
2		8 250	8 250	0.857	7 070
3		6 188	6 188	0.794	4 913
4		4 641	4 641	0.735	3 411
5		13 921	13 921	0.681	9 480
					(75 126)

The present value of the cost of borrowing is £75 126.

2 *Machine A:*

Year	*0 (£000)*	*1 (£000)*	*2 (£000)*	*3 (£000)*	*4 (£000)*	*5 (£000)*	*6 (£000)*
Additional sales		116.60	123.60	131.01	138.87	147.20	
Labour costs		(10.50)	(11.03)	(11.58)	(12.16)	(12.76)	
Power costs		(9.27)	(9.55)	(9.83)	(10.13)	(10.43)	
Net operating cash flow		96.83	103.02	109.60	116.59	124.01	
Capital allowances		(50.00)	(37.50)	(28.13)	(21.09)	(63.28)	
Net taxable cash flow		46.83	65.52	81.48	95.49	60.73	
Taxation			(14.52)	(20.31)	(25.26)	(29.60)	(18.83)
Add back capital allowances		50.00	37.50	28.13	21.09	63.28	
Capital	(200)						
Net project cash flows	(200)	96.83	88.51	89.29	91.33	94.41	(18.83)
Discount factors	1.000	0.870	0.756	0.658	0.572	0.497	0.432
Discounted cash flows	(200)	84.20	66.92	58.71	52.22	46.94	(8.14)
Net present value, m/c A	100.85						

The NPV for machine A is £100 850.

Machine B:

Year	*0 (£000)*	*1 (£000)*	*2 (£000)*	*3 (£000)*	*4 (£000)*	*5 (£000)*	*6 (£000)*
Additional sales		116.60	123.60	131.01	138.87	147.20	
Labour costs		(7.35)	(7.72)	(8.10)	(8.51)	(8.93)	
Power costs		(4.12)	(4.24)	(4.37)	(4.50)	(4.64)	
Net operating cash flow		105.13	111.64	118.54	125.86	133.63	
Capital allowances		(62.50)	(46.88)	(35.16)	(26.37)	(54.09)	
Net taxable cash flow		42.63	64.76	83.38	99.49	79.54	
Taxation			(13.22)	(20.08)	(25.85)	(30.84)	(24.66)
Add back capital allowances		62.50	46.88	35.16	26.37	54.09	
Capital	(250)					25.00	
Net project cash flows	(250)	105.13	98.42	98.46	100.01	127.80	(24.66)
Discount factors	1.000	0.870	0.756	0.658	0.572	0.497	0.432
Discounted cash flows	(250)	91.42	74.42	64.74	57.18	63.52	(10.66)
Net present value, m/c B	90.62						

The NPV for machine B is £90 620. Machine A should be chosen by Logar plc rather than machine B, since machine A has a higher NPV.

3 (a) The worst likely return is £10 000 per annum for five years.

$10\,000 \times 3.791 = £37\,910$. This has a probability of 12 per cent.

The best possibility is £50 000 per annum for seven years.

$50\,000 \times 4.868 = £243\,400$. This has a probability of 12 per cent.

(b) £10 000 per year for five years = $10\,000 \times 3.791 = £37\,910$

Probability = $0.2 \times 0.6 = 12$ per cent, so EV = $37\,910 \times 0.12 = £4549$

£10 000 per year for seven years = $10\,000 \times 4.868 = £48\,680$

Probability = $0.2 \times 0.4 = 8$ per cent, so EV = $48\,680 \times 0.08 = £3894$

£30 000 per year for five years = $30\,000 \times 3.791 = £113\,730$

Probability = $0.6 \times 0.5 = 30$ per cent, so EV = $113\,730 \times 0.3 = £34\,119$

£30 000 per year for seven years = $30\,000 \times 4.868 = £146\,040$

Probability = $0.6 \times 0.5 = 30$ per cent, so EV = $146\,040 \times 0.3 = £43\,812$

£50 000 per year for five years = $50\,000 \times 3.791 = £189\,550$

Probability = $0.2 \times 0.4 = 8$ per cent, so EV = $189\,550 \times 0.08 = £15\,164$

£50 000 per year for seven years = $50\,000 \times 4.868 = £243\,400$

Probability = $0.2 \times 0.6 = 12$ per cent, so EV = $243\,400 \times 0.12 = £29\,208$

Total EV = $4549 + 3894 + 34\,119 + 43\,812 + 15\,164 + 29\,208 = £130\,746$

4 (a) Try 17 per cent: $((((20\,000 \times 5) - 24\,875) \times 4.659)) - 350\,000 = 7$

Hence IRR = 17 per cent

(b) If cost of capital is 15 per cent, the project life giving zero NPV can be found from tables, using the cumulative present value factor of 4.659 determined while calculating the IRR. This project life is between eight and nine years, and so interpolating:

Project life = $8 + ((4.659 - 4.487)/(4.772 - 4.487)) = 8.6$ years

This is a decrease of 1.4 years or 14 per cent.

(c) If sales price = S

$((((20\,000 \times (S - 3.50)) - 24\,875)) \times 5.019) - 350\,000 = 0$

Hence S = $(((350\,000/5.019) + 24.875)/20\,000) + 3.50 = £8.23$

This is a reduction of 27 pence or 3.2 per cent.

5 (a) Calculation of optimum replacement cycle using the EAC method.

Cycle	*1*	*2*	*3*	*4*
Initial cost	(50 000)	(50 000)	(50 000)	(50 000)
Year 1 operating costs	(12 500)	(12 500)	(12 500)	(12 500)
Year 1 maintenance costs	0	0	0	0
Year 1 scrap value	26 786			
Year 2 operating costs		(13 552)	(13 552)	(13 552)
Year 2 maintenance costs		(2 392)	(2 392)	(2 392)
Year 2 scrap value		14 349		
Year 3 operating costs			(14 236)	(14 236)
Year 3 maintenance costs			(3 203)	(3 203)
Year 3 scrap value			7 830	
Year 4 operating costs				(15 252)
Year 4 maintenance costs				(4 449)
Year 4 scrap value				3 813
Present cost of cycle	(35 714)	(64 094)	(88 053)	(111 771)
Cumulative present value factors	0.893	1.690	2.402	3.037
Equivalent annual cost	(39 993)	(37 925)	(36 658)	(36 803)

The optimum replacement cycle is every three years, as this has the lowest EAC.

(b) Calculation of optimum replacement cycle using the LCM method. The present cost of each cycle (i.e. Year 0 value) was calculated in part (a). The lowest common multiple of 1, 2, 3 and 4 is 12.

	Number of replacement cycles			
Year	*12 × 1*	*6 × 2*	*4 × 3*	*3 × 4*
1	(35 714)	(64 094)	(88 053)	(111 771)
2	(31 888)			
3	(28 471)	(51 096)		
4	(25 421)		(62 674)	
5	(22 697)	(40 733)		(71 032)
6	(20 265)			
7	(18 094)	(32 472)	(44 610)	
8	(16 155)			
9	(14 424)	(25 887)		(45 142)
10	(12 879)		(31 753)	
11	(11 499)	(20 637)		
12	(10 267)			
	(247 774)	(234 919)	(227 090)	(227 945)

The optimum replacement cycle is every three years, as this has the lowest present cost.

CHAPTER 5

Answers to Questions

1 In corporate finance, a key concept is the relationship between risk and return. The higher the risk associated with a given investment, the higher will be the return required in exchange for investing in it. Debentures are debt finance paying a fixed annual return and are secured on assets of the company. They therefore have a much lower risk than ordinary equity, which is unsecured and which has no right to receive a dividend. If a company fails, the ordinary shareholders may receive nothing at all. In exchange for this higher risk, ordinary shareholders will require a higher return.

2 Some of the important rights which are available to shareholders in their position as owners of a company are mentioned in Section 5.1.1.

3 There are several ways a company may obtain such a quotation: namely, an offer for sale at fixed price, an offer for sale by tender, an intermediaries offer, a placing and an introduction. These are discussed in Section 5.2.1.

4 There are a variety of advantages and disadvantages to be considered by an unquoted company considering seeking a stock exchange listing.

Advantages of obtaining a quotation:

- opens up new avenues for the company to raise finance;
- increases the marketability of the company's shares;
- raises the profile of the company;
- the company may obtain a better credit rating;
- the company can use its shares to fund future take-over activity.

Disadvantages of obtaining a quotation:

- the costs of flotation have to be met;
- the cost of compliance with listing regulations;
- the company may be open to a hostile take-over bid;
- dilution of control will result from wider share ownership;
- the company may have to satisfy increased shareholder expectations.

5 Pre-emptive rights mean that the company has an obligation to offer any new issue of shares to the existing shareholders before making a public offer. The importance to shareholders of pre-emptive rights is that it prevents there being a significant change in the structure of ownership and control of the company, since the shares are offered to existing shareholders (although not necessarily taken up) in proportion to their existing holdings.

6 The advantage to a company of a rights issue is that, depending on market conditions, it may be a cheaper method of raising equity finance than a public offer. This is partly because the issue costs of a rights issue are lower than in the case of a public offer. A disadvantage is that, if insufficient funds are raised from the rights issue, the company must take further steps to secure the finance that it needs. This will be a more expensive and lengthy process than would be the case with a single placing of shares.

7 Rights issue price = £2.50 × 0.8 = £2.00
Theoretical ex-rights price = ((4 × 2.50) + 2.00)/5 = £2.40
Value of rights per existing share = (2.40 – 2.00)/4 = 0.1, i.e. 10p per share
The correct answer is therefore (a).

8 The correct answer is (d), a scrip issue, also known as a bonus issue. If you are unsure about this, study Section 5.4 carefully.

9 Preference shares do not enjoy great popularity as a source of finance because they are less tax efficient than debt. They are also riskier than debt, since there is no right to receive a preference dividend, although cumulative preference shares will preserve the right to receive unpaid dividends. More recently, more exotic varieties of preference shares have enjoyed an increased popularity, such as auction market preferred stock, a type of variable rate preference share.

10 You should have chosen (c), that a cumulative preference share carries forward the right to receive unpaid preference dividends. The right to be converted into ordinary shares at a future date (a) is carried by convertible preference shares, and the right to receive a share of residual profits (b) is carried by participating preference shares. All three types of preference shares will entitle their holders to a fixed rate of dividend (d). Voting rights at the company's annual general meeting (e) may be attached to preference shares, but it is unlikely.

Answers to Questions for review

1 The shares of Brand plc have a nominal value of 50p and a book value of £200 000 so there are 400 000 shares.

	£
Current market value of Brand = 400 000 × 1.90 =	760 000
Funds raised through rights issue	160 000
Final market value	920 000

	£
Earnings before rights issue = 600 000 × 0.15 =	90 000
Earnings from new funds = 160 000 × 0.15 =	24 000
Total earnings after rights issue	114 000

Issue price of £1.80
Number of new shares = 160 000/1.80 = 88 889
Total shares in issue = 400 000 + 88 889 = 488 889
Theoretical ex-rights price = 920 000/488 889 = £1.88
New EPS = 100 × (114 000/488 889) = 23.3 pence
Form of rights issue = 400 000/88 889 = 4.5, i.e. 2 for 9

Issue price of £1.60
Number of new shares = 160 000/1.60 = 100 000
Total shares in issue = 400 000 + 100 000 = 500 000
Theoretical ex-rights price = 920 000/500 000 = £1.84
New EPS = 100 × (114 000/500 000) = 22.8 pence
Form of rights issue = 400 000/100 000 = 4, i.e. 1 for 4

Issue price of £1.40
Number of new shares = 160 000/1.40 = 114 286
Total shares in issue = 400 000 + 114 286 = 514 286
Theoretical ex-rights price = 920 000/514 286 = £1.79
New EPS = 100 × (114 000/514 286) = 22.2 pence
Form of rights issue = 400 000/114 286 = 3.5, i.e. 2 for 7

It is to be expected, since the return on shareholders' funds has not changed, that the theoretical ex-rights price would be below the current share price, and the calculations have confirmed this. Why were the proposed rights issue prices at discounts of five, 10 and 16 per cent to the current share price, i.e. less than the commonly quoted discount of 20 per cent? Anyway, the actual share price after the rights issue would also depend on other factors, such as the view taken by the market of the use to be made of the new funds and the effect of the issue on EPS. The current EPS is (90 000/400 000) × 100 = 22.5p and two of the proposed issue prices give an increase on this figure. Only when the issue price falls below the current shareholders' funds per share (600 000/400 000 = £1.50) does dilution of earnings per share occur.

2 The key point here is that Maltby's P/E ratio remains unchanged.
Current number of shares = £4m/0.5 = 8m shares
Current EPS = (£7m/8m) × 100 = 87.5 pence
Current PER = (3.50/0.875) = 4
Rights issue price = 3.50 × 0.8 = £2.80
The rights issue is a 1 for 4 issue, so new number of shares is 10m
Theoretical ex-rights price = ((3.50 × 4) + 2.80)/5 = 16.80/5 = £3.36
Funds raised = £2.80 × 2m = £5.6m

Redemption of debentures
Debentures redeemed = £5.6m/1.12 = £5m
Interest saved = 5m × 0.16 = £800 000
Tax saving lost = 800 000 × 0.31 = £248 000
Net saving = 800 000 – 248 000 = £552 000
New earnings = 7 000 000 + 552 000 = £7 552 000
New EPS = (7.552m/10m) × 100 = 75.52 pence
New share price = 75.52 × 4 = 302 pence

Investment project
Earnings on new funds = 5.6m × 0.2 = £1.12m
New earnings = 7m + 1.12m = £8.12m
New EPS = (8.12m/10m) × 100 = 81.20 pence
New share price = 81.20 × 4 = 325 pence

Conclusion
Both options result in a share price which is less than the theoretical ex-rights price. The theoretical ex-rights price, providing rights are either taken up or sold, results in no change in shareholder wealth. Both options, then, result in a reduction in shareholder wealth. Since the fundamental financial objective of the company is the maximisation of shareholder wealth, neither option can be recommended as being in the best interests of shareholders.

3 The answer to this question can be found in Section 5.4.2.

CHAPTER 6

Answers to Questions

1 The answer to this question can be found by referring to the discussion at the start of Section 6.1.

2 (a) A restrictive covenant places limitations on the actions of managers in order to safeguard the investment made by providers of debt finance.

(b) Sums of money are put into a debenture sinking fund on a regular basis so that the accrued amount plus interest can be used to redeem debentures.

(c) A redemption window is a period of time during which debentures or loan stock can be redeemed.

3 (a) Deep discount bonds are loan stock issued at a large discount to par value, which will be redeemed at or above par on maturity. They may be attractive to companies who need a low servicing cost during the life of the bond and who will be able to meet the high cost of redemption at maturity. Investors might be attracted to the large capital gain on offer, which will have tax advantages for some.

(b) Zero coupon bonds are bonds issued at a discount to par value which pay no interest. The investor obtains a capital gain from the difference between the issue price and the redemption value. Attractions for companies are similar to those for deep discount bonds.

(c) A warrant is a right to buy new shares at a future date at a fixed, predetermined price. Warrants are usually issued as part of a package with unsecured loan stock in order to make it more attractive. They are detachable from the stock and can be sold and bought separately. Investors may find them attractive because they offer potentially high gains compared with investing in the underlying shares.

(d) Convertibles are loan stock which can be converted into ordinary shares at the option of the holder. The interest rate on convertibles is therefore lower, since the holder has the option to participate in the growth of the company, unlike the holder of ordinary loan stock.

4 The answer to this question can be found by referring to Section 6.3.1.

5 The conversion premium is the premium per share on converting a convertible security into equity. The rights premium is the premium per share of a convertible security over equivalent loan stock with a similar coupon, arising due to the option to convert carried by the convertible security. The relationship between the conversion premium, the rights premium and the market value of a convertible security can be illustrated by a diagram (*see* Exhibit 6.1).

6 The company will consider the length of time remaining to maturity; the general level of interest rates and the term structure of interest rates; the rate of return on other securities, especially ordinary equity; expectations of likely movements in interest rates and inflation rates; and the required return of investors in debentures.

7 Advantages:

- convertibles may be attractive to particular investors;
- interest rates on convertibles are usually lower than on straight debentures;
- interest charges on debentures are tax-allowable;
- debentures increase gearing but might decrease the cost of capital;
- convertible debentures can be self-liquidating;

- conversion will not harm the capital structure and may even help it.

Disadvantages:

- there may be restrictive covenants attached to convertible debentures;
- issuing debentures decreases debt capacity;
- dilution of EPS may occur on conversion;
- conversion may cause dilution of control of existing shareholders.

8 As the price of the underlying share changes, there is a larger proportionate movement in the price of the warrant than in the price of the underlying share. In consequence, it is possible to make a greater proportionate gain (or loss) by investing in warrants, than by investing in the underlying share. This is called the gearing effect of warrants.

9

Year	*Cash flow*	*£*	*10% discount factor*	*Present value (£)*
1–3	Interest	9	2.487	22.38
3	Principal	100	0.751	75.10
				97.48

Current ex-interest market value is £97.48

If the stock is irredeemable, ex-interest market value = £9/0.1 = £90

10 For an explanation of the difference between a finance lease and an operating lease, *see* Section 6.7.1. As for the importance of the distinction for corporate finance, operating leases are useful where equipment is required for a short time, or where there is risk of obsolescence. The lessee may also be relieved of the cost of servicing and maintenance. Finance leases may be cheaper than purchase, especially if the lessee pays little or no tax. The lessor can obtain tax relief on the capital cost of the leased asset and pass the benefits on to the lessee in the form of lower lease payments. Other benefits claimed for leasing include the 'off-balance-sheet' nature of some kinds of lease finance and access for small firms to expensive equipment.

Answers to Questions for review

1 Here, we have to find out how much Bugle plc will be prepared to pay for the bonds, given that they require a 15 per cent rate of return.

(a) *Stock 1*:

Fair price = $(12/1.15) + ((100 + 12)/1.15^2)$ = £95.12

Since the market price is £95, the bond is worth buying.

(b) *Stock 2*:

Fair price = $(8/1.15) + ((110 + 8)/1.15^2)$ = £96.18

Since the market price is £95, this bond is also worth buying.

2 The answer to this question can be found by referring to Exhibit 6.1.

3 (a)

(i) If converted now: $3.20 \times 25 =$ £80.00

If sold in the market: £93.00

(ii) Convert in two years:

expected share price = $3.20 \times 1.14^2 =$ £4.16

value if converted = $25 \times 4.16 =$ £104.00

present value = $104 \times 0.797 =$ £82.89

interest received = $10 \times 1.690 =$ £16.90

total present value = $82.89 + 16.90 =$ £99.79

(iii) If held until maturity: $(10 \times 5.650) + (100 \times 0.322) =$ £88.70

On these figures, the investor will convert in two years, since this gives the greatest present value of returns.

(b) In explaining the importance of the distinction between convertibles and warrants to investors, the following points could be discussed:

- with a warrant, the bond-holder keeps the original loan stock, whereas with a convertible the loan stock must be given up if conversion is chosen;
- warrants can be detached from the underlying stock and sold, but conversion rights on convertible loan stock are not detachable;
- both warrants and convertibles allow investors to participate in the future growth of the company;
- warrants entitle the holder to obtain shares whether or not any loan stock is held. The right to convert is only held if the stock is held;
- because of the gearing effect of warrants, they can be used for speculative investment in return for a small outlay.

4 The answer to this question is contained in Sections 6.7.2 and 6.7.3.

5 The appropriate discount rate is the after-tax cost of borrowing, which is 14 per cent × (1 – 0.33) = 9.38 per cent ≈ 9 per cent

Leasing:

Year	*Cash flow*	£	*9% discount factor*	*Present value (£)*
0–2	Lease payments	(320)	2.759	(882.88)
1–3	Tax savings	105.6	2.531	267.27
				(615.61)

Buying (assuming Turner is not tax exhausted):

Year	Cash flow	£	9% discount factor	Present value (£)
0	Purchase	(1000)	1.000	(1000)
1	Tax saving	82.500	0.917	75.65
2	Tax saving	61.875	0.842	52.10
3	Tax saving	185.625	0.772	143.30
				(728.95)

The cost of leasing is £615.61 and the cost of borrowing is £728.95, so Turner should lease rather than buy the machine.

CHAPTER 7

Answers to Questions

1 (a) Although income and capital gains are taxed at the same rate, capital gains will be slightly more attractive due to the annual capital gains tax allowance of £6300. Therefore the statement is correct.

(b) This statement is correct. Investors receive a net dividend after tax at the standard rate of income tax. Those in the higher income tax bracket then have to make a further payment to the Inland Revenue.

(c) This statement is correct. By paying a dividend a company is triggering the early payment of part of its corporation tax liability via ACT.

2 The correct choice is answer (e). The argument that shareholders could manufacture their own dividends by selling off part of their shareholding was used by Miller and Modigliani in 1961 to argue that the dividend policy of a company was irrelevant. All of the other points can be used to support a case for dividends having an effect on the value of the equity shares of a company.

3 First, convert the share price to ex-dividend: P_0 = £3.45 – 20p = £3.25

Using the Gordon growth model:

$$\pounds 3.25 = (0.20 \times (1 + g)/(0.15 - g))$$

Re-arranging, g = 0.2875/3.45 = 8.33 per cent

4 First, assume that g = 0. Therefore, using the Gordon model:

$K_e = D_0/P_0 = 30/200 = 15$ per cent

If the next dividend of 40p is to be paid in Year 4 and held constant thereafter, then since g = 0 the value of the share in Year 3 is 40/0.15 = £2.67

Discounted back to the current time: $P_0 = 2.67/(1.15)^3$ = £1.756

The share price has dropped by £2.00 – £1.756 = 24.4p

Option (a) is therefore the correct answer.

5 Option (a) is the correct response. Companies like to keep nominal dividends increasing steadily or, at worst, when profits decrease, at least maintain the nominal dividend paid in the previous period.

6, 7 Here the discussion should centre around the fact that Miller and Modigliani's assumptions are simplifications of the real world. These assumptions, while not mirroring the real world, do not totally invalidate the model. Given these assumptions, the conclusions made by the model are perfectly logical. The nature of some of the assumptions only weakens the conclusions of the model, without actually invalidating the model.

8 Clearly an increase in institutional share ownership has concentrated control of UK companies. This fact, coupled with the fact that institutional investors require a regular dividend stream from their investments, has led the institutional investors to become involved in trying to influence the dividend policy of companies.

9 (a) *Residual theory of dividends.* Dividends may be paid out if the capital investment needs of the company are fully met and there are funds left over. While corporate profits are cyclical, capital investment plans involve long-term commitment, so it follows that dividends may be used to take up the slack.

Financial managers cannot follow both a policy of stable dividends and a policy of long-term commitment to capital investment, unless they are willing to raise new finance in times of need to achieve both. Given the objective of shareholder wealth maximisation, if a company can invest in profitable projects and earn a higher return than shareholders could in their alternative investment opportunities, then shareholders should be willing to subscribe new equity finance.

(b) *Clientele effect.* This term refers to the argument that companies attract particular types of shareholder due to their dividend decisions. It states that companies establish a track record for paying a certain level of dividend and that shareholders recognise this. Because of their shareholders' preferences, companies find it difficult to change their dividend policies suddenly.

(c) *Signalling properties of dividends.* With asymmetry of information, dividends can be seen as signals from the company's managers to shareholders and the financial markets. With some exceptions, empirical studies show that dividends convey some new information to the market.

(d) *The 'bird-in-the-hand' argument.* This arises from the existence of uncertainty. If the future were certain and there were no transaction costs, potential dividends retained by a company for the purpose of investment would lead to share price increases reflecting increases in wealth. With uncertainty, however, risk-averse investors are not indifferent to the division of earnings into dividends and capital gains in the share price.

Answers to Questions for review

1 You could have discussed the following factors:

- the need to remain profitable;
- the company's liquidity position;
- the ease with which the company can access further sources of finance;
- investors' preference for a stable dividend policy.

2 (a) Using the Gordon model, with D_0 = 20p and K_e = 14 per cent

For g: $13 \times (1 + g)^4 = 20$, hence

$$g = \sqrt[4]{\frac{20}{13}} - 1 = 11.4 \text{ per cent}$$

$$P_0 = (20 \times (1 + 0.1140))/(0.14 - 0.114) = £8.57$$

(b) New value of K_e = 15.4 per cent

New $P_0 = (20 \times (1 + 0.114)/(0.154 - 0.114) = £5.77$

(c) Therefore, a 10 per cent increase in the required rate of return from 14 per cent to 15.4 per cent has led to a 33 per cent change in share price. This indicates that a small change in the required rate of return for a share leads to a large percentage change in the share price.

3 The answer to this question is given in Section 7.6.1.

4 (a) Company A, which has paid no dividends for five years, is pursuing a sensible policy for a rapidly growing company. All its earnings are being reinvested and so it has reduced its need for external finance to a minimum. Since the company is probably investing a great deal, its tax liability is likely to be small. Paying dividends would incur payment of ACT which might be unrelieved.

Company B's policy of distributing 50 per cent of earnings seems to offer predictability. In fact, its earnings may fluctuate considerably. A dividend cut usually causes a share price fall, since the market views it as being a negative signal. If Company B is mature, with low volatility in earnings, its dividend policy may be acceptable.

Company C's policy falls between those of A and B, in that a small dividend is paid. The predictability of the dividend will be welcomed by shareholders. It also gives the company the advantage of having retained earnings available for investment. Scrip issues may increase a company's market value by increasing the marketability of its shares. Shareholder concessions are a means of attracting small shareholders who can benefit from them personally, and have no impact on dividend policy.

(b) Company A would be attractive to investors who prefer to get a return through capital growth. Company B would be attractive to investors who prefer a high proportion of their return in the form of income, even if it is variable from year to year. A diversified portfolio would reduce the effect of variability in the dividend. Company C would be attractive to private investors, as most of the return is in the form of capital growth and there are shareholder concessions.

Each company *may* maximise the wealth of its shareholders. If Miller and Modigliani are correct, the three companies will maximise shareholder wealth because the value of each company is unaffected by its dividend policy. Alternatively, each company's group of shareholders may favour their particular company's policy, and so maximise their wealth, because the dividend policy of each is appropriate to their tax position.

CHAPTER 8

Answers to Questions

1 Market value of equity, E = 500 000 × 1.50 = £750 000
Market value of debt, D = nil
Cost of equity capital, K_e = dividend/market value of share = 27/150 = 0.18
Since there is no debt capital, WACC = K_e = 18 per cent

2 K_d = 12/94 = 12.8 per cent
K_d (after tax) = 12.8 × (1 – 0.35) = 8.3 per cent

3 E = 1 000 000 × 0.49 = £490 000
D = 100 000 × 72/100 = £72 000
K_e = 9/49 = 0.1837 and so K_e is 18.37 per cent
K_d = Interest/Market value = 10/72 = 0.1389 and so K_d is 13.89 per cent
WACC $= ((K_e \times E) + (K_d \times D(1 - t)))/(E + D)$
$= ((18.37 \times 490\ 000) + (13.89 \times 72\ 000 \times 0.67))/562\ 000$
= 17.21 per cent

4 When we mention WACC in this context, we can assume we are talking about an historic WACC, i.e. one referring to the cost of funds already raised. There are certain conditions that must be met in order for it to be appropriate to use an historic cost of capital to appraise new projects, as follows:

- the new project must have a similar level of risk to the average risk of a company's existing projects;
- the amount of finance needed for the new project must be small relative to the amount of finance already raised;
- the company must be intending to finance the new project by using a similar financing mix to its historical financing mix.

5 The correct answer is (c). If capital markets are perfect and taxation did not exist, we are in a world corresponding to Miller and Modigliani's first model. As the company increases its level of debt, the increase in the cost of its equity finance will be exactly offset by increasing amounts of cheaper debt finance.

6 Here we are assuming that the world of Miller and Modigliani's second paper exists. Therefore the two companies should have similar WACCs. Because York is all-equity financed, its WACC is the same as its cost of equity finance, i.e. 16 per cent. It follows that Johnson should have a WACC equal to 16 per cent also.

Therefore: $(1/3 \times 10 \text{ per cent}) + (2/3 \times K_e) = 16$ per cent

Hence: $K_e = 19$ per cent

7 The correct answer is (c). The traditional approach does *not* assume perfect markets and therefore recognises the existence of bankruptcy risk. This is reflected in the upward slope of the cost of debt curve and the steepening of the cost of equity curve at high levels of gearing.

8 The answer depends on how the company has been financed.

If the company is financed mainly from short-term sources, it cannot ignore an increase in interest rates and may choose to switch to long-term financing. This will be at a higher rate and profitability will be diminished.

If the company is financed mainly from long-term sources, an increase in interest rates will not affect its profits directly. However, higher interest rates may depress economic activity and its profits may fall accordingly.

If the company is financed mainly from retained earnings or equity, an increase in the required return of shareholders will lead to pressure for higher dividends. The company may have insufficient funds to meet such demands.

9 The traditional theory of capital structure proposes that an optimal capital exists, and so under this theory a company can increase its total value by the sensible use of gearing. The traditional theory argues that:

- K_e rises with increased gearing due to the increasing financial and bankruptcy risk;
- K_d rises only at high gearing levels when bankruptcy risk increases;
- replacing more expensive equity finance with less expensive debt finance decreases the company's WACC, up to a point;
- once an optimum level of gearing is reached, K_e increases by a rate which more than offsets the effect of using cheaper debt, and so WACC increases.

10 Miller and Modigliani argued that weighted average cost of capital remains unchanged at all levels of gearing. The value of a company is dependent on expected performance and commercial risk and so its market value, and hence its cost of capital, is independent of its capital structure. The cost of equity K_e increases in such a manner that it exactly offsets the use of cheaper debt finance, and so WACC is constant. This can be demonstrated through the arbitrage proof. Arbitrage prevents the possibility of perfect substitutes selling at different prices, and two companies identical except for their capital structures are, for Miller and Modigliani, perfect substitutes. Using the assumption that individuals and companies can borrow at the same rate, they demonstrated how arbitrage would cause the WACC of two such companies to become identical through the buying and selling actions of investors.

Answers to Questions for review

1 $K_e = (7 \times (1 + 0.08)/49) + 0.08 = 0.1543 + 0.08 = 0.2343 \approx 23$ per cent

$K_p = D_p/P_0 = (0.075 \times 50)/32 = 0.1172 \approx 12$ per cent

$K_d = I/P_o = (0.1 \times 100)/92 = 0.1087 \approx 11$ per cent

A market-based weighting is preferred to one based on book values.

		£
E	= 1 000 000 × 0.49 =	490 000
E_p	= 250 000 × 0.32 =	80 000
D	= 100 000 × 0.92 =	92 000
		662 000

WACC = (23 × (490/662)) + (12 × (80/662)) + (11 × (1 – 0.33) × (92/662))
= 17.02 per cent + 1.45 per cent + 1.02 per cent
= 19.5 per cent

2 Capital gearing can be determined as (Debt/(Equity + Debt))
Using book values, capital gearing = (9000/13 000) × 100 = 69 per cent
Market value of equity = 8m × 3.50 = £28m
Market value of debt = 9m × 1.12 = £10.08m

Using market values, capital gearing = (10.08/38.08) × 100 = 26.5 per cent
A market-based determination of gearing is generally considered to be superior to an estimate based on book values because:

- book values are historical cost values and so are likely to be out of date;
- book values reflect decisions taken long ago and may not be relevant;
- market values reflect current evaluations of the risk of the company;
- market values reflect current required returns in the capital markets.

3 (a) First, Kitson should sell his £1000 of shares in Short and borrow enough funds to copy the gearing ratio of Short. Short's gearing ratio is 2000/8000 = 25 per cent, so Kitson should borrow £333, making his gearing 333/1333 = 25 per cent.

The next stage is to invest all the £1333 in Carbon's shares and compare the returns before and after the change.

New dividend income with Carbon shares:

Return: 1333 × (500 000/3 125 000) =	£213.28
Interest on borrowings: 10 per cent of £333 =	(£33.30)
Net return:	£179.98

Old return with Short shares:

Return: 1000 × (1 000 000/6 000 000) =	£166.67

Therefore Kitson makes a net profit of £13.31 on the transaction.

(b) For Carbon, £500 000 income, after tax at 40 per cent, will leave £300 000 to pay out as dividends.

Total market value of shares = 300 000/0.16 = £1 875 000

Market value of each share is £1 875 000/3 250 000 = 57.6p

For Short, total profit equals £1.2m but tax will be paid on only £1.0m of this due to interest paid of £0.2m. Hence only £600 000 will be available for dividends.

Assuming that Short's K_e increases to 18 per cent in order to equate the two companies' WACCs:

Total market value of shares = 600 000/0.18 = £3 333 333

Market value of each share is £3 333 333/5 000 000 = 66.7p

4 *Option (a)*. Income of £2000 is distributed to shareholders who require a return of nine per cent. The market value of equity is therefore 2000/0.09 = £22 222.

Option (b). Interest on debt of 5000 × 3 per cent = £150 is paid, so dividends to shareholders are 2000 – 150 = £1850. Since the required return of shareholders is 10 per cent, the market value of equity is 1850/0.10 = £18 500. Since the market value of debt is £5000, the total value of the company is 18 500 + 5000 = £23 500.

Option (c). Interest on debt of 9000 × 6 per cent = £540 is paid, so dividends to shareholders are 2000 – 540 = £1460. Since the required return of shareholders is 13 per cent, the market value of equity is 1460/ 0.13 = £11 231. As the market value of debt is £9000, the total value of the company is 11 231 + 9000 = £20 231.

Since the value of the company is greatest under option (b), this represents the optimal financing choice.

5 There are a number of problems that will be encountered when trying to calculate a WACC for a company.

- How do we find the cost of equity? There are two alternatives – the dividend growth model and the CAPM – both of which have potential drawbacks.
- How do we find the cost of debt? Companies have many forms of debt, and company accounts do not always give the appropriate interest that they are paying, for example to their bank. In addition, the maturity date of the debt may not be specified, or it may have split redemption dates.
- The market values of debt and equity may be hard to find. For example, some forms of debt may be tradable, but may not have a continuously trading market, while other forms of debt may not be traded.
- Some debt instruments are rather complex and it may not be possible to find their cost or market value, for example convertibles and floating rate debt.
- Should short-term debt be included in the WACC calculation, or is it a working capital issue?
- Company balance sheets may further be complicated by the use of non-sterling debt, or currency and interest rate swaps.

CHAPTER 9

Answers to Questions

1 Risk may be divided into systematic risk and unsystematic risk. Systematic risk refers to the extent to which a company's cash flows are affected by factors not specific to the company. It is determined by the sensitivity of the cash flows to the general level of economic activity and by its operating gearing.

Unsystematic risk refers to the extent to which a firm's cash flows are affected by company-specific factors, such as the quality of its managers, the level of its advertising, the effectiveness of its R&D, and the skill of its labour.

By careful choice of the investments in a portfolio, unsystematic risk can be diversified away. Systematic risk, however, cannot be diversified away, since it is experienced by all companies. The risk of a well-diversified portfolio will be similar to the systematic risk of the market as a whole.

2 Investments may not perform as expected. In a well-diversified portfolio, investments that perform well will tend to balance those that do not, and only systematic risk will remain. The systematic risk of the portfolio will be the same as the average systematic risk of the market as a whole. If an investor wants to avoid risk altogether, he must invest in risk-free securities.

A company's managers may feel that shareholders' interests will be best served by spreading risk through diversification. A shareholder with a well-diversified portfolio, however, will already have eliminated unsystematic risk. For such shareholders, diversification at the company level is of no value.

For a shareholder who does not hold a well-diversified portfolio, and who has not eliminated unsystematic risk, such diversification may be of some value.

3 If the set of all possible portfolios that can be formulated from a large number of given securities is considered, there are a large number of portfolios which are the most desirable to a rational investor. These are the portfolios that offer the highest return for a given level of risk, or the lowest risk for a given level of expected return. Such portfolios are known as *efficient portfolios* and lie along the *efficient frontier* of the set of all possible portfolios in a graph of portfolio returns against portfolio risk. However, it is not possible to say which portfolio an individual investor would prefer, as this would depend solely on his attitude to risk and return.

The efficient portfolio which is best suited to the risk-return characteristics of a particular individual investor is an *optimal portfolio* for that investor. It represents a tangency point of the individual investor's utility or indifference curve on the efficient frontier.

4 The limitations of portfolio theory as an aid to investment are:

- the assumption that investors can lend and borrow at the risk-free rate is unrealistic;
- transaction costs deter investors from making changes to portfolios;
- the composition of the market portfolio is difficult to determine;
- should not the market portfolio include all securities in all capital markets?
- securities are not divisible in practice;
- how can we determine the expected risks and returns of securities?
- how do investors make choices from the wide variety of possibilities?
- how can investors determine their own utility function?

5 The answer is (c). This company will have the highest level of *financial* risk due to the high level of gearing and the highest level of *business* risk, given the nature of the building material industry.

6 The answer is (c). The total risk of a company can be split into unsystematic and systematic risk. The company in question may have a very high level of specific risk but only a low level of systematic risk and hence a low equity beta.

7 Currently, $\beta_e = 1.30$ D = 0.25 E = 0.75

Hence: $\beta_a = \beta_e \times (E/(E + D(1 - C_T)))$

$= 1.30 \times 0.75/(0.75 + (0.25 \times 0.65))$

$= 0.975/0.9125 = 1.0685$

If now D = 0.33 and E = 0.67 then:

$\beta_e = \beta_a \times (1 + (D(1 - t)/E)) = 1.0685 \times 1.320 = 1.41$

The new equity beta is therefore 1.41.

8 The risk-free rate is approximated in practice by using the yield on government securities such as Treasury bills. As for the capital market line, it will not be a straight line in practice because investors, while being able to lend at the risk-free rate, cannot borrow at the risk-free rate. Therefore, the CML will kink downwards to the right-hand side of the market portfolio.

9 R_m = 16 per cent R_f = 10 per cent $Cov_{ls} = 7.5$ $\sigma_m^2 = 4.5$

$\beta_{ls} = Cov_{ls}/\sigma_m^2 = 7.5/4.5 = 1.67$

$E(R_{ls}) = R_f + \beta_{ls}(R_m - R_f) = 10 + (1.67 \times (16 - 10)) = 20$ per cent

The required rate of return on Lime Spider's shares is therefore 20 per cent.

10 The asset beta is the weighted average of the betas of equity and debt. Since the simplifying assumption that the beta of debt is zero is made, but the market value of debt is non-zero, the asset beta will always be lower than the equity beta unless, of course, the company is all-equity financed.

Answers to Questions for review

1 If a risk-free asset is combined with a multi-asset portfolio, the best combination of risky and risk-free assets occurs along a line which begins with a portfolio containing only the risk-free asset and which is tangential to the efficient frontier of portfolios containing only risky assets. This line is called the capital market line.

The point of tangency with the efficient frontier is called the market portfolio, since it contains all risky assets. This is because, if we assume that all investors make the same forecasts and therefore come to the same conclusions, all investors will choose to hold this risky portfolio. The conclusion, then, is that all investors will want to hold a slice of the market portfolio, in combination with the risk-free asset. The number of shares that an individual investor needs to hold in order to have a well-diversified portfolio is only about twenty. It is therefore practical for an individual investor to obtain an efficient portfolio which maximises their utility. The optimal portfolio for the investor will be located on the capital market line at the point of tangency with the investor's personal utility curve.

Portfolio theory therefore provides a framework for the investor to construct a market portfolio that diversifies away unsystematic risk and then, by combining the market portfolio with the risk-free asset, maximises utility.

2 (a) Return of X alone $= (30 \times 0.3) + (25 \times 0.4) + (20 \times 0.3)$
$= 9 + 10 + 6 = 25$ per cent

Return of Y alone $= (50 \times 0.2) + (30 \times 0.6) + (10 \times 0.2)$
$= 10 + 18 + 2 = 30$ per cent

Return of 60 per cent X and 40 per cent Y $= (0.6 \times 25) + (0.4 \times 30) = 15 + 12 = 27$ per cent

(b) Risk can be measured by the standard deviation of the returns.

Standard deviation of X

Probability	*Return (%)*	$(R - \bar{R})$	$P \times (R - \bar{R})^2$
0.3	30	5	7.5
0.4	25	0	0.0
0.3	20	–5	7.5
			15.0

The standard deviation of X $= \sqrt{15.0} = 3.873$ per cent.

Standard deviation of Y

Probability	*Return (%)*	$(R - \bar{R})$	$P \times (R - \bar{R})^2$
0.2	50	20	80
0.6	30	0	0
0.2	10	–20	80
			160

The standard deviation of Y $= \sqrt{160} = 12.649$ per cent.

Standard deviation of 60 per cent X and 40 per cent Y:

Using the portfolio theory expression for σ_p as follows:

$$\sigma_p = [(0.6^2 \times 15) + (0.4^2 \times 160) + (2 \times 0.6 \times 0.4 \times 3.873 \times 12.649 \times 0.15)]^{1/2}$$
$$= [5.4 + 25.6 + 3.527]^{1/2} = 5.876 \text{ per cent}$$

3 *Supertronic plc*

$\beta_a = \beta_g \times (E/(E + D(1 - t)))$
$\beta_a = 1.33 \times 0.5/(0.5 + (0.5 \times 0.65))$
$= 0.665/0.825 = 0.806$

Electroland plc

$\beta_a = \beta_g \times (E/(E + D(1 - t)))$
$\beta_a = 1.30 \times 0.6/(0.6 + (0.4 \times 0.65))$
$= 0.780/0.860 = 0.907$

But $\beta_a = 0.907 = (0.8 \times \beta_{a1}) + (0.2 \times \beta_{a2})$
$= (0.8 \times \beta_{a1}) + (0.2 \times 1.4)$

Hence $\beta_{a1} = (0.907 - 0.280)/0.8 = 0.784$

Transelectro plc

$\beta_a = \beta_g \times (E/(E + D(1 - t)))$

$\beta_a = 1.05 \times 0.65/(0.65 + (0.35 \times 0.65))$

$= 0.6825/0.8775 = 0.778$

Average proxy asset beta:

$(0.806 + 0.784 + 0.778)/3 = 2.368/3 = 0.789$

Regearing: $\beta_g = \beta_g \times (1 + (D(1 - t)/E))$

$= 0.789 \times (1 + ((0.3 \times 0.65)/0.7))$

$= 0.789 + 1.2786 = 1.01$

$E(R_i) = R_f + \beta_g (R_m - R_f) = 10 + (1.01 \times (14 - 10)) = 14$ per cent

Since the expected return of the project of 18 per cent is greater than the calculated required rate of return, the project should be accepted.

4 (a) The portfolio beta is the weighted average of the individual security betas.

Share	*No. shares*	*Share price (£)*	*Market value (£)*		*Beta*	*Weighted beta*
Kitson	70 000	3.75	262 500	×	1.27	0.1697
Pembridge	150 000	4.25	637 500	×	1.53	0.4964
Taylor	100 000	2.50	250 000	×	1.01	0.1285
Short	80 000	4.50	360 000	×	0.95	0.1740
Johnson	130 000	3.50	455 000	×	0.82	0.1899
			1 965 000			1.1585

Since $\beta_p = 1.16$ and so is greater than 1, the portfolio is riskier than the market.

(b) We need to compare the returns predicted by the CAPM with expected returns (*see* table below). Shares with expected returns less than those predicted by their betas are underperforming and should be disposed of.

Company	*Beta*	*E(R_j)%*	*E(R)%*	*E(R) – E(R_j)%*	*Advice*
Kitson	1.27	18.89	17.0	(1.89)	Sell
Pembridge	1.53	20.71	21.0	0.29	Hold
Taylor	1.01	17.07	19.0	1.93	Hold
Short	0.95	16.65	14.5	(2.15)	Sell
Johnson	0.82	15.74	20.0	4.26	Buy

5 Problems that could have been discussed in connection with applying the CAPM in investment appraisal include:

- determining the excess market return;
- determining the risk-free rate of return;
- estimation of the equity and overall betas for a company;
- determination of the beta for a project;
- the CAPM is a single-period model;
- the CAPM is an ex-ante model;
- national surrogates for market return may be internationally inappropriate.

CHAPTER 10

Answers to Questions

1 It is important to match the financing with the life of assets. We can analyse assets into fixed assets, permanent current assets and fluctuating current assets. Permanent current assets, being 'core' current assets which are needed to support normal levels of sales, should be financed from a long-term source. The working capital policy chosen should take account of the relative risk of long- and short-term finance to the company and the need to balance liquidity against profitability. An aggressive financing policy will use short-term funds to finance fluctuating current assets as well as finance part of the permanent current assets. A conservative financing policy will use long-term funds to finance permanent current assets as well as to finance part of the fluctuating current assets. An aggressive financing policy will be more profitable, but riskier.

2 The components of the cash conversion cycle (CCC) are the inventory conversion period (ICP), the debtor conversion period (DCP), and the creditor deferral period (CDP), and the relationship between them is:

$$CCC = ICP + DCP + (-CDP)$$

Investment in working capital must be financed and the longer the cash conversion cycle, the more capital is tied up and the higher the cost. A company could reduce the working capital tied up by optimising the components of the cash conversion cycle. So, for example, shortening the inventory conversion period could reduce the working capital requirement and increase profitability.

3 Overtrading arises when a company seeks to do too much too quickly, without sufficient long-term capital to support its operations. While a company which is overtrading may well be profitable, it is likely to meet difficulties with liquidity, and may be unable to meet its financial obligations to creditors and others as they fall due. Strategies that could be considered by management wishing to address the problem of overtrading include the introduction of new capital, possibly from shareholders; better control and management of working capital; and a reduction in business activity in order to consolidate the company's position and build up capital through retained earnings.

4 Factors offer a range of services in the area of sales administration and the collection of cash due from debtors, including administration of sales invoicing and accounting, collection of cash due, chasing up late payers, advancing cash against the security of debtors due, and offering protection against non-payment via non-recourse factoring. Invoice discounting, however, involves the sale of selected invoices to another company. Its main value lies in the improvement in cash flow that it offers.

5 Cash flow problems can arise from:

- making losses, since continuing losses will lead to cash flow problems;
- inflation, since historical profit may be insufficient to replace assets;
- growth, since this calls for investment in fixed assets and working capital;
- seasonal business, due to imbalances in cash flow;

- significant one-off items of expenditure, such as repayment of debt capital.

Cash flow problems can be eased in several ways. Examples include postponing capital expenditure (e.g. extending vehicle replacement life), accelerating cash inflows (e.g. offering cash discounts, chasing up slow payers), shelving investment plans, selling off non-core assets and reducing cash outflows. Economies could be found in normal operations as well.

6 There are three reasons why a company may choose to have reserves of cash. Companies need to have a cash reserve to balance short-term cash inflows and ouflows; this is called the transactions motive for holding cash. The precautionary motive for holding cash refers to the fact that a company may choose to have cash reserves in order to meet unexpected demands. Companies may also build up cash reserves to take advantage of investment opportunities that may occur; this is called the speculative motive for holding cash.

7 Short-term cash surpluses should be invested on a short-term basis without risk of capital loss. In selecting an investment method, the finance director should take into consideration the size of the surplus; the ease of realisation of the investment selected; the maturity, risk and yield of different investments; and any penalties for early liquidation.

Short-term instruments which could be discussed include money market deposits, Treasury bills, bank certificates of deposit, gilt-edged stock and bank deposits.

8 The risk of bad debts could be minimised if the creditworthiness of new customers is assessed and reviewed on a regular basis. Relevant information should be obtained from a variety of sources, including bank references, trade references, published information, such as accounts and the press, and credit reference agencies. In addition, the credit analysis system should adopt a cost-effective approach, so that the extent of the credit assessment should reflect the size of the order, the likelihood of subsequent business, and the amount of credit requested.

9 Proposed changes to credit policy should be evaluated in the light of the additional costs and benefits that will result from their being undertaken. For example, the cost of the introduction of cash discounts can be compared with the benefits of faster settlement of accounts in terms of reduced interest charges, and possibly also the additional business that may result. The change should only be undertaken if the marginal benefits arising from the new policy exceed its marginal costs.

10 Companies can exercise control over the levels of their working capital by formulating and implementing policies concerning inventory, debtors, cash and creditors. Such policies will take account of the factors that influence these components of working capital, as follows.

- *Debtors*. Credit period allowed by a company and its competitors, speed of invoicing and other aspects of administrative efficiency, the use of discounts for early settlement, debtor collection methods, the forecast volume of sales.
- *Stock*. The length of the production process, the rate of turnover of raw materials, the turnover period of finished goods, delivery lead time, the budgeted and actual volumes of output and sales.

- *Creditors*. The extent to which a company can delay payments to suppliers, the volume of purchases, the availability of cash discounts for early payment.
- *Cash*. Interest rates and available short-term investments, the availability of credit, the ease with which a company can access funds.

Answers to Questions for review

1 Your recommended policy should have been based on the EOQ model.
F = £100 per order
S = 60 000 tonnes per year
H = £0.10 per tonne per year
Substituting: $Q = (2 \times 100 \times 60\,000/0.10)^{1/2}$ = 10 954 tonnes per order
Number of orders per year = 60 000/10 954 = 5.5 orders
Re-order level = 2 × 60 000/50 = 2400 tonnes
Total cost of optimal policy = holding costs + ordering costs
= (0.1 × 10 954)/2 + (100 × 60 000)/10 954
= 547.70 + 547.74 = £1095

To compare the optimal policy with the current policy, the average level of stock under the current policy must be found. An order is placed when stock falls to 10 000 tonnes, but the lead time is two weeks. The stock used in that time is (60 000 × 2)/50 = 2400 tonnes. Before delivery, inventory has fallen to (10 000 – 2400) = 7600 tonnes. Orders are made twice per year, and so the order size = 60 000/2 = 30 000 tonnes. The order will increase stock level to 30 000 + 7600 = 37 600 tonnes. Hence the average stock level = 7600 + (30 000/2) = 22 600 tonnes. Total costs of current policy = (0.1 × 22 600) + (100 × 2) = £2460 per year.

The recommended policy, then, costs £1365 per year less than the current policy.

2 Annual costs:

Raw materials:	700 000 × 0.20 =	£140 000
Direct labour:	700 000 × 0.35 =	£245 000
Overheads:	700 000 × 0.15 =	£105 000

Working capital requirement:

	£	£
Stocks of raw materials: 140 000 × (2/52) =		5 385
Work-in-progress:		
materials: 140 000 × (4/52) =	10 769	
labour: 245 000 × (4/52) × ½ =	9 423	
overheads: 105 000 × (4/52) × ½ =	4 038	
		24 230
Finished goods: 490 000 × (3/52) =		28 269
Debtors: 700 000 × (8/52) =		107 692
Creditors: 140 000 × (4/52) =		(10 769)
Working capital required:		154 807

Note that work-in-progress is assumed to be half complete as regards labour and overheads, but fully complete as regards raw materials, i.e. all raw material is added at the start of production.

3 New level of sales will be 1 500 000 × 1.15 = £1 725 000
Variable costs are 80% × 75% = 60% of sales
Contribution from sales is therefore 40% of sales

	£	£
Proposed investment in debtors = 1 725 000 × 60/365 =		283 562
Current investment in debtors = 1 500 000 × 30/365 =		123 288
Increase in investment in debtors		160 274
Increase in contribution = 15% × 1 500 000 × 40% =		90 000
New level of bad debts = 1 725 000 × 4% =	69 000	
Current level of bad debts = 1 500 000 × 1% =	15 000	
Increase in bad debts		(54 000)
Additional financing costs = 160 274 × 12% =		(19 233)
Savings by introducing change in policy		16 767

The financing policy is financially acceptable, although the savings are not great.

4

	£	£
Current level of debtors = 1 600 000 × 45/365 =		197 260
Proposed level of debtors:		
Not taking the discount = 60% × 1 600 000 × 45/365 =	118 356	
Taking the discount = 40% × 1 600 000 × 10/365 =	17 534	
		135 890
Change in level of debtors		61 370
Saving in financing costs = 61 370 × 11% =		6 751
Administrative cost savings		4 450
Total savings		11 201

Calculation of maximum discount:
1 600 000 × 40% × maximum discount = 11 201
Hence maximum discount = 11 201/(1 600 000 × 0.4) = 0.0175 or 1.75%

The maximum discount that could be offered is therefore 1.75%.

CHAPTER 11

Answers to Questions

1 The reason why mergers are rare relative to the occurrence of take-overs is that for a merger to take place the transaction needs to involve two companies of equal size, with

no one player being dominant. Also both companies need to cancel their shares and issue new shares. These criteria are very rarely met, as it is unlikely two companies of equal size will be involved and, even so, one company may still be seen to be dominant. From a cost point of view it is easier and cheaper to exchange one company's shares for another than to cancel both companies' shares and distribute new shares.

2 The economic reasons for taking over another company centre on the belief that shareholder wealth will be enhanced by the deal. This increase in wealth can arise from a number of sources, as follows:

- synergy, whereby the value of the combined entity exceeds its parts;
- economies of scale, e.g. in distribution and production;
- the elimination of inefficient management;
- entry in to new markets, for example instead of starting from scratch;
- to provide critical mass;
- to provide growth;
- to provide market share.

3 The financial benefits that may be gained by shareholders via a take-over will include:

- acquisition of an undervalued target (unlikely if markets are efficient);
- benefit from relative tax considerations;
- increase in EPS or boot-strapping (cannot be accepted as a justification).

4 A number of arguments have been advanced against using acquisitions and mergers as a way of achieving growth:

- the bid may be referred to the MMC and so be delayed and even refused;
- the bid may be contested and result in a bloody battle;
- the only beneficiaries from mergers and take-overs are shareholders in the target company;
- financing a take-over is expensive;
- it is difficult to achieve post-merger integration.

5 There is no consensus view on why mergers and take-overs come in waves, but a number of contributory factors have been identified:

- a bull market can encourage the use of shares to finance take-overs;
- increasing liquidity and profitability can encourage companies to look for acquisition targets;
- deregulation of financial markets has made access to finance easier;
- low levels of gearing allow companies to use debt to finance acquisitions.

6 Using P/E ratios to value companies is a rough rule of thumb and must be used with caution. EPS is an accounting figure that can be subject to manipulation and creative accounting. In addition, earnings will vary over time and not stay at their current level, so the EPS figure may need to be normalised to reflect this. Problems with using the P/E

ratio method include the difficulty of selecting an appropriate P/E ratio to apply, and the fact that the ratio combines a current value (share price) with an historic value (EPS).

The accuracy of the Gordon growth model relies heavily on forecast future dividend payments and the calculated shareholders' required rate of return. Both of these figures are difficult to estimate with any real accuracy. There are also difficulties in using the model in this context because it considers the dividends that flow to individual investors, rather than the company's ability to generate cash flows from its assets.

7 The DCF valuation method is preferred by academics because it is directly related to the ideal of shareholder wealth maximisation. Practical difficulties with this method include:

- estimating future cash flows;
- the choice of an appropriate discount rate;
- the selection of an appropriate time period over which to evaluate;
- how to forecast accurately any economies of scale and synergies;
- taking account of the risk of the target company;
- estimating the future cost of capital.

The appropriate discount rate with which to discount expected cash flows is the acquiring company's cost of capital.

8 The answer to this question can be found in Section 11.5.4.

9 Possible post-bid defences that you could have described include:

- formulation of a defence document;
- announcing forecasts of increased profits;
- announcing an increase in dividends;
- looking for a 'white knight';
- getting rid of the 'crown jewels'.

10 Possible reasons why the shareholders of predator companies rarely benefit from take-overs include the following:

- if the bid is contested, the acquisition can cost the predator more than it originally intended to pay, reducing its shareholders' wealth;
- predicted economies of scale and synergy may fail to materialise;
- the predator company's management may lack knowledge and expertise in the business they have acquired;
- the quality of the acquired assets may turn out to be lower than expected;
- cultural problems may be experienced between predator and victim;
- if the take-over is for cash, the predator company may be drained of liquidity and face a high level of gearing. This restricts its ability to accept attractive projects.

Answers to Questions for review

1 (a) The major justifications put forward to explain *horizontal mergers* centre on the fact that the merging companies are in the same industry and so are likely to benefit from economies of scale. They may also benefit from synergy between operations as well. Horizontal mergers can also be justified as a way of breaking into new geographical markets. Market share can also be a viable reason, so that companies can earn monopoly profits, but the bidder must beware of referral to the MMC. There may be financial economies and tax benefits from mergers, but increasing EPS is not a valid justification.

(b) Here the major justification is that a company can either secure control of vital raw materials or guarantee an outlet for, and control the distribution of, its product. This helps companies to reduce the power of suppliers or to decrease the revenue lost to distributors. Economies of scale or synergy are less likely to occur than with horizontal take-overs.

(c) It is very difficult to see the rationale for conglomerate take-overs, as there will be few economies of scale or synergy due to the unrelated nature of the merging businesses. The take-over cannot be justified from the point of view of risk reduction, as shareholders are likely to hold diversified portfolios. Nor can the take-over be justified as the acquisition of a bargain, since if capital markets are efficient, the target's share price will reflect its true value.

2 (a) Calculation of the value of Staygood using P/E ratios:
Staygood's share price = 12 × 37p = £4.44
We will assume that the market will expect Restwell to achieve a level of return on Staygood comparable to that which it makes on its own assets. Hence:
Total market value = 5m × £4.44 = £22.2m

(b) To use the Gordon growth model we must find g and K_e.

Here g is given by $\sqrt[5]{\frac{27}{15}} - 1 = 12.47$ per cent

K_e for Staygood is 20 per cent higher that Restwell, therefore:

K_e = 15 per cent × 1.20 =	18 per cent
Therefore P_0 = (27 × (1.1247))/(0.18 – 0.1247) =	£5.49
Total market value = 5m × £5.49 =	£27.46m

(c) Using future cash flows and discounting these to infinity using Restwell's WACC as a discount rate:
Present value = (£2.5m /(0.12 – 0.05)) + ($5/1.12^2$) = £39.7m

3 Powell's market value, using its P/E ratio and earnings, is 5.8m × 10 = £58m
The earnings of Stimac plc will be (£10m + £5.8m) × 1.08 = £17.06m
Using a P/E ratio of 9, the value of Stimac is £17.06m × 9 = £153.54m

The 10m shares of Powell will be swapped for 30m Carsley shares, making 70m shares in the new company in total. Therefore, the wealth of Powell's shareholders will now be £153.54m × (30m/70m) = £65.8m.

Powell's shareholders are £7.8m better off (78 pence per share).

4 There are a large number of factors that will influence a company on the way it decides to structure its financing of a take-over bid, as follows.

- *The tax position of the victim company's shareholders.* If they are tax exempt, they may prefer a cash offer as they will not incur capital gains tax. If they are liable for capital gains then they may prefer a share-for-share offer. If there is a diverse range of investors in different tax-paying positions then a mixed bid may be more appropriate.
- *The predator company's level of liquidity and ability to borrow funds.* This will determine whether it will be able to find sufficient funds in order to make a cash offer.
- *The predator company's share price.* If its share price is high compared to the victim company's share price, the predator company will not have to issue too many shares if it makes a share-for-share offer, reducing any potential dilution of EPS and control.
- *The attitudes and preferences of shareholders.* The predator company's shareholders many not want it to borrow for a cash offer because this may increase financial risk beyond what they are prepared to tolerate. A cash offer may be unattractive to the victim company's shareholders because they no longer have a participating interest in the company that they originally bought shares in.

CHAPTER 12

Answers to Questions

1 (a) Here the company is facing transaction exposure. If the pound weakens against the deutschmark, the sterling cost of the company's coal imports will increase. Therefore, the risk here is downside in nature.

(b) The type of exchange rate risk being faced here is economic risk. The UK toy company is facing upside risk here, because a depreciation in the pound against the dollar will make the US company's imports less attractive to domestic customers.

(c) Here the UK company faces translation risk. The risk is downside in nature because, as the pound appreciates against the franc, the translated sterling value of the factory will decrease, increasing the company's liabilities relative to its assets.

2 Translation risk is best managed by using matching. For example, if purchasing an asset in a foreign country, raise the funds for the purchase in the foreign currency, so both the asset and liability are in the same currency.

There are a number of ways to hedge transaction risk internally. Matching, for example, could mean paying for imports in the same currency that a company invoices its exports in. Alternatively, a company could invoice customers in the domestic currency and find a supplier which does the same. The problem with this method, though, is that the company may lose foreign sales and also restrict the potential suppliers it can purchase from. Companies can also manage transaction risk by leading and lagging payments according to their expectations of exchange rate movements.

3 The company needs to purchase sufficient dollars to deposit on the money markets so that when the deposit matures, there are exactly enough dollars to pay its $345 000 liability. Therefore:

$$Z \times (1 + 8.5 \text{ per cent}/4) = \$345\ 000$$

Here Z = \$337 821 which at the current spot rate will cost £189 787.

4 The major difference between OTC options and traded options is that the latter come in the form of contracts standardised with respect to amount and duration, while the former are non-standardised and negotiable with respect to amount and duration. Traded options are available from LIFFE while OTC options are provided by banks. One of the consequences of traded options being standardised is that they can be sold on to other parties. OTC options can be tailormade to match the characteristics of the exposure a company wants to hedge.

5 If we sell futures contracts and interest rates increase, we close out our position in the future by buying futures contracts at a lower price, therefore making a gain. We therefore need to sell futures contracts to offset the increased cost of borrowing. How many contracts should we sell? Our transaction is equal to 12 contracts, but we are borrowing for a six-month period, so we need to sell 24 contracts in order fully to hedge our exposure. The correct response is therefore (c).

6 Interest rate risk is concerned with the sensitivity of profit and operating cash flows to changes in interest rates. A company will need to analyse how its profits and cash flows are likely to change in response to forecast changes in interest rates, and take a decision as to whether action is necessary. Factors which could influence the decision to hedge interest rate risk include:

- the expected volatility of interest rates;
- the sensitivity of profits and cash flows to interest rate changes;
- the balance between fixed and floating rate debt in a company's capital structure;
- the financial plans of the company.

7 A company can use internal measures such as matching if it has cash inflows and outflows which can be matched in respect of timing and amount. If it wishes to transfer risk to a third party, however, it will need to use external hedging instruments. The following factors will determine which external hedging instruments will be used:

- whether the company wishes to profit from favourable rate movements or wants to lock in to a particular interest rate;
- the view the company takes on future interest rate movements and volatility;
- the timing, nature and duration of the interest rate exposure;
- the extent to which the company wishes to hedge its interest rate exposure;
- the knowledge and experience of the company's treasury staff;
- the relative costs associated with the different derivatives.

8 Here the correct answer is (c). A bank-created floor is only sought if a company wants to guard against interest rates going down. The rest of the responses will all successfully hedge against interest rate increases.

9 The drawbacks include the following points:

- a company may find it difficult to find an appropriate swap partner which has equal but opposite requirements to itself;
- once engaged in a swap agreement it is not possible to benefit from favourable movements in the exchange rate;
- the swap partner has to be vetted so as to reduce the possibility of counterparty default.

10 Here the most valuable option is (e), the $1.42 put option. The holder of this option can exchange dollars into sterling at a much more favourable rate than the current spot rate. In fact (e) is the only option that is 'in the money'.

Answers to Questions for review

1 The factors that you could have discussed include the following:

- if a company is uncertain as to the direction in which interest rates will move, it could take an OTC option to allow it to take advantage of favourable interest rate movements. This is not possible with a futures contract, which would lock the company into a particular interest rate;
- while paying a premium for an OTC option, a company will save itself the initial margin required by a futures contract, as well as any subsequent variation margin;
- an OTC option will make it easier for a company to match the hedge to the duration and size of its exposure. The standardised nature of futures contracts may lead the company to having to over- or under-hedge;
- the company may feel happier dealing with a bank that it is familiar with in order to obtain an OTC option, rather than approaching a new market such as LIFFE to deal in futures contracts;
- the efficiency of using futures to hedge interest rate changes may be hampered by the existence of basis risk.

2 (a) Using the forward market: $364 897/1.5455 = £236 103

(b) Using the money markets:
Carrycan must make a dollar deposit now.
Six-month dollar deposit rate = 4.5/2 = 2.25 per cent
$Z \times 1.0225$ = $364 897
Hence Z = $356 867
Cost of buying $356 867 at current spot rate is 356 867/1.5617 = £228 512
Six-monthly sterling deposit rate = 5.5/2 = 2.75 per cent
Six months' interest lost on £228 512 = (£228 512 × 0.0275) = £6284
Total cost = 222 512 + 6284 = £234 796

(c) Using currency put options:
Each contract will deliver 1.7 × 12 500 = $21 250
Number of contracts required = 364 897/21 250 = 17.17, i.e. 17 contracts
Cost = 0.096 × 12 500 × 17 = $20 400
Sterling cost of options = 20 400/1.5617 = £13 063
Sterling required = 17 × £12 500 = £212 500 to deliver $361 250

Shortfall = 364 897 – 361 250 = \$3647
Cost in sterling using forward rate = 3647/1.5455 = £2360
Total cost of using options = 13 063 + 212 500 + 2360 = £227 923

Therefore the foreign currency options are the cheapest method for the company to use to hedge its transaction exposure.

3 You could have discussed the following factors:

- the time to expiry of the option;
- interest rates, particularly the risk-free rate of return;
- the price of the underlying asset, e.g. interest rate futures;
- the exercise price of the option;
- the volatility of interest rates and exchange rates;
- market expectations about future changes in interest and exchange rates.

4 (a) Say for instance LIBOR = 10 per cent. Company B's floating rate is three per cent more expensive than Company A's rate, but its fixed rate is 12.5 per cent more expensive than A's. Hence Company A has a comparative advantage in fixed rate loans, and Company B has a comparative advantage in floating rate loans.

(b) Net potential gain = (LIBOR – (LIBOR + 0.3)) + (13.5 – 12) = –0.3 + 1.5 = 1.2 per cent, i.e. 0.6 per cent benefit to each company.

Company B pays:
Company A's fixed rate borrowing (12 per cent) plus 0.9 per cent, therefore company B' s actual fixed rate = 12.9 per cent (compared to 13.5 per cent).
Company A pays:
Company B's floating borrowing rate of LIBOR + 0.3 and also receives 0.9 per cent, therefore company A's actual floating rate = LIBOR – 0.6 (compared to LIBOR).

5 Slammer plc has a comparative advantage in fixed rates, as it can obtain a fixed rate loan 0.5 per cent cheaper than Can plc, while it can obtain a floating rate loan only 0.2 per cent cheaper than Can plc. If the two companies arranged an interest rate swap, Slammer plc could borrow at a fixed rate of 11.5 per cent and Can plc would pay the fixed rate interest, while Can plc could borrow at a floating rate of LIBOR plus 0.4 per cent and Slammer plc would pay the floating rate interest. Since Can plc is saving 0.5 per cent on fixed rates, but Slammer plc is paying 0.2 per cent more than its possible floating rate, the net benefit is 0.3 per cent, which is 0.15 per cent for each company if divided equally. Can plc should therefore have a net cost or effective borrowing rate of 11.85 per cent and so should pay Slammer plc 0.35 per cent. This will make Slammer plc's net cost or effective borrowing rate LIBOR + 0.05 per cent, which is a saving of 0.15 per cent over its opportunity cost. We can show this in table form as follows:

Alternative costs	*Slammer plc*	*Can plc*
Fixed rate	11.50%	—
Floating rate	—	LIBOR + 0.4%
Swap: fixed rate	(11.75%)	11.75%
Swap: floating rate	LIBOR + 0.4%	(LIBOR + 0.4%)
Effective borrowing rate	LIBOR + 0.05%	11.85%
Opportunity cost	LIBOR + 0.2%	12.0%
Relative saving	0.15%	0.15%

CHAPTER 13

Answers to Questions

1 The answer to this question can be found in Section 13.1.1.

2 The answer to this question can be found in Section 13.1.2.

3 The answer to this question can be found in Section 13.2.

4 The answer to this question can be found in Section 13.2.3.

5 The answer to this question can be found in Section 13.3.1.

6 The primary objective of the management of a company undertaking foreign direct investment should be to maximise the wealth of its shareholders. The evaluation at the parent company level is therefore the key to whether a proposal should be accepted or not.

7 The following difficulties may be encountered by analysts:

- How can they determine an appropriate value of beta?
- With reference to which market should it be calculated?
- What value of the market premium should be used?
- Which risk-free rate should be selected?
- What if the share price of the company changes: should the cost of capital be recalculated?

8 The main factors influencing the choice and mix of financing used in foreign direct investment are gearing, taxation, political risk and currency risk. The financing decision should aim to minimise the cost of capital in order to maximise the value of the firm.

9 The company can use one of several techniques. It could look at the country's political risk index and compare it to that of other countries. It could use the Delphi technique, statistical analysis, a checklist approach or visit the country concerned. If it seeks to assess political risk in a systematic way, the results of the assessment are more likely to be useful.

10 Apart from doing nothing, the first option to consider is that of insurance against political risk, whether through a private company or through a government department such as the ECGD. The second option is possible negotiation of a concession agreement with the host government, as long as it is a government that can be trusted to keep such an agreement. A third option is to select financing and operating policies which reduce the political risk faced in a particular country. An example of such a financing policy is the use of a significant amount of local debt. An example of such an operating policy is locating different stages of production in different countries, to make expropriation less likely.

Answers to Questions for review

1 (a) We need to see if the project is acceptable to the parent company.

Year	*0*	*1*	*2*	*3*	*4*	*5*
Operating profit (G$)		250	450	550	650	800
Interest (G$)		(15)	(15)	(15)	(15)	(15)
		235	435	535	635	785
Taxation (G$)		47	87	107	127	157
		188	348	428	508	628
Capital invested (G$)	(600)					600
Working capital (G$)	(250)					
Loan (G$)	250					(250)
Project after tax (G$)	(600)	188	348	428	508	978
Exchange rate (G$/£)	3	4	5	6	7	8
Payable to UK (£)	(200)	47.0	69.6	71.3	72.6	122.2
UK tax (£)		(5.9)	(8.7)	(8.9)	(9.1)	(9.8)
	(200)	41.1	60.9	62.4	63.5	112.4
20% discount factor	1.000	0.833	0.694	0.579	0.482	0.402
Present value (£)	(200)	34.2	42.3	36.1	30.6	45.2
Net present value (£)	(11.6)					

Since the NPV is negative, the project is not acceptable on financial grounds.

(b) A general discussion of political risk, illustrated by examples from the scenario of the question, is called for.

2 (a) If Redek Mornag chooses to increase exports to Laresia, it will be limited by its current surplus capacity, unless it decides to increase its productive capacity in the UK. Since it currently exports to Laresia, increasing exports is a low-risk strategy, as it already has local business contacts and established channels of distribution. However, profitability will be reduced by transport and insurance costs. There is also the possibility that import controls will be introduced if Laresia's balance of trade deteriorates.

(b) Licensing would mean that import and other controls would not present a problem, but the returns are likely to be small. There is also the danger that the licensee could set up in opposition to Redek Mornag, having acquired the necessary knowledge and expertise through operating under licence, and it could be difficult to do much about this.

(c) Constructing a manufacturing facility demonstrates commitment to the country of Laresia, and offers the possibility of higher profits than either exporting or licensing. Government incentives for such a move may be available and it might be possible to take advantage of the latest production techniques. Local wage rates are also likely to be lower.

3 In distinguishing between international and domestic capital investment decisions, the following points could be considered:

(a) The difference between project cash flows and parent cash flows
   (i) the need for a two-stage evaluation process;
   (ii) remittable and distributable cash flows;
   (iii) the nature and type of parent cash flows;
   (iv) the difficulties in identifying relevant cash flows;
   (v) the effect of investment on other operations.

(b) Difficulties in valuing investment by the parent company
   (i) transfer of capital as equipment and inventory;
   (ii) use of opportunity cost.

(c) The problem of exchange rates, e.g. estimation difficulties re future exchange rates.

(d) Taxation
   (i) differential tax regimes;
   (ii) withholding taxes;
   (iii) allowances for taxes paid elsewhere.

(e) Foreign investment and the cost of capital
   (i) risk premium;
   (ii) international diversification and systematic risk.

(f) Restrictions on the repatriation of funds
   (i) exchange controls;
   (ii) royalties and management fees.

(g) International investment decisions and risk
   (i) political risk, exchange rate and interest rate risk;
   (ii) risk analysis and risk management methods.

4 At the local level, we have:

Year	*0* (*K000*)	*1* (*K000*)	*2* (*K000*)	*3* (*K000*)	*4* (*K000*)	*5* (*K000*)
Operating cash flows		3000	3000	3000	3000	3000
WDAs		(1050)	(1050)	(1050)	(1050)	(1050)
Interest		(100)	(100)	(100)	(100)	(100)
Profit before tax		1850	1850	1850	1850	1850
Withholding tax		(277.5)	(277.5)	(277.5)	(277.5)	(277.5)
After-tax cash flows		1572.5	1572.5	1572.5	1572.5	1572.5
Initial investment	(5250)					
Working capital	(1000)					
Loan capital	1000					(1000)
Sale of subsidiary						4200
Add back WDAs		1050	1050	1050	1050	1050
Project cash flows	(5250)	2622.5	2622.5	2622.5	2622.5	5822.5
12% discount factors	1.000	0.893	0.797	0.712	0.636	0.567
Present values	(5250)	2342	2090	1867	1668	3301

NPV = (5 250 000) + 2 342 000 + 2 090 000 + 1 867 000 + 1 668 000 + 3 301 000
= K6 020 000

But the NPV at the parent company level is what is important.

Year	*0*	*1*	*2*	*3*	*4*	*5*
Remitted to UK (K000)	(5250)	2622.5	2622.5	2622.5	2622.5	5822.5
Exchange rate, K/£	3.50	4.00	4.40	4.70	4.90	5.00
	£000	*£000*	*£000*	*£000*	*£000*	*£000*
Sterling equivalent	(1500)	656	596	558	535	1164
UK tax		(74)	(67)	(62)	(60)	(59)
	(1500)	581	529	495	475	1105
Exports lost, after tax		(50)	(50)	(50)	(50)	(50)
Parent cash flow	(1500)	532	479	445	425	1055
18% discount factors	1.000	0.847	0.718	0.609	0.516	0.437
Parent cash flow	(1500)	451	344	271	219	461

NPV = (1 500 000) + 451 000 + 344 000 + 271 000 + 219 000 + 461 000 = £246 000

The investment appears to be financially acceptable.

5 Political risk, which is the possibility of favourable or adverse political action, has the following features:

- it is increased if the host nation and the multinational company have differing objectives;
- it is increased in areas with political and social instability;
- measuring political and social instability is difficult.

Possible difficulties arising from political risk include:

- exchange controls;
- currency restrictions;
- restrictions on local borrowing;
- expropriation or nationalisation of assets;
- tax discrimination;
- import controls.

GLOSSARY

Accounting rate of return: the average annual accounting profit generated by an investment relative to the required capital outlay.

Accounts receivable: money owed to a company by the customers to whom it has supplied goods and services.

Acquisition: the purchase of one company by another.

Agency: the theoretical relationship that exists between the owners of a company and the managers as agents they employ to run the company on their behalf.

Agency costs: the costs arising as a result of an *agency* relationship.

American option: an option that can be exercised at any time up to, and on, its expiry date.

Amortised loan: a loan where interest and principal are paid off through regular, equal payments.

Annuity: a regular payment of a fixed amount of money over a finite time period.

Arbitrage: the simultaneous buying and selling of assets or securities in different markets in order to yield a risk-free gain.

Asset beta: the sensitivity to systematic factors of the cash flows accruing to a particular set of productive assets.

Asymmetry of information: the situation where one party is in an advantageous position compared to another due to its possession of privileged information.

Auction market preferred stock (AMPS): a form of preference share where the dividend yield is periodically adjusted by a process of auction.

Authorised share capital: this represents the book value of shares that a company is allowed to issue in accordance with its articles of association.

Basis risk: the risk that a specific percentage movement in the cash market will not be equally and oppositely matched by a move in the futures market when hedging interest and exchange rate risk.

Bear market: a market in which share prices are being driven down by the selling activities of pessimistic investors.

Beta: a measure of the sensitivity of a security's returns to systematic risk.

Bonus issue: also known as a *scrip issue*, this represents an issue of new shares to existing shareholders, in proportion to their existing holdings, without the subscription of new funds.

Book value: the value allocated to an asset or liability in the financial statements of a company.

Boot-strapping: the practice whereby a company with a high price/earnings ratio can engineer an increase in its earnings per share by taking over a company with a lower price/earnings ratio.

Business risk: the variability of a company's operating profits given the line of business it is operating in.

Call option: an option that allows the holder to buy an asset at a predetermined price.

Cap: an agreement that fixes a maximum rate of interest at which a party can borrow.

Capital allowances: a tax allowance given against the purchase of certain fixed assets.

Capital gains: the difference between the

original purchase price of a security and its current market price.

Capital market line: the linear risk/return trade-off for investors spreading their money between the market portfolio and risk-free assets.

Capital markets: financial markets where long-term securities are bought and sold.

Capital rationing: the situation when a company has to limit the number of projects it invests in due to insufficient funds being available to invest in all desirable projects.

Cash conversion cycle: the time period between a company paying cash out for its costs of production and receiving cash from the sale of its goods.

Cash market hedge: where a company hedges an exposure to risk by making an equal and opposite cash market transaction.

Certificate of deposit: a tradable security issued by banks to investors who deposit a given amount of money for a specified time period.

Chartism: the practice of studying past share price movements in order to make future capital gains through the buying and selling of shares.

Clientele effect: the theory that suggests that investors are attracted to companies that satisfy their requirements, for example as regards dividends.

Collar: an agreement that keeps either a borrowing or a lending rate between specified upper and lower limits.

Convertible bonds: bonds that can, at some specified date(s), be converted into a predetermined number of ordinary shares.

Convertible preference shares: preference shares that can, at some specified date(s), be converted into a predetermined number of ordinary shares.

Corporate bond: a long-term debt security paying periodic interest with repayment of the principal on maturity.

Corporate governance: the way in which companies are controlled and directed by their stakeholders.

Correlation coefficient: a relative measure of the degree to which the returns of two investments move in the same direction as each other.

Cost of capital: the rate of return required by investors supplying funds to a company and so the minimum rate of return required on prospective projects.

Cost of debt: the rate of return required by the suppliers of debt finance.

Cost of equity: the rate of return required by the suppliers of equity finance.

Coupon rate: the rate of interest paid by a bond relative to its par or face value.

Covariance of returns: an absolute statistical measure of how the returns of two securities are linked to each other, both in terms of direction and magnitude.

Creative accounting: the practice of manipulating company accounts in order to make a company's performance appear more favourable that it actually is.

Creditor hierarchy: the pecking order in which a company's creditors are paid should it go into liquidation.

Cum dividend market price: the market price of a share whose purchase gives the right to receive a recently declared dividend.

Cum rights price: the market value of a share if the current rights have yet to expire.

Currency futures: derivative instruments that allow companies to lock in to current exchange rates with respect to the future purchase or sale of currencies.

Debenture: a bond secured against the assets of the borrowing company.

Debtor collection period: the average number of days it takes for a company to receive payment from its debtors.

Deep discount bonds: bonds that are issued

at a significant discount to their par value and pay a coupon lower than bonds issued at par.

Default risk: the risk that a borrower will not fulfil their commitments with respect to the payment of interest or repayment of principal.

Derivatives: financial securities the values of which are based upon other securities or assets such as bonds, shares, commodities and currencies.

Discount rate: the rate used in the process of discounting future cash flows.

Disintermediation: the process whereby companies raise finance and lend through financial markets directly, rather than through financial institutions.

Diversifiable risk: risk that can be avoided by spreading funds over a portfolio of investments.

Drop lock bonds: floating rate bonds that have a minimum interest rate.

Efficient frontier: the set of optimum portfolios when investing in risky securities.

Enhanced scrip dividends: a *scrip dividend* worth more than the cash dividend alternative.

Envelope curve: the risk/return combinations available to investors when investing in risky assets.

Exchange rate risk: the risk of adverse movements in exchange rates leading to companies experiencing actual or balance sheet losses.

Exercise price: the price at which an option holder can purchase or sell the specified financial asset.

Eurobonds: long-term debt securities issued outside the country in which the issuer is located.

Factoring: the collection of a company's debts by a specialist company, with finance advanced against the security of amounts owed by debtors.

Finance lease: a long-term agreement where the lease period is equivalent to the useful economic life of the leased asset.

Financial risk: the risk of fluctuations in interest rates causing reductions in a company's after-tax earnings and hence its ability to pay dividends.

Financial engineering: the combining or splitting of different financial instruments to create new or synthetic securities.

Fixed charge: debentures secured against a specific company asset.

Floating charge: debentures secured against a pool of company assets.

Floor: similar to a *cap* but here the agreement fixes a minimum rate of interest at which a party can borrow.

Forward rate agreements: contracts which allow companies to fix, in advance, future borrowing and lending rates, based on a nominal principal over a given time period.

Free riders: parties who enjoy the benefits of corrected management behaviour without contributing to the associated costs.

Fundamental analysis: the use of financial information to determine the 'intrinsic value' of a share and hence profit from shares incorrectly priced by the market.

Futures contracts: an agreement to buy or sell a standard quantity of a specific financial instrument or foreign currency at a future date and price agreed between two parties.

Gap exposure: the exposure to interest rate risk arising when a company has liabilities and assets whose coupon rates are based on similar floating rates, but the underlying floating rates are revised with differing frequencies.

Gilt-edged government securities: low-risk, long-term securities issued by the government.

Goal congruence: the situation where agents and principals have identical objectives.

Golden parachutes: generous redundancy

terms for directors of a company, used to deter predator companies from dismissing them after a take-over.

Hedging: the mitigation of exposure to risk by undertaking equal and opposite transactions.

Hybrid finance: a financial security that exhibits the characteristics of both debt and equity.

Indifference curves: a series of curves that join up points of equal utility for an individual investor.

Insider dealing: the use of privileged information to buy and sell securities in order to obtain abnormal returns.

Institutional investors: large financial intermediaries, such as insurance companies, unit trusts, investment trusts and pension funds, who invest large amounts of money in company shares.

Interbank market: a money market that facilitates banks' short-term borrowing and lending.

Interest rate risk: the risk of a company's profits being adversely affected by movements in interest rates.

Junk bonds: unsecured corporate bonds which pay high coupon rates to compensate investors for their high default risk.

Lagging: the delaying of foreign currency transactions in order to benefit from favourable movements in exchange rates.

Lead time: the time delay between placing an order for a raw material and its delivery.

Leveraged take-over: a take-over the cost of which is predominantly financed by debt.

Lodgement delay: the time delay between paying money and cheques into bank accounts and the accounts registering the payment.

London Interbank Offered Rate (LIBOR): key interbank money market interest rate.

Long position: the position taken when an investor purchases and holds a security.

Marginal trading: where the share price of a company is determined by the trading of only a small proportion of its issued share capital.

Market capitalisation: the market value of a company's shares multiplied by the total number of its shares in issue.

Market portfolio: the optimal portfolio of high-risk assets with which to combine holdings of risk-free assets.

Market risk: the relative effect on the returns of an individual security of changes in the market as a whole.

Matching: an internal hedging technique where liabilities and assets are matched in order to mitigate exposure.

Mergers: the coming together of two separate organisations to form one unified entity.

Merchant bank: a bank that specialises in wholesale transactions as opposed to smaller retail transactions.

Mezzanine finance: debt finance, often used in the finance of take-overs, that has risk and return characteristics somewhere between those of ordinary debt and equity.

Money markets: a series of markets which specialise in the borrowing and lending of short-term funds.

Netting: the process of offsetting credit balances against debtor balances in order to minimise inter-company indebtedness.

Nominal value: the face value of an asset in monetary terms.

Non-executive directors (NEDs): directors brought in from outside a company to sit on its board and oversee its operations, but who are not involved in its day-to-day operations.

Non-pecuniary benefits: benefits other than those in the form of cash.

Non-recourse factoring: a factoring agreement where the factor, rather than the company, carries the risk of bad debts.

Off-balance-sheet financing: the use of financing techniques, such as operating leases, that do not have to be capitalised on the balance sheet.

Official List: the list of companies that are registered on the London Stock Exchange.

Operating lease: a short-term agreement where the lease period is substantially less than the useful economic life of the leased asset.

Opportunity cost: the benefit foregone by not utilising an asset in its next best use.

Option: an agreement giving the holder the right, but not the obligation, to buy or sell a specified amount of a commodity or financial instrument over a specific time period and at a specified price.

Over the counter: refers to derivatives that are tailormade by banks to suit the requirements of their customers.

Overtrading: the situation where a company experiences liquidity problems due to it trading beyond the capital resources it has available.

Par value: the face value of a security.

Peppercorn rent: the reduced rent paid by a lessee following the conclusion of the primary period of a finance lease.

Permanent current assets: current assets which are maintained at a core level over time, such as buffer stock.

Perpetuity: the payment of equal cash flows at regular intervals which continue into the indefinite future.

Poison pill: a financial transaction, such as a share issue, that is triggered when an aggressor company attempts to take over another company, hence making the takeover more expensive.

Political risk: the risk that the political situation of a country will adversely affect the value of a company's operations.

Pre-emptive right: the right enjoyed by existing shareholders of a company whereby they are legally entitled to the first refusal on any new shares that it may issue.

Present value: the value of a future cash flow in current terms, once it has been discounted by the appropriate discount rate.

Primary markets: markets where securities are issued for the first time.

Profitability index: the ratio of a project's net present value relative to its initial investment.

Real cost of capital: a company's cost of capital which makes no allowance for the effects of inflation.

Redemption yield: the return required by an investor over the life of a security, taking into account both revenue and capital gains.

Replacement cost: the cost of replacing an asset with one of similar age and condition.

Restrictive covenants: clauses included in bond deeds designed to place restrictions on a company's future financing in order to protect existing creditors' interests.

Retail price index: the weighted average of the prices of a basket of goods which is taken as a guide to inflation.

Retained earnings: cash retained by a company for reinvestment purposes.

Risk averse: a term used to describe investors who are not keen to take risk, regardless of the potential returns.

Risk-free rate of return: the yield earned on securities which are considered to be free from risk, such as some government securities.

Risk premium: the return in excess of the risk-free rate that is required by an investor before accepting a high-risk investment.

Running yield: also called interest or flat yield, this is calculated by simply dividing the coupon of a security by its current market price.

Scrip dividend: an issue of new shares to existing shareholders in lieu of a cash dividend.

Scrip issue: *see* Bonus issue.

Secondary markets: markets where securities, once issued, are subsequently traded.

Securitisation: the process whereby companies, instead of raising finance by borrowing from financial institutions, convert assets into securities for sale in the marketplace.

Security market line: the linear relationship between systematic risk and return as defined by the capital asset pricing model.

Sensitivity analysis: the technique of analysing how changes in an individual project variable affect a project's overall net present value.

Share option schemes: schemes which involve the giving of share options to employees of a company in order to provide an incentive.

Share split: the issuing of a number of new shares in return for each existing share held by investors.

Sinking fund: an amount of money put aside annually for use in redeeming debentures that mature in the future.

Special dividends: a substantial dividend payment that is not expected to be repeated in the near future.

Sterling commercial paper: short-dated money market instruments that companies can issue to raise finance.

Stock: in the UK stock is another term for a bond, while in the US it is taken to mean a share.

Stock splits: US terminology for a *share split*.

Strike price: the price at which an option holder can purchase or sell the specified financial asset.

Sunk costs: costs that have already been incurred and therefore cannot be retrieved.

Swaps: an agreement between two parties to exchange interest payments based on an agreed principal.

Swaptions: derivatives which give the holder the option to become involved in a swap agreement.

Synergy: the creation of wealth by the combination of complementary assets.

Systematic risk: also known as *market risk*, this represents the relative effect on the returns of an individual security of changes in the market as a whole.

Tax exhaustion: the position where a company has insufficient profits with which to take advantage of the capital allowances available to it.

Technical analysis: the use of past share price data and statistical analysis to predict future share prices.

Tick: a standardised unit measuring movement in the price of futures contracts, defined as 0.01 per cent of the contract size.

Time value of money: the concept that £1 received in the future is not equivalent to £1 received today due to factors such as risk and opportunity cost.

Traded option: a standardised agreement giving the holder the right, but not the obligation, to buy or sell a specified amount of a commodity or financial instrument over a specific time period and at a specified price.

Transaction risk: the risk that, when making transactions in a foreign currency, the exchange rate will move in an unfavourable direction.

Transfer pricing: the manipulation of the rate at which one subsidiary charges another subsidiary for its products in order to minimise the company's overall corporate tax bill.

Translation risk: the balance sheet risk experienced by companies with assets and liabilities denominated in currencies other than that of the home country.

Treasury bills: virtually risk-free short-dated securities issued by governments.

Undercapitalisation: *see* Overtrading.

Underwriting: the process whereby companies issuing securities arrange for financial institutions to buy up any unsold securities.

Unsystematic risk: the risk that is specific to a company and hence can be diversified away by spreading money over a portfolio of investments.

Upside risk: the possibility of a favourable outcome due to the movement of a financial variable.

Utility curves: *see* Indifference curves.

Vanilla: a term often used to describe the purest and most straightforward version of a derivative, i.e. a vanilla swap.

Venture capital: 'risk' capital supplied by specialist organisations to smaller companies that would otherwise struggle to raise capital due to their high risk.

Warehousing: the situation where a financial institution acts as an intermediary for a swap deal even though no suitable counterparty has yet been found.

Warrants: tradable share options issued by companies, commonly attached to an issue of bonds.

Weighted average cost of capital: the average rate of return determined from all sources of finance employed by a company, which can be used as a discount rate for investment appraisal decisions and as a key factor to consider in decisions concerning new finance.

White knight: a favourable take-over partner that may be sought by a company which is the subject of an unwanted take-over bid.

Withholding tax: a tax levied by an overseas country on profits repatriated to the home country.

Working capital: the difference between a company's current assets and liabilities, also referred to as net working capital.

Writing down allowance: *see* Capital allowance.

Yield to maturity: *see* Redemption yield.

Zero coupon bonds: bonds issued at a considerable discount to their face value and as a consequence paying no coupon.

Zero sum game: a situation where, for one party to gain by a certain amount, another party must lose by a similar amount.

INDEX